Diversity and Accommodation

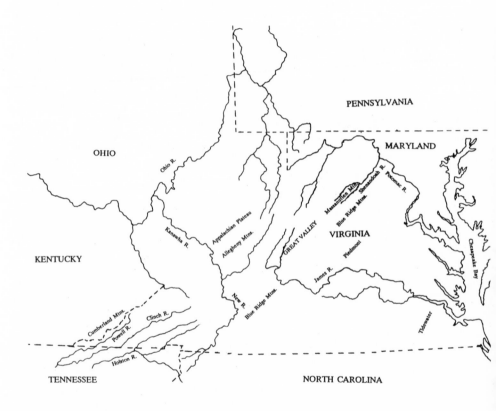

PENNSYLVANIA

MARYLAND

OHIO

Ohio R.

VIRGINIA

KENTUCKY

Kanawha R.

Appalachian Plateau

Allegheny Mtns.

GREAT VALLEY

Massanutten Mtn.

Blue Ridge Mtns.

Shenandoah R.

Potomac R.

Piedmont

Chesapeake Bay

James R.

Cumberland Mtns.

Powell R.

Clinch R.

New R.

Blue Ridge Mtns.

Tidewater

Holston R.

TENNESSEE

NORTH CAROLINA

Diversity and Accommodation

Essays on the Cultural Composition of the Virginia Frontier

Edited by
Michael J. Puglisi

The University of Tennessee Press • Knoxville

Frontispiece: The Virginia Appalachian Frontier.

The paper in this book meets the minimum requirements of the
American National Standard for Permanence of Paper for Printed

Library Materials. ∞ The binding materials have been chosen
for strength and durability.

✪ Printed on recycled paper.

Library of Congress Cataloging-in-Publication Data

Diversity and accommodation: essays on the cultural composition of the Virginia frontier /
edited by Michael J. Puglisi.—1st ed.
            p.   cm.
Proceedings of a conference held in October 1992 in Emory, Virginia.
Includes bibliographical references and index.
ISBN 0-87049-969-6 (cloth: alk. paper)
            1. Virginia—History—Colonial period, ca. 1600–1775—Congresses. 2. Virginia—
History—1775–1865—Congresses. 3. Frontier and pioneer life—Virginia—Congresses.
4. Ethnicity—Virginia—Congresses. 5. Pluralism (Social sciences)—Virginia—Congresses.
6. Acculturation—Virginia—Congresses. 7. Minorities—Virginia—History—Congresses.
I. Puglisi, Michael J.
F229.D58 1997
975.5'02—dc20   96-35612
                                                                      CIP

Contents

Part III. Native Americans and African Americans on the Frontier

Part IV. Community Ties in Southwest Virginia

Part V. Material Reflections of Culture

Illustrations

Figures

Maps

Tables

Preface

In 1990, while attending a conference appropriately titled "New Directions in Virginia History" in Richmond, Warren Hofstra and Bob Mitchell agreed to meet me for breakfast one morning to talk about an idea I was hatching to hold a conference on the cultural composition of the Virginia frontier. The two of them, who were experienced in directing similar projects, encouraged my idea. Over coffee and blueberry muffins, the seeds of this volume began to germinate. During the next year, we solicited participants and began formulating themes. Support came from the administration of Emory and Henry College, and a grant request to the Virginia Foundation for the Humanities and Public Policy received a positive response. In October 1992, the contributors to this volume came together in Emory, Virginia, with other participants. For two days, both in formal paper sessions and in less formal social gatherings, we shared our thoughts on just what influences ethnicity and culture had in shaping the society of the early Virginia backcountry.

From the start, in planning the conference from which these essays originated, a few realities became apparent. First, because of the nature of the recent scholarship on the early backcountry and the scholars who were involved in producing it, the conference inevitably was going to include the contributions of various disciplinary perspectives. Second, again reflecting current trends in the field, the dominant themes were going to revolve around dynamics such as pluralism, toleration, acculturation, and accommodation, rather than isolation, intolerance, or ethnocentrism. The realities of existence on the frontier precluded exclusive clannishness and separate spheres of activity, even if the settlers of the region had been interested in such a course. The interdisciplinary dialogue that has taken place in recent scholarship has been instrumental in re-creating the vibrancy and fluidity of the evolution of backcountry society and calling into question the neatly packaged yet overly simplistic stereotypes of the past. This volume attempts to further that effort for the Virginia frontier.

Multiple expressions of gratitude need to be extended whenever a book is published; particularly in a collection such as this, the person whose name appears on the cover is merely one among many. I would like to begin by thanking the staff of the Virginia Foundation for the Humanities and Public Policy for their assistance with the original grant which funded the conference. I also thank my former colleagues at Emory and Henry College, without whose support the project would not have been a success. I must especially cite Richard Pfau, then dean of the faculty at Emory and Henry, for his constant encouragement. All those who participated in the sessions by presenting papers or by offering comments and all those who attended have contributed to the body of scholarship which emerged from the conference. To the contributors included in this volume, I must offer thanks for their hard work and endurance while the manuscript took shape, as well as for their diligence and tolerance in responding to my demanding and sometimes unrealistic deadlines. I particularly wish to thank Bob Mitchell and Warren Hofstra for their continued advice and moral support throughout the process. There have been others along the way—among them Ken Koons and David Hsiung—who, by their counsel and example, have helped (more than they know) to shape my thinking on this project. I also must acknowledge the contributions of Karen Gundert in preparing the manuscript. At the University of Tennessee Press, I want to thank Meredith Morris-Babb for her unflagging interest, enthusiasm, and guidance while the manuscript was under consideration and Stan Ivester and Scot Danforth for thoroughly and expertly guiding the manuscript through the copyediting stages. Finally, and most sincerely, my gratitude and appreciation go to my wife, Claudia, and my children, Mike, Tony, and Margaret, who give me the energy and the motivation to even attempt such an undertaking.

Part I

Toward a Social History of the Virginia Frontier

Introduction

Images and Realities of Cultural Diversity on the Virginia Frontier

Michael J. Puglisi

The historiography of the Virginia backcountry has very much paralleled the actual historical exploration and settlement of the region. In each case, progress was slow, and initial information on the backcountry came only in limited, fragmented, and generalized portions. By the third quarter of the seventeenth century, a small but varied group of entrepreneurs had begun showing interest in the Piedmont region, beyond the fall line, and explorers such as Abraham Wood and John Lederer approached the seemingly insurmountable barrier of the Blue Ridge Mountains. Then, in 1671, Thomas Batts and Robert Fallam broke the barrier and brought back the first sketchy reports of the region beyond the hills.[1] At the time of the 1716 Knights of the Golden Horseshoe expedition and even later, for the most part Virginians had only a few accounts based on isolated, incomplete, and biased information to form their perceptions of what became known as the backcountry.

Likewise, with painfully few exceptions, early attempts at scholarship on the historical development of the Virginia frontier tended to portray a stereotypical image of the region as either quaint, heroic, or backward. These early-twentieth-century historians based their generalizations on outstanding persons, events, or architectural structures rather than upon mass realities. Further, they relied heavily on local traditions and oral relations and seemed primarily interested in genealogical descent and the appearance of religious or patriotic virtues.[2] The image commonly presented was one of romanticized, sturdy backwoods heroes who fought off the elements as well as hostile Indians, who eked out an existence with all odds against them, and whose feats and deeds could have easily formed the foundation of a James Fenimore Cooper epic. These hardy pioneers, cast from the mold of the Daniel Boone hero genre, supposedly lived an isolated existence, lacking any trappings or comforts of civilized society such as money, commerce, or contact with the outside world on the eastern side of the mountains. Boone, with his "love of adventure and unseen places, physical prowess, resourcefulness and moral courage in the face of danger," represented to many writers the very embodiment of the personality and spirit which characterized their image of the frontier settlers. Somehow, these writers also credited the frontier population with innately possessing, in the tradition of Frederick Jackson Turner, all of the qualities of pure democracy, based upon "an independence of action that scorns all authority not emanating from the people." In the process of exploring the wilderness, planting their land, making a living, and providing for their families, these heroes of the first frontier "conquered an empire and built a new nation" dedicated to the principles by which they lived.[3]

Even the real hardships of backcountry existence itself were romanticized in these accounts; independent-minded settlers were "Surrounded by constant danger and separated from one another by walls of trees and sometimes mountains. . . ."[4] They were "fearless men and women who did not flinch before the terrors of the wilderness," who "had to content themselves with the most primitive food, clothing, household furnishings and kitchen utensils," who hunted and "raised a few vegetables," but who somehow survived by their wits and brought order and progress where none existed before them.[5] John Caruso, whose book *The Appalachian Frontier* is widely considered a classic, flatly stated that "The settlers lived a life of poverty and hard work." Without citing any probate inventories or tax records, he maintained that most of them were "destined to go to their graves ignorant of plank floors, feather beds, riding carriages and side saddles." "Living in a primitive stage of society," he suggested, pioneers "gave little consideration to wealth, position and family tradition," but rather were contented with the benefits of their "innate civility."[6]

What made these people so different from their brothers and cousins in other parts of the colonies? John Campbell pronounced them predisposed to the challenge: "on the whole a sturdy, virile people, fitted by nature and experience to meet the hardships of pioneer life." Samuel Kercheval argued that it was a "natural result of this kind of rural life . . . to produce a hardy and vigorous race of people."[7] Caruso agreed. "Constantly jumping over brambles or fallen trees," he reported, frontier boys "developed agility in escaping Indians and extricating [themselves] from their ruses." Even more, living in the backcountry environment allowed them to develop abilities like walking over "fallen leaves without crushing one or breaking a twig" and deducing "by the report of a rifle whether it belonged to an Indian or to a white man."[8] Either way, these frontier settlers were cast in larger than life and innately virtuous images by writers of the nineteenth and early twentieth centuries.

Stereotypes also extended to characterizations of groups of settlers by early historians. Speaking of German settlers in the Shenandoah Valley, Kercheval proclaimed that "The peaceable and orderly deportment of this hardy and industrious race of people, together with their perfect submission to the restraints of civil authority, has always been proverbial."[9] While the German immigrants were portrayed as model farmers who preferred to mark off their orderly and productive farms in the flat limestone basins of the Shenandoah Valley floor, the Scotch-Irish appeared as rugged individualists who favored the independence provided by the isolation of the uplands, along with less labor-intensive pursuits such as subsistence agriculture and livestock grazing.[10] Either of these generalizations could be used to portray virtuous or dubious habits, depending upon the motives of the writer. Caruso's treatment of the Scotch-Irish is illustrative. He argued that, as a whole, they were "a striking example of the powerful influence which heredity and environmental factors exert on the psychological make-up of a people." On the positive side, centuries of a hunting and gathering existence, along with participation in "sanguinary feuds," "developed in them a self-reliance and a physical endurance" which prepared them to meet "the formidable challenge of the American frontier." They possessed an "undying confidence in their own manhood" and thereby won the admiration of even the Shawnee Indians, "who acknowledged them as superiors." Caruso explained the Scotch-Irish reputation for feisty behavior as "an indomitable spirit of personal independence which impelled them to resist any encroachment on their individual rights." On the other hand, he called them "hard-boiled and sometimes cruel" and noted a "defiant,

aggressive and grasping nature which," he analyzed, "compensated for
feelings of insecurity and inferiority." Portraying an unfounded stereotype as fact, the author stated, "They kept the Sabbath and everything
else they could lay their hands on."[11] Needless to say, this generalization is far too broad a statement to be truly useful for historical examination, and yet it paints a widely accepted picture. As European settlers
received this sort of treatment in historical accounts, the non-white
characters in the frontier story suffered even greater misrepresentation.

Generally, Indians appeared in the early histories only as adversaries and props for the settlers' own heroics. Perhaps the kindest statement about the natives was Kercheval's characterization of them as an
"unfortunate race of people," though taken in context, this phrase seems
more pejorative than sympathetic.[12] The word "Indian" in these accounts generally fell in close proximity to words like "hostile," "savage,"
and "massacres." The settlers who fought them, however, were universally
"men notorious for their valor." There was Captain Jeremiah Smith,
who in 1756 "raised a party of twenty brave men"—alas, no timid men
to be found—but "with his own hand" killed a French captain and drove
off the Indian attackers. Consider "Mr. Bingaman," described as "remarkably stout and active," who in the face of a fierce Indian attack "defended his family with great resolution and firmness," though not with
complete success, as he retreated after his wife and children were killed.[13]
Not to be outdone, pioneer women also displayed heroic qualities when
faced with such challenges. Sally Ridley Buchanan, for instance, though
pregnant, insured victory during the 1792 "Siege of Buchanan's" in
Davidson County, Tennessee. A "courageous, kind, and honourable
woman, 'much respected by all,'" she tirelessly supported the male defenders of the fort by passing among them with "a bottle of whiskey in
one hand [and] bullets in her tucked-up apron," refusing to rest until
the last shot had been fired and the attackers repulsed.[14] And there was
always room for the romantic story. During a 1776 assault on the
Watauga settlements, "pretty Kate Sherill" found herself locked out of
the fort; she was saved by John Sevier, who "leaped to the top of the
stockade, shot her foremost pursuer, and, leaning over . . . lifted her to
safety." For good measure, in a predictable conclusion, Sevier ended up
marrying Sherill some months later.[15] They all had to do their part, and
by most accounts did so splendidly, against supposedly ceaseless Indian
attacks. Joseph Doddridge wrote in the nineteenth century that settlement of the frontier was difficult enough, "but when, in addition to all
the unavoidable hardships attendant on this business, those resulting
from an extensive and furious warfare with savages are superadded, toil,

privations and sufferings are then carried to the full extent of the capacity of men to endure them."[16] Given such stacked odds, how could the Indians appear to be anything but hostile and savage, or the settlers opposing them anything less than heroic.

African Americans were virtually absent from the pages of early Virginia backcountry historiography, leading to the mistaken assumption that they were absent from the landscape itself, and therefore played little or no role in the history of the region. Like Indians, blacks were addressed only peripherally, in the shadows cast by white settlers, and, in many cases, the only references to them revolved around the generalization that the backcountry was primarily settled by immigrants who were small farmers, practiced subsistence and mixed agriculture, and in their virtue were predisposed against the institution of slavery.[17]

Just as the Virginia backcountry eventually became opened to large-scale settlement—and consequently a clearer understanding of the realities of life there, at least for the settlers themselves, was achieved—scholarship on the backcountry has also reached a more vibrant and more accurate level, at least among scholars active in the field. In a sense, both backcountry society and scholarship matured over time. Carl Bridenbaugh introduced a new perspective on backcountry studies in his classic *Myths and Realities: Societies of the Colonial South*.[18] In spite of its shortcomings, Bridenbaugh's work represented somewhat of a "discovery" in the course of backcountry studies. Most important, he examined the region in the larger context of the entire colonial South, stressing the region's connection to, rather than isolation from, the Tidewater and Piedmont areas. He introduced into the scholarship social dynamics such as travel and communications networks, conscious commercial activity, town evolution, and the early appearance of a social system distinguished by disparities of wealth and status. In other words, he characterized backcountry development in terms that were surprisingly similar to development in other regions. Important as it was, however, *Myths and Realities* did not have an immediate, universal impact, and new works based on the traditional histories continued to appear.[19]

The next milestone in the advance of Virginia backcountry scholarship appeared in 1977 with the publication of Robert Mitchell's *Commercialism and Frontier: Perspectives on the Early Shenandoah Valley*. Mitchell found that "seldom were [backcountry settlers] reduced to a raw state of economic evolution distinguished by geographical isolation, complete self sufficiency, and marginal living standards." At most, this initial phase lasted only briefly, and was replaced quickly by "a steadily increasing commercial bias."[20] Mitchell measured commercialism not by a simple formula of production and consumption, but rather by assessing interest, effort, and response to perceived opportunities for commercial activity. In doing so, he concluded that commercial considerations represented a high priority in settlement patterns and land acquisition from the start and possibly were more important considerations than even ethnic, cultural, or religious predispositions.[21] In addition, Mitchell replaced the heroic actions of hardy frontiersmen with the calculating ventures of merchants, merchant-farmers, and land speculators, whom he termed "the real frontier risk takers."[22] Rather than the assumptions of isolation and economic backwardness, *Commercialism and Frontier* explored networks of commercialism and assimilation of eastern influences in the region.

What Mitchell did for the Shenandoah Valley, Richard Beeman did for the Southside, that portion of the backcountry east of the Blue Ridge yet still geographically remote enough from the Tidewater to be considered on the frontier by contemporaries and historians alike. In *The Evolution of the Southern Backcountry: A Case Study of Lunenburg County, Virginia, 1746–1832,* Beeman described a locality whose community building process was complicated by differences in the ethnic backgrounds, lifestyles, and religious orientations of its early transient population. While a dominant social and political elite was slow to develop, a hierarchical system based on relative wealth and prominence quickly appeared, and the interests of these local leaders who sat as justices of the peace in the county court clearly revolved around "the establishment of those rudimentary services and facilities that were essential to the economic and social life of the region."[23] Beeman portrayed Lunenburg County as an "open-ended frontier society" with "limited concentrations of wealth" or "hereditary priviledge" and few slaves, which in time became an oligarchic participant in the tobacco plantation slave system.[24] In addition to showing the importance of eastern economic influences, as had Mitchell, perhaps Beeman's greatest contribution was the important lesson that there was no single, universal experience or pattern of development that characterized the Virginia backcountry—much less the entire colonial frontier—and that serious study requires recognition and analysis of particular localities and groups in the region.

Mitchell's and Beeman's important works on the Virginia frontier fit into the larger context of backcountry studies in other colonies, as do the contributions in this volume. In another parallel between the history and the historiography of the backcountry, scholarship on the region—and its cultural constituencies and their adaptations to the new environment—began in southeastern Pennsylvania and has progressively flowed toward the southwest, along the frontier. The location of the "backcountry," of course, constantly changed as new immigrants and their descendants moved farther inland from the coastal settlements, and, in terms of the settling of the southern frontier, the first "backcountry" appeared in southeastern Pennsylvania. During the 1970s, a number of works appeared that addressed fundamental ethnic, social, and cultural issues in the emerging backcountry. Among the most notable were James T. Lemon's *The Best Poor Man's Country* and Stephanie Grauman Wolf's *Urban Village*.[25] While neither study focused specifically on the role of ethnicity and cultural relations, these social dynamics proved foundational to both works.

Lemon found that the society of early rural Pennsylvania very much reflected frontier characteristics, with its defense of individualism, its racially and ethnically heterogeneous population, and its mixed agricultural base. With his analysis of such factors as the influences on settlement patterns, the search for spatial mobility by settlers, and the major economic forces at work in the region, Lemon could not ignore cultural indicators. He found that while settlement patterns revealed ethnic and religious clustering, there was no group determinism attached to soil type or topography, as tradition had suggested. In addition, ethnic conflict was minimal in the region because, regardless of their backgrounds, the settlers shared similar social and economic goals. Finally, Lemon chronicled an initially high degree of mobility in the population.[26]

Like Lemon, Wolf's major focus was not ethnicity but rather the emergence of an urban-oriented economic and social system in southeastern Pennsylvania. Even in the streets of Germantown, however, she identified characteristics similar to those cited by Lemon that foreshadowed the frontier movement west and south into the backcountry proper. The "urban village" contained a "highly heterogeneous population of great mobility" in which pluralism reigned as the avenue toward economic success.[27] The image is one of immigrants arriving in Philadelphia and passing through Germantown—perhaps with a brief stay—on their way to new horizons.

In addition to the valuable insights provided by these two works, they also pointed toward new questions and directions in social history, especially in the area of backcountry studies. First, they provided a necessary alternative to the study of community in American society, pointing out that the then dominant genre of the New England town study was not the only model available. Most American communities were not homogenous and stable, and, in fact, the cohesive, compact village setting was not the only context in which meaningful community relations could exist. Second, they affirmed that the cultural and religious baggage carried by eighteenth-century immigrants from Germany and the fringes of Great Britain had to be considered as influences on the fringes of the American colonies, as the groups shared similar aspirations in a new environment while simultaneously guarding and adapting their familiar ways to meet the challenges which confronted them. Michael Zuckerman, in his collection of essays on intergroup relations in southeastern Pennsylvania and the Delaware Valley, applied the term "pluralistic" in characterizing these early frontier situations, arguing that "[i]n a plural society, every group is a people among peoples"; therefore, "every group's identity must be problematic." He suggested that analyzing the conditions under which ethnically diverse immigrants maintained, compromised, or abandoned particular aspects of their cultural and religious traditions raises "crucial questions for the character of group life in America."[28] These questions have become the foundation for backcountry studies in other colonies in recent years.

Just as backcountry society spread from its so-called hearth in southeastern Pennsylvania and reached its peak on the southern frontier, backcountry studies have multiplied in number and complexity in the Appalachian region. The current scholarship on the Virginia backcountry, of which the essays in this collection are representative, both reflects the lessons of the earlier works cited above and fits into the influx of southern backcountry studies. Unfortunately, a majority of the studies have focused on political development and associated periods of conflict, particularly in reference to tensions between east and west surrounding the coming of the Revolution, rather than on social development and cultural relations.[29] Bridenbaugh drew a sketch, wrote Daniel Thorp, of a society marked by "occasional outbursts of violence . . . against a backdrop of different ethnic and religious groups learning to live peacefully with one another" and challenged subsequent historians to tell the detailed stories; according to Thorp, through the 1980s, only half of the challenge—concerning the "outbursts of violence"—had been met.[30]

More recently, several very good works have appeared on the scene that promote cultural analysis as the basis for interpreting the development of social relations on the frontier and emphasizing the importance of pluralism in the region. For instance, Thorp's study of the Wachovia

Moravian community in North Carolina provides a fine example of a cultural group orchestrating patterns of coexistence and peaceful interchange with other settlers, while guarding its own identity. The Moravians, Thorp found, sought "to protect many elements of their community from outside influences [but] also made a deliberate effort to get along with their neighbors and to integrate themselves into the legal, political, and economic systems around them." They knew that they were a part of a "larger non-Moravian world" and chose to participate, for their own benefit and prosperity, but without damaging their own community cohesion, by developing "closely supervised links between themselves" and the surrounding populations.[31] Rather than melting away beyond recognition, the author maintained, cultures on the frontier learned to tolerate one another and gradually accepted intercourse in mutually beneficial areas; group boundaries existed, but they were not impenetrable. Like Lemon, Thorp discovered a general absence of ethnic conflict because the Moravians and their neighbors had similar aspirations, and they all faced the same threats and challenges on the frontier.[32]

Some of the best scholarship on the backcountry in recent years has appeared in the form of journal articles and essays, as well as in papers presented at a series of conferences (like the one that inspired the core of this collection) that were designed to encourage, support, and broadcast new approaches to the study of the early southern frontier.[33] The fruits of one of these meetings resulted in perhaps the most significant collection on the region to date, Mitchell's *Appalachian Frontiers: Settlement, Society and Development in the Preindustrial Era.* Filling a definite void in backcountry studies, the work contains several essays based on the examination of cultural relations on the frontier. Sally Schwartz revisited the question of "Religious Pluralism in Colonial Pennsylvania," finding that the pluralistic accommodations which were consciously formulated by William Penn were carried by settlers to southern Appalachia, along with a willingness to make compromises on such issues as reasonable limits on freedom of conscience, qualifications for political participation, and acceptance of strange laws so long as they did not impinge on religious beliefs.[34] Kenneth Keller examined the supposed distinctiveness of the Scotch-Irish on the southern frontier and concluded that their most distinguishing characteristic, which defined them as a group, was their adherence to Presbyterianism. He posited that religion, more than ethnicity, gave the Scotch-Irish their identity, but that the frontier environment allowed them to participate politically and economically, while maintaining their Presbyterian practices.[35] Finally, Elizabeth Kessel surveyed the German population of western Maryland and showed how the settlers simultaneously adapted to the environment and preserved their identity while participating in commercial grain agriculture. According to Kessel, they maintained group unity by migrating in kinship groups and practicing endogamy, but adhered to other cultural norms, particularly those with economic implications, only when such behavior proved viable in the new environment.[36] These examples illustrate the nature of social research on the early backcountry, revealing the pervasive theme of pluralism, which is also apparent in this collection.

Other notable works have approached the question of cultural interaction from a more general perspective, addressing the larger region as a whole or the experiences of an entire ethnic group without reference to a particular case study. Three controversial works in this category appeared at approximately the same time. While Grady McWhiney posited that Celtic culture dominated the entire southern backcountry by the late eighteenth century and provided the foundation for southern culture, in general, David Hackett Fischer supported the theory of a direct transfer of cultural traits and folkways from the British borderlands to the American frontier, arguing that collective British folkways represented the fundamental determinant of American social development.[37] Terry Jordan and Matti Kaups added a different interpretation, maintaining the importance of transplanted European traditions, but citing the influences of Finnish and Swedish immigrants as the defining characteristics of backcountry culture from the Delaware Valley through the southern Appalachians.[38] Each of these works provided a unique perspective on the study of the backcountry, and collectively they inspired considerable debate, but none was able to prove its point conclusively.

Other important books have been received less sensationally. In *Palatines, Liberty, and Property,* A. G. Roeber re-examined traditional interpretations of the German Lutheran experience in various parts of America, particularly in the backcountry areas. While the author's primary concern was the political assimilation of German Lutherans during the eighteenth century, he based his study on the avenues and degrees by which German settlers felt culturally secure enough to take part in the political debate by the time of the Revolution, without entirely abandoning their group identity.[39] The same kinds of analysis have proven valuable in examining the experiences of non-European groups, as evidenced by such ethnohistorical works as James Merrell's study of the Catawba Indians' struggle to maintain their cultural integrity in the ever increasingly English world of the southern Piedmont, and Tom Hatley's analysis of a century of complex relationships between the backcountry Cherokees and the colonists of South Carolina.[40] Each of these studies reflects the importance of recognizing cultural pluralism as a reality in the dynamics of frontier society.

In 1991, Bernard Bailyn and Philip Morgan published a collection of essays entitled *Strangers Within the Realm: Cultural Margins of the First British Empire*.[41] The essays addressed marginal areas from Scotland and Ireland to the West Indies, including the North American frontier. The collection is held together by the basic belief that the study of marginal cultures is important because they "acquired distinctive and permanent characteristics [that] eventually formed core worlds of their own that, in many cases, generated margins even more complex than they themselves had been." The editors presented a paradigm of "*shifting* frontiers," in which "Relationships were in constant motion."[42] As Maldwyn Jones pointed out, backcountry areas witnessed the emergence of cultural syntheses—in addition to the maintenance of "cultural continuities"—brought about by the "various borrowings, adaptations, and compromises" that resulted from the "interaction [of groups] with their environments" and with each other.[43] Bailyn and Morgan responded to a perceived need for a "multicultural, pluralistic approach to British colonial history" and referred to the "pioneering nature" of their work.[44] This current collection on the cultures of the Virginia backcountry is, to a considerable extent, part of that mission. It is also a part of the growing body of culturally based backcountry scholarship being produced in other states.

One further distinctive characteristic of this vibrant activity in backcountry scholarship is that much of it has been interdisciplinary or multidisciplinary in nature. Significant works have been produced by geographers, anthropologists, and archaeologists, in addition to works by historians in a wide range of subfields from ecological history and ethnohistory to social history and material culture. Often working collaboratively, in recent years backcountry scholars have created a productive environment marked by a free flow of ideas. This disciplinary mingling is evident in this volume, whose contributors include nine historians, two geographers, two archaeologists, and a linguist.

In addition to the specific findings produced in individual projects, interdisciplinary and multidisciplinary studies create an even greater impact on the field in general. By introducing new perspectives and insights across disciplinary lines and by fostering a dialogue among scholars, they encourage further investigation. The chief victim of the trend toward interdisciplinary studies has been the complacency that often results from adherence to a particular methodology or ideological perspective. No longer accepted are the vast generalizations and broad stereotypes that characterized the early literature, as scholars have been challenged to examine and re-examine old assumptions in light of new information and theories. This collection is a product of that spirit of interdisciplinary investigation. From its origins as a conference theme, the goal has been an examination of the realities of the cultural composition of the Virginia frontier. Reacting to the stereotypes of cultural clannishness and exclusivity, researchers have provided revised views, which take into account such dynamics as adaptation and accommodation.

Any study which approaches the topic of cultural composition and evolution in a frontier area must begin, at least implicitly, with a revised understanding of the term "frontier." Frontier studies in the twentieth century have focused on Frederick Jackson Turner's 1893 "Frontier Thesis," that generally portrayed the frontier in terms of a boundary line separating settlement and civilization on one side from wilderness and incivility on the other. In a cultural sense, scholars now view frontier areas not as barriers or dividers, but rather as mixing zones, where different cultures, environments, experiences, economies, motives, and perspectives come into contact. Thus, frontiers are not merely geographical boundaries but can exist between groups within a given region or locale.[45] Groups of people rarely, if ever, live in complete isolation, and exchange invariably takes place, either passively and unwittingly or overtly and purposefully. Social, cultural, and ethnic groups influence one another by their very presence, if nothing else.

Given this perspective, study of the cultural composition of the backcountry cannot rest with the stereotypes, generalizations, and assumptions that dominated the literature of previous decades. The images of ethnic and cultural separation, of German clannishness and Scotch-Irish individualism, though based on kernels of truth, are far too restrictive and simplistic. Distinct ethnic and cultural groups did exist on the Virginia frontier, and they represented a significant influence on the development and heritage of the region, but accommodation, mixing, exchange, and coexistence were always present and were more important dynamics than the traditional view has portrayed them to be. This theme is apparent throughout this collection, as authors present research which indicates significant levels of mutual interaction, beginning with the earliest European incursions into the region and the early Indian initiative in the early trade relationships. Current scholarship also dispels the myth of exclusivity among European cultural groups on the frontier; culture and ethnicity were important identifiers, but the groups did not exist in isolation from one another, whether physically, socially, or economically. African Americans represented a larger presence (though, of course, not necessarily by choice) in the backcountry than was previously assumed and thereby exerted a definite influence on the development of the region. Nor were backcountry settlers completely cut off from society and economy east of the mountains, as early writers implied, though the influence of relative frontier isolation must be recognized. These are just a few of the findings reflected in the following chapters, all of which revolve around the theme of exchange and accommodation on the frontier. Examination of this concept requires the sort of detailed study of particular neighborhoods or communities represented in the following essays, with a final goal of uncovering the realities of frontier existence. Reflecting the clear influence of the groundbreaking works discussed above, the contributors to this volume have applied the perspectives and methodologies of social history, including the appreciation of interdisciplinary and multidisciplinary insights, to backcountry studies. As such, the first essay is appropriate both because of the qualifications of its author and for its content.

Robert Mitchell addresses the current state of backcountry studies by calling for a new empirical approach to the topic, an approach he characterizes as progressing "from the ground up." He poses probing questions for the current and future agenda of frontier scholarship, such as what challenges settlers encountered in their new environment, what their transformation of the landscape indicates about their resource usage and cultural perspectives, and how the new regional economies which resulted were reflected in the human landscape. Stating that these are the types of questions which backcountry scholars ought to be asking, Mitchell, a historical geographer, advises that the answers can only come through a collaborative effort among all of the social sciences, particularly history, geography, and anthropology, thus his admonition for re-creating a realistic picture of the past "from the ground up."

Mitchell's approach clearly rests on the belief that the natural environment and the human environment were interrelated and, in fact, inseparable. Both nature and society are systems under constant process, and in the frontier environment, those processes were inextricably intertwined. Given this perspective, backcountry studies must take this concept of process into account. Further, backcountry community studies would do well to apply the concept of process to their analysis of space or place, incorporating such considerations as environmental conditions, the reflections of settlement on the landscape, and the transformation of localities, not only in appearance but in function, composition, and meaning. Doing so allows new dimensions in explaining why colonists chose to settle where they did, what considerations went into the development of neighborhoods and towns, and how residents of the backcountry perceived both their insular world and their relationship with the larger world.

By his own admission, Mitchell's prescription for backcountry studies creates some problems. Locally focused studies have the potential to indicate diversity and difference rather than conformity or continuity, which will result in case studies that do not necessarily fit into the cohesive fabric of American history and, on the whole, will make the surface perhaps less smooth, but the larger picture much fuller in the long run. This possibility makes the effort all the more worthwhile, of course, and undoubtedly all the more exciting and fulfilling for those involved in the discoveries.

The chapters which follow are arranged around readily recognizable topics of the Virginia frontier experience, in an effort to provide clarity while still indicating a sense of progression in the development of backcountry society. The initial introduction of European cultures and settlement progressed from north to south in the region, and so the first section revolves around themes distinctive to the early dynamics of relatively recent arrivals in the Shenandoah Valley. While settlers from Ulster and the Rhineland dominated, both in numbers and in prominent activity, it is important to address the presence, roles, and influences of Native American and African American cultures throughout the Virginia frontier. Therefore, a section is devoted to examining these topics at various times and locations as the forces which affected cultural and ethnic relations developed. Following the major path of settlement, the next section addresses the complex social and political dynamics that combined local cultural distinctions, larger regional interests, and the influences of the frontier environment in southwest Virginia. Finally, the remaining essays analyze material reflections of cultural backgrounds—as well as adaptations—apparent in backcountry architecture.

One theme that becomes markedly apparent in this collection of scholarship is that Mitchell is correct when he states that detailed studies of place and landscape in the backcountry will complicate the image of the region during the eighteenth and early nineteenth centuries. There certainly was not just one frontier experience; different ethnic and cultural groups brought their own outlooks to America. Natural and human environments shaped experiences in counties and communities along the way. Dynamics of persistence, accommodation, and acculturation proved as variable as the places in which they occurred and the people who created them. Perhaps Ann McCleary sums it up best with her statement that on the Virginia frontier, diverse settlers from Ireland, Germany, England, and Africa "shared a common land, blending old memories and new experiences to forge a distinctive culture that clearly reflected its ethnic roots." Only through detailed analysis of life in the region from various perspectives and employing innovative approaches can scholars come to a better understanding of what cultural influences settlers carried with them, how those influences affected the process of cultural development, and in what forms they survived with the evolution of new cultural patterns in the region. This collection constitutes a step toward achieving those ends.

Notes

1. See John Lederer, *The Discoveries of John Lederer,* ed. William P. Cumming (Charlottesville: Univ. Press of Virginia, 1958); "Explorations Beyond the Mountains," *William and Mary Quarterly* 1st ser., 15 (1907): 234–41; Clarence Alvord and Lee Bidgood, *The First Explorations of the Trans-Allegheny Region by the Virginians, 1650–1674* (Cleveland: Arthur H. Clarke Co., 1912); Alan V. Briceland, *Westward from Virginia; The Exploration of the Virginia–Carolina Frontier, 1650–1710* (Charlottesville: Univ. Press of Virginia, 1987).
2. See Samuel Kercheval, *A History of the Valley of Virginia,* 4th ed. (Strasburg, Va.: Shenandoah Publishing House, 1925); F. B. Kegley, *Kegley's Virginia Frontier* (Roanoke, Va.: Southwest Virginia Historical Society, 1938); John C. Campbell, *The Southern Highlander and His Homeland* (New York: Russell Sage Foundation, 1921); John W. Wayland, *The German Element of the Shenandoah Valley of Virginia* (Charlottesville: The Michie Co., 1907); John A. Caruso, *The Appalachian Frontier: America's First Surge Westward* (New York: Bobbs-Merrill Co., 1959). For an exception, see Freeman H. Hart, *The Valley of Virginia in the American Revolution* (Chapel Hill: Univ. of North Carolina Press, 1942).
3. Caruso, *Appalachian Frontier,* 70, 211; Caruso prefaced his book with Walt Whitman's heroic poem "Pioneers! O Pioneers!"
4. Ibid., 221.
5. See Virginius Dabney, *Virginia: The New Dominion* (Garden City, N.Y.: Doubleday and Co., 1971), 94. Dabney relied heavily on Kercheval. Harriette Simpson Arnow, *Flowering of the Cumberland* (Lexington: Univ. Press of Kentucky, 1963). Even if early writers noted progress in frontier society, that fact was not widely recognized, as Eller has pointed out the persistence of the stereotype of backwardness and primitiveness in the region. Ronald D Eller, *Miners, Millhands, and Mountaineers: Industrialization of the Appalachian South, 1880–1930* (Knoxville: Univ. of Tennessee Press, 1982), xvi-xviii.

6. Caruso, *Appalachian Frontier*, 83, 208.

7. Campbell, *Southern Highlander*, 23; Kercheval, *History of the Valley*, 151.

8. Caruso, *Appalachian Frontier*, 232.

9. Kercheval, *History of the Valley*, 61.

10. See Karl B. Raitz and Richard Ulack, *Appalachia: A Regional Geography* (Boulder: Westview Press, 1984), 115, 117, 124-25. For examples of counter presentations of a non-stereotypical nature, see Kenneth W. Keller, "What is Distinctive About the Scotch-Irish?" in *Appalachian Frontiers: Settlement, Society and Development in the Preindustrial Era*, ed. Robert D. Mitchell (Lexington: Univ. Press of Kentucky, 1991), 69–86; Warren R. Hofstra, "Land, Ethnicity, and Community at the Opequon Settlement, Virginia, 1730–1800," *Virginia Magazine of History and Biography* 98 (1990): 423–48; Grady McWhiney, *Cracker Culture: Celtic Ways in the Old South* (Tuscaloosa: Univ. of Alabama Press, 1988), 23–51.

11. Caruso, *Appalachian Frontier*, 39–40.

12. Kercheval, *History of the Valley*, 45. The notable exception is Caruso, who stated, "The white men cared little that their invasion would mean starvation for the Indians." He went on to relate Sir William Johnson's 1774 evaluation of "idle fellows . . . too lazy to cultivate lands," who preferred to hunt, thereby interfering with the natives' ability to subsist, and noting that they "begin to feel the scarcity this has occasioned, which greatly encreases their resentment." Caruso, *Appalachian Frontier*, 122–23; Caruso also called the murder of eight Mingo Indians from Chief John Logan's tribe, which precipitated Lord Dunmore's War, "one of the most inhuman episodes in the epic of the pioneers" (ibid., 125–26).

13. Kercheval, *History of the Valley*, 72–85. Similar stories abound in virtually every early history of the region. See also Wills DeHaas, *History of the Early Settlement and Indian Wars of Western Virginia* (Wheeling, 1851).

14. Arnow, *Flowering of the Cumberland*, 25–27.

15. Caruso, *Appalachian Frontier*, 115.

16. Joseph Doddridge, *Notes on the Settlement and Indian Wars of the Western Part of Virginia and Pennsylvania, from the Year 1763 Until the Year 1783 Inclusive, Together With a View of the State of Society and Manners of the First Settlers of the Western Country* (1824), in Kercheval, *History of the Valley*, 246.

17. See, for example, Campbell, *Southern Highlander*, 94.

18. Carl Bridenbaugh, *Myths and Realities: Societies of the Colonial South* (Baton Rouge: Louisiana State Univ. Press, 1952).

19. For instance, Dabney, *Virginia*, which relied heavily on earlier histories; Arnow, *Flowering of the Cumberland*; Caruso, *Appalachian Frontier*.

20. Robert D. Mitchell, *Commercialism and Frontier: Perspectives on the Early Shenandoah Valley* (Charlottesville: Univ. Press of Virginia, 1977), 3–4.

21. Ibid., 40, 143, 239–40.

22. Ibid., 52–53, 216.

23. Richard R. Beeman, *The Evolution of the Southern Backcountry: A Case Study of Lunenburg County, Virginia, 1746–1832* (Philadelphia: Univ. of Pennsylvania Press, 1984), 46, 30–31, 48–49, 90.

24. Ibid., 225. For an evaluation of this perspective, see Albert H. Tillson Jr., "The Southern Backcountry: A Survey of Current Research," *Virginia Magazine of History and Biography* 98 (1990): 387–422.

25. James T. Lemon, *The Best Poor Man's Country: A Geographical Study of Early Southeastern Pennsylvania* (Baltimore: Johns Hopkins Univ. Press, 1972); Stephanie Grauman Wolf, *Urban Village: Population, Community, and Family Structure in Germantown, Pennsylvania, 1683–1800* (Princeton: Princeton Univ. Press, 1976).

26. Lemon, *Best Poor Man's Country*, xiii–xv, 22–23, 43, 61–64. For a later discussion of geography and ethnic settlement patterns in central Pennsylvania, see Kenneth E. Koons, "Families and Farms in the Lower Cumberland Valley of Southcentral Pennsylvania, 1850–1880," (D.A. diss.: Carnegie Mellon Univ., 1986), 71–135.

27. Wolf, *Urban Village*, 10, 72–73.

28. Michael Zuckerman, ed., *Friends and Neighbors: Group Life in America's First Plural Society* (Philadelphia: Temple Univ. Press, 1982), 23. For other attempts to search for alternate community models, see Richard Beeman, "The New Social History and the Search for 'Community' in Colonial America," *American Quarterly* 24 (1977): 422–43; Darrett B. Rutman and Anita H. Rutman, *A Place in Time: Middlesex County, Virginia, 1650–1750* (New York: Norton, 1984).

29. Several very fine and valuable works fall into this category. For example, see A. Roger Ekirch, *Poor Carolina: Politics and Society in Colonial North Carolina, 1726–1776* (Chapel Hill: Univ. of North Carolina Press, 1981); Ronald Hoffman, Thad W. Tate, and Peter J. Albert, eds., *An Uncivil War: The Southern Backcountry during the American Revolution* (Charlottesville: Univ. Press of Virginia, 1985); Albert H. Tillson Jr., *Gentry and Common Folk: Political Culture on the Virginia Frontier, 1740–1789* (Lexington: Univ. Press of Kentucky, 1991). For a critique of this historiographical trend, see Daniel B. Thorp, *The Moravian Community in Colonial North Carolina: Pluralism on the Southern Frontier* (Knoxville: Univ. of Tennessee Press, 1989), 1–3.

30. Thorp, *Moravian Community*, 2.

31. Ibid., 4–5.

32. Ibid., 199–203.

33. "Conference on the Appalachian Frontier," Harrisonburg, Va., 1985; "Re-examining America's Frontier Heritage," Winchester, Va., 1991; "Cultural Diversity on the Virginia Frontier," Emory, Va., 1992; "The Southern Colonial Backcountry: Beginning an Interdisciplinary Dialogue," Columbia, S.C., 1993; "After the Backcountry: Rural Life and Society in the Nineteenth-Century Valley of Virginia," Lexington, Va., 1995.

34. Sally Schwartz, "Religious Pluralism in Colonial Pennsylvania," in *Appalachian Frontiers*, ed. Mitchell, 51–68.

35. Keller, "What Is Distinctive About the Scotch-Irish?" in *Appalachian Frontiers*, ed. Mitchell, 69–86.

36. Elizabeth A. Kessel, "Germans in the Making of Frederick County, Maryland, 1730–1800," in *Appalachian Frontiers*, ed. Mitchell, 87–104.

37. McWhiney, *Cracker Culture*; David Hackett Fischer, *Albion's Seed: Four British Folkways in America* (New York: Oxford Univ. Press, 1989).

38. Terry G. Jordan and Matti Kaups, *The American Backwoods Frontier: An Ethnic and Ecological Interpretation* (Baltimore: Johns Hopkins Univ. Press, 1989).

39. A. G. Roeber, *Palatines, Liberty, and Property: German Lutherans in Colonial British America* (Baltimore: Johns Hopkins Univ. Press, 1993).

40. James H. Merrell, *The Indians' New World: Catawbas and Their Neighbors From*

European Contact through the Era of Removal (Chapel Hill: Univ. of North Carolina Press, 1989); Tom Hatley, *The Dividing Paths: Cherokees and South Carolinians through the Era of Revolution* (New York: Oxford Univ. Press, 1993). See also Thomas Hatley, "Cherokee Women Farmers Hold Their Ground," in *Appalachian Frontiers*, ed. Mitchell, 37–51. Also, Timothy Silver has produced an ecological history that focuses on the synergism between Indians, Africans, and Europeans in the South Atlantic environment. Timothy H. Silver, *A New Face on the Countryside: Indians, Colonists, and Slaves in South Atlantic Forests, 1500–1800* (Cambridge: Cambridge Univ. Press, 1990).

41. Bernard Bailyn and Philip D. Morgan, eds., *Strangers Within the Realm: Cultural Margins of the First British Empire* (Chapel Hill: Univ. of North Carolina Press, 1991). Essays in this collection that are directly relevant to the American backcountry include James Merrell, "'The Customes of Our Countrey': Indians and Colonists in Early America," 117–56; Philip D. Morgan, "British Encounters with African-Americans, circa 1600–1780," 157–219; A. G. Roeber, "'The Origin of Whatever Is Not English Among Us': The Dutch-speaking Peoples of Colonial America," 220–83; Maldwyn A. Jones, "The Scotch-Irish in British America," 284–313.

42. Bailyn and Morgan, ed., *Strangers Within the Realm*, 1, 19.

43. Jones, "Scotch-Irish," 313.

44. Bailyn and Morgan, eds., *Strangers Within the Realm*, 10.

45. See Jack D. Forbes, "Frontiers in American History and the Role of the Frontier Historian," *Ethnohistory* 15 (1968): 203–35.

Works Cited

Alvord, Clarence, and Lee Bidgood. *The First Explorations of the Trans-Allegheny Region by the Virginians, 1650–1674*. Cleveland: Arthur H. Clark Co., 1912.

Arnow, Harriette Simpson. *Flowering of the Cumberland*. Lexington: Univ. Press of Kentucky, 1963.

Bailyn, Bernard and Philip D. Morgan, editors. *Strangers Within the Realm: Cultural Margins of the First British Empire*. Chapel Hill: Univ. of North Carolina Press, 1991.

Beeman, Richard R. *The Evolution of the Southern Backcountry: A Case Study of Lunenburg County, Virginia, 1746–1832*. Philadelphia: Univ. of Pennsylvania Press, 1984.

———. "The New Social History and the Search for 'Community' in Colonial America." *American Quarterly* 24 (1977): 423–43.

Briceland, Alan V. *Westward from Virginia: The Exploration of the Virginia–Carolina Frontier, 1650–1710*. Charlottesville: Univ. Press of Virginia, 1987.

Bridenbaugh, Carl. *Myths and Realities: Societies of the Colonial South*. Baton Rouge: Louisiana State Univ. Press, 1952.

Campbell, John C. *The Southern Highlander and His Homeland*. New York: Russell Sage Foundation, 1921.

Caruso, John A. *The Appalachian Frontier: America's First Surge Westward*. New York: Bobbs-Merrill Co., 1959.

Dabney, Virginius. *Virginia: The New Dominion*. Garden City, N.Y.: Doubleday and Co., 1971.

Ekirch, A. Roger. *Poor Carolina: Politics and Society in Colonial North Carolina, 1726–1776*. Chapel Hill: Univ. of North Carolina Press, 1981.

Eller, Ronald D. *Miners, Millhands, and Mountaineers: Industrialization of the Appalachian South, 1880–1930*. Knoxville: Univ. of Tennessee Press, 1982.

Fischer, David Hackett. *Albion's Seed: Four British Folkways in America*. New York: Oxford Univ. Press, 1989.

Forbes, Jack D. "Frontiers in American History and the Role of the Frontier Historian." *Ethnohistory* 15 (1968): 203–35.

Hart, Freeman H. *The Valley of Virginia in the American Revolution, 1763–1789*. Chapel Hill: Univ. of North Carolina Press, 1942.

Hatley, Thomas. "Cherokee Women Farmers Hold Their Ground." In *Appalachian Frontiers: Settlement, Society and Development in the Preindustrial Era*, edited by Robert D. Mitchell, 37–51. Lexington: Univ. Press of Kentucky, 1991.

Hatley, Tom. *The Dividing Paths: Cherokees and South Carolinians through the Era of Revolution*. New York: Oxford Univ. Press, 1993.

Hoffman, Ronald, Thad W. Tate, and Peter J. Albert, editors. *An Uncivil War: The Southern Backcountry during the American Revolution*. Charlottesville: Univ. Press of Virginia, 1985.

Hofstra, Warren R. "Land, Ethnicity, and Community at the Opequon Settlement, Virginia, 1730–1800." *Virginia Magazine of History and Biography* 98 (1990): 423–48.

Jordan, Terry G., and Matti Kaups. *The American Backwoods Frontier: An Ethnic and Ecological Interpretation*. Baltimore: Johns Hopkins Univ. Press, 1989.

Kegley, F. B. *Kegley's Virginia Frontier*. Roanoke, Va.: Southwest Virginia Historical Society, 1938.

Keller, Kenneth W. "What Is Distinctive About the Scotch-Irish?" In *Appalachian Frontiers: Settlement, Society and Development in the Preindustrial Era*, edited by Robert D. Mitchell, 69–86. Lexington: Univ. Press of Kentucky, 1991.

Kercheval, Samuel. *A History of the Valley of Virginia*. 4th edition. Strasburg, Va.: Shenandoah Publishing House, 1925.

Kessel, Elizabeth A. "Germans in the Making of Frederick County, Maryland, 1730–1800." In *Appalachian Frontiers: Settlement, Society and Development in the Preindustrial Era*, edited by Robert D. Mitchell, 87–104. Lexington: Univ. Press of Kentucky, 1991.

Koons, Kenneth E. "Families and Farms in the Lower Cumberland Valley of Southcentral Pennsylvania, 1850–1880." D.A. diss., Carnegie Mellon Univ., 1986.

[Lederer, John]. *The Discoveries of John Lederer*. Edited by William P. Cumming. Charlottesville: Univ. Press of Virginia, 1958.

Lemon, James T. *The Best Poor Man's Country: A Geographical Study of Early Southeastern Pennsylvania*. Baltimore: Johns Hopkins Univ. Press, 1972.

McWhiney, Grady. *Cracker Culture: Celtic Ways in the Old South*. Tuscaloosa: Univ. of Alabama Press, 1988.

Merrell, James H. *The Indians' New World: Catawbas and Their Neighbors from European Contact through the Era of Removal*. Chapel Hill: Univ. of North Carolina Press, 1989.

Mitchell, Robert D. *Commercialism and Frontier: Perspectives on the Early Shenandoah Valley*. Charlottesville: Univ. Press of Virginia, 1977.

Raitz, Karl B., and Richard Ulack. *Appalachia: A Regional Geography*. Boulder, Colo.: Westview Press, 1984.

Roeber, A. G. *Palatines, Liberty, and Property: German Lutherans in Colonial British America*. Baltimore: Johns Hopkins Univ. Press, 1993.

Rutman, Darrett B., and Anita H. Rutman. *A Place in Time: Middlesex County, Virginia, 1650–1750*. New York: W. W. Norton and Co., 1984.

Schwartz, Sally. "Religious Pluralism in Colonial Pennsylvania." In *Appalachian Frontiers: Settlement, Society and Development in the Preindustrial Era*, edited by Robert D. Mitchell, 51–68. Lexington: Univ. Press of Kentucky, 1991.

Silver, Timothy H. *A New Face on the Countryside: Indians, Colonists, and Slaves in South Atlantic Forests, 1500–1800*. Cambridge: Cambridge Univ. Press, 1990.

Thorp, Daniel B. *The Moravian Community in Colonial North Carolina: Pluralism on the Southern Frontier*. Knoxville: Univ. of Tennessee Press, 1989.

Tillson, Albert H., Jr. *Gentry and Common Folk: Political Culture on the Virginia Frontier, 1740–1789*. Lexington: Univ. Press of Kentucky, 1991.

———. "The Southern Backcountry: A Survey of Current Research." *Virginia Magazine of History and Biography* 98 (1990): 387–422.

Wayland, John W. *The German Element of the Shenandoah Valley of Virginia*. Charlottesville, Va.: The Michie Co., 1907.

Wolf, Stephanie Grauman. *Urban Village: Population, Community and Family Structure in Germantown, Pennsylvania, 1683–1800*. Princeton: Princeton Univ. Press, 1976.

Zuckerman, Michael, editor. *Friends and Neighbors: Group Life in America's First Plural Society*. Philadelphia: Temple Univ. Press, 1982.

Chapter 1

"From the Ground Up"

Space, Place, and Diversity in Frontier Studies

Robert D. Mitchell

American historians entered the twentieth century as the exclusive gatekeepers of the American past, unified in their intent by the grand synthesis generated by Frederick Jackson Turner's frontier thesis. As we end the century, however, we not only lack such consensus but also the waters of the past have been muddied by communities of new participants, particularly from anthropology, geography, and sociology.[1] Recent attempts to synthesize America's first two centuries of documentary history thus have been dominated not by one voice but by many. The result has been not one portrait but a series of varied, often conflicting, and frequently contradictory images of the past. Many scholars seem comfortable with the idea of history as a "lumpy and contested" arena. Yet, if we are to judge from recent reactions to the suggested guidelines for the future teaching of American history in schools, the American public remains uneasy about adopting alternative interpretations of the national story line.[2]

Frontier scholars also should remain skeptical of a new synthesis, but for more specific reasons. If authors' premises and perspectives are the clues to understanding their procedures and conclusions, then "ground truth" is the ultimate measure of their generalizations. What actually happened on the ground as European migrants colonized the great swath of interior territory between south-central Pennsylvania and southeastern Georgia between 1730 and 1780? What evidence is there to support the views that this southern backcountry was, for example, simply a regressive, backward-looking periphery of British imperial expansion (Bernard Bailyn); or a heavily forested environment ripe for the preadapted log traits of southern Sweden and Finland (Terry Jordan and Matti Kaups); or the receptacle for a transplanted border culture from North Britain or, more narrowly, from the Celtic fringe of Britain (David Hackett Fischer and Grady McWhiney); or the geographical extension of already established regions along the colonial Atlantic Seaboard (Donald Meinig) that were dependent on, and quickly absorbed into, the seaboard settlements by the outbreak of the American Revolution (Jack Greene)?[3]

"Breaking into the backcountry," as Greg Nobles has phrased it, requires adopting a different set of procedures. Nobles emphasizes the tension between frontier independence and regional and national integration as the key to "a coherent synthesis" of the late colonial frontier. Frontier regions experienced similarities sufficient to suggest a common backcountry culture that reflected both an awareness of difference and "an impetus for integration" with both eastern colonial and European centers.[4] For Warren Hofstra, in his review of the Virginia backcountry, this independence was coupled with a striving for improvement or a competency within the context of a highly pluralistic frontier cultural environment. As he expresses it: "The issue is not what people brought to the settlement frontier, but what they made of it."[5] This place-making issue lies at the heart of frontier studies because it forces us to ask fundamental questions about the social appropriation of space, and the creation of socially meaningful places containing natural features, built structures and forms, and place-name evidence of human presence.

Space is not simply an inert physical receptacle for human action but acquires the attribute of spatiality through human encounter. That is, space comprises sets of dynamic environments interpreted by social groups and transformed into places as a result of purposeful human activities. Places have location, dimension, identity, integration, localized focusing power, and the capacity to change over time. They are both objects and receptacles for human experiences.[6] An emphasis on place attributes and place-to-place variation in the arrangement of phenomena also forces us to transcend the uniqueness of individual places and to emphasize their singularity; that is, to compare those phenomena and processes that link places in time and over space. Frontier studies lend themselves particularly well to this mode of inquiry, as Nobles has demonstrated. Newly settled areas emerge as independent entities and exhibit extensive regional differences in the short term. Over the longer term, however, these frontier places tend to become more integrated into larger regional and eventually national entities but at different rates and without necessarily losing their geographical identities. Places, in this sense, are subject to historically contingent processes.[7]

It is the neglect of a sense of place and the reluctance to interpret frontier areas initially on their own terms that is particularly unsatisfying about the grand syntheses of the last ten years. A failure to appreciate situatedness and the importance of locale, a dismissal of environmental circumstances, a blind faith in trait diffusion processes, and a preference for structural explanations over matters of choice and intentionality have all contributed to portraits of southern colonial frontiers that are ultimately irreconcilable.

It is also clear, however, that a new empirical inquiry into the relationships between environment, settlement, and society in frontier contexts cannot be achieved solely by using traditional historical procedures. Just as a new social history proposed to reinterpret the past from the perspective of ordinary people operating in particular locales—"from the bottom up," so to speak—so a new geographical history would reconstruct places "from the ground up."[8] If place does indeed matter, then the attributes of places are of critical concern to those who occupy them.[9] These attributes are the outcome of the reciprocal interactions between natural and social processes generated by initial aboriginal settlement and subsequently modified by the migration and spread of European colonists across a reappropriated American space. We will explore these points by examining the creation of Virginia's Appalachian frontiers during the late colonial era.

Settlement and Encounter

Between 1730 and 1780, about 380,000 Euro-American settlers had settled along the Southern frontier between western Maryland and northeastern Georgia, including some 140,000 in the Valley of Virginia between the Blue Ridge to the east and the Allegheny Plateau to the west.[10] Three attributes of the Virginia section of this frontier zone were particularly significant: the absence of resident native populations; the novelty of a mountainous environment; and increasing distance from the Atlantic coast. Evaluating the significance of these attributes constitutes the structure of the rest of this essay.

In contrast to the contact zones of New York–Pennsylvania and the western Carolinas, the Valley of Virginia had no resident Amerindian settlements at the beginning of the eighteenth century. When Swiss travelers traversed the northern section of the valley, later known as the Shenandoah Valley, between 1704 and 1710, they found the region sufficiently attractive environmentally and devoid of native encounters to plan agricultural colonies for settlers from central Europe.[11] Although the plans failed to materialize, the lack of resident native groups generally has been interpreted as a factor encouraging a more rapid colonial settlement of the region than would otherwise have occurred. This conclusion is based on two standard tenets of frontier studies that have only recently been challenged. The first is that the interior migration of European colonizers was a zero-sum process in which each colonial advance meant further native retreat. The area was simply there for the taking. Second, that this "westward movement" can be captured simply in maps of newly acquired territories and expressed in terms of increasing colonial population densities per square mile. Euro-American occupancy was both inevitable and irreversible.[12]

European encounter with the territory immediately west of the Blue Ridge was a considerably more complex process. Two points are crucial. First, the migration of Europeans and, later, Tidewater colonists into the earliest settled region of the Shenandoah Valley represented the reoccupation of an area recently depopulated of Amerindians as a consequence of both long-term struggles between native groups and the geopolitical strategies of British and French governments directed toward control of the vast territory between the Virginia Blue Ridge and Carolina Piedmont, and the upper Ohio Valley. Second, despite the continuous colonial settlement of the Shenandoah Valley after 1730, the region remained contested space until the resolution of the French and Indian War in 1763.

In our attempts to comprehend the position of Amerindian societies within this critical territory, we have acquired some appreciation of native conceptions of "nature" but have only begun to understand their conceptions of space and territory and how they affected the outcome of cross-cultural encounters.[13] Initial evidence from traditional narrative tales and native linguistic structures suggests that "space" was not a strongly defined concept among native peoples. When expressed in treaty negotiations and in cartographic form, for example, space tended to be linear and one-dimensional and was thus subject to considerable misinterpretation by Europeans trained to think of maps as two-dimensional, viewed-from-above, depictions of reality.[14] Amerindian maps appear to have been much simpler, lacking coordinates and grids, and more fluid, with references to distance, direction, and height being related to positions of the sun and the winds and to travel days and seasonal changes. As in many oral societies, events and actions took precedence over locations and distributions.[15]

It is important to remember these ideas when we examine the chronology of cultural encounters on Virginia's western frontiers. Thus, at the beginning of the eighteenth century, the Shenandoah Valley was one of several north–south conduits containing trails for long-distance contacts between Iroquois groups in northern New York, Virginia's tributary groups on the Piedmont, and the Catawbas, Creeks, and Cherokees in the southern Piedmont and Appalachians. Increasing French interest in the Ohio and Mississippi valleys after 1700 led to a French strategy of negotiating trading contacts and more formal alliances with local native societies.[16] The response of Virginia's governments was to keep close control of surviving tributary groups on the Piedmont and to maintain good relations with the Iroquois in particular.

The Tuscarora War between 1711 and 1713, however, shattered Governor Alexander Spotswood's policy of regulation and containment, and recent research by Warren Hofstra suggests that this forced a rethinking of the colony's frontier policy.[17] By 1716, Spotswood had developed the idea of "buffer settlements" on the Piedmont as the best device for protecting the colony's Tidewater settlements against possible Amerindian or French attack. Since neither tributary tribal groups nor frontier militia units seemed reliable for such purposes, Spotswood recommended that Virginia settle the Piedmont with loyal foreign Protestants, take full control of the region up to the passes in the Blue Ridge, and negotiate with the Iroquois.[18]

There were two major consequences of this approach. In 1720, the Virginia Assembly created two new frontier counties on the Piedmont, Spotsylvania in the north and Brunswick in the south. Significantly, it was the former that was organized first, and its western boundary extended to the east bank of the Shenandoah River thus appropriating the northern gaps through the Blue Ridge.[19] Two years later, Virginia was party to the Treaty of Albany with the Iroquois. Its most important geographical implication was Iroquois acceptance of a westward shift in their principal routes to the south from the Piedmont to the Valley of Virginia.[20] This acceptance of restricted rights of access, however, did not mean that the Iroquois and other groups west of the Blue Ridge, including the Shawnee and the Delaware, rescinded their rights of control and use within the newly defined western territory.

This distinction between access and control did not manifest itself until the 1730s when movements of the Iroquois and the Cherokees increasingly led to conflicts with pioneer European settlers in the Shenandoah Valley, who began petitioning the Virginia Assembly for help. These settlers had not simply wandered into an "open wilderness" but had been encouraged to occupy the region as a result of the land settlement policies of Spotswood's successor, William Gooch. Although it is accurate to describe this policy as one of actively "planting" foreign Protestants as a new settlement buffer west of the Blue Ridge, what is remarkable about the process is how generous Gooch was with land grants and how disinterested he was in regulating the actual form settlement should take.[21] Gooch, undoubtedly, was under considerable pressure to obtain frontier settlers. Not only was there growing tension over Amerindian movements, but a new Lord Fairfax, proprietor of the Northern Neck between the Potomac and Rappahannock Rivers, began pressing his claim to extend his proprietary west of the Blue Ridge into territory that Gooch was already parceling out among new immigrants from Pennsylvania, New Jersey, and New York.[22]

A major consequence of these conflicts was the Virginia Assembly's decision in December 1738, at a time of particularly hostile encounters between Amerindians and Europeans, to organize the colony's territory west of the Blue Ridge into the new frontier counties of Frederick in the north and Augusta in the south.[23] Although there was no immediate attempt to establish any county apparatus, the Iroquois in particular were upset by this further extension of colonial hegemony, and during the next four years several colonial settlers and natives were killed in skirmishes in both frontier counties. It was the Virginia government's desire to provide protection to its frontier settlers that seems to have encouraged the assembly to establish the first county court in Frederick in April 1743, more than four years after its founding, and to initiate the formation of a county militia.[24] Within a year, Virginia had signed a new treaty with the Iroquois at Lancaster, Pennsylvania.

Recognition by the Iroquois that they give up all territorial claims to the Shenandoah Valley but retain the right to pass in peace through the region along the stipulated "Warrior's Path" closed a critical era in

European-native relations between Virginians and natives.[25] Acting on this understanding, both Iroquois and European colonists continued to coexist relatively peacefully until increasing French interest in occupying the upper Ohio Valley in 1754 inaugurated a new chapter in European-native relations and altered the geographical importance of the Shenandoah Valley. Redrawing the map of Virginia in 1751, Joshua Fry and Peter Jefferson made evident how maps could represent the extension of power. The only references to native presence west of the Blue Ridge were to the "Indian Road by the Treaty of Lancaster" and "Shawno [old] Fields" on the upper Potomac River.

Settlement and Environment

What kinds of environments did colonial pioneers encounter as they began to fashion new places on Virginia's western frontiers after 1730? And what specific challenges did they meet in colonizing Virginia's Appalachians? The three premises driving the environmental history of colonial America are that European colonists did not encounter a "virgin land" unaffected by aboriginal occupation; that most of the land was covered with hardwood or pine forests; and that Euro-American settlers encountered no serious natural obstacles to the diffusion of European agricultural practices.[26]

Determining the characteristics of contact environments is not an easy task because it requires the collaboration of historians with ecologists, geographers, and archaeologists in the creation of integrated methodologies that rarely have been applied to the study of colonial America.[27] Collaborative research of this kind is critical for two reasons. It allows us to locate people at specific settlement sites as a base line for measuring how settlers actually arranged themselves across a landscape and how the distribution pattern changed over time, and it provides a means for re-creating what the landscape comprised in terms of land cover as a base line for measuring the ecological changes induced by Euro-American colonization.

A critical key to such reconstruction is the production of a cadaster, a map showing the location, size, shape, and spatial arrangement of all surveyed land tracts recorded for an area undergoing colonization. The first conceptual changes in the reoccupation of early American frontiers were the transformation of "wilderness," or "waste land" in European terms, into productive environments and the reapportionment of the land into units of fixed private or, less commonly, communal property.

Cadastral reconstruction is a forbidding task, especially if the documentary record of land grants is highly fragmented or incomplete. Yet there is no other method of locating settlers at specific sites and being able to interpret the spatial connections between sites as they were transformed into farm, village, and town places.

The Shenandoah Valley lends itself well to such research because its early land records are intact and it was the earliest settled area of the southern colonial frontier, having been occupied by Europeans at least since 1730, ten years before the settlement of adjacent parts of Maryland, and fifteen years prior to the opening up of the North Carolina piedmont. By 1780, the Shenandoah Valley contained between fifty-five thousand and sixty thousand residents. This fifty-year span allows us to evaluate the environmental impact of its first two generations of Euro-American settlers. More specifically, an analysis of the one thousand extant patents, deeds, and surveys for Frederick County, the first functioning county west of the Blue Ridge, contained within the much-reduced county boundaries of 1772 provides a manageable data base for reconstruction.[28]

These land grants, when compiled into a continuous cadaster, cover 362,360 acres or 566 square miles across the valley floor, an area more than half the size of Rhode Island.[29] Mountainous areas, most notably the western slopes of the Blue Ridge, the ridges of the Allegheny Front to the west, and the narrow ridge of Massanutten Mountain running down the center of the valley, were avoided and remained unpatented until the 1790s. The surveys contained 7,802 witness-tree markers designating specifically identified points in the metes-and-bounds surveys, and some 40 percent contained further data on land cover and settlement, including visual or textual references to dwelling sites, roads, mills, meadows, marshes, glades, and the like. Land granting began in 1730, reached a peak of activity between 1746 and 1755, and declined during and immediately after the French and Indian War. Settlement information can often be verified through follow-up fieldwork and archaeological reconnaissance.

A major concern of this research was to evaluate the long-standing belief that the central Appalachians, and particularly the Shenandoah Valley, was more extensively affected by periodic, aboriginal-induced burnings for hunting purposes prior to Euro-American contact. So entrenched is this belief that, beginning with the first published history of the valley in 1833, the "prairie myth" has been repeated by most commentators up to the present time.[30] Samuel Kercheval's *A History of the*

Valley of Virginia, based in part on oral histories given by settlers who had lived in the region during the late eighteenth century, initiated the tradition that the floor of the valley was "a vast prairie" where trees were confined to areas along stream channels. One implication of such open, grass-covered environments was that they were much easier to occupy by colonial farmers, thus further facilitating the settlement of the region. If extensive open areas existed we should expect to find local surveyors using more stakes and stones and fewer trees as markers along property survey lines.

A second concern was to evaluate the proposition that environmental factors were particularly crucial in the decisions made by pioneers to site their farms during the first generation, while social factors became more crucial as the area became more effectively occupied. Even where settlers arrived in family and ethnic groups, their most immediate concern would have been to locate the most suitable farmstead site with respect to maximum access to resources, such as level land, good soils, fresh water, and woodland for fuel and building purposes, and minimum exposure to risks, such as poor soils or stream flooding.

Reconstruction of land cover from the surveys revealed a complex forest-grassland mosaic in which deciduous hardwoods predominated, pines were more closely associated with shale soils or steeper and higher terrain, and less wooded or more open grassy areas were located more commonly along stream channels. Land cover at contact time, in short, was precisely the reverse of Kercheval's description.[31]

Surveyors used fifty-one different types of markers between 1730 and 1750. Forty-six of these markers were varieties of trees with stones, stakes, piles, posts, and poles making up the remainder. In general, the larger the area surveyed, the greater the frequency of tree species. The proportion of marks represented by trees remained fairly constant at 90 to 94 percent throughout the century. The most commonly marked tree by far was white oak, followed by pine, hickory, red oak, black oak, chestnut oak, and Spanish oak. There were some clear trends, however. White oak represented more than 40 percent of trees identified during the 1730s, but less than 25 percent by 1780, while pine increased from less than 10 percent to 20 percent during the same time period. Hickory and most oak species declined in a similar fashion to white oak, with the exception of chestnut oak, which increased from less than 5 percent to 20 percent.

If we interpret the evidence literally, at the time of pioneer colonial settlement the forests on the floor of the northern Shenandoah Valley comprised about 70 percent oaks, 14 percent hickories, 6 percent pines, 3 percent walnuts, and 7 percent other species. The modern-day forests of the region are still dominated by oaks, but the relatively limited references to hickories and chestnuts during the contact period is surprising. This may be the result of surveyor bias in species identification, but the rare references to easily identifiable chestnuts is particularly striking.

Another unexpected reference was to "saplings," or very young trees. One would have anticipated an increasing frequency of their occurrence toward the end of the colonial era as the contact forest was replaced by regrowth woodlands. Yet saplings were more likely to be mentioned during the 1730s than during the 1770s. This may indicate that the forest was in an early stage of succession because of previous native-induced burnings, or, if fire was suppressed or deer reduced in abundance, saplings could have been less frequent. It may also indicate increasing surveyor bias against marking saplings, which through experience were likely to be less permanent than larger trees.

The presence of more open lands and the processes creating them are more problematic. Throughout the Appalachian system few areas are naturally devoid of forest growth. Floodplains and areas with perched water tables often support grassy areas, while steep mountain slopes are frequently covered with boulders rather than trees. In areas underlain by limestone where surface drainage is minimal, as on the floor of the northern Shenandoah Valley, scattered springs may lead to the formation of small, marshy areas, while deposits of marl from dissolved limestone in streams can cause or extend floods along streambanks and thus make it difficult for trees to reestablish themselves. The naturalist John Bartram, for example, while crossing Opequon Creek near Winchester in 1759, observed "ye effects of ye incrusting limestone waters . . . incrusts round brush or leaves or stones or anything in its course frequently stopping its course and overflowing ye adjacent low grounds. . . ."[32]

Determining the distribution of grassy areas depends on reconstructing the frequency and location of indicators of more open land such as non-tree survey markers, surveyors' indications of marsh and meadow areas on the surveyed tracts, and references to more open land in the form of barrens, bogs, glades, marshes, meadows, poison fields, or thickets. More than 70 percent of such references, specifically to bogs, glades, marshes, and meadows, occur along stream channels, with references to barrens commonly associated with an outcrop of shale lands along the center of the valley floor. Comments on thickets were associated with this shale zone or with traverses along mountain foothills. Occasional allusions to poison fields (poison oak or sumac?) appear to be in connection with transition areas between woodland and more open areas. Preliminary indications suggest that open grassy areas may have covered 10 to 12 percent of the valley floor, but at no time is there evidence of such areas covering scores of acres of open land.

These conclusions are particularly important in view of the environmental perceptions generally ascribed to colonial immigrants from western and central Europe. They do not coincide with the view expressed by some scholars that settlers held open grassy areas in a particularly positive light. On the contrary, good land quality was associated with the presence of open hardwood forests; pine-covered areas were regarded as distinctly inferior; and grass-covered terrain was viewed with caution unless it appeared suitable for pasture.[33]

The association of oak-hickory forest with good agricultural land and pines with poorer prospects was common among visitors to the Shenandoah Valley. John Bartram wrote, "where ye woods Consisting at first of Oaks Hicories Poplars Walnuts and c. A mark of much better land than what bears pines," while Nicholas Cresswell observed in 1774 that "limestone in general, abounds with Shumack, Walnut and Locust trees which are certain indications that the Lands are rich."[34] Barrens were associated with pine growth rather than with an absence of vegetation. Moravian travelers on their way to North Carolina during the early 1750s remarked of the area just south of Frederick County that "the country was pretty barren, overgrown with pine trees."[35] Philip Fithian, on the other hand, found on the land along Opequon Creek in 1775 "large and rich meadows—Many have good Grass on the Uplands."[36]

The belief that vegetation cover was the best indicator of the suitability of underlying soils for agriculture was deeply entrenched. By the 1780s, Brissot de Warville, who had traveled extensively in the Appalachian valleys, could write: "There are three or four kinds of land: bottom land, near the Potomac, the Shenandoah, and the Conococheague Rivers; virgin limestone land of top quality; land already under cultivation; and what is called slate land, which contains no limestone and is much inferior. In the very center of the [Shenandoah] valley there are leagues of land covered with rock and not fit for farming called the Barrens."[37] And a decade later Isaac Weld described the environmental consequences of Euro-American settlement in the vicinity of Winchester, the Frederick County seat, as "so thickly settled, and consequently so much cleared that wood is now beginning to be thought valuable. . . . It is only, however, in this particular neighborhood that the country is so much improved; in other places there are immense tracts of woodlands still remaining, and in general the hills are all left uncleared."[38] The extent to which pioneer settlers used environmental indicators about soils and land cover in their settlement decisions, however, requires a more detailed examination of the site selections made by pioneer colonists as they moved into the Shenandoah Valley after 1730.

Settlement, Environment, and Society

Nicholas Cresswell, in his 1770 account of establishing a farm just north of old Frederick County, declared that good land in large tracts in the Shenandoah Valley was still available and inexpensive "tho' perhaps one third of it is cleared from woods."[39] Extending this observation to the entire northern valley suggests a substantial transformation of land cover by the end of the colonial era. Wood apparently was becoming scarce around Winchester by 1790. By this time, Winchester, with its 1,650 residents, was the largest settlement west of the Blue Ridge. This county seat and market town dominated a settlement pattern of smaller towns and villages, comprising a total of 7,500 nonfarm residents, that serviced the northern valley's farm population of about 43,000.

How had the place-making process produced such a settlement system and to what extent had environmental concerns influenced its pioneer origins? Answering this question requires the use of three different methodologies. First, by using the distribution of land grants along upper Opequon Creek we can link settlement sites and structures that could be verified on the landscape, and by mapping early land grants along the limestone-shale contact zone in the center of the valley we can evaluate the importance of soils and terrain in settlement decisions. Second, by using data from land and probate records it is possible to reconstruct how pioneer rural communities functioned and how they used local resources. And, third, by reconstructing the founding of Winchester and the creation of its very distinctive cadaster we can understand the processes crucial to its origins, its growth, and its centralizing power.

In 1734, Jost Hite, a Palatine immigrant who had moved south from Pennsylvania, patented a 5,018-acre tract along upper Opequon Creek six miles south of the future site of Winchester. He sold off parts of this tract to thirteen families between 1736 and 1750. His choice of location was environmentally sound. He chose the best-watered limestone land in the upper reaches of a stream that had few surface tributaries (map 1.1).[40] All thirteen original tracts were situated perpendicular to the creek to provide direct access to water and to a variety of local

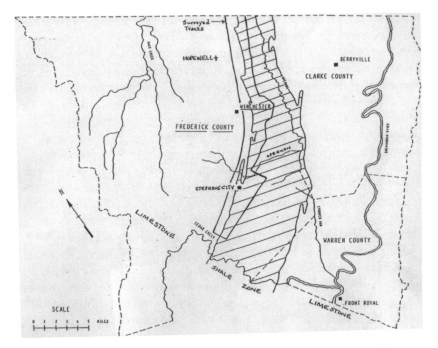

Map 1.1. Limestone-shale interface, Shenandoah Valley. Courtesy of The University of Tennessee Cartography Laboratory.

edge habitats. The early land surveys indicated an abundance of oaks and hickories as well as natural meadows along the creek and at least one glade on a level upland.

Twelve of the tracts transformed into farms had farmsteads situated one-half to three-quarters of a mile apart and sited on low-lying terraces above floodplain level. Two brothers-in-law, Thomas Marquis and John Wilson, for example, jointly owned a 518-acre tract on which they built a "spring house" on a slight rise above a meadow.[41] This structure still stands today. Most pioneer families had come from northern Ireland, but German-speaking families also acquired tracts along the creek interspersed with their Scotch-Irish neighbors. Diversity was present from the outset. John Snapp's survey, for example, shows his farmstead on the edge of a streamside meadow, and Stephen Hotsinpiller excavated a stone-cellar vault, which can still be seen today, in a knoll near a meadow below his farmstead. The relationship between water access, terrace sites, well-drained soils, meadows, and adjacent woodlands was crucial to the decisions made by pioneer families in locating farmsteads within their large survey tracts.

Mapping properties along the limestone-shale interface proved particularly revealing. The current state of the literature on settlement and soils suggests that there was no clearly defined ethnic difference in choosing settlement sites and that most settlers preferred limestone soils and avoided shale lands.[42] Pioneer colonization of Opequon confirms the absence of ethnic distinctions, notably between Scotch-Irish and German-speaking settlers, but available evidence suggests a modification in the second generalization. One group of thirty-one topographically mapped tracts indicated eleven primarily on limestone land, three primarily on shale, but seventeen located astride the limestone-shale contact zone (map. 1.1). It is true that the limestone sections of these seventeen tracts were generally used first, but the most distinctive fact is again the search for edge habitats to provide a broader range of resource possibilities.

Archeological evidence from local limestone and shale areas indicates that pioneer farmsteads were located four times more frequently on limestone than on shale soils.[43] In one six-tract locale along the contact zone, none appropriated the most dissected shale lands but all included rolling uplands on both limestone and shale. John Frost's survey, for example, identified twelve witness-tree markers, comprising seven white oaks, and two hickories on limestone, and one pine on shale. Neighbor Lewis Neill, like Frost, had his tract located across the contact zone with a house site on limestone, but Neill's father had gone further on his adjacent tract by locating a mill on a stream in his shale land. The availability of mill sites on surface streams in the more dissected, steeper-sloping shale lands helps to explain why pioneer settlers chose interface locations. By the end of the colonial era, mills in Frederick County had become concentrated along eastern tributaries of Opequon Creek on shale lands.[44]

Several properties in the limestone-shale contact zone enclosed springs along the interface. There is some indication that the principal north–south Amerindian trail through the valley, the "Warrior's Path," followed this contact zone, presumably to take advantage of the water supplies and edge habitats it provided. It seems reasonable to conclude that many pioneer colonists followed similar reasoning in exploiting this ecotone. But once settled, colonial paths took shape within a different social context from those of more transient natives.

The creation of paths through woods and across cleared properties to link farmsteads was one of two final measures taken to create viable rural communities in the backcountry. The path cleared along the contact zone was enlarged during the early 1740s to accommodate carts and wagons. This was the valley's contribution to "the Great Wagon Road," identified on contemporary land surveys as well as on the Fry-Jefferson map, that eventually linked Philadelphia and Charleston via the Valley of Virginia and the Carolina Piedmont.[45] The other component that provided a focus for the formation of pioneer communities was the establishment of fixed sites for worship. The two earliest sites in Frederick County were the Presbyterian church, founded on the upper Opequon in 1736 on land originally owned by Jost Hite, and Hopewell meeting house, established twelve miles to the north in 1734 on land owned by John Ross, a Quaker contemporary of Hite's.[46] Several of the pioneer families who occupied tracts along the limestone-shale interface between 1735 and 1750 were members of the Hopewell community, but apparently they preferred to make the six-mile round trip from their farms to the meeting house rather than relocate.

The structure of pioneer rural communities in Frederick County, therefore, was predicated on site choices that tended to maximize access to a diverse resource base. While pioneer families also displayed kinship and ethnic ties in their formation of communities, no culturally exclusive settlements emerged and local churches and meeting houses often functioned interdenominationally. Spatially, such communities have been described as open-country neighborhoods.[47] Economically, they comprised self-sufficient households during the pioneer era when distances from eastern centers were formidable and transport links tenuous. An examination of twelve estate inventories for the upper Opequon community between 1730 and 1750 indicates a mixed-farming economy based on wheat, rye, corn (maize), hay, and flax, together with widespread use of cattle, horses, sheep, and pigs.[48] Maize was the only addition to an otherwise European farm repertoire. Farm and woodworking tools were common, but the most notable items were spinning wheels mentioned in ten inventories and looms mentioned in three. On a larger scale, 165 surviving inventories for Frederick County between 1736 and 1751 not only confirmed the pattern for Opequon but also indicated commercial production of a second native crop, tobacco, by the late 1740s, occasional use of servants or slaves, periodic references to ready cash, and widespread involvement in local debt networks.[49]

Several synthetic studies have argued that whatever independence southern backcountry populations demonstrated was associated with geographic isolation fostered by remote mountainous environments and considerable distances from centers of civil order and authority. Lawlessness and violence inevitably ensued. For Bailyn, the violence of eighteenth-century life was an extension of the lawlessness expressed on the outlying peripheries of seventeenth-century Britain; for Fischer and McWhiney, violence was emblematic of the militant border culture of North Britain or the Celtic fringe typified by the behavior of the Scotch-Irish; while for Jordan and Kaups, American backwoods culture spread beyond settled society by pioneers who displayed a lack of appreciation or respect for centralizing institutions.[50]

In the Shenandoah Valley, however, we have two intriguing and somewhat different interpretations of pioneer society in Augusta County in the southern part of the region. Albert Tillson has argued for a "separate political culture" in which pioneer leaders who initially imposed social order had to recognize and accommodate to a general population that rejected traditional eastern values of gentry dominance and paternalism. Frontier order was grounded in localism, rural neighborhoods, and church adjudication.[51] Turk McCleskey, on the other hand, has painted a portrait of pioneer society in which a social elite of land speculators and surveyors imposed a local frontier version of eastern Virginia's hierarchical and deferential society on a relatively law-abiding population.[52]

The need for civil order through the operation of local government institutions was expressed from the outset in Frederick County. This institutional setting provided the context for the implementation of the final component in the region's settlement evolution with the founding of Winchester in 1744. The existing literature on urbanization in the eighteenth-century South links the formation of urban systems to the characteristics of regional economies.[53] Specifically, because the plantation-staple economies of tobacco and rice-producing areas had few processing or marketing requirements, there was little need for services generally associated with towns. In mixed-farming regions in the backcountry, however, where wheat or corn became important exports, the greater need for processing, transportation, and marketing services generated opportunities for market towns, which formed into a number of urban systems between western Maryland and the Carolinas. This explanation works well at a regional scale of analysis, but it does not explain the origins of individual towns. Examining town formation "from the ground up" requires a different strategy, one that is sensitive both to the individuality of town founding and to the broader institutional context within which towns emerged in the Virginia backcountry.

Pioneer life in Frederick County was dispersed, decentralized, self-sufficient, and geographically isolated. The functioning of local government initially was no exception to this pattern. Although the county was founded in 1738, local justices held court meetings in various private residences for the first six years. In the search for a suitable courthouse site, James Wood, the first county clerk and deputy county surveyor, took the initiative and laid out twenty-six lots along two streets on part of his 1,241-acre tract, which included a small western tributary of Opequon Creek approximately midway between the Hopewell and Opequon neighborhoods.[54] To make his site attractive to county justices, Wood donated four adjacent lots to the county for public use and declared that purchasers of the other lots would be required to build on them within two years. Within one year purchasers acquired at least sixteen lots and had constructed two stores and an ordinary. A village, therefore, quickly emerged, although travelers were quick to remark on its largely "barren" site and poor water supply. The unequivocal location of the county seat set in motion a flurry of new road orders, improved road connections over the Blue Ridge, and the rerouting of the main road from the north, later "the Great Wagon Road," through the fledgling settlement.[55]

"Urbanism," as a commitment to live in a more concentrated, non-farm setting, had quickly taken hold.[56] Village life originated from the distinctive way in which Virginia's frontier settlers responded to the imposition of county institutions. Deriving their traditions from the western fringes of the British Isles and Germany, and having them reinforced by sojourns in the Middle colonies, they had a clear response to social and political order. In contrast to eastern Virginia, where the founding of new counties usually gave rise to "courthouse places" consisting of no more than a courthouse and jail in one structure, a pillory and stocks, and perhaps a lawyer's office, settlers in Frederick County responded rapidly to the opportunities provided by nonfarm centers.

Although the village grew slowly, with a log courthouse and jail not completed until late in 1751, the physical presence of Lord Fairfax at this time, with his fond recollections of Kent County in England and its county seat of Maidstone, sent the western frontiers off on a different trajectory. Fairfax, on whose land Winchester was founded, struck an agreement with James Wood, and the addition of new town lots on a gridlike layout encouraged Frederick County to petition successfully for a town charter in 1752.[57] The charter enhanced the village's local market activities by permitting semiannual fairs that would attract many farmers, travelers, and merchants. By 1753, the new town had between two hundred and three hundred residents and a small cadre of storekeepers, merchants, and artisans.[58] A year later, George Washington made Winchester his military headquarters for the Southern District against the French and their Amerindian allies and supervised the construction of Fort Loudoun at the north end of town. Winchester thus also became a garrison town, and the presence of a militia stimulated demand for additional accommodations, foodstuffs, livestock feed, and other services from the town and surrounding countryside. Indeed, Winchester's growing mercantile community really dated from the war period, when it attracted additional merchants and storekeepers and broke its isolation with eastern centers. Not only were trade connections consolidated with Alexandria, seventy-five miles away, but also the town's bustling activities attracted the attention of Philadelphia merchant firms two hundred miles away.[59] The droving of cattle from the southern backcountry to Philadelphia, for example, which had begun during the late 1740s, was diverted to Winchester during the war and then resumed supplying the Philadelphia market after 1763.

The application of staple theory to Winchester's growth would suggest that the movement of farm commodities through the town was crucial to its development. Close examination of regional trade during the 1760s, however, reveals a different picture. The town grew initially because it was a chartered county seat, a garrison town, and it attracted merchants and artisans. While the cattle trade did move through the town on an annual basis, the only economic stimuli it provided was a supply of hides for Winchester's emerging tanning and leather industry and a demand for feedstuffs for northward-moving herds.[60] The commercial wheat trade, which became the region's principal export after 1763, would seem to be a better candidate for staple theory. Yet, even more striking was the fact that local wheat was not milled in town, where there was no water for a mill race, but rather at mills principally in the shale zone a mile and a half to the east. It was millers and wagoners in the countryside who exported wheat and flour to Alexandria. Where Winchester played a crucial role was in financing this commodity trade by its merchants, who had credit accounts with merchants in Alexandria and Philadelphia, and who were responsible for centralizing the region's import trade in dry goods in the town. This was the particular entrepôt function that Winchester performed to guarantee its supremacy within the emerging urban hierarchy of smaller towns and villages of the post-colonial era.[61]

A Discontinuous Past?

The occupation of new worlds by Europeans after 1500 initiated a dramatic and traumatic phase of global settlement history that will continue to influence our world into the twenty-first century. The broad continental outlines, as well as many of the regional consequences of new contacts between peoples and environments, have been evaluated often provocatively by generations of scholars particularly in North America. Thirty years ago, historians of colonial New England initiated a new social perspective in their township studies, originally at the local level and later at a colony-wide level. The one clear conclusion to be drawn from these studies was the tension created between a Puritan sense of community and conformity and the often bewildering diversity to be found within individual towns. Some scholars despaired of ever achieving a new level of generalization about early New England experiences.[62] Yet, as this research agenda spread to the study of the Middle colonies and especially to the study of the Chesapeake colonies, a new era of empiricism began to create more thorough portrayals of the complexities of colonial encounters.

The study of the adaptive processes involved in creating new colonial societies finally reached into the eighteenth-century backcountry during the 1980s, but within a rather different intellectual context. The lessons learned from intensive local studies and the rise of environmental history have presented historians with a new challenge, albeit one which historical geographers and archaeologists have been dealing with for some time. That challenge is to be more sensitive to matters of place, to the location of phenomena, to the environmental dimensions of new encounters, to the settlement landscapes created by colonization, and to the transformation of place in the creation of new societies.

Such sensitivity requires new sociologies and new methodologies. It relies on close cooperation of scholars from different fields and subdisciplines and on an appreciation of the value and the challenge of alternative viewpoints. It depends on the often tedious reconstruction of morphologies by mapping cadasters and settlement sites, on a basic understanding of the implications of human modifications of natural processes, and on the personal as well as the institutional dimensions of settlers making spatial choices. And it necessitates an appreciation of both the specific space-time contexts within which settlement takes place and the broader processes of colonization and change that link all locales at regional and national scales. It entertains the hope that interested scholars may even be able to agree upon a common set of research questions.

Yet, above all, a renewed empiricism may keep us humble about the limitations of historical inquiry. Local studies, even if grounded in larger issues and informed by theory, will continue to emphasize diversity, difference, and discontinuity. The world will remain lumpier, more messy, and more confusing at the local level than the smoother continuity evoked by long-term synthesis. A newly grounded geographical history, as described here, has the potential for creating a more chaotic past that challenges the presumed unity and continuity of American history. Can we continue to accept the legitimacy of one comprehensive and cohesive national experience in the face of many atomistic and competitive histories? And if we cannot, how do we convey this idea to an American public without generating confusion and ultimate rejection?

If history "from the ground up" is to mean anything it means multiple histories that may not "fit" well into a precast mold. It means not only local and regional history but histories of the interaction of communities, ethnicities, and social groups. It means not only social history but histories of people in both voluntary and involuntary associations. It means recognizing differences and distinctions, but also seeking similarities and linkages where they can be demonstrated to exist. Perhaps what we are striving for are "place histories," not just "histories of places," locales as transformed by human actions, in all their complexities known, inferred, and as yet unimagined. If this is so, then the past is not so much, in the words of David Lowenthal, "a foreign country," as our most precious and most vulnerable cultural artifact.[63]

Notes

The author wishes to acknowledge the help provided by Warren Hofstra and an anonymous reviewer whose critiques of my initial effort have made this a much improved essay.

1. Eric H. Monkkonen, ed., *Engaging the Past: The Uses of History across the Social Sciences* (Durham: Duke Univ. Press, 1994).

2. *National Standards for United States History: Exploring the American Experience* (Los Angeles: National Center for History in the Schools, UCLA, 1994).

3. Bernard Bailyn, *The Peopling of British North America: An Introduction* (New York: Alfred A. Knopf), 1986; Terry G. Jordan and Matti Kaups, *The American Backwoods Frontier: An Ethnic and Ecological Interpretation* (Baltimore: Johns Hopkins Univ. Press, 1989); David Hackett Fischer, *Albion's Seed: Four British Folkways in America* (New York: Oxford Univ. Press, 1989); Grady McWhiney, *Cracker Culture: Celtic Ways in the Old South* (Tuscaloosa: Univ. of Alabama Press, 1988); D. W. Meinig, *The Shaping of America: A Geographical Perspective on 500 Years of History*, vol. 1, *Atlantic America, 1492–1800* (New Haven: Yale Univ. Press, 1986); Jack P. Greene, *Pursuits of Happiness: The Social Development of Early Modern British Colonies and the Formation of American Culture* (Chapel Hill: Univ. of North Carolina Press, 1988).

4. Gregory H. Nobles, "Breaking into the Backcountry: New Approaches to the Early American Frontier," *William and Mary Quarterly* 3d ser., 46 (1989): 641–70.

See also Albert H. Tillson Jr., "The Southern Backcountry: A Survey of Current Research," *Virginia Magazine of History and Biography* 98 (1990): 386–422.

5. Warren R. Hofstra, "The Virginia Backcountry in the Eighteenth Century: Origins and Outcomes," *Virginia Magazine of History and Biography* 101 (1993): 494. The pluralism of place is emphasized in Jack P. Greene, "Independence, Improvement, and Authority: Toward a Framework for Understanding the Histories of the Southern Backcountry during the Era of the American Revolution," in *An Uncivil War: The Southern Backcountry during the American Revolution,* ed. Ronald Hoffman, Thad W. Tate, and Peter J. Albert, (Charlottesville: Univ. Press of Virginia, 1985), 3–36.

6. The literature on space and place is vast, but see Fred Lukermann, "Geography as a formal intellectual discipline and the way in which it contributes to human knowledge," *Canadian Geographer* 8 (1964): 167–72; Yi-Fu Tuan, *Space and Place: The Perspective of Experience* (Minneapolis: Univ. of Minnesota Press, 1977); Robert David Sack, *Conceptions of Space in Social Thought: A Geographic Perspective* (London: Macmillan Press, 1980); Henri Lefebvre, *The Production of Space,* trans. Donald Nicholson-Smith (Oxford: Blackwell Publishers, 1991); J. Nicholas Entrikin, *The Betweenness of Place: Towards a Geography of Modernity* (Baltimore: Johns Hopkins Univ. Press, 1991).

7. Allan Pred, "Place as Historically Contingent Process: Structuration and the Time-geography of Becoming Places," *Annals of the Association of American Geographers* 74 (1982): 279–97; Allan Pred, *Place, Practice, and Structure: Social and Spatial Transformation in Southern Sweden, 1750–1850* (Cambridge: Polity Press, 1986), 5–31.

8. For a somewhat different interpretation of "geographical history," see Carville Earle, *Geographical Inquiry and American Historical Problems* (Stanford: Stanford Univ. Press, 1992), 496–500.

9. There have been several critical evaluations of local studies that have indicated some disillusionment with their overall contribution to a new social history. See, for example, Darrett B. Rutman, "The Social Web: A Prospectus for the Study of the Early American Community," in *Insights and Parallels: Problems and Issues of American Social History,* ed. William L. O'Neill (Minneapolis: Univ. of Minnesota Press, 1973), 57–89, and Richard R. Beeman, "The New Social History and the Search for 'Community' in Colonial America," *American Quarterly* 29 (1977): 422–43.

10. Compiled from U.S. Bureau of the Census, *Historical Statistics of the United States Colonial Times to 1970* (Washington, D.C.: U.S. Government Printing Office, 1975), pt. 2, ser. Z1–19.

11. Charles E. Kemper, "Documents Relating to Early Projected Swiss Colonies in the Valley of Virginia, 1706–1709," *Virginia Magazine of History and Biography* 29 (1921):1–17, 180–82, and Kemper, "Documents Relating to a Proposed Swiss and German Colony in the Western Part of Virginia," ibid., 183–90, 287–91.

12. These ideas, made explicit in Turner's frontier thesis, remain implicit in all of the major synthetic works of the last ten years except in Meinig's approach, where recognition of a persistent "Indian" presence is magnified considerably in his second volume dealing with the antebellum era. See D. W. Meinig, *The Shaping of America: A Geographical Perspective on 500 Years of History,* vol. 2, *Continental*

America, 1800–1867 (New Haven: Yale Univ. Press, 1993). For continued attempts to define "frontier" in terms of Euro-American population densities, see John Fraser Hart, "The Spread of the Frontier and the Growth of Population," *Geoscience and Man* 5 (1974): 73–81, and Carville Earle, "The Rate of Frontier Expansion in American History, 1650–1890," in *Lois Green Carr: The Chesapeake and Beyond—A Celebration,* Discussion Papers (Crownsville, Md.: Maryland Historical and Cultural Publications, 1992), 183–204.

13. A more sensitive approach to encounters between natives and Europeans is reflected in James H. Merrell, *The Indians' New World: Catawbas and Their Neighbors from European Contact through the Era of Removal* (Chapel Hill: Univ. of North Carolina Press, 1989); Peter H. Wood, G. Waselkov, and T. Hatley, eds., *Powhatan's Mantle: Indians in the Colonial Southeast* (Lincoln: Univ. of Nebraska Press, 1989); Tom Hatley, *The Dividing Paths: Cherokees and South Carolinians Through the Era of Revolution* (New York: Oxford Univ. Press, 1993).

14. See the pathbreaking work of Joel Sherzer, *An Areal-Typological Study of American Indian Languages North of Mexico,* No. 20 (Amsterdam: North Holland Linguistic Series, 1976), and Hugh Brody, *Maps and Dreams: Indians and the British Columbia Frontier* (London: Norman and Hobhouse, 1982). The pioneer in North American cultural cartography is G. Malcolm Lewis, "Indian Maps," in *Old Trails and New Directions: Papers of the Third North American Fur Trade Conference,* ed. Carol M. Judd and Arthur J. Ray (Toronto: Univ. of Toronto Press, 1980), 9–23; Lewis, "Misinterpretation of Amerindian Information as a Source of Error on Euro-American Maps," *Annals of the Association of American Geographers* 77 (1987): 542–63; Lewis, "Metrics, Geometrics, Signs and Language: Sources of Cartographic Miscommunication Between Native and Euro-American Cultures in North America," *Cartographica* 31 (1994): 98–106.

15. There is at least one striking exception, the Catawba Deerskin Map dating from the early 1720s. Reproduced in Merrell, *The Indians' New World,* 93.

16. Daniel H. Usner Jr., *Indians, Settlers, and Slaves in a Frontier Exchange Economy* (Chapel Hill: Univ. of North Carolina Press, 1992); Michael N. McConnell, *A Country Between: The Upper Ohio Valley and Its Peoples, 1724–1774* (Lincoln: Univ. of Nebraska Press, 1992).

17. Warren R. Hofstra, "'The Extention of His Majesties Dominions on the frontere': Settlement, Colonial Policy, and the Clash of Nations West of the Blue Ridge," paper presented at the conference "'Away I'm Bound Away': Virginia and the Westward Movement," Virginia Historical Society, Richmond, 1993. For native perspectives on this issue, see Frances Jennings, *The Ambiguous Iroquois Empire: The Covenant Chain Confederation of Indian Tribes with English Colonies from Its Beginnings to the Lancaster Treaty of 1744* (New York: W. W. Norton, 1984), 210–12; Merrell, *The Indians' New World,* 74–80, 89–91, 97–98, 113–22; Daniel K. Richter, *The Ordeal of the Longhouse: The Peoples of the Iroquois League in the Era of European Colonization* (Chapel Hill: Univ. of North Carolina Press, 1992), 32–38, 236–80. For Virginia perspectives, see Warren M. Billings, John E. Selby, and Thad W. Tate, *Colonial Virginia: A History* (White Plains, N.Y.: KTO Press, 1986), 175–81; Leonidas Dodson, *Alexander Spotswood: Governor of Colonial Virginia, 1710–1722* (Philadelphia: Univ. of Pennsylvania Press, 1932), 70–111.

18. Billings, Selby, and Tate, *Colonial Virginia,* 175–94; Dodson, *Alexander Spotswood,* 99–100, 228–44.

19. William W. Hening, comp., *The Statutes at Large: Being a Collection of All the Laws of Virginia, from the First Session of the Legislature in 1619*, 13 vols. (Richmond, New York, and Philadelphia, 1819–23), 4: 77–79; Morgan P. Robinson, *Virginia Counties: Those Resulting from Virginia Legislation* (Richmond: Virginia State Library, 1916), 94–95.

20. Billings, Selby, and Tate, *Colonial Virginia*, 195–96; Dodson, *Alexander Spotswood*, 99–109; Jennings, *Ambiguous Iroquois Empire*, 278–81, 294–98; Richter, *Ordeal of the Longhouse*, 240–43.

21. Robert D. Mitchell, *Commercialism and Frontier: Perspectives on the Early Shenandoah Valley* (Charlottesville: Univ. Press of Virginia, 1977), 25–31; Robert D. Mitchell and Warren R. Hofstra, "How Do Settlement Systems Evolve? The Virginia Backcountry during the Eighteenth Century," *Journal of Historical Geography* 21 (1995): 132–33.

22. The land and territorial struggles between Fairfax and the Crown and between Fairfax and Jost Hite were among the most celebrated cases in late colonial America. Their outcomes in favor of Fairfax allowed him to extend his proprietorial claims west of the Blue Ridge, although the dispute with the Hite grantees was not settled fully until after the Revolution. See Stuart E. Brown Jr., *Virginia Baron: The Story of Thomas 6th Lord Fairfax* (Berryville, Va.: Chesapeake Book Co., 1965); Josiah L. Dickinson, *The Fairfax Proprietary* (Front Royal, Va.: Warren Press, 1959); Mitchell, *Commercialism and Frontier*, 28–31; Warren R. Hofstra, "Land Policy and Settlement in the Northern Shenandoah Valley," in *Appalachian Frontiers: Settlement, Society, and Development in the Preindustrial Era*, ed. Robert D. Mitchell (Lexington: Univ. Press of Kentucky, 1991), 106–12.

23. Hening, *Statutes*, 5: 78–80.

24. H. R. McIlwaine, et al., *Executive Journals of the Council of Colonial Virginia*, 6 vols. (Richmond: Virginia State Library, 1925–66), 5: 112–17.

25. Ibid., 5: 191; H. R. McIlwaine, ed., *Journals of the House of Burgesses of Virginia, 1742–1747, 1748–1749* (Richmond: Virginia State Library, 1909), 75–76; Jennings, *Ambiguous Iroquois Empire*, 365–75.

26. Carl O. Sauer, "The Settlement of the Humid East," in *Climate and Man: Yearbook of Agriculture 1941* (Washington, D.C.: U.S. Dept. of Agriculture, 1941), 157–66; Roderick Nash, *Wilderness and the American Mind*, 3d ed. (New Haven: Yale Univ. Press, 1983); William Cronon, *Changes in the Land: Indians, Colonists, and the Ecology of New England* (New York: Hill and Wang, 1983); Alfred W. Crosby, *Ecological Imperialism: The Biological Expansion of Europe, 900–1900* (New York: Cambridge Univ. Press, 1986).

27. But see Donald Worster, "Transformations of the Earth: Toward an Agroecological Perspective in History," *Journal of American History* 76 (1990): 1087–1106; Worster, "Seeing beyond Culture," *Journal of American History* 76 (1990): 1142–47. The present author is currently working within a multidisciplinary environment. See Robert D. Mitchell, Warren R. Hofstra, and Edward F. Connor, "Reconstructing the Colonial Environment of the Upper Chesapeake Watershed," in *History of the Chesapeake Ecosystem*, ed. Philip D. Curtin (Baltimore: Johns Hopkins Univ. Press, forthcoming).

28. The multidisciplinary research team that compiled and analyzed this data base comprises a forester-surveyor, an ecologist, a historical archaeologist, a social historian, and a historical geographer. The initial research was funded by the National Geographic Society, grant no. 4381–90.

29. The surveys were extracted from the Northern Neck Survey Books located in the Library of Virginia, Richmond, and from surviving survey books for Frederick County contained in the Frederick County Courthouse in Winchester and in the collections of the Virginia Historical Society in Richmond.

30. Samuel Kercheval, *A History of the Valley of Virginia*, 4th ed. (Strasburg, Va.: Shenandoah Publishing House, 1925), 52, 305; William H. Foote, *Sketches of Virginia, Historical and Biographical* (Philadelphia: Lippincott, 1850), 13; Hu Maxwell, "The Use and Abuse of Forests by the Virginia Indians," *William and Mary Quarterly* 1st ser., 19 (1910): 73–103; John W. Wayland, *The German Element of the Shenandoah Valley of Virginia* (Charlottesville: The Michie Co., 1907), 5; William Couper, *History of the Shenandoah Valley* (New York: Lewis Historical Publishing Co., 1952), vol. 1: 1; and Jean Gottmann, *Virginia in Our Century* (Charlottesville: Univ. Press of Virginia, 1969), 233–34.

31. See also Mitchell, Hofstra, and Connor, "Reconstructing the Colonial Environment."

32. John Bartram, Bartram Papers, vol. 1, Historical Society of Pennsylvania, Philadelphia.

33. Brian P. Birch, "The Environment and Settlement of the Prairie-Woodland Transition Belt—A Case Study of Edwards County, Illinois," *Southampton Research Series in Geography* 6 (1971): 3–31; Brian P. Birch, "British Evaluation of the Forest Openings and Prairie Edges of the North-Central states, 1800–1850," in *The Frontier: Comparative Studies*, ed. W. W. Savage Jr. and S. I. Thompson, vol. 2 (Norman: Univ. of Oklahoma Press, 1979), 167–92; Michael J. O'Brien, et al., *Grassland, Forest and Historical Settlement: An Analysis of Dynamics in Northeast Missouri* (Lincoln: Univ. of Nebraska Press, 1984).

34. John Bartram, Bartram Papers; Nicholas Cresswell, *The Journal of Nicholas Cresswell, 1774–1777* (New York: Dial Press, 1924), 49.

35. William J. Hinke and Charles E. Kemper, eds., "Moravian Diaries of Travels through Virginia," *Virginia Magazine of History and Biography* 12 (1904–5): 144.

36. Philip Vickers Fithian, *Journal, 1775–1776*, eds. Robert G. Albion and Leonidas Dodson (Princeton: Princeton Univ. Press, 1934), 19.

37. J. P. Brissot de Warville, *New Travels in the United States of America, 1788*, ed. Durand Echeverria (Cambridge: Belknap Press of Harvard Univ. Press, 1964), 358.

38. Isaac Weld, *Travels through the States of North America*, 2 vols. (London: John Stockdale, 1807), vol. 1: 231.

39. Cresswell, *Journal*, 197.

40. Warren R. Hofstra, "Land Policy and Settlement in the Northern Shenandoah Valley," in *Appalachian Frontiers*, ed. Mitchell, 112–13.

41. References to specific surveys are based on the alphabetically arranged Northern Neck surveys in the Archives Division of the Library of Virginia, Richmond.

42. James T. Lemon, *The Best Poor Man's Country: A Geographical Study of Early Southeastern Pennsylvania* (Baltimore: Johns Hopkins Univ. Press, 1972), 61–64; Mitchell, *Commercialism and Frontier*, 40–44.

43. Clarence R. Geier and Warren R. Hofstra, "An Archaeological Survey of and Management Plan for Cultural Resources in the Vicinity of the Upper Opequon Creek" (Richmond: Virginia Dept. of Historic Resources, 1991); Warren Hofstra and Clarence Geier, "The Abrams Creek–Redbud Run Project: A Cul-

tural Resource Inventory Study of Archaeological Sites in the Shale Area East of Winchester, Virginia," (Richmond: Virginia Dept. of Historic Resources, 1992).

44. This can be observed on "Thomas Fisher's Map of Winchester, March 10, 1778," in Robert F. Oaks, "Philadelphians in Exile: The Problem of Loyalty during the American Revolution," *Pennsylvania Magazine of History and Biography* 96 (1972): 319.

45. "The Great Wagon Road" is clearly designated on James Wood's 1,241-acre survey dated June 1752, Northern Neck surveys, part of which was the site of Winchester.

46. Mitchell, *Commercialism and Frontier*, 28–29; Hofstra, "Land Policy," 112–14.

47. Conrad M. Arensberg, "American Communities," *American Anthropologist* 57 (1955):1143–62; Mitchell and Hofstra, "Settlement Systems."

48. Warren R. Hofstra, "The Opequon Inventories, Frederick County, Virginia, 1749–1796," *Ulster Folklife* 35 (1989): 42–71; Warren R. Hofstra, "Land, Ethnicity, and Community at the Opequon Settlement, Virginia, 1730–1800," *Virginia Magazine of History and Biography* 98 (1990): 423–38.

49. Frederick County Will Books 1–3.

50. Bailyn, *Peopling of British North America*, 112–13; Fischer, *Albion's Seed*, 623–30; McWhiney, *Cracker Culture*, vi–xiv; Grady McWhiney and Perry D. Jamieson, *Attack and Die: Civil War Military Tactics and the Southern Heritage* (Tuscaloosa: Univ. of Alabama Press, 1982), 174ff.; Jordan and Kaups, *American Backwoods Frontier*, 1–7.

51. Albert H. Tillson Jr., *Gentry and Common Folk: Political Culture on a Virginia Frontier, 1740–1789* (Lexington: Univ. Press of Kentucky, 1991).

52. Turk McCleskey, "Rich Land, Poor Prospects: Real Estate and the Formation of a Social Elite in Augusta County, Virginia, 1738–1770," *Virginia Magazine of History and Biography* 98 (1990): 449–86.

53. Joseph A. Ernst and H. Roy Merrens, "'Camden's Turrets Pierce the Skies!': The Urban Process in the Southern Colonies during the Eighteenth Century," *William and Mary Quarterly* 3d ser., 30 (1973): 549–74; Carville Earle and Ronald Hoffman, "Staple Crops and Urban Development in the Eighteenth-Century South," *Perspectives in American History* 10 (1976): 7–78; Charles J. Farmer, *In the Absence of Towns: Settlement and Country Trade in Southside Virginia* (Lanham, Md.: Rowman and Littlefield, 1993).

54. Frederick County Order Book 1: 264.

55. Frederick County Order Book 1.

56. Mitchell and Hofstra, "Settlement Systems."

57. Hening, *Statutes*, 6: 268–70.

58. Hinke and Kemper, "Moravian Diaries," 141.

59. This is exemplified by Bryan Bruin's real estate activities in and around Winchester as recorded in Frederick County Deed Books 4–16, and his trading activities in Philadelphia as recorded in Bryan Bruin-Owen Jones correspondence in Owen Jones Letterbook (1759–81), Owen Jones Papers, Pennsylvania Historical Society, Philadelphia.

60. Mitchell, *Commercialism and Frontier*, 147–49, 197–201.

61. Ibid., 194–99; Mitchell and Hofstra, "Settlement Systems," 139–41; Warren R. Hofstra and Robert D. Mitchell, "Town and Country in Backcountry Virginia: Winchester and the Shenandoah Valley, 1730–1800," *Journal of Southern History* 59 (1993): 619–46.

62. John Murrin, "Review Essay," *History and Theory* 11 (1972): 226–75; Edward M. Cook Jr., "Geography and History: Spatial Approaches to Early American History," *Historical Methods Newsletter* 13 (1980): 19–28.
63. David Lowenthal, *The Past Is a Foreign Country* (Cambridge: Cambridge Univ. Press, 1985).

Works Cited

Arensberg, Conrad M. "American Communities." *American Anthropologist* 57 (1955): 1143–62.

Bailyn, Bernard. *The Peopling of British North America: An Introduction.* New York: Alfred A. Knopf, 1986.

Bartram Papers. Historical Society of Pennsylvania, Philadelphia.

Beeman, Richard R. "The New Social History and the Search for 'Community' in Colonial America." *American Quarterly* 29 (1977): 422–43.

Billings, Warren M., John E. Selby, and Thad W. Tate. *Colonial Virginia: A History.* White Plains, N.Y.: KTO Press, 1986.

Birch, Brian P. "The Environment and Settlement of the Prairie-Woodland Transition Belt—a Case Study of Edwards County, Illinois." *Southampton Research Series in Geography* 6 (1971): 3–31.

———. "British Evaluation of the Forest Openings and Prairie Edges of the North-Central States, 1800–1850." In *The Frontier: Comparative Studies,* edited by W. W. Savage Jr. and S. I. Thompson, 167–92. Norman: Univ. of Oklahoma Press, 1979.

Brissot de Warville, J. P. *New Travels in the United States of America, 1788.* Edited by Durand Echeverria. Cambridge: Belknap Press of Harvard Univ. Press, 1964.

Brody, Hugh. *Maps and Dreams: Indians and the British Columbia Frontier.* London: Normal and Hobhouse, 1982.

Brown, Stuart E., Jr. *Virginia Baron: The Story of Thomas 6th Lord Fairfax.* Berryville, Va.: Chesapeake Book Co., 1965.

Cook, Edward M., Jr. "Geography and History: Spatial Approaches to Early American History." *Historical Methods Newsletter* 13 (1980): 19–28.

Couper, William. *History of Shenandoah Valley.* 3 vols. New York: Lewis Historical Publishing Co., 1952.

Cresswell, Nicholas. *The Journal of Nicholas Cresswell, 1774–1777.* New York: Dial Press, 1924.

Cronon, William. *Changes in the Land: Indians, Colonists, and the Ecology of New England.* New York: Hill and Wang, 1983.

Crosby, Alfred W. *Ecological Imperialism: The Biological Expansion of Europe, 900–1900.* New York: Cambridge Univ. Press, 1986.

Curtin, Philip D., editor. *History of the Chesapeake Ecosystem.* Baltimore: Johns Hopkins Univ. Press, forthcoming 1996.

Dodson, Leonidas. *Alexander Spotswood: Governor of Colonial Virginia, 1710–1722.* Philadelphia: Univ. of Pennsylvania Press, 1932.

Earle, Carville. *Geographical Inquiry and American Historical Problems.* Stanford: Stanford Univ. Press, 1992.

———. "The Rate of Frontier Expansion in American History, 1650–1890." In *Lois Green Carr: The Chesapeake and Beyond—A Celebration.* Discussion Papers. Crownsville, Md.: Maryland Historical and Cultural Publications, 1992.

Earle, Carville, and Ronald Hoffman. "Staple Crops and Urban Development in the Eighteenth-Century South." *Perspectives in American History* 10 (1976): 7–78.

Entrikin, Nicholas J. *The Betweenness of Place: Towards a Geography of Modernity.* Baltimore: Johns Hopkins Univ. Press, 1991.

Ernst, Joseph A., and H. Roy Merrens. "'Camden's Turrets Pierce the Skies!': The Urban Process in the Southern Colonies during the Eighteenth Century." *William and Mary Quarterly* 3d ser., 30 (1973): 549–74.

Farmer, Charles J. *In the Absence of Towns: Settlement and Country Trade in Southside Virginia.* Lanham, Md.: Rowman and Littlefield, 1993.

Fischer, David Hackett. *Albion's Seed: Four British Folkways in America.* New York: Oxford Univ. Press, 1989.

Fithian, Philip Vickers. *Journal, 1775–1776.* Edited by Robert G. Albion and Leonidas Dodson. Princeton: Princeton Univ. Press, 1934.

Foote, William H. *Sketches of Virginia, Historical and Biographical.* Philadelphia: Lippincott, 1850.

Frederick County Will Books and Order Books, Frederick County Courthouse, Winchester, Va.

Geier, Clarence R., and Warren R. Hofstra. "An Archaeological Survey of and Management Plan for Cultural Resources in the Vicinity of the Upper Opequon Creek." Richmond: Virginia Dept. of Historic Resources, 1991.

Gottmann, Jean. *Virginia in Our Century.* Charlottesville: Univ. Press of Virginia, 1969.

Greene, Jack P. "Independence, Improvement, and Authority: Toward a Framework for Understanding the Histories of the Southern Backcountry during the Era of the American Revolution." In *An Uncivil War: The Southern Backcountry during the American Revolution,* edited by Ronald Hoffman, Thad W. Tate, and Peter J. Albert, 3–36. Charlottesville: Univ. Press of Virginia, 1985.

———. *Pursuits of Happiness: The Social Development of Early Modern British Colonies and the Formation of American Culture.* Chapel Hill: Univ. of North Carolina Press, 1988.

Hart, John Fraser. "The Spread of the Frontier and the Growth of Population." *Geoscience and Man* 5 (1974): 73–81.

Hatley, Tom. *The Dividing Paths: Cherokees and South Carolinians Through the Era of Revolution.* New York: Oxford Univ. Press, 1993.

Hening, William W., comp. *The Statutes at Large: Being a Collection of All the Laws of Virginia, from the First Session of the Legislature in 1619.* 13 vols. Richmond, New York, and Philadelphia, 1819–23.

Hinke, William J., and Charles E. Kemper, editors. "Moravian Diaries of Travels through Virginia." *Virginia Magazine of History and Biography* 12 (1904–05): 134–53.

Hoffman, Ronald, Thad W. Tate, and Peter J. Albert, editors. *An Uncivil War: The Southern Backcountry during the American Revolution.* Charlottesville: Univ. Press of Virginia, 1985.

Hofstra, Warren R. "The Opequon Inventories, Frederick County, Virginia, 1749–1796." *Ulster Folklife* 35 (1989): 42–71.

———. "Land, Ethnicity, and Community at the Opequon Settlement, Virginia, 1730–1800." *Virginia Magazine of History and Biography* 98 (1990): 423–38.

———. "Land Policy and Settlement in the Northern Shenandoah Valley." In *Appalachian Frontiers: Settlement, Society, and Development in the Preindustrial Era,* edited by Robert D. Mitchell, 106–12. Lexington: Univ. Press of Kentucky, 1991.

————. "'The Extension of His Majesties Dominions on the frontere': Settlement, Colonial Policy, and the Clash of Nations west of the Blue Ridge." Paper delivered at the conference "'Away I'm Bound Away': Virginia and the Westward Movement," Virginia Historical Society, Richmond, 1993.

————. "The Virginia Backcountry in the Eighteenth Century: Origins and Outcomes." *Virginia Magazine of History and Biography* 101 (1993): 485–508.

Hofstra, Warren R., and Clarence Geier. "The Abrams Creek–Redbud Run Project: A Cultural Resource Inventory Study of Archaeological Sites in the Shale Area East of Winchester, Virginia." Richmond: Virginia Dept. of Historic Resources, 1992.

Hofstra, Warren R., and Robert D. Mitchell. "Town and Country in Backcountry Virginia: Winchester and the Shenandoah Valley, 1730–1800." *Journal of Southern History* 59 (1993): 619–46.

Jennings, Frances. *The Ambiguous Iroquois Empire: The Covenant Chain Confederation of Indian Tribes with English Colonies from Its Beginnings to the Lancaster Treaty of 1744.* New York: W. W. Norton, 1984.

Jones, Owen. Papers. Pennsylvania Historical Society, Philadelphia.

Jordan, Terry G., and Matti Kaups. *The American Backwoods Frontier: An Ethnic and Ecological Interpretation.* Baltimore: Johns Hopkins Univ. Press, 1989.

Judd, Carol M., and Arthur J. Ray, editors. *Old Trails and New Directions: Papers of the Third North American Fur Trade Conference.* Toronto: Univ. of Toronto Press, 1980.

Kemper, Charles E. "Documents Relating to Early Projected Swiss Colonies in the Valley of Virginia, 1706–1709." *Virginia Magazine of History and Biography* 29 (1921): 1–17, 180–82.

————. "Documents Relating to a Proposed Swiss and German Colony in the Western Part of Virginia." *Virginia Magazine of History and Biography* 29 (1921): 183–90, 287–91.

Kercheval, Samuel. *A History of the Valley of Virginia.* 4th edition. Strasburg, Va.: Shenandoah Publishing House, 1925.

Lefebvre, Henri. *The Production of Space.* Translated by Donald Nicholson-Smith. Oxford: Blackwell, 1991.

Lemon, James T. *The Best Poor Man's Country: A Geographical Study of Early Southeastern Pennsylvania.* Baltimore: Johns Hopkins Univ. Press, 1972.

Lewis, G. Malcolm. "Indian Maps." In *Old Trails and New Directions,* edited by Carol M. Judd and Arthur J. Ray, 9–23. Toronto: Univ. of Toronto Press, 1980.

————. "Misinterpretation of Amerindian Information as a Source of Error on Euro-American Maps." *Annals of the Association of American Geographers* 77 (1987): 542–63.

————. "Metrics, Geometrics, Signs and Language: Sources of Cartographic Miscommunication Between Native and Euro-American Cultures in North America." *Cartographica* 31 (1994): 98–106.

Lowenthal, David. *The Past Is a Foreign Country.* Cambridge: Cambridge Univ. Press, 1985.

Lukermann, Fred. "Geography as a Formal Intellectual Discipline and the Way in which it Contributes to Human Knowledge." *Canadian Geographer* 8 (1964): 167–72.

Maxwell, Hu. "The Use and Abuse of Forests by the Virginia Indians." *William and Mary Quarterly* 1st ser., 19 (1910): 73–103.

McCleskey, Turk. "Rich Land, Poor Prospects: Real Estate and the Formation of a Social Elite in Augusta County, Virginia, 1738–1770." *Virginia Magazine of History and Biography* 98 (1990): 449–86.

McConnell, Michael N. *A Country Between: The Upper Ohio Valley and Its Peoples.* Lincoln: Univ. of Nebraska Press, 1992.

McIlwaine, H. R., et al. *Executive Journals of the Council of Colonial Virginia.* 6 vols. Richmond: Virginia State Library, 1925–66.

———, editor. *Journals of the House of Burgesses of Virginia, 1742–1747, 1748–1749.* Richmond: Virginia State Library, 1909.

McWhiney, Grady. *Cracker Culture: Celtic Ways in the Old South.* Tuscaloosa: Univ. of Alabama Press, 1988.

McWhiney, Grady, and Perry D. Jamieson. *Attack and Die: Civil War Military Tactics and the Southern Heritage.* Tuscaloosa: Univ. of Alabama Press, 1982.

Meinig, D. W. *The Shaping of America: A Geographical Perspective on 500 Years of History,* vol. 1. *Atlantic America, 1492–1800.* New Haven: Yale Univ. Press, 1986.

———. *The Shaping of America: A Geographical Perspective on 500 Years of History,* vol. 2. *Continental America, 1800–1867.* New Haven: Yale Univ. Press, 1993.

Merrell, James H. *The Indians' New World: Catawbas and Their Neighbors from European Contact through the Era of Removal.* Chapel Hill: Univ. of North Carolina Press, 1989.

Mitchell, Robert D. *Commercialism and Frontier: Perspectives on the Early Shenandoah Valley.* Charlottesville: Univ. Press of Virginia, 1977.

———, editor. *Appalachian Frontiers: Settlement, Society, and Development in the Preindustrial Era.* Lexington: Univ. Press of Kentucky, 1991.

Mitchell, Robert D., and Warren R. Hofstra. "How Do Settlement Systems Evolve? The Virginia Backcountry During the Eighteenth Century." *Journal of Historical Geography* 21 (1995): 123–47.

Mitchell, Robert D., Warren R. Hofstra, and Edward F. Connor. "Reconstructing the Colonial Environment of the Upper Chesapeake Watershed." In *History of the Chesapeake Ecosystem.* Edited by Philip D. Curtin. Baltimore: Johns Hopkins Univ. Press, forthcoming.

Monkkonen, Eric H. *Engaging the Past: The Uses of History across the Social Sciences.* Durham: Duke Univ. Press, 1994.

Murrin, John. "Review Essay." *History and Theory* 11 (1972): 226–75.

Nash, Roderick. *Wilderness and the American Mind.* 3d ed. New Haven: Yale Univ. Press, 1983.

National Standards for United States History: Exploring the American Experience. Los Angeles: National Center for History in the Schools, UCLA, 1994.

Nobles, Gregory H. "Breaking into the Backcountry: New Approaches to the Early American Frontier, 1750–1800." *William and Mary Quarterly* 3d ser., 46 (1989): 641–70.

Oaks, Robert F. "Philadelphians in Exile: The Problem of Loyalty during the American Revolution." *Pennsylvania Magazine of History and Biography* 96 (1972): 298–325.

O'Brien, Michael J., et al. *Grassland, Forest, and Historical Settlement: An Analysis of Dynamics in Northeast Missouri.* Lincoln: Univ. of Nebraska Press, 1984.

O'Neill, William L., editor. *Insights and Parallels: Problems and Issues of American Social History.* Minneapolis: Univ. of Minnesota Press, 1973.

Pred, Allan. "Place as Historically Contingent Process: Structuration and the Time-geography of Becoming Places." *Annals of the Association of American Geographers* 74 (1982): 279–97.

———. *Place, Practice, and Structure: Social and Spatial Transformation in Southern Sweden, 1750–1850.* Cambridge: Polity Press, 1986.

Richter, Daniel K. *The Ordeal of the Longhouse: The Peoples of the Iroquois League in the Era of European Colonization.* Chapel Hill: Univ. of North Carolina Press, 1992.

Robinson, Morgan P. *Virginia Counties: Those Resulting from Virginia Legislation.* Richmond: Virginia State Library, 1916.

Rutman, Darrett B. "The Social Web: A Prospectus for the Study of the Early American Community." In *Insights and Parallels,* edited by William L. O'Neill, 57–89. Minneapolis: Univ. of Minnesota Press, 1973.

Sack, Robert David. *Conceptions of Space in Social Thought: A Geographic Perspective.* London: Macmillan, 1980.

Sauer, Carl O. "The Settlement of the Humid East." In *Climate and Man: Yearbook of Agriculture 1941,* 157–66. Washington, D.C.: U.S. Dept. of Agriculture, 1941.

Savage, W. W., and S. I. Thompson, eds. *The Frontier: Comparative Studies,* vol. 2. Norman: Univ. of Oklahoma Press, 1979.

Sherzer, Joel. *An Areal-Typological Study of American Indian Languages North of Mexico,* No. 20. Amsterdam: North Holland Linguistic Series, 1976.

Tillson, Albert H., Jr. "The Southern Backcountry: A Survey of Current Research." *Virginia Magazine of History and Biography* 98 (1990): 387–422.

———. *Gentry and Common Folk: Political Culture on a Virginia Frontier, 1740–1789.* Lexington: Univ. Press of Kentucky, 1991.

Tuan, Yi-Fu. *Space and Place: The Perspective of Experience.* Minneapolis: Univ. of Minnesota Press, 1977.

U.S. Bureau of the Census. *Historical Statistics of the United States Colonial Times to 1970,* 2 vols. Washington, D.C.: U.S. Government Printing Office, 1975.

Usner, Daniel H., Jr. *Indians, Settlers, and Slaves in a Frontier Exchange Economy.* Chapel Hill: Univ. of North Carolina Press, 1992.

Wayland, John W. *The German Element of the Shenandoah Valley of Virginia.* Charlottesville: Univ. Press of Virginia, 1907.

Weld, Isaac. *Travels through the States of North America,* 2 vols. London: John Stockdale, 1807.

Wood, Peter H., G. Waselkov, and T. Hatley, editors. *Powhatan's Mantle: Indians in the Colonial Southeast.* Lincoln: Univ. of Nebraska Press, 1989.

Worster, Donald. "Transformation of the Earth: Toward an Agroecological Perspective in History." *Journal of American History* 76 (1990): 1087–1106.

———. "Seeing beyond Culture." *Journal of American History* 76 (1990): 1142–47.

Part II

Cultural Perspectives in the Shenandoah Valley

The Shenandoah Valley has been one of the areas of the Virginia backcountry traditionally covered by the literature, but the topics addressed in the following essays do not reflect traditional approaches. Employing the perspectives of social history and the insights of interdisciplinary analysis, these chapters examine realities of life on the frontier. Gone are the romantic portrayals of heroic pioneers chopping their way through the wilderness and the anecdotal images of quaint Old World legacies, replaced instead by analysis of cultural, environmental, social, and economic dynamics as they operated in the pragmatic lives of the Valley's early European residents.

Frederick Jackson Turner established the development of society on the frontier as the primary area of inquiry for scholars in the field. The following chapters reflect the current manifestation of that theme, the search for community, the interactions that shaped it, and the identifiers that defined it. In 1989 Gregory Nobles noted that this process of "community building on the frontier" is an area that scholars need to explore more thoroughly because on the frontier, with its diverse and fluid population, "communal relations were the most important source of both collective identity and cultural conflict."[1] Cultural groups in the Virginia backcountry could not remain isolated from one another; they shared the same landscape and challenges, and they had to interact, particularly in the context of economic activity. Nobles also pointed out that "economic conditions cannot be considered apart from social relations," noting the frequent intersection of "cultural assumptions and economic expectations."[2] While cultural considerations may have predisposed an inclination toward separation, economic aspirations mandated interaction, and thus the two influenced community dynamics. Conclusions about the development of community and cultural identity on the frontier can only come about through detailed case studies, such as the ones provided in the chapters in this section.

Warren Hofstra takes us back to the northern Shenandoah Valley to trace the beginnings of European influence on the landscape. He bases his analysis on the theory that "Landscape is a physical artifact of culture: singular as a cultural expression and plural as a composite consequence of the actions of numerous individuals." Cultural pluralism was a fact of life on the Virginia frontier, but Hofstra amends the traditional interpretation by stating that whatever polarity existed was drawn not along ethnic lines between Germans and Scotch-Irish, but rather on economic activity, particularly between the towns that developed and the countryside. This fact, he points out, marked the chief difference between the cultural landscape of the backcountry and that of eastern Virginia, where towns were few and economic activity took place at scattered plantations.

The backcountry went through four stages of development, according to Hofstra. First, as settlers transformed wilderness into "property," they achieved self-sufficiency "collectively in the local exchange of goods and services." Hofstra provides a corrective to the stereotypical picture of Germans marking off well-ordered farms on the valley floor while Scotch-Irish settlers fled to the isolation of the upland hollows. Settlement was dispersed, based more on economic potential than on ethnic predisposition, and the groups mixed on a daily basis in the local economy, all the while maintaining their individual cohesion through inheritance systems, religious practice, and marriage patterns. In the second phase, towns emerged, but they were initially "poorly integrated into [the] rural economies." Only in the next stage, when markets for agricultural commodities developed in the Atlantic economy, did this begin to change. Then backcountry settlers could look to export their goods and enjoy the benefits of being consumers in an expanding international economy. The culmination of this development came when backcountry towns began performing significant market functions, particularly establishing commercial links with the important port cities along the coast, in response to the ever-increasing interest of backcountry residents in foreign trade and the "growing rural demand for imported manufactured goods."

Hofstra portrays collective activity rather than ethnic exclusivity as the major factor defining backcountry development. Collective activity, however, did not preclude ethnic differences. These became most apparent in the market towns, where the groups were forced into more concentrated contact and their primary reason for being there was economic competition. German and Scotch-Irish settlers guarded their cultural identity, even when they practiced cooperation and toleration for each other's mutual benefit.

In the following chapter, Richard MacMaster further examines the cultural pluralism evident in the Shenandoah Valley through the perspective of religious diversity and affiliation. Ethnic groups intermixed in the region, but they tended to settle in identifiable enclaves or neighborhoods, focused on the existence of appropriate congregations. According to MacMaster, the explanation for this pattern lies in the nature of the migration itself. Rather than the stereotypical hero figure who pushed onward alone or with only a nuclear family for support into an uninhabited wilderness, MacMaster portrays the typical migrant as a member of a larger group of kin or neighbors who moved together and searched for—or created—hospitable communities in which to settle.

Communities constantly redefined themselves as new families appeared and others disappeared from the neighborhoods; they even shifted geographically in response to settlement patterns, population concentrations, and changes in the focus of economic, cultural, and religious activity. As does Hofstra, MacMaster points out that pluralism existed in the Shenandoah Valley, and regular contact occurred across cultural boundaries, but that institutions, such as religion, worked to maintain group identities. It is essential to recognize the *process* of community formation and evolution in the backcountry because the nature and diversity of frontier society made communities there vibrant, ever-changing, and dynamic.

Kenneth Keller looks for the roots as well as the decline of ethnic communalism in the Virginia backcountry by tracing the experiences of immigrants from the Rhineland. He finds, not surprisingly, that the habits and daily activities of inhabitants along the Rhine did not differ greatly from those of inhabitants along the Shenandoah; in both cases, such practices as small-scale commercial agriculture, domestic manufacture as an economic supplement, and equal partible inheritance characterized life in German communities. All of these qualities predisposed Rhenish immigrants on the frontier to a commercial outlook. By the time that settlers reached the Virginia backcountry, they had generally acquired years of experience with the American economy and with the cultural pluralism of the region thanks to their migrations through Pennsylvania and Maryland, and this experience only strengthened the capitalist perspective that they imported with them.

While other scholars emphasize the continuity of ethnic identity, in spite of interethnic activities, Keller focuses on the decline of ethnic identity during the late eighteenth century. He further develops a theme hinted at by MacMaster; by the last decades of the eighteenth century, strict boundaries that had earlier existed in such areas as endogamous marriage patterns, denominational exclusivity, and ethnically distinct neighborhood settlement began to blur. A variety of factors related to the dominance of the English administrative structures and the demographic diversity on the Virginia backcountry, according to Keller, resulted in the "rapid decline of communal identity" among descendants of German immigrants.

Taken together, these three essays provide a texture to society in the early Shenandoah Valley that was generally missing from earlier histories. The authors tie the legacies of cultural orientations to the physical landscape of geography and the human landscape of community, all of which were inseparable in the realities of life in the backcountry. This perspective provides a more believable picture of the actors involved, and one which makes sense in the context of the motives, influences, and desires that drive human behavior in society.

Notes

1. Gregory H. Nobles, "Breaking into the Backcountry: New Approaches to the Early American Frontier, 1750–1800," *William and Mary Quarterly* 3d ser., 46 (1989): 643; See also John McCusker and Russell Menard, *The Economy of British America, 1607–1789* (Chapel Hill: Univ. of North Carolina Press, 1985), 200–202.
2. Nobles, "Breaking into the Backcountry," 654.

Chapter 2

Ethnicity and Community Formation on the Shenandoah Valley Frontier, 1730–1800

Warren R. Hofstra

Debates provoked by the Columbian Quincentenary provide an ideal setting for the consideration of cultural diversity on the Virginia frontier. On the one hand, the five-hundredth anniversary of European expansion into the Western Hemisphere has inspired a celebration of American multiculturalism; on the other, it has stimulated a more cynical observance of the cultural devastation inflicted by European imperialism on non-European peoples. In either case the contemporary quincentenary has provided a welcome and necessary corrective to the Columbian celebrations in the 1890s, which exalted the "triumph" of western industry and the "superiority" of European civilization. A subsequent century of cultural intolerance bringing death and suffering to unprecedented millions and the resurgence of ethnic hostility in Eastern Europe in the 1990s make an appreciation of cultural diversity more and more essential. But from the outlook of the eighteenth-century frontier—from the viewpoint of the land itself and its aboriginal inhabitants—newcomers from Europe may not have appeared all that different from one another. Even cultural pluralism as a model for backcountry society might presuppose a greater significance for ethnic differences than were merited.

By 1800 a cultural landscape had emerged west of the Blue Ridge that embraced all immigrant groups consistently as a common expression of the objectives Europeans held in taking up American lands within an English colonial administrative system. Outsiders viewing this landscape would have recognized few differences between areas occupied by peoples from the north of Ireland, from the central Rhine Valley, from England, or from eastern Virginia.[1] Eighteenth-century travelers may have been fascinated with the distinctiveness of these peoples, but none distinguished separate areas of settlement by physical appearance alone. John F. D. Smyth, for instance, found that "many of the Irish here can scarcely speak in English; and thousands of the Germans understand no language but High Dutch; however they are all very laborious, and extremely industrious, having improved this part of the country beyond conception."[2]

The cultural landscape represents the outcome of this improving process. Landscape is a physical artifact of culture: singular as a cultural expression and plural as a composite consequence of the actions of numerous individuals. Landscape embodies the totality of the sites, forms, and routes of human activity; it is the sum of dwellings, farmsteads, barns, sheds, fences, fields, roads, towns, streets, and buildings. Beyond the pattern of these elements on the physical terrain, landscape encompasses the manner in which that terrain itself and the natural environment are modified by culture. Landscape also embodies the social, economic, and political institutions in which people interact according to law and custom to shape this pattern.[3]

Although the landscape of western Virginia was itself undistinguished by ethnic differences, it was, however, defined by a fundamental polarity between town and country. The relationship between these two basic settlement forms was considerably more complex than central-place theory would suggest for a preindustrial setting in which the countryside was ideally the place of production and the town the center of trade and manufacture.[4] Much trade, in fact, took place in the countryside. Virginia towns proved incapable of exercising exclusive privileges over trade and craft functions, and farmers, in addition to marketing much of their produce outside town markets, regularly supplemented farming with artisan activities. Water power necessitated the distribution of mills as centers of agricultural processing and marketing across the countryside. Dispersal was, in fact, a defining element of this landscape, and dense road patterns developed to facilitate communications between the places of human activity. Stores and ordinaries at crossroads became centers of economic and social exchange. Roads connected the countryside to towns in highly distinctive radial patterns that extended the public commercial arena of civic life across rural space.[5] By siting houses directly on roads, farmers locked themselves into the rational, collective public order of town life, itself articulated in grids of lots and streets. In both town and country, symmetrical and logically ordered house forms such as the I-house became the most common architectural expression among all ethnic groups.[6]

The landscape of the Virginia backcountry developed in four stages. What the initial European occupants of the land accomplished during the first stage, beginning in the early 1730s, was the transformation of perceived wilderness, or "waste land," as they called it, into property. By delimiting property in irregular units according to the English metes-and-bounds survey system, they segregated the natural resources available to one settler from those of another. They defined property in law as fee simple ownership, conferring exclusive privileges to profit from the development of the land and to convey it by deed or will. Family settlement obligations attached to land orders and grants by the Virginia government facilitated rapid occupation of the land.[7] Lacking requirements to establish towns and failing to perceive threats from Native Americans, Europeans dispersed in enclosed family farms and rural communities where self-sufficiency was achieved collectively in the local exchange of goods and services. Towns emerged in the second stage, ten to fifteen years later, as county seats. Although early county towns in the Shenandoah Valley, such as Winchester and Staunton, lacked distinctive trade functions, stores soon appeared to take advantage of economic activities accompanying court days. As garrisons during the Seven Years' War, backcountry towns developed markets for provisioning troops. But by the 1760s and 1770s, towns remained poorly integrated into rural economies.

The development of commercial markets for agricultural commodities throughout the Atlantic trading basin would change this situation during the third stage of landscape evolution. Hemp bounties, the provisions trade, especially for meat in the West Indies, and significant increases in European grain prices after 1760 provided farmers with commercial markets for fibers, livestock, and grains or flour for the first time.[8] The marketing of these commodities remained embedded in the countryside, but first- and second-generation immigrant families were now able to enter a money and credit economy in which a growing capacity to consume coincided with an international consumer revolution in manufactured goods.[9] By the last decades of the eighteenth century and the final stage of landscape evolution, towns began to assume significant market functions as merchants with credit relations throughout a large region extending from Philadelphia to Norfolk organized a retail and wholesale trade to meet the growing rural demand for imported manufactured goods. Trade thus linked dispersed rural communities into town-centered regional economies in which money, banks, and internal improvements became vital factors of economic growth.

Several critical elements characterized the cultural landscape that emerged across these four stages. First, the town and country landscape of the Shenandoah Valley was significantly different from cultural landscapes east of the Blue Ridge. Certainly an absence of towns characterized the to-bacco-growing regions of Virginia by 1700.[10] Although an "urban experience of considerable magnitude" had by the Revolution produced a network of tobacco towns and fall-line ports to service the Scottish factor trade, the diminished service economies of these towns and the location of import and artisan functions on dispersed plantations generated a cultural landscape unfamiliar to the people of western Virginia.[11] At the close of the eighteenth century the travels of Lutheran minister Paul Henkel took him on a course "through Old Virginia, east of the Blue Ridge. For eight days we traveled in a strange land," he wrote.[12]

The landscape that European immigrants created west of the Blue Ridge also varied considerably from the homelands they departed across the Atlantic. In the north of Ireland enclosed farms covered most arable regions, but townlands averaging approximately 330 acres formed the basic land unit, and estates composed of multiple townlands contained large numbers of tenants who occupied often as little as six to ten acres and supported families on linen weaving.[13] Agricultural villages, meanwhile, predominated in Germany, and farm families worked surrounding plots of land.[14]

The landscape of the early Shenandoah Valley resembles the twentieth-century, rural-farm, small-town America that is both idealized and villainized in modern literature, politics, and popular culture. Simplification of road networks to accommodate the automobile, however, has created a far more private, less public, rural environment today than existed in the eighteenth century.[15]

A final critical element of the landscape of eighteenth-century western Virginia merits more extensive investigation and frames the second part of this essay's argument concerning relationships of ethnicity and community formation. The landscape may have embodied all ethnic groups in common and been fabricated by Ulster, English, Anglo-American, and German immigrants together, but within it real ethnic differences marked the social relations that defined communities. Outsiders may have discerned few physical differences among settlement areas, but insiders were fixed within rural communities in which ethnic backgrounds shaped daily life. The parameters of tolerance and conflict, then, defined social relations between groups.

The experience of German-speaking peoples in the lower Shenandoah Valley will be used to illustrate these ideas for several reasons. First, Scotch-Irish communities have been extensively examined elsewhere and will serve as a basis of comparison for German communities.[16] Second, prolonged cultural cohesion among German settlers presents an excellent opportunity for studying sustained community relations.[17]

ﻰ

In the journals of his travels and preachments, Lutheran minister John Casper Stoever Jr. identified three areas of early German settlement in the Shenandoah Valley: Massanutten, along the South Fork of the Shenandoah River at the site of Swiss immigrant Jacob Stover's colony in modern Page County; Shenandoah, on the Shenandoah's North Fork in the vicinity of present-day Strasburg; and Opequon, on the lands of Jost Hite along the upper watershed of the Opequon Creek.[18] As a native of Bonfeld in the Kraichgau region of south-central Germany, Hite joined the 1709 exodus to England under the aegis of Queen Anne, journeyed to America to labor in a naval stores project in New York, and by the 1720s held extensive landholdings in Pennsylvania.[19] Learning of land opportunities in Virginia, Hite secured land orders from the Virginia Council for 140,000 acres west of the Blue Ridge in the early 1730s and, by the spring of 1732, had settled with fifteen to twenty German and Scotch-Irish families along the Opequon.[20] From these and additional families that joined the colony during the next decade, study populations of eleven Scotch-Irish and eleven German families have been drawn.[21]

The German families included those of Hite and his daughters, who married Jacob Chrisman, George Bowman, and Paul Froman. With them were the families of Stephen Hotsinpiller, Peter Mauk, Christian Nisewanger, John Poker, John Snapp, Peter Stephens, and Abraham Wiseman. Hite's children took up lands along Cedar Creek, a tributary of the Shenandoah River. The land dealings of the Hite family, often extensive and complex, characterized German speakers who entered more fully into the public life of Anglo-Virginia and served as cultural mediators for the other German families. The latter all settled on tracts of land ranging from 168 to 674 acres within the drains of the upper Opequon where Hite had patented more than five thousand acres.[22]

Whereas the eleven Scotch-Irish families composed a single kin group, kinship patterns among first-generation German families, with the exception of the Hites, were less discernible.[23] Several of these families, including the Snapps and Mauks in one case, and Hotsinpillers and Nisewangers in another, journeyed to America on the same ship, however, and Hotsinpillers and Nisewangers both married into the family of Melchior Brumback from Germanna, Virginia.[24] Despite these relationships, neither German nor Scotch-Irish families clustered in contiguous tracts along the Opequon. Each German family had at least one Scotch-Irish neighbor, and because families located farmsteads in relation to topographical features within tracts, not social or military considerations, dwellings tended to be spaced in one-quarter- to one-half-mile intervals along creek terraces.[25] What emerged was a decentralized settlement consistent with the first stage of landscape evolution in which members of different ethnic groups dispersed in taking up land rather than clustering in ethnic neighborhoods.

Dispersal did not mean isolation, and roads quickly emerged that led from farmstead to farmstead, literally from door to door, in a pattern that interconnected members of all ethnic groups to rural economic centers at mills and ordinaries. Hite himself requested permission from the court of Orange County in April 1738 to keep an ordinary at his house and that same year joined with forty-five neighbors in a petition to establish a public road from his mill to a ferry on the Shenandoah River.[26] Significantly the road petition contained the signatures of men from four of the eleven German families at Opequon and five Scotch-Irish families. That ethnic groups collaborated in fashioning the emerging rural landscape of farms, mills, and roads and that the settlements of both Germans and Scotch-Irish became significant points of attachment on the landscape in the road-building process was further indicated when the Frederick County Court in 1750 appointed John Hite and Robert Allen to "mark and lay off" a public road along the course of the Opequon Creek to Hite's mill and when, five years later, the court appointed Joseph Glass to replace Thomas Marquis as overseer for the portion of the road from John Beckett's to Hite's.[27] Allen, Glass, Beckett, and Marquis were all prominent members of the first generation of Scotch-Irish settlers. Hite was, of course, German.

Trade patterns help explain the structure of this emerging road system. Not only did Germans and Scotch-Irish at Opequon live next to one another at settlements that communicated directly by road, but they also traded regularly with one another. The economic activities of the Hotsinpiller and Bowman families exemplified the workings of this system.

Stephen Hotsinpiller arrived in Philadelphia on the ship *Mortonhouse* in August 1728 and in 1736 purchased a 450-acre tract of land from Jost Hite, where he farmed and practiced the trade of blacksmith.[28] The assets of his estate, inventoried upon his death in 1776, indicated not only the diversity of his economic pursuits but also the opportunities this diversity provided for exchange with neighbors. Enumerated in the estate were livestock, including cattle, horses, and hogs; crops of rye, wheat, oats, and corn; and stored provisions of flour, bacon, and beef. In addition to blacksmithing, Hotsinpiller produced hemp, flax, and wool for textiles and distilled considerable quantities of liquor.[29] The extent of surplus available for trade is difficult to determine from the inventory alone, but in May when the appraisal was conducted Hotsinpiller still had fourteen bushels of wheat stored, one cask of flour, and eleven acres of wheat in the ground. The eleven acres alone would have been sufficient to feed a family of ten for a year, and Hotsinpiller's family at the time of his passing was considerably smaller.[30] That Hotsinpiller engaged in trade with neighbors was further indicated in the inventory by a wagon, money weights, a steelyard, and debts to Robert Allen and John Poker, one Scotch-Irish and the other German.[31] Stephen Hotsinpiller's son John not only acquired a significant portion of his father's land and his blacksmith trade, but when he died in 1780 his estate paid debts in small sums (generally less than a pound) to fifteen individuals, including four Germans and four Scotch-Irish.[32]

George Bowman acquired considerable landholdings along Cedar Creek about ten miles south of Hotsinpiller.[33] The slaves, wagon, still, carpenter's tools, and money scales included in his estate appraised in 1769 suggest a number of ways in which he engaged in trade. He also operated a mill and held bills, bonds, notes, and book accounts with neighbors for more than £2,000. Among the debts paid by the estate, 20 percent went to Germans and 30 percent to Scotch-Irish.[34] George Bowman Jr. inherited the mill, and when he died scarcely a year after his father, he held notes from six individuals, at least two of whom were Scotch-Irish. Between 1770 and 1781 his estate received cash payments from thirty-nine debtors and made twenty-one disbursements to creditors. Among those whom Bowman owed were at least eleven Germans and five Scotch-Irish. Clearly ethnicity was not a factor in determining the clientele at Bowman's mill.[35]

The endeavors of the Hotsinpillers and Bowmans, then, help explain the emergence of rural communities during the first stage of landscape evolution. Members of diverse ethnic groups interacted in making this landscape of dispersed, enclosed family farms, regularly spaced farmsteads, residential intermixing, and roads that interconnected all settlements, notwithstanding ethnicity, with the centers of the rural economy at mills and ordinaries. Mixed farming, initially outside a market economy, produced some surplus and craft specialization, but no single family was independent. All were, to some measure, interdependent, trading goods and services on a regular basis to insure the self-sufficiency of the community.[36] That the rural landscape was common to all ethnic groups was a product precisely of this interdependence.

Farm building, agricultural production, and economic exchange for most families generally did not exceed needs to maintain yearly subsistence and provide for the continuity of the family unit through inheritance.[37] Within the mutuality of exchange networks—within the common landscape—resided the objective of each family to secure in a competence the assets necessary for independence. For German and Scotch-Irish immigrants this independence had real meaning as freedom from the subject relations of tenancy, indebtedness, and powerlessness that had made the family in Europe a unit of labor exploitation and wealth expropriation.[38] Although the landscape remained undelineated by ethnic distinctions, the ethnic associations that emanated from the family defined the nature of domestic life and social relations.

The manner in which German settlers at Opequon employed instruments of inheritance clearly indicated the significance they attached to sustaining the cohesion of the family. Partible division of property among both sons and daughters characterized testate patterns in the region of Germany from which most of the Opequon settlers originated. By placing the property interests of children above those of widows, German testators maintained property within the lineal family.[39] Among the German families at Opequon, eight men of the first generation drafted wills between 1747 and 1777.[40] In no case did husbands leave property exclusively in the control of widows. If widows remarried, this property would pass into the hands of new husbands and other families. In three of the six wills mentioning wives, widows received only a life interest in the homeplace, which upon death or remarriage reverted to a son. In another common pattern George Bowman left the homeplace to a son with rights of occupancy to his widow. Only two men named wives among executors, but seven designated sons. Four of the eight directed that their estates be divided equally among their children either as property or legacies, and the other four left land to some or all sons with obligations to pay legacies to remaining children including daughters. Only Stephen Hotsinpiller bequeathed property outside the family to cultural institutions.

The bequests of John Poker, who wrote his will in 1747 and died before 1751, provide a good example of testate patterns intended to perpetuate the nexus of land and family. With the exception of a token five shillings and a cow and calf left to his eldest son, Michael, because "he has had his portion before left by his mother in Garminy," Poker bequeathed all his estate both real and personal to "his loving wife Barbary" during her natural life with the condition that "if she sees cause to get married again I give her two cows and calves and nothing more." The land passed to sons Philip and George with an obligation to pay each of the other children in "Equal shares of the money so that it may be Equally divided Share & Share alike."[41]

With the property they inherited and acquired, sons perpetuated the inheritance practices of fathers. Eleven sons drafted wills between 1769 and 1808. Of nine that mentioned wives, eight left widows only a life interest in real or personal property, and one divided his entire estate among his children with detailed instructions to each for his widow's annual provisions. Seven sons left their homeplaces to one of their sons after the life interest of the widow expired and various combinations of land and legacies to other children without apparent discrimination between sons and daughters except that sons more commonly received land and daughters legacies. Three simply directed that their estates be divided equally among all children.[42]

In their selection of marriage partners, the children of German immigrants demonstrated not only the same primacy of family displayed in inheritance patterns but also the close connection between family and ethnicity. Only one marriage occurred between German and Scotch-Irish families at Opequon, and in numerous instances in which second-generation marriage partners can be determined, Germans selected mates from their own ethnic group. All of Stephen Hotsinpiller's seven daughters married into German families, three of John Snapp's five daughters did so, and the sons of Peter Stephens married into the Nisewanger, Bowman, and Chrisman families.[43]

With regard to the social relations surrounding family, Germans also maintained a separate sphere. Nearly all of the Scotch-Irish families at Opequon can be associated with the Opequon Presbyterian Church.[44] No meeting house is known for German settlers, but the marriage and baptism records of John Casper Stoever Jr., who made eleven visits to Opequon between 1734 and 1741, point out the congregational associations of these men and women. Stoever performed baptism ceremonies for nine of the eleven German families at Opequon. Various members of the community stood as sponsors for the newborn.

Jost Hite, Susanna Wiseman, wife of Abraham Wiseman, and Barbara Snapp, wife of John Snapp Sr., on one occasion in 1736 sponsored Rosina, the infant daughter of John Poker. In another instance John Poker and Barbara Snapp stood as sponsors for John Snapp's nephew. Despite the absence of a regular minister at the Opequon Presbyterian Church, Stoever performed no baptismal or marriage services for the Scotch-Irish congregation there.[45]

Nonfamily members named as executors in wills give some indication of whom Germans chose as their closest friends and associates. Executors performed the familial functions of insuring that legacies were paid, widows were provided for, and children were educated. Most testators, of course, named sons as executors, but in cases among first-generation German families at Opequon when fathers named friends as executors they were invariably German. Peter Mauk, for instance, asked his "beloved Friend" Christopher Wandle to insure that "nothing may be Wasted and that all my Debts be Paid before my Estate be divided."[46]

❧

Within the common landscape that Germans and Scotch-Irish made and inhabited at Opequon, then, ethnicity had real meaning. Despite dispersion and a high degree of residential intermixing, separate spheres were maintained in social relations of family, land, kinship, marriage, congregation, and friendship. In their mutual economic dependence members of separate ethnic groups would of necessity have had to maintain considerable tolerance for one another. To the extent that they governed themselves collectively, the mechanisms of tolerance would have likewise been implanted in local political institutions. By rapidly extending the primary instruments of local governance in the county court, vestry, and militia to the backcountry, the colonial government in Williamsburg insured that, to a large measure, the region would regulate its own affairs. Virginia did not govern its frontiers as a colony, backcountry counties were not accorded inferior status in the legislature, and the area was not presided over by a civilian or military governor whose primary responsibility would be to eastern centers of power as the federal Congress would later manage its western territories. Within the institutions of local government, therefore, German and Scotch-Irish settlers, who constituted a majority in the Shenandoah Valley, together with members of other ethnic groups, had the opportunity to engage one another directly in the collective pursuit of public order.[47]

As early as 1734 Jost Hite received appointment as a justice in the court of Orange County, and in 1743 when the first commission of the peace for Frederick County was sworn, four members of the Scotch-Irish families at Opequon became justices. As new commissions were installed during the next decade, Germans such as Jacob Hite and Lewis Stephens began to play prominent roles on the court. Members of both the Scotch-Irish and German communities at Opequon similarly served on grand juries and on the parish vestry. In 1764 three of Jost Hite's sons, for instance, became vestrymen. Militia companies probably provided the greatest opportunity for ethnic interaction. During the height of the Indian raids in 1756, Lewis Stephens's company contained three men of the first-generation Scotch-Irish families at Opequon and two from the German families.[48]

The Columbian Quincentenary in focusing attention on European expansion has certainly emphasized multiculturalism and promoted cultural pluralism as a model for cultural accommodation today. Similarly, in the depiction of a common cultural landscape that Germans, Scotch-Irish, English, and others made together for their separate development resides the danger of assuming that tolerance was an inevitable consequence of pluralism. But just as the virulence of ethnic hostility in Eastern Europe has shocked the modern world, so ethnic conflict from time to time rocked the eighteenth-century backcountry.

Evidence of ethnic conflict appears to have been most closely associated with the final stage of landscape evolution, the development of towns. Residential intermixing was certainly more compressed in towns, and a competitive economic environment would have presented greater opportunity for social friction. That civic unity may not have encompassed ethnicity was suggested by travelers such as Harry Toulmin, who on his arrival in Winchester in 1793 observed that "It contains 1,660 inhabitants. But they are a motley set of Germans, Irish, Scots, and Anglo-Americans." Other visitors reinforced Toulmin's impression. The founder of American Methodism, Francis Asbury, commented that "the inhabitants are much divided; made up, as they are, of different nations, and speaking different languages, they agree in scarcely anything, except it be to sin against God." On another occasion, in the 1780s, the trustees of the Winchester Academy complained that "the various religions and languages which prevail among the people [were] preventing their union, in the support of this useful institution."[49]

Violence occasionally marked relations between ethnic groups. On July 11, 1759, for instance, "a certain disturbance and affray arose and happened" between a group of English and Scotch-Irish inhabitants and a group of German residents. In the end the Germans "were much beaten and hurt." Court papers give no indication of the cause of the "riot," as it was termed, but the case rose to Virginia's General Court. The first historian of the Shenandoah Valley, Samuel Kercheval, writing in the 1830s left a vivid account of the folk culture that developed in Winchester around ethnic conflict:

> The national prejudices which existed between the Dutch and Irish produced much disorder and many riots. It was customary for the Dutch on St. Patrick's Day, to exhibit the effigy of the saint, with a string of Irish potatoes around his neck, and his wife Sheeley, with her apron loaded also with potatoes. This was always followed by a riot. The Irish resented the indignity to their saint, and his holy spouse, and a battle followed. On St. Michael's Day the Irish would retort, and exhibit the saint with a rope of sour krout about his neck. Then the Dutch, like the Yankee, "felt chock full of fight" and at it they went pell mell and many a black eye, bloody nose, and broken head, was the result.[50]

Discussion of ethnicity in early America has veered from the position that ethnic identity was insignificant in social relations by 1800 to arguments that the ethnic traits of eighteenth-century immigrants not only persisted throughout the nineteenth century but also drove the process of regional definition in antebellum America. Proponents of the former position suggest that ethnicity did not matter in the way Americans interacted in trade, politics, and community formation. The alternative view holds that the cultures or folkways common to immigrant source areas such as north Britain or the Celtic periphery of the British Isles overspread broad areas of the North American interior and explain sectional tensions in United States history.[51] The experience of German settlers at Opequon, however, indicates that ethnicity remained significant in social relations throughout the eighteenth century, but that where and how ethnicity mattered was more complex than debates over persistence would suggest. What persisted among all ethnic groups at Opequon was the desire for the economic independence of the household and the perpetuation of the family on the land. Where competence in these matters required interaction and accommodation, families of all ethnic groups settled near one another, traded with one another, and governed in common. Nonetheless, family as the core of the household also defined a separate sphere in which ethnicity dictated marriage partners and shaped patterns of inheritance, denominational practice, and friendship. Thus, Germans, Scotch-Irish, English, and Anglo-American men and women not only shared a common landscape but created that landscape out of their common interests. At times that landscape could become a contested terrain for rituals of ethnic conflict. For the most part, however, these peoples worked the landscape together, ordering and allocating the resources necessary to maintain the separate spheres of family and kin.

Notes

1. A possible exception to this pattern exists in the area surrounding Millwood in present-day Clarke County, which was populated by prominent Tidewater families in the 1780s who operated large slave-based plantations and built distinctive Georgian and Greek Revival manor houses. See Willard F. Bliss, "The Tuckahoe in the Valley" (Ph.D. diss.: Princeton Univ., 1946); Mary G. Farland and Beverley B. Greenhalgh, *In the Shadow of the Blue Ridge: Clarke County, 1732–1952* (Richmond, Va.: William Byrd Press, 1978); Warren R. Hofstra, *A Separate Place: The Formation of Clarke County, Virginia* (White Post, Va.: Clarke County Sesquicentennial Committee, 1986).

2. John F. D. Smyth, *A Tour in the United States of America*, 2 vols. (London: G. Robinson, 1784; New York: New York Times and Arno Press, 1968), 2: 258. Numerous travelers drew vivid distinctions between ethnic groups, but these had more to do with character traits than landscape and with notions of ethnic preferences in land selection. See Isaac Weld, *Travels through the States of North America*, 2 vols. (London: John Stockdale, 1807; New York: Johnson Reprint, 1968), 1: 222–26, 214–15; Harry Toulmin, *The Western Country in 1793: Reports on Kentucky and Virginia*, ed. Marion Tinling and Godfrey Davies (San Marino, Calif.: Huntington Library, 1948), 22.

3. For additional discussion of landscape definitions, see John B. Jackson, *Discovering the Vernacular Landscape* (New Haven: Yale Univ. Press, 1984); John R. Stilgoe, *Common Landscape of America, 1580 to 1845* (New Haven: Yale Univ. Press, 1982).

4. The literature on central-place theory and the geography of urban location is sizable and complex. For the theory's original explication, see Walter Christaller, *Central Places in Southern Germany*, trans. Carlisle W. Baskin (Jena: Gustav Fisher, 1933; Englewood Cliffs, N.J.: Prentice Hall, 1966); and for applications to American settings, see Brian J. L. Berry, *Geography of Market Centers and Retail Distribution* (Englewood Cliffs, N.J.: Prentice Hall, 1967); James T. Lemon, "Urbanization and the Development of Eighteenth-Century Southeastern Pennsylvania and Adjacent Delaware," *William and Mary Quarterly* 3d ser., 24 (1967): 501–42; Lemon, *The Best Poor Man's Country: A Geographical Study of Early Southeastern Pennsylvania* (Baltimore: Johns Hopkins Univ. Press, 1972; New York: W. W. Norton, 1976), 118–49.

5. Early-nineteenth-century internal improvement maps, for instance, showed fourteen roads converging on the town of Winchester. See Herman Böÿe, "A Map of the State of Virginia . . ." Library of Virginia, Richmond; reprinted in E. M. Sanchez-Saavedra, *Description of the Country: Virginia's Cartographers and Their Maps, 1607–1881* (Richmond: Virginia State Library, 1975); James Madi-

son, "A Map of Virginia Formed from Actual Surveys," 1807, Library Company of Philadelphia, Philadelphia, Pa.

6. Edward A. Chappell, "Acculturation in the Shenandoah Valley: Rhenish Houses of the Massanutten Settlement," *Proceedings of the American Philosophical Society* 124 (1980): 56; Warren R. Hofstra, "Adaptation or Survival? Folk Housing at Opequon Settlement, Virginia," *Ulster Folklife* 37 (1991): 36–61; Hofstra, "Private Dwellings, Public Ways, and the Landscape of Early Rural Capitalism in Virginia's Shenandoah Valley," in *Gender, Class, and Shelter: Perspectives in Vernacular Architecture, V,* ed. Elizabeth Collins Cromley and Carter L. Hudgins (Knoxville: Univ. of Tennessee Press, 1995), 211–24.

7. For further treatment of Virginia land policy, see Warren R. Hofstra, "Land Policy and Settlement in the Northern Shenandoah Valley," in *Appalachian Frontiers: Settlement, Society, and Development in the Preindustrial Era,* ed. Robert D. Mitchell (Lexington: Univ. Press of Kentucky, 1990), 105–26; Turk McCleskey, "Rich Land, Poor Prospects: Real Estate and the Formation of a Social Elite in Augusta County, Virginia, 1738–1770," *Virginia Magazine of History and Biography* 98 (1990): 449–86; Manning C. Voorhis, "The Land Grant Policy of Colonial Virginia, 1607–1774," (Ph.D. diss.: Univ. of Virginia, 1940), 108–65.

8. Freeman H. Hart, *The Valley of Virginia in the American Revolution* (Chapel Hill: Univ. of North Carolina Press, 1942), 8–13; Robert D. Mitchell, *Commercialism and Frontier: Perspectives on the Early Shenandoah Valley* (Charlottesville: Univ. Press of Virginia, 1977), 147–49, 161–78, 183–87, 234–35.

9. In the considerable literature on the consumer revolution in Britain and America, see especially T. H. Breen, "An Empire of Goods: The Anglicization of Colonial America, 1690–1776," *Journal of British Studies* 25 (1986): 467–99; Cary Carson, Ronald Hoffman, and Peter J. Albert, eds., *Of Consuming Interests: The Style of Life in the Eighteenth Century* (Charlottesville: Univ. Press of Virginia for the United States Capitol Historical Society, 1994); Neil McKendrick, John Brewer, and J. H. Plumb, *The Birth of a Consumer Society: The Commercialization of Eighteenth-Century England* (Bloomington: Indiana Univ. Press, 1985); Carole Shammas, "Consumer Behavior in Colonial America," *Social Science History* 6 (Winter 1982): 67–86.

10. Lois Green Carr, "'The Metropolis of Maryland': A Comment on Town Development Along the Tobacco Coast," *Maryland Historical Magazine* 69 (Summer 1974): 124–45; Ronald E. Grim, "The Absence of Towns in Seventeenth-Century Virginia: The Emergence of Service Centers in York County," (Ph.D. diss.: Univ. of Maryland, College Park, 1977); Kevin P. Kelly, "'In dispers'd Country Plantations': Settlement Patterns in Seventeenth-Century Surry County, Virginia," in *The Chesapeake in the Seventeenth Century: Essays on Anglo-American Society,* ed. Thad W. Tate and David L. Ammerman (Chapel Hill: Univ. of North Carolina Press, 1979), 183–205; John C. Rainbolt, "The Absence of Towns in Seventeenth-Century Virginia," *Journal of Southern History* 35 (1969): 343–60; Edward M. Riley, "The Town Acts of Colonial Virginia," *Journal of Southern History* 16 (1950): 306–23.

11. Carville V. Earle and Ronald Hoffman, "Staple Crops and Urban Development in the Eighteenth-Century South," in *Perspectives in American History* 10 (1976): 7–78; Earle and Hoffman, "The Urban South: The First Two Centuries," in *The City in Southern History: The Growth of Urban Civilization in the South,* ed. Blaine A. Brownell and David R. Goldfield (Port Washington, N.Y.: Kennikat

Press, 1977), 23–51; James O'Mara, *An Historical Geography of Urban System Development: Tidewater Virginia in the 18th Century,* Dept. of Geography, Atkinson College, York Univ., Downsview, Ontario, Geographical Monographs No. 13 (1983).

12. "Chronological Life of Paul Henkel," ed. and trans. William J. Finck, typescript, p. 47. Tusing Collection, New Market, Va., as quoted in Klaus Wust, *The Virginia Germans* (Charlottesville: Univ. Press of Virginia, 1969), 100.

13. William H. Crawford, "The Evolution of Ulster Towns, 1750–1850," in *Plantation to Partition: Essays in Ulster History in Honour of J. L. McCracken,* ed. Peter Roebuck (Belfast: Blackstaff Press, 1981), 140–56; Crawford, "Economy and Society in Eighteenth Century Ulster" (Ph.D. diss.: Queen's Univ. of Belfast, 1982); Philip S. Robinson, *The Plantation of Ulster: British Settlement in an Irish Landscape, 1600–1670* (Dublin: Gill and MacMillan, New York: St. Martin's Press, 1984; Belfast: Ulster Historical Foundation, 1994), 85.

14. Lemon, *Best Poor Man's Country,* 106–8; A. G. Roeber, *Palatines, Liberty, and Property: German Lutherans in Colonial British America* (Baltimore: Johns Hopkins Univ. Press, 1993), 27–61.

15. Clarence R. Geier and Warren R. Hofstra, "An Archaeological Survey of and Management Plan for Cultural Resources in the Vicinity of the Upper Opequon Creek," Virginia Dept. of Historic Resources, Richmond, 1991, 48–64.

16. Warren R. Hofstra, "The Opequon Inventories, 1749–1796," *Ulster Folklife* 35 (1989): 42–71; Hofstra, "Land, Ethnicity, and Community at Opequon Settlement, Virginia, 1730–1800," *Virginia Magazine of History and Biography* 98 (1990): 423–48; Hofstra, "Adaptation or Survival?" 36–61.

17. Mark Häberlein, "German Migrants in Colonial Pennsylvania: Resources, Opportunities, and Experience," *William and Mary Quarterly* 3d ser., 50 (1993): 555–74; Elizabeth A. Kessell, "Germans in the Making of Frederick County, Maryland," in *Appalachian Frontiers,* ed. Mitchell, 87–104; Mitchell, *Commercialism and Frontier,* 104–9, 240; A. G. Roeber, "'The Origin of Whatever Is Not English among Us': The Dutch-speaking and the German-speaking Peoples of Colonial British America," in *Strangers Within the Realm: Cultural Margins of the First British Empire,* ed. Bernard Bailyn and Philip D. Morgan (Chapel Hill: Univ. of North Carolina Press, 1991), 220–83; Wust, *Virginia Germans,* 43–44.

18. A useful compilation of Stoever's records appears in William E. Eisenberg, *This Heritage: The Story of Lutheran Beginnings in the Lower Shenandoah Valley, and of Grace Church Winchester* (Boyce, Va.: Carr Publishing Company, 1954), 312–21; see also Mitchell, *Commercialism and Frontier,* 25–31; Wust, *Virginia Germans,* 37.

19. Henry Z. Jones, Ralph Conner, and Klaus Wust, *German Origins of Jost Hite: Virginia Pioneer, 1685–1761* (Edinburg, Va.: Shenandoah History, 1979).

20. Hite purchased land orders issued to John and Isaac Van Meter for forty thousand acres and acquired orders of his own for one hundred thousand acres, see H. R. McIlwaine, Wilmer L. Hall, and Benjamin J. Hillman, eds., *Executive Journals of the Council of Colonial Virginia,* 6 vols. (Richmond: Virginia State Library, 1925–66), 4: 223–24, 253.

21. Issues of ethnicity and community formation among the eleven Scotch-Irish families have been explored extensively in Hofstra, "Land, Ethnicity, and Community," 423–48.

22. For Hite's 5,018-acre patent, see Patent Book 15: 343 (hereafter cited as PB).

For land records of the seven families that settled along the Opequon, see Stephen Hotsinpiller, Orange County Deed Book 1: 431 (hereafter cited as ODB); Peter Mauk, ODB 6: 258; Christian Nisewanger, ODB 1: 436; John Poker, Frederick County Deed Book 2: 90 (hereafter cited as FDB); John Snapp, Northern Neck Land Grant Book G: 371 (hereafter cited as NNLGB); Peter Stephens, PB 15: 336, NNLGB H: 207; Abraham Wiseman, ODB 6: 249. Patent Books and Northern Neck Land Grant Books are located at the Library of Virginia, Richmond; Orange County Records are located in the Orange County Courthouse in Orange, Va.; and Frederick County records are in the Frederick County Courthouse, Winchester, Va. Only the first pages of public documents are referenced because they are indexed that way in county records. Anglicized spellings for German names are used in the text as they appear in public records.

23. Hofstra, "Land, Ethnicity, and Community," 434–36.
24. Ralph B. Strassburger and William J. Hinke, *Pennsylvania German Pioneers*, 2 vols. (Norristown, Pa.: Pennsylvania German Society, 1934; Baltimore: Genealogical Publishing House, 1980), 1: 19, 107–9; B. C. Holtzclaw, *Ancestry and Descendants of the Nassau-Siegen Immigrants to Virginia* (Culpeper, Va.: Memorial Foundation of the Germanna Colonies in Virginia, 1978), 57–58, 63–64.
25. Geier and Hofstra, "Archaeological Survey," 39–93; Hofstra, "Adaptation or Survival?" 36–38.
26. For Hite's petition for an ordinary license, see Orange County Order Book 1: 293 (hereafter cited as OOB) and Ann Brush Miller, *Historic Roads of Virginia: Orange County Road Orders, 1734–1749* (Charlottesville: Virginia Highway and Transportation Research Council, 1984), 30. Hite's 1738 road petition to the Orange County Court is quoted in William J. Hinke and Charles E. Kemper, eds., "Moravian Diaries of Travels through Virginia," *Virginia Magazine of History and Biography* 12 (1905): 142; see also OOB 1: 439; 2: 3; Miller, *Orange County Road Orders*, 36, 39.
27. The road order called for a road from Hoop Petticoat Gap to Hite's mill. Archaeological field investigations and a review of initial surveys strongly suggest that this was the road along the Opequon Creek that interconnected all the initial occupation sites in the Opequon settlement. See Frederick County Order Book 3: 299, 6: 193 (hereafter cited as FOB).
28. Holtzclaw, *Descendants of the Nassau-Siegen Immigrants*, 57–58; ODB 1: 431. In the deed Hotsinpiller describes himself as a blacksmith.
29. Frederick County Will Book 4: 327 (hereafter cited as FWB).
30. Annual food needs at Opequon are indicated by bequests of Frederick Mauk and George Hotsinpiller, who in wills of 1779 and 1794 required that their widows be provided with 14 or 15 bushels of wheat a year. A yield of 150 bushels of wheat could easily be expected from the limestone soils of Hotsinpiller's land. See FWB 4: 440; 5: 468.
31. For Hotsinpiller's estate account, see FWB 5: 176.
32. For land transactions between Stephen and John Hotsinpiller, see FDB 12: 165; 15: 394; 16: 243. John Hotsinpiller's inventory contained smith's tools appraised at £300, the most valuable single item in the estate. See FWB 4: 549. His debts are detailed in the estate accounts. See FWB 4: 646–48.
33. Bowman patented 1,000 acres on Cedar Creek in 1734, see PB 15: 338, plus a

total of 1,042 acres in four additional tracts in the surrounding area, see NNLGB H: 455, 613, 633, 642.

34. For George Bowman Sr.'s will, inventory, and accounts, see FWB 3: 431, 482; 5: 248.

35. For George Bowman Jr.'s will, inventory and account, see FWB 3: 506; 4: 120; 6: 389.

36. The issue of individualism was taken up by James T. Lemon in his account of the cultural geography of rural colonial Pennsylvania and in a subsequent series of exchanges with James A. Henretta. See Lemon, *Best Poor Man's Country*, xv–xvi; Henretta, "Families and Farms: *Mentalité* in Pre-Industrial America," *William and Mary Quarterly* 3d ser., 35 (1978): 3–32; Lemon, with a reply by Henretta, "Comment on James A. Henretta's 'Families and Farms: *Mentalité* in Pre-Industrial America,'" *William and Mary Quarterly* 3d ser., 37 (1980): 688–700. The best summaries of the voluminous literature of the ensuing debate are found in Allan Kulikoff, "The Transition to Capitalism in Rural America," *William and Mary Quarterly* 3d ser., 46 (1989): 120–44; and Michael Merrill, "Putting 'Capitalism' in Its Place: A Review of Recent Literature," *William and Mary Quarterly* 3d ser., 52 (1995): 315–26.

37. Henretta, "Families and Farms," 19.

38. Daniel Vickers, "Competency and Competition: Economic Culture in Early America," *William and Mary Quarterly* 3d ser., 47 (1990): 3–29. For a discussion of the significance of achieving independence in eighteenth-century society, see Jack P. Greene, "Independence, Improvement, and Authority: Toward a Framework for Understanding the Histories of the Southern Backcountry during the Era of the American Revolution," in *An Uncivil War: The Southern Backcountry during the American Revolution*, ed. Ronald Hoffman, Thad W. Tate, and Peter J. Albert (Charlottesville: Univ. Press of Virginia for the United States Capitol Historical Society, 1985), 3–36; Greene, *Pursuits of Happiness: The Social Development of Early Modern British Colonies and the Formation of American Culture* (Chapel Hill: Univ. of North Carolina Press, 1988), 15–16, 98, 195–97; Henretta, "Families and Farms," 18–19.

39. In dividing property more or less equally among all children, providing only for the livelihood of widows, and generally placing the private interests of the family above those of the community and its cultural institutions, German testators at Opequon established inheritance patterns similar to the ones created by Germans at Hebron settlement in the Virginia Piedmont. See Roeber, *Palatines, Liberty, and Property*, 149–55. For comparison to inheritance practices in Germany, Georgia, and South Carolina, see ibid., 46–58, 166–72, 224–30. See also Roeber, "The Origins and Transfer of German-American Concepts of Property and Inheritance," *Perspectives in American History*, New Series, 3 (1987): 115–71. Partible inheritance, protection of the property rights of children, and provision for the life maintenance of widows beyond the rights of dower also characterized inheritance practices among Germans in Frederick County, Maryland. See Kessell, "Germans in the Making of Frederick County," 101–2.

40. An unusually high percentage compared to German patterns, but not uncharacteristic of America. See Roeber, *Palatines, Liberty, and Property*, 149–50, 169–69. For wills, see George Bowman, FWB 3: 431; Jacob Chrisman, FWB 4: 402; Jost Hite, FWB 2: 487; Stephen Hotsinpiller, FWB 4: 321; Peter Mauk, FWB

4: 87; John Poker, FWB 1: 436; John Snapp Sr., FWB 3: 35; Peter Stephens, FWB 2: 266.

41. FWB 1: 436.

42. For wills of the second generation, see George Bowman Jr., FWB 3: 506; Isaac Hite, FWB 6: 55; George Hotsinpiller, FWB 5: 468; John Hotsinpiller, FWB 4: 500; Frederick Mauk, FWB 4: 440; John Nisewanger, FWB 5: 200; Jacob Poker, FWB 6: 497; John Poker, FWB 12: 480; John Snapp Jr., FWB 5: 152; Lawrence Stephens, FWB 4: 338; Lewis Stephens, FWB 8: 198.

43. In the only case of matrimony between German and Scotch-Irish settlers at Opequon, Barbara Wilson, daughter of first-generation settler Robert Wilson, married Peter Stephens, grandson of Peter Stephens, but the marriage ended in separation. See Robert Wilson's will, FWB 4: 444. For Hotsinpiller's family connections, see Stephen Hotsinpiller's will, FWB 4: 321; for John Snapp Sr.'s will, see FWB 3: 35; and for Peter Stephen's will, see Dan V. Stephens, *Peter Stephens and Some of His Descendants* (Fremont, Nebr.: Hammond and Stephens, 1936), 14.

44. Members of nine of these families signed a deed as trustees for a burying plot at the Opequon Presbyterian Church in 1745. See FDB 1: 275.

45. Eisenberg, *This Heritage,* 312–21.

46. FWB 4: 87.

47. On the issue of the extension of political institutions to the Virginia backcountry, see Richard R. Beeman, "The Political Response to Social Conflict in the Southern Backcountry: A Comparative View of Virginia and the Carolinas during the Revolution," in *An Uncivil War,* ed. Hoffman, Tate, and Albert, 213–39; Carl Bridenbaugh, *Myths and Realities: Societies of the Colonial South* (Baton Rouge: Louisiana State Univ. Press, 1952), 155–67; Nathaniel Turk McCleskey, "Across the First Divide: Frontiers of Settlement and Culture in Augusta County, Virginia, 1738–1770," (Ph.D. diss.: College of William and Mary, 1990).

48. For references to the Frederick County commissions of the peace, see FOB 1: 1; 5: 294. For additional information on Frederick County courts, vestries, and grand juries, see Thomas K. Cartmell, *Shenandoah Valley Pioneers and Their Descendants: A History of Frederick County, Virginia* (Winchester, Va.: Eddy Press, 1909; Berryville, Va.: Chesapeake Book Company, 1963), 17–26, 180–86. Militia companies are detailed in court-martial records transcribed in FDB 18.

49. Toulmin, *The Western Country,* 57; Francis Asbury, *Journal of Rev. Francis Asbury,* 3 vols. (New York: Lane and Scott, 1852), 1: 461; Legislative Petition, Winchester City, Nov. 10, 1788, Library of Virginia, Richmond. That accounts of ethnic conflict in Winchester have survived in the historical record may be more indicative of their exceptional rather than exemplary quality. Studies of relations among ethnic groups in Pennsylvania and North Carolina, although revealing some sources of conflict, stress accommodation and peaceable relations. According to James Lemon, for instance, "we can see that despite certain conflicts these people with a common western European background and similar goals were able to cooperate with one another most of the time regardless of denominational and national differences." See *Best Poor Man's Country,* 22–23. See also James G. Leyburn, *The Scotch-Irish: A Social History* (Chapel Hill: Univ. of North Carolina Press, 1962), 190–91; Daniel B. Thorp, *The Moravian Community in Colonial North Carolina: Pluralism on the Southern Frontier* (Knoxville:

Univ. of Tennessee Press, 1989), 178–98; Stephanie Grauman Wolf, *Urban Village: Population, Community, and Family Structure in Germantown, Pennsylvania, 1683–1800* (Princeton: Princeton Univ. Press, 1976), 127–53; Jerome H. Wood Jr., *Conestoga Crossroads: Lancaster, Pennsylvania, 1730–1790* (Harrisburg: Pennsylvania Historical and Museum Commission, 1979), 159–247.

50. Winchester Riot, July 11, 1759, Bonds, Qualifications, and Commissions, Frederick County Court Papers, Library of Virginia, Richmond; Wust, *Virginia Germans*, 178; Samuel Kercheval, *A History of the Valley of Virginia*, 5th ed. (Strasburg, Va.: Shenandoah Publishing House, 1973), 176.

51. That ethnicity as a factor in social relations declined in significance by 1800 appears most strongly in the work of James Lemon and Robert Mitchell. See Lemon, *Best Poor Man's Country*, and Mitchell, *Commercialism and Frontier*. The contrary position that ethnic traits persisted and defined American sectional development has been more recently developed by David Hackett Fischer. See *Albion's Seed: Four British Folkways in America* (New York: Oxford Univ. Press, 1989); see also Terry Jordan and Matti Kaups, *The American Backwoods Frontier: An Ethnic and Ecological Interpretation* (Baltimore: Johns Hopkins Univ. Press, 1989); Forrest McDonald and Grady McWhiney, "The Antebellum Southern Herdsman: A Reinterpretation," *Journal of Southern History* 41 (1975): 147–66; McDonald and McWhiney, "The South from Self-Sufficiency to Peonage: An Interpretation," *American Historical Review* 85 (1980): 1095–1118; McWhiney, *Cracker Culture: Celtic Ways in the Old South* (Tuscaloosa: Univ. of Alabama Press, 1988); McWhiney and McDonald, "Celtic Origins of Southern Herding Practices," *Journal of Southern History* 51 (1985): 165–82.

Works Cited

Asbury, Francis. *Journal of Rev. Francis Asbury*, 3 vols. New York: Lane and Scott, 1852.

Beeman, Richard R. "The Political Response to Social Conflict in the Southern Backcountry: A Comparative View of Virginia and the Carolinas during the Revolution." In *An Uncivil War: The Southern Backcountry during the American Revolution*, edited by Ronald Hoffman, Thad W. Tate, and Peter J. Albert, 213–39. Charlottesville: Univ. Press of Virginia, 1985.

Berry, Brian J. L. *Geography of Market Centers and Retail Distribution*. Englewood Cliffs, N.J.: Prentice Hall, 1967.

Bliss, Willard F. "The Tuckahoe in the Valley." Ph.D. diss., Princeton Univ., 1946.

Böÿe, Herman. "A Map of the State of Virginia . . ." Library of Virginia, Richmond, Va. Reprint, E. M. Sanchez-Saavedra. *Description of the Country: Virginia's Cartographers and Their Maps, 1607–1881*. Richmond: Virginia State Library, 1975.

Breen, T. H. "An Empire of Goods: The Anglicization of Colonial America, 1690–1776." *Journal of British Studies* 25 (1986): 467–99.

Bridenbaugh, Carl. *Myths and Realities: Societies of the Colonial South*. Baton Rouge: Louisiana State Univ. Press, 1952.

Carr, Lois Green. "'The Metropolis of Maryland': A Comment on Town Development Along the Tobacco Coast." *Maryland Historical Magazine* 69 (1974): 124–45.

Carson, Cary, Ronald Hoffman, and Peter J. Albert, editors. *Of Consuming Interests: The Style of Life in the Eighteenth Century*. Charlottesville: Univ. Press of Virginia, 1994.

Cartmell, Thomas K. *Shenandoah Valley Pioneers and Their Descendants: A History of*

Frederick County, Virginia. Winchester, Va.: Eddy Press, 1909; Berryville, Va.: Chesapeake Book Company, 1963.

Chappell, Edward A. "Acculturation in the Shenandoah Valley: Rhenish Houses of the Massanutten Settlement." *Proceedings of the American Philosophical Society* 124 (1980): 55–89.

Christaller, Walter. *Central Places in Southern Germany.* Translated by Carlisle W. Baskin. Jena: Gustav Fisher, 1933; Englewood Cliffs, N.J.: Prentice Hall, 1966.

"Chronological Life of Paul Henkel." Edited and translated by William J. Finck. Typescript, p. 47. Tusing Collection. New Market, Va. As quoted in Klaus Wust. *The Virginia Germans.* Charlottesville: Univ. Press of Virginia, 1969, 100.

Crawford, William H. "The Evolution of Ulster Towns, 1750–1850." In *Plantation to Partition: Essays in Ulster History in Honour of J. L. McCracken,* edited by Peter Roebuck, 140–56. Belfast: Blackstaff Press, 1981.

———. "Economy and Society in Eighteenth Century Ulster." Ph.D. diss., Queen's Univ. of Belfast, 1982.

Earle, Carville V., and Ronald Hoffman. "Staple Crops and Urban Development in the Eighteenth-Century South." In *Perspectives in American History* 10 (1976): 7–78.

———. "The Urban South: The First Two Centuries." In *The City in Southern History: The Growth of Urban Civilization in the South,* edited by Blaine A. Brownell and David R. Goldfield, 23–51. Port Washington, N.Y.: Kennikat Press, 1977.

Eisenberg, William E. *This Heritage: The Story of Lutheran Beginnings in the Lower Shenandoah Valley, and of Grace Church Winchester.* Boyce, Va.: Carr Publishing Company, 1954.

Farland, Mary G., and Beverley B. Greenhalgh. *In the Shadow of the Blue Ridge: Clarke County, 1732–1952.* Richmond, Va.: William Byrd Press, 1978.

Fischer, David Hackett. *Albion's Seed: Four British Folkways in America.* New York: Oxford Univ. Press, 1989.

Frederick County Court Papers. Bonds, Qualifications, and Commissions. Library of Virginia, Richmond.

Frederick County Deed Books, Order Books, and Will Books. Frederick County Courthouse, Winchester, Va.

Geier, Clarence R., and Warren R. Hofstra. "An Archaeological Survey of and Management Plan for Cultural Resources in the Vicinity of the Upper Opequon Creek." Virginia Dept. of Historic Resources, Richmond, 1991.

Greene, Jack P. "Independence, Improvement, and Authority: Toward a Framework for Understanding the Histories of the Southern Backcountry during the Era of the American Revolution." In *An Uncivil War: The Southern Backcountry during the American Revolution,* edited by Ronald Hoffman, Thad W. Tate, and Peter J. Albert, 3–36. Charlottesville: Univ. Press of Virginia, 1985.

———. *Pursuits of Happiness: The Social Development of Early Modern British Colonies and the Formation of American Culture.* Chapel Hill: Univ. of North Carolina Press, 1988.

Grim, Ronald E. "The Absence of Towns in Seventeenth-Century Virginia: The Emergence of Service Centers in York County." Ph.D. diss., Univ. of Maryland, College Park, 1977.

Häberlein, Mark. "German Migrants in Colonial Pennsylvania: Resources, Opportunities, and Experience." *William and Mary Quarterly* 3d ser., 50 (1993): 555–74.

Hart, Freeman H. *The Valley of Virginia in the American Revolution.* Chapel Hill: Univ. of North Carolina Press, 1942.

Henretta, James A. "Families and Farms: *Mentalité* in Pre-Industrial America." *William and Mary Quarterly* 3d ser., 35 (1978): 3–32.

Hinke, William J., and Charles E. Kemper, editors. "Moravian Diaries of Travels through Virginia." *Virginia Magazine of History and Biography* 11 (1903–4): 113–31, 225–42, 370–93; 12 (1904–5): 55–82, 134–53, 271–84.

Hofstra, Warren R. *A Separate Place: The Formation of Clarke County, Virginia.* White Post, Va.: Clarke County Sesquicentennial Committee, 1986.

———. "The Opequon Inventories, 1749–1796." *Ulster Folklife* 35 (1989): 42–71.

———. "Land, Ethnicity, and Community at Opequon Settlement, Virginia, 1730–1800." *Virginia Magazine of History and Biography* 98 (1990): 423–48.

———. "Land Policy and Settlement in the Northern Shenandoah Valley." In *Appalachian Frontiers: Settlement, Society, & Development in the Preindustrial Era,* edited by Robert D. Mitchell, 105–26. Lexington: Univ. Press of Kentucky, 1990.

———. "Adaptation or Survival? Folk Housing at Opequon Settlement, Virginia." *Ulster Folklife* 37 (1991): 36–61.

———. "Private Dwellings, Public Ways, and the Landscape of Early Rural Capitalism in Virginia's Shenandoah Valley." In *Gender, Class, and Shelter: Perspectives in Vernacular Architecture, V,* edited by Elizabeth Collins Cromley and Carter L. Hudgins, 211–24. Knoxville: Univ. of Tennessee Press, 1995.

Holtzclaw, B. C. *Ancestry and Descendants of the Nassau-Siegen Immigrants to Virginia.* Culpeper, Va.: Memorial Foundation of the Germanna Colonies in Virginia, 1978.

Jackson, John B. *Discovering the Vernacular Landscape.* New Haven: Yale Univ. Press, 1984.

Jones, Henry Z., Ralph Conner, and Klaus Wust. *German Origins of Jost Hite: Virginia Pioneer, 1685–1761.* Edinburg, Va.: Shenandoah History, 1979.

Jordan, Terry, and Matti Kaups. *The American Backwoods Frontier: An Ethnic and Ecological Interpretation.* Baltimore: Johns Hopkins Univ. Press, 1989.

Kelly, Kevin P. "'In dispers'd Country Plantations': Settlement Patterns in Seventeenth-Century Surry County, Virginia." In *The Chesapeake in the Seventeenth Century: Essays on Anglo-American Society,* edited by Thad W. Tate and David L. Ammerman, 183–205. Chapel Hill: Univ. of North Carolina Press, 1979.

Kercheval, Samuel. *A History of the Valley of Virginia.* 5th ed. Strasburg, Va.: Shenandoah Publishing House, 1973.

Kessell, Elizabeth A. "Germans in the Making of Frederick County, Maryland." In *Appalachian Frontiers: Settlement, Society, and Development in the Preindustrial Era,* edited by Robert D. Mitchell, 87–104. Lexington: Univ. Press of Kentucky, 1990.

Kulikoff, Allan. "The Transition to Capitalism in Rural America." *William and Mary Quarterly* 3d ser., 46 (1989): 120–44.

Lemon, James T. "Urbanization and the Development of Eighteenth-Century Southeastern Pennsylvania and Adjacent Delaware." *William and Mary Quarterly* 3d ser., 24 (1967): 501–42.

———. *The Best Poor Man's Country: A Geographical Study of Early Southeastern Pennsylvania.* Baltimore: Johns Hopkins Univ. Press, 1972; New York: W. W. Norton, 1976.

———. With a Reply by James A. Henretta. "Comment on James A. Henretta's 'Families and Farms: *Mentalité* in Pre-Industrial America,'" *William and Mary Quarterly* 3d ser., 37 (1980): 688–700.

Leyburn, James G. *The Scotch-Irish: A Social History.* Chapel Hill: Univ. of North Carolina Press, 1962.

Madison, James. "A Map of Virginia Formed from Actual Surveys," 1807. Library Company of Philadelphia, Philadelphia, Pa.

McCleskey, Nathaniel Turk. "Across the First Divide: Frontiers of Settlement and Culture in Augusta County, Virginia, 1738–1770." Ph.D. diss., College of William and Mary, 1990.

————. "Rich Land, Poor Prospects: Real Estate and the Formation of a Social Elite in Augusta County, Virginia, 1738–1770." *Virginia Magazine of History and Biography* 98 (1990): 449–86.

McDonald, Forrest, and Grady McWhiney. "The Antebellum Southern Herdsman: A Reinterpretation." *Journal of Southern History* 41 (1975): 147–66.

————. "The South from Self-Sufficiency to Peonage: An Interpretation." *American Historical Review* 85 (1980): 1095–1118.

McIlwaine, H. R., Wilmer L. Hall, and Benjamin J. Hillman, editors. *Executive Journals of the Council of Colonial Virginia*, 6 vols. Richmond: Virginia State Library, 1925–66.

McKendrick, Neil, John Brewer, and J. H. Plumb. *The Birth of a Consumer Society: The Commercialization of Eighteenth-Century England.* Bloomington: Indiana Univ. Press, 1985.

McWhiney, Grady. *Cracker Culture: Celtic Ways in the Old South.* Tuscaloosa: Univ. of Alabama Press, 1988.

McWhiney, Grady, and Forrest McDonald, "Celtic Origins of Southern Herding Practices." *Journal of Southern History* 51 (1985): 165–82.

Merrill, Michael. "Putting 'Capitalism' in Its Place: A Review of Recent Literature." *William and Mary Quarterly* 3d ser., 52 (1995): 315–26.

Miller, Ann Brush. *Historic Roads of Virginia: Orange County Road Orders, 1734–1749.* Charlottesville: Virginia Highway and Transportation Research Council, 1984.

Mitchell, Robert D. *Commercialism and Frontier: Perspectives on the Early Shenandoah Valley.* Charlottesville: Univ. Press of Virginia, 1977.

Northern Neck Land Grant Books. Library of Virginia, Richmond.

O'Mara, James. *An Historical Geography of Urban System Development: Tidewater Virginia in the 18th Century.* Dept. of Geography, Atkinson College, York Univ., Downsview, Ontario, Geographical Monographs No. 13 (1983).

Orange County Deed Books and Order Books. Orange County Courthouse, Orange, Va.

Patent Books. Library of Virginia, Richmond.

Rainbolt, John C. "The Absence of Towns in Seventeenth-Century Virginia." *Journal of Southern History* 35 (1969): 343–60.

Riley, Edward M. "The Town Acts of Colonial Virginia." *Journal of Southern History* 16 (1950): 306–23.

Robinson, Philip S. *The Plantation of Ulster: British Settlement in an Irish Landscape, 1600–1670.* Dublin: Gill and MacMillan, New York: St. Martin's Press, 1984; Belfast: Ulster Historical Foundation, 1994.

Roeber, A. G. "The Origins and Transfer of German-American Concepts of Property and Inheritance." *Perspectives in American History*, New Series, 3 (1987): 115–71.

————. "'The Origin of Whatever Is Not English among Us': The Dutch-speaking and the German-speaking Peoples of Colonial British America." In *Strangers Within the Realm: Cultural Margins of the First British Empire*, edited by Bernard Bailyn and Philip D. Morgan, 220–83. Chapel Hill: Univ. of North Carolina Press, 1991.

————. *Palatines, Liberty, and Property: German Lutherans in Colonial British America.* Baltimore: Johns Hopkins Univ. Press, 1993.

Shammas, Carole. "Consumer Behavior in Colonial America." *Social Science History* 6 (1982): 67–86.

Smyth, John F. D. *A Tour in the United States of America,* 2 vols. London: G. Robinson, 1784; New York: New York Times & Arno Press, 1968.

Stephens, Dan V. *Peter Stephens and Some of His Descendants.* Fremont, Nebr.: Hammond and Stephens, 1936.

Stilgoe, John R. *Common Landscape of America, 1580 to 1845.* New Haven: Yale Univ. Press, 1982.

Strassburger, Ralph B., and William J. Hinke. *Pennsylvania German Pioneers,* 2 vols. Norristown, Pa.: Pennsylvania German Society, 1934; Baltimore: Genealogical Publishing House, 1980.

Thorp, Daniel B. *The Moravian Community in Colonial North Carolina: Pluralism on the Southern Frontier.* Knoxville: Univ. of Tennessee Press, 1989.

Toulmin, Harry. *The Western Country in 1793: Reports on Kentucky and Virginia.* Edited by Marion Tinling and Godfrey Davies. San Marino, Calif.: Huntington Library, 1948.

Vickers, Daniel. "Competency and Competition: Economic Culture in Early America." *William and Mary Quarterly* 3d ser., 47 (1990): 3–29.

Voorhis, Manning C. "The Land Grant Policy of Colonial Virginia, 1607–1774." Ph.D. diss., Univ. of Virginia, 1940.

Weld, Isaac. *Travels through the States of North America,* 2 vols. London: John Stockdale, 1807; New York: Johnson Reprint, 1968.

Winchester City Legislative Petitions. Library of Virginia, Richmond.

Wolf, Stephanie Grauman. *Urban Village: Population, Community, and Family Structure in Germantown, Pennsylvania, 1683–1800.* Princeton: Princeton Univ. Press, 1976.

Wood, Jerome H., Jr. *Conestoga Crossroads: Lancaster, Pennsylvania, 1730–1790.* Harrisburg: Pennsylvania Historical and Museum Commission, 1979.

Wust, Klaus. *The Virginia Germans.* Charlottesville: Univ. Press of Virginia, 1969.

Chapter 3

Religion, Migration, and Pluralism

A Shenandoah Valley Community, 1740–1790

Richard K. MacMaster

Religious diversity and pluralism made Virginians who lived between the Blue Ridge and the Allegheny Mountains different from people in other sections of the colony. That, at any rate, was the opinion of the Rev. James Ireland, when, in 1804, he dictated his reminiscences of the religious revival in the 1760s and 1770s. According to Ireland:

> The people inhabiting these valleys, were better informed, arising from the following considerations, they were a divided people as to religious persuasions, consisting of Baptists, Presbyterians, Methodists, Quakers, Menonists, Tunkers, and Churchmen, with a variety of others. As persecution was not a reigning principle among them, and they lived in a common state of sociability, it gave them an opportunity of being acquainted with each other's principles and practices, by which their ideas became more enlarged and their judgments more generally informed than those of the [eastern] division.

Civility and secular interests characterized those Virginians who lived "from the Blue Ridge of Mountains down towards the bay," and they were considered "the politest part of the people," but they did not concern themselves with religion, unless to oppose it in others. Ireland had even less regard for the inhabitants of the Allegheny frontier. He dismissed them as "an uncultivated people," "rude and illiterate," and "a compound of the barbarian and the indian."[1]

The Shenandoah Valley counties also stood apart from other sections of Virginia in their experience of the eighteenth-century revival. Rhys Isaac identified "the evangelical revolt" as "the most dramatic and far-reaching event in the transformation of Virginia," and Richard Beeman observed that even in the backcountry of Southside Virginia "the rise of enthusiastic, evangelical religion" had profound social consequences and "posed a striking challenge to Anglican gentry culture." Some Valley congregations felt the pain of division over a new minister or a new hymn book, and Baptist, Methodist, and United Brethren evangelists gathered new converts, but nowhere was the evangelical movement a threat or a challenge to the existing order. There was not even the coming together of Presbyterians and Anglicans against all enthusiasts that Beeman found in Lunenburg County. What James Ireland termed "a common state of sociability" prevailed.[2]

Eighteenth-century Shenandoah Valley people behaved much as their former neighbors in southeastern Pennsylvania had. They accepted other Christians, certainly other Protestants, as fellow believers who differed from themselves in minor ways. Especially among German settlers, two or three denominations would share a meeting house that often doubled as a school for children of all faiths. Funerals and, increasingly, marriages brought neighbors of varied backgrounds together. Many retained strong denominational loyalties, others favored a nondenominational pietism, but all accepted church membership as a voluntary choice. Wartime demands for military service cast a shadow over this idyllic picture, however, when Quakers and Mennonites expressed conscientious objection to taking up arms. Some ethnic groups settled so thickly, both in Pennsylvania and Virginia, as to limit their contacts with others, and, even in mixed areas, language remained a barrier. In the Shenandoah Valley, as in southeastern Pennsylvania, a lively land market broke down many of those barriers and brought settlers of different backgrounds into formerly solid ethnic enclaves. This was the case in Shenandoah County.

Although he later served churches in other sections of the Shenandoah Valley, James Ireland spent a significant part of his life near present New Market in the southern part of Shenandoah County. This rural neighborhood along Holman's Creek, the North River of the Shenandoah, and

Smith's Creek was an area of almost continual settlement and resettlement in the eighteenth century. New families moved into the section regularly and others disappeared from the county. But those who persisted in the community were as likely to sell out and move a short distance. The community was thus continually defining and redefining its boundaries as one ethnic or religious group shifted its center or admitted people of other backgrounds into its neighborhood. There was no apparent weakening of religious commitment on the part of those identified with one congregation or another. Baptists generally remained Baptists, Quakers remained Quakers, although some did join another church, especially in times of revival. (The revival itself had a marked nondenominational tone, stressing a common evangelical piety.) But the likelihood of marriage across denominational lines greatly increased when neighbors were of different faiths. A Quaker or Mennonite might have a Baptist son-in-law; a Lutheran could have family members who were Mennonites or Quakers. Friendships and business relationships naturally increased cross-denominational contacts among neighbors. The process of migration—both long- and short-distance movement—contributed an essential ingredient to understanding the "common state of sociability" that characterized this and other Shenandoah Valley communities.

Residential mixing of ethnic and religious groups influenced attitudes of tolerance. As Sally Schwartz has demonstrated, in contrast with Virginia, "positive responses to religious as well as ethnic diversity increased" in Pennsylvania in the 1760s and 1770s, and Pennsylvanians tended to be "undogmatic about their denominational affiliation." One Pennsylvania German summarized his experience of "many diverse religious opinions" at a rural funeral: "Here we mingled like fish at sea, but peaceably. He who would let it be noticed that he was inimical to another because of religion, would be regarded as a fool, although one frankly tells another his mind." His immediate neighbors were a Mennonite preacher and a Catholic priest; both were his friends.[3] The Hereford or New Goshenhoppen community in Berks County, where he lived, had a reputation for friendly relations; it was a community where people of different religious groups lived in close proximity. Other Pennsylvania communities with sharper lines of demarcation showed less tolerance.[4]

James Ireland's enthusiasm for Shenandoah Valley pluralism doubtless reflected his own experience. The son of a Scottish lawyer and a graduate of the famous Latin High School in Edinburgh, Ireland embarked for America as a result of a "juvenile indiscretion." He found employment as a schoolmaster near the present town of New Market in Shenandoah County. He found enjoyment in "balls, dancing, and chanting to the sound of the violin," and his own accomplishments in this field soon gained him the confidence and esteem not only of the young ladies and gentlemen of the neighborhood but also of their elders, who invited him to join in "swearing, drinking, and frolicking" and "horse-racing." The way lay open to the young schoolmaster for advancement in society, a good marriage, and perhaps a clerical or legal career.[5]

His life took a different turn through an invitation from an acquaintance "who taught vocal music" to accompany him to one of his singing schools. It was held "about 22 miles from his residence, at the house of one Colonel Pugh." The two young men rode together down the Valley to Colonel Joseph Pugh's house, near Woodstock. Ireland's unnamed friend "was married to a minister's daughter in Maryland," and his own father was a minister, "both of the Baptist persuasion." These details make it possible to identify the music teacher as John Alderson Jr., who lived on Smith's Creek, just north of New Market.

Ireland was such a success in the singing school at Colonel Pugh's that he recruited pupils for his own school. One young lady, who chose to board with a friend near New Market so as to attend Ireland's school, was instrumental in starting a prayer meeting. Soon the schoolmaster and several of his friends began meeting together for earnest prayer. Others were amused that "James Ireland is going to get converted."[6]

His conversion was not instantaneous, but stretched over a period of struggle in 1768 and 1769. Ireland's experience mirrored that of others in the neighborhood, so that reports spread "of the work of the Lord that had broke out amongst us" and "the flourishing state of religion at Smiths Creek." Ireland himself "took up lodging at a good old Presbyterian friend's house, whose residence was contiguous to Massanutten mountain." This friend was Adam Jackman, who had married Jane Carroll, daughter of William Carroll, an early Quaker settler on Smith's Creek. The schoolmaster would "retire every morning with my Bible and prayer book" to the wooded slope of the mountain.

He was attracted to the Separate Baptists, even traveling over the Blue Ridge to hear John Pickett preach in Fauquier County, but he remained unconvinced of the need for baptism by immersion. The "little bonded society on Smiths Creek" with whom he found Christian fellowship was equally reluctant to take on denominational identity. This circumstance "produced a degree of trouble and anxiety for a short time." Ireland and his friends agreed that the work of God "was carried on under the ministry of the Baptists," the enthusiastic Separates and the more sedate Regulars, who were both Calvinists. Eventually they favored the Separate Baptists. "Our little religious body were disposed to join them" and sent Ireland to the Separates across the Blue Ridge, who admitted him as an itinerant preacher.[7]

Ireland returned briefly to Smith's Creek and then accepted a call to preach at Carter's Run in Fauquier County. On his way down the valley, he stopped with Colonel Pugh and Colonel John Tipton, who was one of the church wardens of Beckford Parish, but Ireland "expected to be a prisoner in Culpeper jail that night." The attitude of sheriffs and church wardens toward itinerant Baptist preachers differed from county to county. Ireland was indeed arrested and imprisoned in Culpeper County when he refused to give security that he would neither teach, preach, nor exhort. On his release, he returned to the Shenandoah Valley.[8]

"From my residence on Smiths Creek, I used to pursue my course into what is now called Rockingham County," he recorded and "attended statedly at a place called the White House, where I was instrumental in planting what has since been called the Menonist Baptist Church." Ireland visited the Mennonites in present Page County, awakened in 1770 by the preaching of Baptist John Koontz; they later formed an independent congregation that met at the White House, near Hamburg, under the leadership of Martin Kauffman. The Koontz congregation was known as the Mill Creek Baptist Church. The Menonist Baptists disagreed with other Virginia Baptists in forbidding the swearing of oaths, the use of military force, and the ownership of slaves, retaining key doctrines of the Mennonite Church. This degree of difference was evidently compatible, in Ireland's view, within a wider fellowship of Baptists.[9]

When the Smith's Creek Separate Baptist Church was formally organized about 1774, the congregation called John Ireland and Anderson Moffett to be its preachers. Moffett, who had been born in Fauquier County in 1746, had moved to Shenandoah County and was settled on Smith's Creek just south of present Mount Jackson. His wife was the daughter of Balzer Hupp, a lifelong Mennonite. Moffett was one of those who "adopted the practice of meeting at private houses on Sundays for the purpose of singing and praying and reading the Scriptures" as one of Ireland's "little bonded society."[10]

The Smith's Creek Separate Baptists did not unite with the existing congregation of Regular Baptists in their own neighborhood, although some favored such a union at an earlier stage. They built a new meeting house on land owned by Edwin Young within the present town of New

Market. On August 3, 1778, Edwin Young leased an acre "whereon the meeting house now stands" to Richard Jackman, Adam Jackman, John Jackman, John Newman, Walter Moffett, Cornelius Ruddell, and Anderson Moffett as trustees "for the use of these Separate Baptists." The trustees included men who came from Presbyterian, Anglican, and Regular Baptist backgrounds and who lived in the southern part of Shenandoah County from the county line as far north as present Mount Jackson. The Massanutten Mountain on the east and the thinly settled pine forest on the west bounded a well-defined rural neighborhood drained by Smith's Creek, the North Fork of the Shenandoah River, and Holman's Creek. This was the community that James Ireland knew best, and it is the community that I have chosen to examine for signs of the "common state of sociability" that united this "divided people as to religious persuasions."[11]

As in all frontier communities, the earliest settlers on Smith's Creek welcomed preachers of any denomination to baptize their younger children and marry their older ones. The Lutheran itinerant John Caspar Stoever married three couples and christened eighteen children in June 1737 "at North River Shenandoah vulgo Codkel Town" and returned a year later for additional baptisms. He married "Daniel Hoolman and Elisabeth Carathay" in 1737 and baptized their twins in 1738.[12] John Craig, a Presbyterian pastor in Augusta County, preached occasionally "at Daniel Holdman's" and in 1741 baptized a child of William Clark, who later gave land for an Anglican chapel.[13]

These practices persisted. A shortage of clergy and the diversity of the community caused the Smith's Creek section to lag behind in organizing congregations and calling preachers. Even after churches were built and ministers settled, people felt free to attend preaching or join their neighbors for worship at their meeting houses. Deacon Samuel Newman of the Smith's Creek Baptist congregation wrote in 1756 of visits by John Alderson about 1753 to different settlements "where the people were much affected, and prepared to receive further instructions from his mouth," and of a preaching tour in 1755 by John Gano, "who was received by the love and likeing of almost all sorts of people."[14] Hugh Judge attended Smith's Creek Quaker meeting in 1782, "which was large, numbers being present of other societies."[15] Quaker marriage certificates from Smith's Creek in the 1780s reveal the same openness to people of other religious societies. Lutherans, Mennonites, and even Baptist minister Anderson Moffett signed as witnesses from the meeting.[16]

By the time the Separate Baptists erected their meeting house, this divided people had built an ample number of churches and meeting houses for themselves. The Virginia Assembly had created Beckford Parish in 1772 when they separated Dunmore (later Shenandoah) County from Frederick County. The new parish inherited two chapels of ease, one near Woodstock, and the other at Rude's Hill. Caspar Hupp, a Mennonite, gave a deed to Burr Harrison and John Tipton, the church wardens, for an acre on the main road from Woodstock to Staunton, beginning "on ye point of a hill above ye old Chappel." Hupp had purchased the land from William Clark, whose father had neglected to register a deed for the chapel land.[17] Hupp's neighbor, Dr. John Henry Neff, who was also a Mennonite, owned the land on which the Quakers had built their meeting house. In 1773 Jackson Allen purchased two acres of land from Dr. John Henry Neff upon which the Smith Creek Meeting House of the Society of Friends was erected.[18] The Regular Baptists had their Smith Creek Meeting House north of present New Market on land owned successively by their deacon, Samuel Newman, and their minister, John Alderson. In 1775 Alderson sold his land, "beginning at a large black oak near the Baptist meeting house," to Christian Wissler, still another Mennonite.[19]

Mennonites probably met for worship in private homes, although they used the Regular Baptist meeting house at a slightly later date. Dunkers, the present Church of the Brethren, invariably worshiped in the houses of their members in the Holman's Creek settlement. Local tradition held that Lutherans and Reformed used the Rude's Hill chapel before they built the first St. Mary's Pine Church in 1787. It is more probable that Lutherans and Reformed church members traveled to Rader's Church in Rockingham County or to the Pine Church on Stony Creek in Shenandoah County. The community included many Lutheran, Reformed, and Presbyterian families from the earliest settlement, but trained ministers were few and churches did not always keep up with their people.[20]

The first Methodist congregation in Shenandoah County and the first in the valley above Berkeley County had built a meeting house at Red Banks, just north of present Mount Jackson, "that new erected Chapple called Bethel," by 1786. The trustees nearly all lived in the immediate neighborhood, but one had his home across the Rockingham County line.[21]

The religious and ethnic diversity of the Smith's Creek–Holman's Creek neighborhood is easy to establish, but James Ireland spoke of "a common state of sociability." These different ethnic and religious groups did not live in isolation from one another, passing like fish in a stream. Robert D. Mitchell concluded from his study of the eighteenth-century Shenandoah Valley that "The residential mixing of ethnically diverse populations was the most dominant trend by the end of the colonial period." While Mitchell found some evidence to support "the long-standing view that the valley's population could be regionalized in terms of national origins," he considered it "more apparent than real." For Mitchell, "the increasing locational intermingling of population within the valley by 1776" raised questions as to "whether discrete national groups still existed" in the Shenandoah Valley and "how far different cultural heritages can be considered a significant factor."[22]

The narrow slice of the Shenandoah Valley we are considering was characterized by this kind of residential mixing from the first settlement. German, Dutch, French, Swiss, English, Welsh, Irish, and Ulster Scot settlers took up contiguous land in the early days. At the same time, as in southeastern Pennsylvania, the "distributional patterns of nationalities and religious denominations" indicated over time that "settlers were strongly attracted by their own cultural groups." Where one German or Swiss or Scot settled, others seemed to take up land in due time. Religion may have been a more significant factor than language or national heritage. Mennonites, Quakers, Lutherans, and Baptists often chose to purchase a farm where others of their faith already lived. The possibility of becoming part of a familiar congregational life and worship would obviously be a factor, rather than any antipathy to settlers of other languages or cultures. As James T. Lemon noted, "Much of German exclusiveness was simply the result of their large numbers and their tendency to arrive in large parties." If Shenandoah Valley settlers chose rural neighborhoods where people of their own faith and language already lived, their numbers were not always large enough to exclude other groups, even if that had been their intention.[23]

Some Shenandoah Valley settlers did create ethnic and religious enclaves as a result of the first migration and settlement. A young minister supplying the North Mountain Presbyterian Church, west of Staunton in Augusta County, in 1776 recognized that "All here are Irish, all are Presbyterians." The settlers along Stony Creek in Shenandoah County eventually formed a solidly German community, predominantly Lutheran and Reformed. Other examples could be easily found. But the settlers along Holman's and Smith's Creeks were far from unique in their mix of ethnic and religious groups.[24] The earliest settlers on Smith's Creek, Holman's Creek, and the North River of the Shenandoah reflected the ethnic and religious diversity of the middle colonies. As in Pennsylvania, where "Penn's refusal to allow the ethnic enclaves desired by early Welsh and

German colonists . . . contributed to mutual toleration as individuals acquired neighbors of different backgrounds and beliefs," the earliest settlements in southern Shenandoah County formed a religious and ethnic mix.[25]

Benjamin Allen and Reuben Allen, sons of a Quaker wheelwright who moved from Dartmouth, Massachusetts, to Shrewsbury, New Jersey, had themselves moved on to Cecil County, Maryland, before coming to the Shenandoah Valley. In 1735 Benjamin Allen bought land along the Shenandoah from Jost Hite that became known as Benjamin Allen's Mill Creek. Reuben Allen acquired 625 acres of land adjoining his brother's tract. Their lands stretched along the Shenandoah south from present Mount Jackson. They were soon joined by Andrew Bird and his family from the Swedish settlement near present Douglassville, Berks County, by Riley Moore and his family from Prince George's County, Maryland, and by William White, another Pennsylvanian, whose lands were at the mouth of Smith's Creek.[26] John Hodge had settled a little further upstream on Smith's Creek by 1737. John Henry Neff, a Mennonite physician, Captain John Dawbin, William Clark, and Daniel Holman had purchased land from Jost Hite along the Shenandoah at Holman's Creek.[27]

The land they bought in good faith from Hite lay within the Fairfax Grant as determined in 1744, so early settlers and newcomers alike needed clear titles from the Proprietary of the Northern Neck. Records of the Proprietary Land Office demonstrate an emerging pattern of ethnic settlement in the 1740s. Christian Funkhouser, a Mennonite, settled on Holman's Creek just above the Neffs and the Holmans. His neighbors upstream were mainly Germans: Rudolph Brock (Brach), Henry Brock, George Brock, Peter Gartner, Henry Bachman, Conrad Rinhart, and Rosina Buckius. Rees Thomas, Evan Jones, Rees Lewis, Evan Thomas, and other Welsh settlers chose the upper reaches of Holman's Creek. Scotch-Irish pioneers had also come to Holman's Creek. Archibald Ruddell, William Maclane, Thomas Moore, a Quaker, John Thompson, and Con Daugherty settled in a group between Captain John Dawbin and Peter Gartner. John O'Neill, Neil O'Neill, Timothy O'Roark, Robert Caldwell, Patrick Grimes, Cornelius O'Bryan, and others of Irish birth settled together on the Shenandoah above the mouth of Holman's Creek.

Other Quakers joined the Quaker Allens along the Shenandoah and Allen's Mill Creek, just north of the Holman's Creek settlements. Joseph Denham (Dennum), John Dodson, Joseph Hawkins, Abraham Collett, George Nichols, and James Hill lived in that neighborhood, as did Moores and Ruddells. Welshman Griffith Thomas and Germans John Bonawitz (Pennywit) and Michael Kelkener settled here, too.

Smith's Creek settlers in the 1740s came of several ethnic and religious backgrounds: William Carroll, a Pennsylvania Quaker, Capt. Peter Scholl from New Jersey, Samuel and Jonathan Newman from Cecil County, Maryland, by way of Pennsylvania. Thomas Looker, Valentine Sevier, William James, Samuel Lusk, Matthias Scheine (Skeen), John and Cornelius Ruddell, William White, and Nicholas Seehorn all had their land titles confirmed by Lord Fairfax in 1748–49.[28]

Clearly, settlers of different backgrounds lived in close proximity, but often in smaller groupings of people of the same ethnic or religious heritage. Neither the residential mixing of people of different heritage nor their apparent desire to identify with that heritage is enough in itself to explain the cultural pluralism that James Ireland described. We need to look at the process of migration itself. Numerous studies published in recent years have established the importance of migration and movement within the colonies. We no longer imagine the isolated individual or family striking out into an unknown territory as typical, although such people clearly existed. The more typical migrants moved with kinfolk or former neighbors, often in stages, and sought to reproduce in the new settlement something of the life they had known in the rural neighborhood they were leaving behind. The concern expressed by Quakers and Baptists about "going off in a disorderly manner" or "locating beyond the verge of established meetings" is implicit in the practice of other denominations and sanctioned the common interest in replicating the community left behind. Migrating families and individuals often chose a settlement where people of their acquaintance already lived or followed relatives in a chain migration over generations. This is the pattern we find along Smith's Creek and Holman's Creek.[29]

If migration from one community to a new one is an event completed within a relatively few years, the character of the old community can be transplanted to the new neighborhood in a determinate way. We might expect the preponderance of Ulster Scots in Augusta or Rockbridge in the first settlement to create the social climate into which newcomers will merge, even when Germans settle there in large numbers. In time the community established by the first settlers may weaken, disintegrate, or disappear as a second wave of migration draws off subsequent generations to new lands. Scotch-Irish sections of Rockingham County became solidly German in this later movement of people. If migration, on the other hand, is a continuous process, spread over a long period of time, each new group of settlers will attempt to replicate their old community before any one so-cial pattern has become dominant.

The tilt of the Shenandoah Valley made it a natural migration route for settlers moving south and west as well as a destination for incoming migrants. Pennsylvanians and Jerseymen in search of good farmland need not press all the way to Carolina to find it. The potential for a good mar-ket in Shenandoah Valley land did not depend on out-migrants selling their land to move to North Carolina or Kentucky. A canny landowner could get a good price for one valley farm and move to another.

Migration was itself a strategy for preserving the family and im-proving its economic prospects. Landowners unable to purchase farms for all their sons in the existing community had the option of setting them up in a trade or acquiring land at a greater or lesser distance from the homeplace.[30]

The pattern of land transfers from the 1750s indicates that sales to newcomers by settlers who had moved elsewhere accounted for only a small percentage of the total. In 1751 Cornelius Cook of Granville County, North Carolina, sold his land to Rees Thomas, and William Rutledge of Granville County sold Cornelius Ruddell the land he had patented. Much more common were transfers of title from one persisting settler to another; John Dawbin, for instance, in 1753 sold Thomas Moore four hundred acres on Holman's Creek he had patented, and other transfers from Tho-mas Moore to Samuel Newman, Swain Rambo to Andrew Bird, Andrew Bird to Jacob Rambo could be instanced.[31]

As settlers bought and sold land on Holman's or Smith's Creeks among themselves, they changed the existing community in small ways. The Quakers were now more concentrated closer to the present Rockingham County line. The Welsh moved up Holman's Creek to-ward Brock's Gap. Mennonites became more prominent on Smith's Creek. More important, all of the apparent centers of ethnic settlement opened to include people of different backgrounds as neighbors.

The pattern prevailed in the 1760s and 1770s. Two additional factors may have contributed to frequent land sales: the heirs of John Mercer suc-cessfully pressed a claim to land on Smith's Creek within the Fairfax Grant, and Burr Hamilton of Prince William County began purchasing farmland along Smith's Creek and the Shenandoah in 1762, piecing together a large plantation. Landowners had added incentives to sell without leaving the area. But those moving south and west also found eager buyers for their lands. Out-migrant Samuel Newman sold his farm to Mennonite Henry Houser on leaving for South Carolina in 1765, and John Sevier, on his way to the Watauga settlement in 1772, sold his lands to Edwin Young and

Joseph Strickler. John Alderson, then in Botetourt County, sold land to Edwin Young and to Christian Whisler in 1775, but the normal transfer was from one persisting resident to another. As a result, the community constantly shifted its boundaries and brought ethnic and religious groups into "a common state of sociability."[32]

In his ground-breaking study of *The Valley of Virginia in the American Revolution*, Freeman Hart nearly equated religious affiliation and ethnic origin.[33] Although there is ample evidence to support this assumption, it obscures the degree to which the churches had become voluntary associations by the middle years of the eighteenth century. Ethnicity and religious identity are not interchangeable, since one could be the result of free choice. Many members of an eighteenth-century Presbyterian congregation in Pennsylvania or Virginia would be of Scotch or Scotch-Irish background, but Presbyterians were not all Scots or Ulstermen, and emigrants from Scotland and Ireland were not all Presbyterians. Church membership in America was a matter of voluntary association. Walter Newman, for example, who came to Pennsylvania from Dublin, Ireland, had all of his children baptized in the Church of England and was most probably of the Anglican faith. Two of his sons united as adults with a Baptist congregation of Welsh ethnicity and another son joined the Lutheran Church.

This is reflected in the Baptist congregation that organized itself in 1756 when the Rev. John Alderson moved to Smith's Creek. Deacon Samuel Newman and his wife had settled on Smith's Creek in 1744, bringing letters from the Montgomery Baptist Church near present Lansdale, Pennsylvania. This was a Welsh congregation, but the pastor preached in Welsh and English. Mary Newman, wife of Samuel's brother Jonathan, was a member of the Southampton Baptist Church in Bucks County. The Newmans, originally members of the Church of England, were baptized and joined the Baptist Church only in 1740, possibly as a result of the revival. Rees Thomas, another charter member, came from the Welsh Baptist Church in Cumru Township, Lancaster (now Berks) County, Pennsylvania, as did three other early members. William Castleberry and his wife belonged to the New Britain Baptist Church in Pennsylvania; his parents were Mennonites. Others who joined in the first year are identified in the records kept by Samuel Newman as "brought up in Quakerism," "A Presbyterian of good report," "formerly a Church of England man," and "brought up a Quaker."

Newman and many of the Smith's Creek members moved to South Carolina in 1765, where he organized the Bush River Baptist Church. Other incoming settlers took their place, and the congregation survived until John Alderson, the minister, and his sons moved to Botetourt County, Virginia, in 1777.[34]

Like the regular Baptists, the Smith's Creek meeting of the Society of Friends (Quakers) gained new members from the community in addition to the ebb and flow of lifelong Quakers migrating to and from the area. Of fifteen families who constituted Smith's Creek Meeting in 1782, four had moved from Pennsylvania meetings of the Society of Friends during the previous five years, and four families of other backgrounds from the Smith's Creek neighborhood had joined the Quaker meeting during the previous five years.[35]

Visiting Friends from other meetings, like Hugh Judge from Pennsylvania and William Matthews from Maryland, found Smith's Creek Meeting in good order and faithful to Quaker testimony during the troubled times of the American Revolution. Jackson Allen, a well-to-do farmer and miller, appeared in Shenandoah County Court in 1776 to answer charges that he had freed his slave in defiance of Virginia law. He was in court more than once and had heavy fines distrained against him for fidelity to Quaker teaching about military service and war taxes, as had his brother Joseph Allen. At least five members of Hopewell Monthly Meeting, which included Smith's Creek, were imprisoned for refusal to undertake military duty. John Allen, on the other hand, had left the Quakers before his marriage to a Presbyterian and served with the militia during the war. The Moore family was equally divided, with some members remaining active in the Friends meeting and others uniting with other churches. Family ties remained strong, as evidenced by wills.[36]

The experience of Smith's Creek Quakers indicates that tolerance and extended family groups that reached across denominational lines do not equate with indifference or a casual approach to religion. The experience of all the religious groups in southern Shenandoah County does suggest that people who lived in "a common state of sociability" with neighbors of other faiths learned to accept one another and to recognize a commonalty with other Christians that made it relatively easy to change church membership at times of marriage or in seasons of revival. These eighteenth-century Valley Virginians had discovered attitudes common to Americans in the nineteenth century.[37]

Notes

1. James Ireland, *The Life of the Rev. James Ireland, Who Was, For Many Years, Pastor of the Baptist Church at Buck Marsh, Waterlick, and Happy Creek in Frederick and Shenandoah County, Virginia* (Winchester, Va., 1819), 181–84.

2. Rhys Isaac, "The Evangelical Revolt: The Nature of the Baptists' Challenge to the Traditional Order in Virginia, 1765–1776," *William and Mary Quarterly* 3d ser., 31 (1974): 345–68; Rhys Isaac, *The Transformation of Virginia 1740–1790* (Chapel Hill: Univ. of North Carolina Press, 1982), 163–64; Richard R. Beeman and Rhys Isaac, "Cultural Conflict and Social Change in the Revolutionary South: Lunenburg County, Virginia," *Journal of Southern History* 46 (1980): 525–50; Beeman, *The Evolution of the Southern Backcountry: A Case Study of Lunenburg County, Virginia, 1746–1832* (Philadelphia: Univ. of Pennsylvania Press, 1984), 97, 104.

3. Sally Schwartz, *"A Mixed Multitude": The Struggle for Toleration in Colonial Pennsylvania* (New York: New York Univ. Press, 1987), 263–66.

4. Richard K. MacMaster, *Land, Piety, Peoplehood: The Establishment of Mennonite Communities in America 1683–1790* (Scottdale, Pa.: Herald Press, 1985), 138, 185–86.

5. Ireland, *Life*, 8, 40–43, 49–51; Isaac, *Transformation*, 86.

6. Ireland, *Life*, 78–82.

7. Ibid., 111, 119, 129–37. Ireland supplied few dates in his autobiography. Robert Semple believed the Separate Baptist Church at Smith's Creek was constituted in 1774 or "about 1774," so that some time elapsed after the original conversions. Robert Semple, *History of the Rise and Progress of the Baptists in Virginia* (Richmond, 1810), 174, 188.

8. Ireland, *Life*, 155–79.

9. Ibid., 189; Semple, *History*, 183–89; MacMaster, *Land, Piety, Peoplehood*, 218–20.

10. Semple, *History*, 189–90; John W. Wayland, "Four Early Baptist Ministers of Northern Virginia," *Religious Herald*, Dec. 15, 1927.

11. Shenandoah County Deeds A: 434. Young confirmed his lease and reserved the acre occupied by "the separate Baptist meeting house" when he sold the remainder of his land to Archibald Rutherford on Sept. 6, 1780. Shenandoah County Deeds, P: 123.

12. J. F. J. Schantz, trans., *The Register of the Rev. John Caspar Stoever* (Philadelphia, 1896), 9.

13. The Rev. John Craig, "Record of Baptisms 1740–1749," Presbyterian Historical Foundation, Montreat, N.C.

14. Newman also recorded a visit to the Smith's Creek Baptist Church by the Rev. Alexander Miller of Cook's Creek Presbyterian Church in present Rockingham County, who filled the meeting house with members of his own congregation and lectured the Baptists on their theological errors. This seems to have been an isolated instance. Linville Creek-Smith Creek Baptist Church Records, Virginia Baptist Historical Society, Richmond, Va.

15. Hugh Judge, *Memoirs and Journal of Hugh Judge* (Byberry, Pa., 1841), 18.

16. *Hopewell Friends History* (Strasburg, Va.: Hopewell Friends, 1938), 378–404.

17. Churchwardens of Beckworth Parish Petition, Oct. 17, 1777, Legislative Petitions, Shenandoah County, Archives Division, Library of Virginia, Richmond. Shenandoah County Deeds A: 434.

18. Shenandoah County Deeds A: 284. The meeting house was confirmed to the Smith's Creek Meeting after the death of Jackson Allen and his son Reuben Allen by Benjamin Allen. Shenandoah County Deeds P: 239.

19. Shenandoah County Deeds B: 276. Young confirmed his lease and reserved

the acre occupied by the "separate Baptist meeting house" when he sold the remainder of his land to Archibald Rutherford on Sept. 6, 1780. Shenandoah County Deeds P: 123.

20. John W. Wayland, *A History of Shenandoah County, Virginia* (Strasburg, Va.: Shenandoah Publishing Co., 1969), 388–91, 424–25; J. Floyd Wine, *Life Along Holman's Creek* (Boyce, Va.: privately published, 1982), 95–98, 112–13; Jacob D. Wine, *A History of the Flat Rock Church of the Brethren* (Forestville, Va.: privately published, 1962), 3–5.

21. Shenandoah County Deeds F: 1.

22. Robert D. Mitchell, *Commercialism and Frontier: Perspectives on the Early Shenandoah Valley* (Charlottesville: Univ. Press of Virginia, 1977), 45; Ireland, *Life*, 189.

23. James T. Lemon, *The Best Poor Man's Country: A Geographical Study of Early Southeastern Pennsylvania* (Baltimore: Johns Hopkins Univ. Press, 1972), 43–49.

24. Robert G. Albion, ed., *Journal and Letters of Philip Vickers Fithian 1775–1776* (Princeton: Princeton Univ. Press, 1934), 139–40; Klaus Wust, ed., *Reformed Zion–Pine Church Record 1788–1827 Stony Creek, Virginia* (Edinburg, Va.: Shenandoah History, 1984), 7.

25. Schwartz, *A Mixed Multitude*, 300.

26. Rudelle Mills Davis and Peggy Davidson Dick, *The Allens, Quakers of Shenandoah* (El Paso, Tex.: privately published, 1984), 5–8.

27. Wine, *Life Along Holman's Creek*, 4.

28. Peggy Shomo Joyner, *Abstracts of Virginia's Northern Neck Warrants & Surveys, Volume I Orange & Augusta Counties, 1730–1754*, vol. 2, *Frederick County, 1747–1780* (Portsmouth, Va.: 1985).

29. Larry Dale Gragg, *Migration in Early America: The Virginia Quaker Experience* (Ann Arbor: University Microfilms International, 1980), 48.

30. Duane E. Ball, "Dynamics of Population and Wealth in Eighteenth-Century Chester County, Pennsylvania," *Journal of Interdisciplinary History* 6 (1976): 621–44.

31. Augusta County Deeds 5: 357, 353, 337, 349; 3: 83, 222, 253.

32. Frederick County Deeds 10: 360; Shenandoah County Deeds A: 380; B: 209, 213, 218.

33. Freeman H. Hart, *The Valley of Virginia in the American Revolution 1763–1789* (Chapel Hill: Univ. of North Carolina Press, 1942), 33–63.

34. Linville Creek–Smith Creek Church Records; Thomas H. Pope, *The History of Newberry County, South Carolina 1749–1860* (Columbia: Univ. of South Carolina Press, 1973), 85–87; Samuel W. Newman, *The Long Trek of the Newman Family 1683–1980* (n.p., 1980), 15–23.

35. Judge, *Memoirs*, 18; *Hopewell Friends History*, 414–18.

36. Shenandoah County Order Book, 1774–1780, 36, 82; Shenandoah County Court Minute Book, 1781–1784, 150; William Matthews to Israel Pemberton, June 16, 1776, Pemberton Papers, Historical Society of Pennsylvania, Philadelphia; William Matthews, Journal, Maryland Historical Society, Baltimore; Judge, *Memoirs*, 16–19; Davis and Dick, *The Allens*, 12–18.

37. On the evidence for wartime commitment on the part of Brethren, Friends, and Mennonites, see Richard K. MacMaster, Samuel L. Horst, and Robert F. Ulle, *Conscience in Crisis: Peace Churches in America 1739–1789* (Scottdale, Pa.: Herald Press, 1979), 523–25.

Works Cited

Albion, Robert G., editor. *Journal and Letters of Philip Vickers Fithian 1775–1776.* Princeton: Princeton Univ. Press, 1934.

Augusta County Deeds. Library of Virginia, Richmond.

Ball, Duane E. "Dynamics of Population and Wealth in Eighteenth-Century Chester County, Pennsylvania." *Journal of Interdisciplinary History* 6 (1976): 621–44.

Beeman, Richard R. *The Evolution of the Southern Backcountry: A Case Study of Lunenburg County, Virginia, 1746–1832.* Philadelphia: Univ. of Pennsylvania Press, 1984.

Beeman, Richard R., and Rhys Isaac. "Cultural Conflict and Social Change in the Revolutionary South: Lunenburg County, Virginia." *Journal of Southern History* 46 (1980): 525–50.

Churchwardens of Beckworth Parish Petition, Oct. 17, 1777. Legislative Petitions, Shenandoah County. Archives Division, Library of Virginia, Richmond.

Craig, The Rev. John. "Record of Baptisms 1740–1749." Presbyterian Historical Foundation, Montreat, N.C.

Davis, Rudelle Mills, and Peggy Davidson Dick. *The Allens, Quakers of Shenandoah.* El Paso, Tex.: privately published, 1984.

Frederick County Deeds. Library of Virginia, Richmond.

Gragg, Larry Dale. *Migration in Early America: The Virginia Quaker Experience.* Ann Arbor, Mich.: University Microfilms International, 1980.

Hart, Freeman H. *The Valley of Virginia in the American Revolution 1763–1789.* Chapel Hill: Univ. of North Carolina Press, 1942.

Hopewell Friends History. Strasburg, Va.: 1938.

Ireland, James. *The Life of the Rev. James Ireland, Who Was, For Many Years, Pastor of the Baptist Church at Buck Marsh, Waterlick, and Happy Creek in Frederick and Shenandoah County, Virginia.* Winchester, Va., 1819.

Isaac, Rhys. "The Evangelical Revolt: The Nature of the Baptists' Challenge to the Traditional Order in Virginia, 1765–1776." *William and Mary Quarterly* 3d ser., 31 (1974): 345–68.

———. *The Transformation of Virginia 1740–1790.* Chapel Hill: Univ. of North Carolina Press, 1982.

Joyner, Peggy Shomo. *Abstracts of Virginia's Northern Neck Warrants & Surveys, Volume I Orange & Augusta Counties, 1730–1754, vol. 2, Frederick County, 1747–1780.* Portsmouth, Va.: 1985.

Judge, Hugh. *Memoirs and Journal of Hugh Judge.* Byberry, Pa., 1841.

Lemon, James T. *The Best Poor Man's Country: A Geographical Study of Early Southeastern Pennsylvania.* Baltimore: Johns Hopkins Univ. Press, 1972.

Linville Creek–Smith Creek Baptist Church Records. Virginia Baptist Historical Society, Richmond, Va.

MacMaster, Richard K. *Land, Piety, Peoplehood: The Establishment of Mennonite Communities in America 1683–1790.* Scottdale, Pa.: Herald Press, 1985.

MacMaster, Richard K., Samuel L. Horst, and Robert F. Ulle. *Conscience in Crisis: Peace Churches in America 1739–1789.* Scottdale, Pa.: Herald Press, 1979.

Matthews, William. Journal. Maryland Historical Society, Baltimore.

Mitchell, Robert D. *Commercialism and Frontier: Perspectives on the Early Shenandoah Valley.* Charlottesville: Univ. Press of Virginia, 1977.

Newman, Samuel P. *The Long Trek of the Newman Family 1683–1980.* N.p., 1980.

Pemberton Papers. Historical Society of Pennsylvania, Philadelphia.

Pope, Thomas H. *The History of Newberry County, South Carolina 1749–1860.* Columbia: Univ. of South Carolina Press, 1973.

Schantz, J. F. J., translator. *The Register of the Rev. John Caspar Stoever.* Philadelphia, 1896.

Schwartz, Sally. *"A Mixed Multitude": The Struggle for Toleration in Colonial Pennsylvania.* New York: New York Univ. Press, 1987.

Semple, Robert. *History of the Rise and Progress of the Baptists in Virginia.* Richmond, 1810.

Shenandoah County Court Minute Book, 1781–1784. Library of Virginia, Richmond.

Shenandoah County Deeds. Library of Virginia, Richmond.

Shenandoah County Order Book, 1774–1780. Library of Virginia, Richmond.

Wayland, John W. "Four Early Baptist Ministers of Northern Virginia." *Religious Herald,* Dec. 15, 1927.

———. *A History of Shenandoah County, Virginia.* Strasburg, Va.: Shenandoah Publishing Co., 1969.

Wine, J. Floyd. *Life Along Holman's Creek.* Boyce, Va.: privately published, 1982.

Wine, Jacob D. *A History of the Flat Rock Church of the Brethren.* Forestville, Va.: privately published, 1962.

Wust, Klaus, editor. *Reformed Zion–Pine Church Record 1788–1827 Stony Creek, Virginia.* Edinburg, Va.: Shenandoah History, 1984.

Chapter 4

The Outlook of Rhinelanders on the Virginia Frontier

Kenneth W. Keller

Recent interest in the evolution of a multicultural American society has revived the study of early settlements of non-English-speaking inhabitants. Among these, perhaps no other group has been the subject of more antiquarian concern than early American German speakers from the Rhineland, who emigrated from Germany, Switzerland, Alsace, and the Low Countries.[1] The scholars who have studied these colonial immigrants from the Rhineland have examined the outlook of these settlers in Pennsylvania and Maryland toward the family, wealth, religion, the printed word, and politics.[2] One region of early German settlement that has not received adequate attention, however, is the Great Valley of Virginia. In many ways, the less densely populated and more remote and marginal Rhinelanders' settlements on the Virginia frontier were different from those Pennsylvania and Maryland. The outlook of Rhinelanders on the Virginia frontier was less focused on communal life and more open to bicultural mingling with the dominant culture of Anglo-American inhabitants.[3]

The most recent studies of the Shenandoah Valley and western Virginia have come from scholars who have speculated about frontier settlement while not focusing specifically upon the Rhinelanders. Robert D. Mitchell's classic *Commercialism and Frontier—Perspectives on the Early Shenandoah Valley* uses a few secondary English-language accounts about the Virginia Germans, like those by Klaus Wust and John Wayland, but it contains no citations to German-language primary sources.[4] Albert H. Tillson Jr.'s *Gentry and Common Folk: Political Culture on a Virginia Frontier, 1740–1789* says little about the Germans, as does Rhys Isaac's *The Transformation of Virginia, 1740–1790.*[5] *Colonial Virginia* by Warren M. Billings, John E. Selby, and Thad W. Tate repeats a few common generalizations about the Virginia Germans, but uses no German sources.[6] One older antiquarian study of the Germans of the Shenandoah Valley exists, but its focus is on description of folklife.[7] From the perspective of recent research in German social, economic, and emigration history and the German-language manuscripts and imprints that survive from the Virginia frontier, the European experience of the Rhinelanders prepared them well for life in America.[8] A comparison of their origins in the Rhineland with their habits on the Virginia frontier shows that the gap between their Old World and New World experience was not so great. In some ways the Rhineland itself, as much as their years in Pennsylvania and Maryland, served as a school for life on the Virginia frontier. And that experience prepared them well for assimilation into Anglo-American culture.

Research by students of German history shows that the Rhineland, from which came the overwhelming proportion of the German speakers, was a region whose peasant inhabitants were not strangers to large-scale, international trade, production for markets beyond local villages, saving of income, and experimentation with crops to provide a cushion in hard times.[9] The Rhine itself was a great commercial artery that provided good communication with the North Sea and a source of information about foreign destinations. The towns along the Rhine traded in wine, woolens, linen, iron, pottery, tile, pitch, and potash. Farmers in the Rhineland grew orchard crops, vegetables such as potatoes, peas, onions, lentils, tobacco, almonds, and grapes, which they converted into wine. Many of these commodities were sold in distant markets in spite of duties levied along the Rhine by various sovereigns. Rural artisans supplied these products and the containers to hold them to larger cities. This trade led to a significant craft and rural manufacturing sector in the generally agricultural economy of the Rhineland. By the eighteenth century, German agriculture was experiencing good times as it recovered from the devastation of the wars of Louis XIV. Probably more important for understanding the outlook of farmer immigrants from the Rhineland was the fact that the Rhine–Main region of Germany and the Palatinate to the south by the French border were the most densely populated sections of Germany. This region was a center of what we would call truck gardening today. Farmers near cities would grow vegetables for sale in urban produce markets. This labor-intensive form of highly specialized agriculture meant that gardeners would regularly take produce to market in cities where it would be delivered to agents who would sell it. Gardeners were accustomed to urban markets and the haggling and dealing with middlemen that went on there. Moreover, local farmers were sensitive to market forces. They shifted from one crop, cereal grains, to ones like tobacco and grapes as these became more profitable.[10] The Rhineland gardeners' world was one of markets, bargaining, and exchange. In the American colonies, though ready access to urban vegetable markets declined as the Rhinelanders moved away from Philadelphia and Pennsylvania's inland towns, they persisted in vegetable gardening. It was no accident that when travelers visited their settlements in America, they remarked that vegetables occupied a more prominent place in their diets than among English speakers.[11]

Another key characteristic of the Rhineland was that it was an area of Germany in which the custom of *Realteilungserbrecht*, or partible inheritance, was practiced. This inheritance practice generally meant that landholding had to be equally divided among all heirs when a farmer died. Over time, the landholdings of the Rhineland got smaller and smaller, so that a farm could no longer support a large family. Rhineland inheritance practices promoted the impulse among Rhenish people to find a supplementary form of income. Farmers had to take up a craft in order to add to family income, so linen weaving or the making of clothing, or working with wood or metal, became a form of livelihood for many Rhinelanders. Rhenish families commonly engaged in domestic manufactures, and when bad harvests or poor prices became too much to bear, families with well-developed skills in home manufacturing emigrated. Families were economic units with diverse artisan skills accustomed to selling the products of their labor. Farmers traded their handicrafts in interior towns, and some of the towns began to specialize in one product, such as wagons, musical instruments, or wine.[12] On the Virginia frontier, the habit of developing domestic manufacturing skills persisted. Virginia Rhinelanders made their clothes by household weaving and used surplus thread and fabric to barter for goods they could not produce. In Virginia, as in the Rhineland, certain towns in the Shenandoah Valley specialized in the making of pottery, stoves, leather, rifles, tinware, furniture, and tombstones.[13]

The habit of equal or partible division of property among heirs transferred easily from the Rhineland to the Virginia frontier. An examination of wills of German-speaking testators in Augusta County from 1749 to 1818 shows a consistent pattern of inheritance in which testators divided property equally among heirs, often among children. Seventy-eight persons in Augusta County with German surnames left wills between 1749 and 1818. Seventy-two of these left their property to be equally divided among heirs, with only four of the testators devising property to wives alone. In six cases, testators demonstrated preferences for one heir over another, as when an eldest son might inherit the family farm, while the others were given cattle or shares of income, or a disobedient son or daughter might be cut off. It was unusual for the testator to liquidate the inheritance by ordering that all property be auctioned off, and the proceeds be divided equally. Testators attempted to parcel out the inheritance in roughly equal amounts. The frequency of preferential forms of partible inheritance appeared only slightly among Augusta County's testators, but most heirs tended to receive equal shares. As Kenneth Koons and others have shown, the tendency for partible inheritance may have become preferential as a scarcity of land developed. Generally, the overwhelming tendency was to continue the tradition of Rhenish *Realteilungserbrecht* in the Shenandoah Valley.[14]

Rhineland habits about religion may have stuck to the immigrants who left for America in the eighteenth century. Most of the Rhenish immigrants who made their way to America were Protestants, and in the main source region of the emigration, the Palatinate, German Reformed, Zwinglian, or Calvinistic Protestantism, not Lutheranism, was strong. German Reformed Protestantism was born in the Palatinate and had its intellectual center at the University of Heidelberg in the Electoral Palatinate east of the Rhine. This form of Protestantism reacted against remaining elements of Catholic worship and theology in Lutheranism and emphasized strict adherence to the Bible, eliminating from the Church all things not specifically authorized therein. The German Reformed churches advocated a form of church government by consistories or presbyteries of clergy and not bishops, and an understanding of the sacraments that was symbolic and less catholic than Luther's. Reformed Protestantism emphasized personal conviction about faith and, probably more so than Lutheranism, the confidence that individuals' reason, guided by the Holy Spirit, could fathom Christian doctrine. Within the Reformed churches in the seventeenth century, there arose the movement known as Pietism. This revitalization movement in Protestantism soon spread from the Reformed Churches to some wings of the Lutheran Church and eventually stimulated religious change that gave birth to other movements, like the Moravian Church, various strains of Anabaptism, and English Methodism.[15] Pietism thrived in the Rhineland. It demanded a warm, heartfelt experience of individual faith, frequent personal study of the Scriptures, an emphasis on stricter personal morality, softening theological differences with other Protestants, ecumenical cooperation with them, institutionalized works of charity in the form of hospitals or orphans' homes, and meetings of believers often led by inspired lay people rather than ordained clergy. In Lutheran areas of the Rhineland, such as in Wuerttemberg and parts of Hessen, Pietism caught on and led to similar developments. Rhinelanders, especially in Reformed regions, were skeptical of formalism, ecclesiastical power, elaborate churches, liturgy, and doctrinal hairsplitting because of this inheritance.[16] The Rhinelanders were to bring these individualistic religious preferences to Pennsylvania and the Virginia frontier. Frontier revivalists who traveled among the Valley Germans found ready audiences for German versions of Wesleyan preaching. German listeners in the Valley of Virginia warmly welcomed William Otterbein, Christian Newcomer, and George Adam Geeting.[17]

The experience of the Rhinelanders in immigrating to the Virginia frontier also prepared them for an outlook that emphasized individual choice. Recent students of the eighteenth-century German immigration to the American colonies, like Marianne Wokeck, Lowell Bennion, and Farley Grubb, emphasize that immigrants to America had to make numerous informed choices about their journey. They had to pick a destination, which could have been in Hungary, Prussia, or Russia, as well as America. Immigration to Hungary and Prussia was seen as less risky than the lengthy voyage to America, though the rewards of the trans-Atlantic trip were potentially greater. Immigrants had to calculate whether the greater opportunity available in America was worth the dangers of a lengthy sea voyage. Most immigrants chose the safer path to go east rather than to go to America. Perhaps those persons most inclined to take risks for the sake of an improved life started on the path that led to Pennsylvania and the Virginia frontier. These emigrants also had to deal with agents, merchants, ship captains, and dealers in Rhineland cities like Worms and Speyer as well as with similar business people in the Dutch port of Rotterdam, from which most of the emigrants sailed. Terms upon which the ships carried the passengers also had to be negotiated. Emigrants had to know about the cost of passage. Some had to negotiate for extended credit. Many of the emigrants were redemptioners, people who chose on their own free will to leave for America, who would find a master for whom they would work once the ship landed in America. Many emigrants brought special artisan skills in high demand in the American colonies; these emigrants could bargain for a reduced term of service in the New World. To get to America the Rhinelanders had to confront a complex, competitive, international, organized system of agents and negotiations: they were used to making rational choices in a market before they arrived in the New World.[18]

Once the immigrants had crossed the Atlantic, their experiences on the way to the Virginia frontier allowed them to adjust rather easily to the new English cultural environment and its economy. The most recent study we have of indentured servants in Pennsylvania suggests that indentured servants were most likely to live in towns and in the city of Philadelphia.[19] If indentured servants from the Rhineland spent their first years in Philadelphia or in one of Pennsylvania's inland towns, they would have been less isolated from English speech, customs, and economic practices. Urban life would have promoted acculturation. According to at least one observer of their life in Pennsylvania, once the immigrants' terms of service ended, they were likely to purchase a farm near a town even though the price of land was relatively high. The Rhinelanders wanted the chance to visit urban markets every week to sell their dairy products, meat, eggs, poultry, or vegetables, as many of them had done in the Rhineland.[20] Easy access to urban markets in their first years in America would also have promoted quicker familiarity with English business practices and customs. In addition, it is likely that most of the Rhineland emigrants, especially after 1760, would have been artisans, not farmers. Farley Grubb's analysis of occupations of these immigrants has led him to conclude that, while many were primarily farmers, the most common occupations outside the farm among them were butcher, baker, and tailor. He concludes that the German-speaking immigrants may have been more skilled than English immigrants and that their literacy rate was second only to those from Scotland and on a par with those from Holland.[21] As tradesmen whose skills were in demand, they would have been less isolated from English ways, as English customers came to them for the products of their labor. For those who did farm, the most common pattern of these Rhineland emigrants was to buy cultivated land from some previous owner, probably an English speaker or Ulsterman. Christoph Daniel Ebeling, one of the first Germans to collect information about America and publish it in his homeland, concluded in the volume about Pennsylvania in his 1797 *Erdbeschreibung*, a geographic description of the United States based on extensive correspondence with numerous Americans, that in Pennsylvania the German immigrants would become the second owner of farms of 200 to 300 acres. They would soon improve the farm by building houses of stone, improve the soil and the cattle. The Rhinelanders in Pennsylvania would have had experience in buying land from English speakers long before they migrated up the Great Valley to the Virginia frontier.[22]

We have no satisfactory statistical evidence on the amount of time the Rhineland settlers spent in Pennsylvania before migrating to Virginia. Church records in the Shenandoah Valley rarely indicated where German settlers had come from, either in Germany or in Pennsylvania, so it is impossible to track any satisfactory sample of Valley Germans back to specific sites in Pennsylvania or the Rhineland. A survey of family genealogies for prominent Valley German families indicated that the families that were wealthy and educated enough to compile genealogies in the nineteenth and twentieth centuries had spent more than just a few years in Pennsylvania before emigrating to the Valley. The Hite family ancestors spent 15 years in New York before migrating to Virginia. The Conrads had a sojourn of 18 years in Pennsylvania before moving south, the Crauns 12, the Stricklers 29, the Wengers 48, the Koiners 49, the Rodeffers 61, and the Showalters 49.[23] The ancestors of some of the most well-known families of Rhineland descent who settled on the Virginia frontier, while remaining German in their folkways, had ample time to establish contact with English speakers and to deal with them in trade before coming to the Virginia frontier.

In the 1730s, then, when the first streams of German-speaking settlers from Pennsylvania and Maryland came up the Great Valley to Virginia, it is very likely that most of these settlers had already lived in America for some time.[24] They came as individuals, not organized by any speculator or promoter, as had early Rhineland migrants to Virginia and the Carolinas. These settlers freely decided as individuals or small family groups to come on their own.[25] They also came in smaller numbers than the flood of immigrants to Pennsylvania. According to the most recent estimates of the size of the German-speaking population of Pennsylvania and Virginia, the Rhinelanders in Virginia made up a much smaller proportion of Virginia's overall population than the Pennsylvania Germans made up of Pennsylvania's population: in Pennsylvania, they formed 38 percent of its 1790 population, while in Virginia, the German-speaking immigrants were only 4.5 percent of the general population. According to Aaron Fogleman, the Virginia Germans' population amounted to fewer than 20,000 people, about one-eighth the size of that of the Pennsylvania Germans.[26] This smaller population of Virginia Rhinelanders also became thinly dispersed. Though the Shenandoah Valley was at its widest 20 miles across, it stretched south for a distance of 180 miles.[27] These German speakers occupied settlements scattered over 3,000 square miles from the Potomac to the headwaters of the Shenandoah River. Others went even farther south, beyond the geographic limits of the Shenandoah, to the James or to the New River, while other groups pushed behind the mountain ridges to isolated coves and hollows in what was to become Pendleton County, West Virginia. Geographic isolation and dispersal made it more difficult for these settlers to keep in touch with larger settlements of German speakers, especially when the migration up the Great Valley began to decline after the War of 1812 made more direct access to the West available.

Most of the Rhinelanders and their descendants on the Virginia frontier were secondary migrants; they had taken their oaths of allegiance to the British king in Pennsylvania or Maryland and did not need to become his subjects when they moved to Virginia. From the time of the organization of Augusta County in 1745 until 1785, only thirty-eight persons with German surnames were naturalized in the Augusta County court.[28] Some new German-speaking settlers continued to come into the upper Valley directly from Germany during the late eighteenth century, but as soldiers' declarations from the Revolutionary era show, most persons with German surnames had come from Pennsylvania, Maryland, or New Jersey.[29] Once they got to the Valley, they continued to speak German, but at the same time they bought and sold land with the original holders, persons of English and Scots-Irish descent, just as they had in Pennsylvania. Records of land purchases in Augusta County and the comments of contemporary observers show that the German speakers bought land from the Scots-Irish from Berkeley and Frederick County to Augusta County.[30] In Augusta County settlers of German descent bought land in the Beverley Manor tract completely surrounded by persons of Scots-Irish descent. The Germans would buy from any seller, regardless of how isolated from other Germans the purchase might make them. For example, Caspar and George Coiner purchased land on eastern Augusta County's Gillespie Run in 1805–6; their neighbors were Hutchinsons, McCunes, Dalhouses, Ramseys, and Bells. Between 1800 and 1812, John Huffmire, Nicholas Link, Daniel Strickler, George Schultz, Philip Greaver, Jacob Zimmermann, and John Griner purchased tracts in the heart of Scots-Irish Beverley Patent; their purchases were not all together in one spot, but scattered throughout the Beverly Patent, surrounded with neighbors with Scots-Irish surnames.[31] If there was an impetus for German purchasers to cluster together or for families to stay in one place, it was surely breaking down by the end of the eighteenth century.

Certainly the emigration of the Rhinelanders during the eighteenth century was a migration of families, although, as the century wore on, more single men tended to migrate. Farley Grubb has found that their immigration included more families and women than did English immigration in the same time.[32] But if family ties were strong among the Rhinelanders and their descendants, or at least stronger than the drive to find acceptable land, one might expect to find high rates of endogamy, or marrying within one's group, among them. But there seems to be less endogamy among the people with German surnames on the Virginia frontier of the late eighteenth century than on the Wisconsin frontier a century later. Richard M. Bernard published a study of endogamy on the Wisconsin frontier in the late nineteenth century; he found that only 13.6 percent of the Wisconsin Germans he studied married outside their own group.[33] Yet, of the 302 marriages involving at least one person with a German surname in Augusta County between 1785 and 1802, 35 percent were with a partner who did not have a German surname. Recent research by Charlene D. Hutcheson involving marriage patterns from 1770 to 1850 in the vicinity of modern Roanoke, farther up the Great Valley, has confirmed that there was a high degree of marriage outside the group among German Lutherans and Reformed people, who married outside their group 70 percent of the time. Scots-Irish inhabitants were more endogamous that Germans.[34] Perhaps there were simply too few persons of German descent in the county to permit a greater number of endogamous marriages. Throughout the Shenandoah Valley, many of the leading families of German descent, like the Hites, the Heiskells, the Sowerses, the Coiners, and the Swopes, married persons of English or Scots-Irish background during this period. Those who assume that the Rhinelanders' families were stable and that they exerted power over children's decisions should understand that recent studies of eighteenth-century German families find them to be unstable, nuclear, and filled with tension.[35] The lure of cheap land and the availability of spouses from other cultural backgrounds were probably stronger forces than cultural affinity on the Virginia frontier.

If communal ties were strong on the Virginia frontier, the institutional network of the German-speaking churches and the German-language press might well have kept them intact. But the state of these transmitters of culture in Virginia was quite different from what it may have been in Pennsylvania or Maryland. Institutions that conveyed German culture were weak on the Virginia frontier. Lutherans, German Reformed, Brethren, and Mennonite alike complained that early ministers were not properly trained. Most German-speaking congregations shared their church buildings with other German-speaking denominations; these union churches were economical solutions to the problem of paying for a meeting house on the frontier, but they did not build a sense of denominational distinctiveness.[36] In some places, denominational lines blurred when persons who were not of German descent took part in religious activities of German-speaking congregations or when German Lutherans and Reformed shared each others' sacraments. At St. Peter's Lutheran Church in Churchville, Virginia, German Reformed and Lutheran congregants took communion together, even though theological disputes between the denominations about Holy Communion had long divided them. The manuscript communion register of this Churchville congregation records that a group labeled "Irish" was admitted to communion. A group of people with English surnames was listed on the register of communicants at St. Peter's in 1796. In 1795 a family the pastor identified as "Englische" was listed as communicants at St. Paul's Lutheran Church, Strasburg. African Americans were also listed in the registers of some of these German-language churches.[37]

The preachers who settled among Lutheran and German Reformed communities in the Valley frequently were not trained theologically and were without any connection to higher denominational institutions. The leader of the earliest Lutheran settlers at the Massanutten Settlement, where the first Europeans to settle in the Shenandoah Valley lived, was Peter Mischler. Of him, Lutheran patriarch Henry Muhlenberg wrote that "neither the necessary shell nor the kernel neither the mediate nor the immediate gifts, for the important office [of pastor] were present." The Lutherans threatened to sue Mischler to keep him from interfering in church affairs, yet he continued to lead Lutheran congregations in Rockingham, Page, and Pendleton Counties. The earliest Lutheran congregations in the vicinity of Staunton were led by Benjamin Henkel, an irregular minister who was never admitted to the Lutheran ministry. Adolph Spindler was the irregular minister of Lutheran congregations in Augusta, Rockingham, and Pendleton Counties from about 1786; he was not ordained a pastor until 1803. The Peaked Mountain, Upper Peaked Mountain, and Stony Creek Reformed congregation was led by Philip Van

Gemuenden, Charles Lange, Henry Giese, William Runkel, and Bernard Willy, all ministers independent of the Reformed Coetus.[38] Friedens Church, a Rockingham County union congregation, had irregular Lutheran and Reformed leaders as well, one of whom the Ministerium regarded as "utterly unfit." As late as the 1770s, congregations like Rader's Church in Rockingham County had to depend on annual visits of ministers sent by the Coetus or the Ministerium.[39] Lutheran and Reformed congregations depended on well-educated, theologically and liturgically trained pastors to function.[40] In the Valley in the eighteenth century, it is clear that they were unable to obtain such religious leaders; the Valley was more likely to be a refuge for canonically irregular men who were not ordained clergy but who had established themselves as preachers in remote, ignored Lutheran and Reformed congregations that sought religious leadership. If the leaders of these congregations were not connected with these higher organs of church government, it is unlikely that much institutional communication took place between the local congregation and other parts of the denomination, and certainly not with European parent churches, Pietist missionary organizations, the Pietist *Stiftungen*—or foundations—in Saxony, the press, seminaries and universities, and charitable activities.

Well into the 1790s, networks of the Virginia congregations of these denominations were only loosely organized and reported to the parent bodies haphazardly. In turn, the higher bodies initiated few contacts with local Virginia congregations. Although the Lutheran Ministerium received occasional letters from the Valley of Virginia, no representative of the Lutheran congregations in Virginia attended the meetings of the Ministerium until 1787, when Christian Streit of Winchester appeared at the meeting of the Ministerium at Lancaster, Pennsylvania. Streit was a graduate of the College of Philadelphia and had received Lutheran theological education from the Swedish Provost Charles Magnus von Wrangel. Pastor Streit lived in the Shenandoah Valley from 1785 to 1812. He was the only theologically educated Lutheran pastor to reside in the Shenandoah Valley for more than a few years in the eighteenth century. In 1787 two licentiates who had preached to scattered Virginia congregations did present credentials from Germany to the Lutheran Ministerium, but it rejected them. Ministerial candidates from Virginia attended meetings of the Ministerium in 1790 and 1791. The Ministerium ordained Paul Henkel in 1792, but he did not attend its annual meeting until 1796. In 1800 he was living in Staunton, but he had left town by 1801. Finally, the Ministerium sent two candidates for ordination to the Valley in 1796.[41] Among the German Reformed, the Coetus received pleas for clergy as early as 1747, but it did not honor the congregations' requests. In 1773 the Coetus announced that neighboring pastors in Pennsylvania or Maryland would visit the Virginia congregations. After the Revolution, the Coetus promised to supply ministers to Virginia, but as late as 1797 it noted that such requests from Virginia could not be complied with. By 1820, there were thirty-one Virginia German Reformed congregations served by only four pastors.[42]

The Virginia congregations were slow in developing their own local organizational network, so little institutional communication developed. More than sixty years after the first Lutherans settled in the Valley, in 1793, a regional organization of Virginia Lutherans had begun to form. A Special Conference of Virginia Lutherans met that year; its proceedings were sent to the Ministerium for examination. Not until 1801 did the Ministerium create a Virginia district that united the Virginia Lutheran congregations and regularly reported its proceedings to the Ministerium. Only in 1772 did the German Reformed Coetus instruct the Virginia congregations to meet together to develop a plan for supporting a minister. No regional network of German Reformed congregations had developed. No Virginia Classis, or regional organization, formed among the German Reformed until 1826, more than thirty years after the Lutherans had organized a Special Conference.[43] None of the proceedings of the Special Conference of Lutherans was printed in the German or any other language until 1806, when the Henkel Press, which had just been established, began to publish them. It must have been difficult for local congregations that did not send lay delegates or pastors to the Lutheran Conference to learn about its decisions respecting church business. Scholars have found no examples of printed German-language proceedings of the German Reformed Church in Virginia, so the communication between local congregations and these regional bodies must have been difficult.[44]

There is also evidence that these local Reformed and Lutheran Congregations did not always follow the worship practices their parent bodies required, nor did they enforce church discipline. The manuscript congregational registers of the Lutheran and Reformed churches are the best German-language records we have of the Rhinelanders and their families on the Virginia frontier. The Lutheran and Reformed Churches in Europe and Pennsylvania followed a liturgical calendar in which Sundays and other church festivals were designated by special names, usually derived from the Latin words of psalms to be used in worship on that day. For example, Laetare Sunday occurred in Lent, Jubilate and Cantate were Sundays after Easter, and Exaudi was the Sunday before the festival of the Ascension, another church holiday. Each Sunday and festival had a special text, or pericope, from which the sermon was to be preached. All members of the Lutheran Ministerium since the 1740s had to pledge to use the liturgical form, or agenda, of the denomination as a requirement for ordination.[45] By the late eighteenth century, some Valley Lutheran and Reformed congregations had abandoned the use of these liturgical names. Friedens Church in Rockingham County, a union congregation in which the building was shared by Lutherans and Reformed, did not use the liturgical year. St. Peter's Lutheran Church in Augusta County, which Reformed people attended and which was occasionally served by Reformed pastors, used the liturgical year in 1796, but had dropped it by 1801. St. Paul's Lutheran Church in Strasburg used the liturgical year from 1776 to 1785, but abandoned it by the nineteenth century in favor of the generic name "Sabbath" for Sunday. These congregations must have been accustomed to a less formal order of worship. Their members were not introduced to the cultus, or ritual practices, of their denominations. These liturgical forms communicated religious teachings and helped spread denominational identity. A simplification of religious ideas and practice was underway among these Valley settlers. The manuscript records of Lutheran congregations in Strasburg and near Staunton show that, by the nineteenth century, these churches adopted "protracted meetings," or revivals, "anxious benches," or special seats for penitent sinners, and revivalist modes of address, such as the terms "brother" and "sister" to refer to other members of the congregation. In the same manuscript records, there is no evidence of church discipline being administered. At most there seems to have been only annual celebration of the Lord's Supper, rather than quarterly or monthly observances.[46]

As far as can be determined, by the end of the eighteenth century, only two of these German Reformed and Lutheran congregations had obtained pipe organs—Grace Church in Winchester in 1795 and St. Paul's in Strasburg in 1794.[47] The European parent churches and numerous congregations in Pennsylvania had pipe organs to promote the vigorous German Protestant tradition of chorale singing.[48] Without these instruments, it must have been difficult to continue using church music derived from European composers in Valley congregations. These religious institutions were marginal and their connections to their denominations were weak no matter how fervently local believers desired ministers or worship services.

Another vital element in promoting culture and a sense of communal identity must surely have been the press. Yet the German-language press in the Valley was weak and a pale imitation of German-language journalism in Pennsylvania. German language printing began in Virginia in 1787 as Matthias Bartgis announced plans for the beginning of a German language press in Winchester. The plans did not bear fruit immediately; no copies of his publications in German have ever been found, and by 1792 he closed his print shop.[49] Short-lived German newspapers appeared in New Market and Staunton. John Wise printed a German paper in Staunton between 1800 and 1802; no copies of it have been found, and its name is not known. Ambrose Henkel's *Virginische Volksberichter* lasted from 1807 to 1809, and Jacob Dietrich's Staunton *Deutsche Virginier Adler* survived from 1808 to 1809. Henkel's New Market paper relied nearly entirely on squibs borrowed from Maryland and Pennsylvania papers and contained little of local origin that Henkel himself did not write. A recent study by David A. Rawson of the New Market, Virginia, post office demonstrated that only two German-language newspapers were received by persons who used it between 1797 and 1842. They were the *Hanover Gazette* from Pennsylvania and the Hagerstown, Maryland, *Westliche Correspondenz*. The overwhelming number of items received there were in English.[50] The Henkel press in New Market became famous, not so much because of its German printing, but because of its bilingual and English-language publication. Its last German imprint appeared in 1854.[51]

The Henkels did sell German-language books published elsewhere, many of which were by the leading Pietist writers. The works of the Pietist Heinrich Jung-Stilling were especially highly advertised in the Henkel newspaper.[52] These works were of general appeal to Lutheran and German Reformed Protestants and emphasized meditation about the crises and joys of daily life, not theological disagreements that would reinforce denominational identity. The popular catechisms for the Reformed and Lutheran churches that the Henkels advertised were in the English language; they also sold English works by Jonathan Edwards, John Newton, and John Bunyan. The Henkels dominated German-language publishing in the Valley, and, though they sold German Reformed books printed elsewhere, their press tended to publish Lutheran works. The German Reformed residents relied upon Lawrence Wartmann, who also published works for the Mennonites and German Baptist Brethren or Dunkers. Wartmann's Harrisonburg press did not begin publishing until 1816, long after the Rhinelanders had begun speaking English.[53] Efforts to distribute such commonly used German-language materials as Bibles met with little success in the early nineteenth century. An Auxiliary Bible Society of Berkeley County organized by 1825 under the leadership of the Lutheran pastor C. Philip Krauth. It procured 29 English Bibles, 20 German Bibles, and 49 New Testaments to distribute in January of 1825. Four months later its efforts to distribute the German Bibles had met with no success: 20 German Bibles remained on hand, but only 16 English Bibles and 9 New Testaments were on its shelves. There was scarcely any audience for German-language Bible reading in Martinsburg.[54]

One surviving ledger from John Wise, an American-born printer of German and American newspapers in Staunton, shows that, by the late eighteenth century, many inhabitants of German descent preferred to subscribe to English-language newspapers. The ledger of John Wise's printing business, which covered the years from 1796 to 1816, lists 494 advertisers and subscribers in his English and German-language newspapers. Wise specifically entered in the ledger whether a subscriber or advertiser purchased a subscription or advertisement in his German paper or in his *Virginia Gazette and Staunton Phenix*. Only 21 persons were listed in his ledger as advertisers or subscribers to his German paper, and only 10 of these had German surnames, and the rest were clients with English or Scots-Irish surnames who placed advertisements for apprentices, lumber, or the sale of cattle to reach potential German-speaking customers. Wise listed 30 persons with German surnames who subscribed only to the English-language paper.[55] By the late eighteenth century in the upper Shenandoah Valley, there were more persons of German descent who preferred to use English.

Another form of German-language publication that appeared in Virginia was the almanac. Surviving Valley German almanacs devoted much attention to commercial and legal affairs in Maryland, Pennsylvania, and Virginia, where readers needed to know the value of various currencies, the distances to market, weights and measures, and the meeting days of the courts. Jacob D. Dietrich published two German almanacs in Virginia in 1805 and 1806. Dietrich had published German-language almanacs in Hagerstown, Maryland, before attempting to publish one in Winchester, Virginia. His *Neue Nord-Americanische Stadt und Land Calender* closely resembled the version of the almanac simultaneously published in Hagerstown.[56] Only two issues of the almanac have survived: one for 1805 and another for 1806. The traditional calendar of days of the astronomical year appeared, along with a liturgical calendar used in Protestant churches. Given names were suggested for each day so that children born that day could receive an appropriate biblical name at baptism. As did compilers of English-language almanacs, Dietrich published in his almanac a description of the planets and constellations and their supposed impact on various body parts.[57] He took up more space with charts and lists that informed his readers of the times of local market fairs in Pennsylvania, Maryland, and Virginia towns, and with announcements of the meeting times of Maryland and Virginia courts. He provided more commercial information by reproducing tables for the calculation of interest and others for reckoning the value of Spanish dollars, pounds, shillings, and pence, and federal dollars. The almanac also included a table of the value of gold and silver in various states. There were also tables of mileage along the main roads to principal towns. Much of the other material was translated from English or Irish newspapers, or German-language renditions of the story of Christopher Columbus, and reports of persons and events in Rochester, New York, and Germantown, Pennsylvania. There was also a short translation from the writings of Kotzubue and a meditation of Seneca on death. What is surprising about Dietrich's almanac is its similarity to English almanacs like Richard Bowen's *Virginia Almanac* from Winchester and the variety of commercial information appearing in it.

Since the Valley Rhinelanders had few books and newspapers, their speech quickly adopted English modifications. German newspaper editors, clergy, and schoolmasters, in whose interest it was to propagate the use of the German language, lamented its decline.[58] Soon Valley German became a peculiar hybrid. Variants of the German language did survive in the Valley into the twentieth century, but it was itself, according to linguist Kurt Kehr, a subdialect of Pennsylvania German, filled with mixtures of English words and sound and spoken in out-of-the-way coves and mountain hollows. This subdialect did not persist through the printed word, which came too late and in too small quantities, but through oral communication among isolated folk.[59] Newspapers of the Valley Germans like the New Market *Volksberichter* and the Staunton *Deutsche Virginia Adler* reflected the pressures of changing to English in the early nineteenth century. Their editors had to coin neologisms to explain to German-speaking readers concepts involving American government. These papers printed equivalent German words for American legal institutions accompanied by the appropriate word English speakers used. The *Deutsche Adler* printed "*Advocat* (lawyer)" or

"*Hayfisch* (shark)," and the *Volksberichter* regularly printed lists of German words and their Americanized meanings, such as the words for "ratification," "administration," "independence," "executive," "embargo," "neutral," "secretary," and "stockade."[60] The *Volksberichter* and *Deutsche Adler* also advertised guides for speaking proper English, such as Christian Becker's German–English language instruction book and the German-English dictionary of the Lancaster, Pennsylvania, printers Hamilton and Ehrenfried.[61]

The form of Virginia politics may also have dampened tendencies to assert distinctive aspects of the Rhinelanders' culture. Tidewater gentry dominated Virginia politics. Virginia's electorate was based upon landholding qualifications, not on simply paying a small county tax, as was the case in Pennsylvania. Though many Rhinelanders did own land and could thus qualify for suffrage, there were many who were servants or landless artisans working in Virginia's towns. They would not have had the right to vote in Virginia. Moreover, there was a lack of printed German-language political information because the Virginia German newspapers were either marginal or not inclined to print political literature. The famous Henkel press of Newmarket avoided printing political writings and concentrated on almanacs and religious publications. The Henkels' *Virginische Volksberichter* rejoiced when Democratic-Republicans won elections in 1808.[62] They did not engage in the bitter partisanship of Pennsylvania German-language papers like the *Readinger Adler* or *Lancaster Correspondent.*[63] Few Virginia counties had German populations large enough to make a difference in an election's results. Though Pennsylvania's politics had been embittered with hostility between dominant Anglicans and Quakers and a "Presbyterian" party of the Scots-Irish and their allies, Virginia's politics centered on the regional rivalry of Tidewater versus the west. After the disestablishment of the Anglican Church in 1786, political debates in Virginia did not focus on conflict between the German speakers and others, but between regions of the Commonwealth at odds over transportation policy, taxation of slaves, and underrepresentation in the legislature. In addition, there were many opportunities for German speakers to serve in lower offices of local government, whether as road surveyors, militia officers, justices of the peace, tax collectors, jurymen, coroners, and appraisers.[64] There is little evidence in the eighteenth century of German speakers expressing frustration because they held lower offices.

Though important cultural institutions were weak for Valley Rhinelanders and their descendants, the developing market economy was of growing importance during the time they faced assimilation into American culture. A market revolution created a modern capitalistic economy in the United States in the era after 1815, and this development happened just as the Rhinelanders' offspring faced the pressures for assimilation into the dominant culture.[65] They were full participants in the development of a market economy, with which their ancestors had experience in the Rhineland. This involvement with the market brought them into contact with persons of many other ethnocultural backgrounds. It can be seen in a variety of ways. The German-language newspapers recognized the dependence of German farmers on distant markets by publishing prices for commodities they produced in distant towns like Richmond, Fredericksburg, Baltimore, Alexandria, and Philadelphia.[66] Although the overwhelming proportion of the Rhinelanders' descendants were farmers, many of them were artisans in the towns and villages of the Valley, where they bought raw materials, advertised, and sold finished goods such as clothing, ironware, bags and bagging, harnesses and shoes, paper, lime, food, tools, wagons, rifles, clocks, and furniture.[67] A few had begun to enter mercantile partnerships by the early nineteenth century, sometimes with persons of Scots-Irish or English backgrounds.[68] They advertised the sale of goods brought in from distant markets, like Philadelphia, East India, or Germany.[69] Other partners had established rural mills or tanneries in the Valley.[70] The ledgers of Valley merchants like Ann Frame, John Wise, Josiah Raymond, James and William Brown, Abraham Shepherd, Henry Shepherd, and Philip Williams show many persons with German surnames transacting business with merchants from the 1790s on. Frequently the persons with German surnames traded cash for goods, though the Rhinelanders' descendants used corn, wheat, flour, home-woven linen, hauling services, pork, iron, and fish purchasing for mercantile goods. In exchange, merchants like Charles Town's Josiah Raymond shipped the farmers' flour to Georgetown and Alexandria.[71] Well into the nineteenth century, the rural farmers of German descent produced home manufactures, which they took to town stores to trade for coffee and sugar.[72]

Newspapers like the *Volksberichter* advertised machines for producing home manufactures from hemp and flax as early as 1809.[73] For German speakers inclined to do business, there were German language handbooks instructing them in arithmetic and bookkeeping, such as the *Geschwinde Rechner* sold by the Henkels.[74] All of these economic patterns show the growing involvement of the Valley Germans in an economy in the transformation to capitalism. It was not a difficult one to make, for their experience had prepared them to join in the trend.

Other folkways and artifacts show the rapid decline of communal identity among the descendants of the Rhinelanders in the Valley of

Virginia. The disappearance of the *Flurküchenhaus* and the spread of Federal Style stone houses and the Mid-Atlantic American I-house building style, or the trend toward naming German children after American patriotic figures, or the growing popularity of American decorative motifs on tombstones, house woodwork, or baptismal and marriage certificates testify to acculturation.[75] They would also show the dominance of economic motivations and personal choice alongside an eagerness to adopt the ways of the dominant culture, especially where it reinforced what was familiar in their Rhenish past. If Pennsylvania and Maryland were vigorous centers of transplanted German Rhineland culture, the Valley of Virginia was too thinly populated with Germans, too exposed to the migration of diverse peoples up the Great Valley, too dependent upon itinerant religious leaders and revivalism, too close to slavery and the plantation system, too distant from distributing centers of German books and newspapers, and too dependent on the export of agricultural surpluses to survive for long with culturally isolated German settlers. The Valley lacked geographically immobile, stable, tightly knit communities dominated by extended families, clergy, patriarchal authority, and the German language. Many substantial aspects of the Rhineland's culture and these immigrants' experience would foster individualism, pursuit of personal goals, and the attraction of money making. Moreover, the Rhineland prepared generations of American frontier settlers as much as the Pennsylvania backcountry had done. Life in the Rhineland had conditioned German-speaking families for their experiences in the Valley of Virginia on the margin of the eighteenth-century European commercial world.

Notes

1. James T. Lemon, *The Best Poor Man's Country: A Geographical Study of Early Southeastern Pennsylvania* (Baltimore: Johns Hopkins Univ. Press, 1972); James T. Lemon, "Early Americans and Their Social Environment," *Journal of Historical Geography* 6 (1980): 115–31. See also Alan Tully, *William Penn's Legacy— Politics and Social Structure in Provincial Pennsylvania, 1726–1755* (Baltimore: Johns Hopkins Univ. Press, 1977), 66–78.
2. Stephanie Grauman Wolf, *Urban Village: Population, Community, and Family Structure in Germantown, Pennsylvania, 1683–1800* (Princeton: Princeton Univ. Press, 1976), 155–59, 287–337; Daniel Snydacker, "Kinship and Community in Rural Pennsylvania, 1749–1820," *Journal of Interdisciplinary History* 13 (1982): 41–61. See also John J. McCusker and Russell R. Menard, *The Economy of British America, 1607–1789* (Chapel Hill: Univ. of North Carolina Press, 1985), 200–208; James A. Henretta, "Families and Farms: *Mentalité* in Pre-Industrial America," *William and Mary Quarterly* 35 (1978): 15–16; A. G. Roeber, "The Origins and

Transfer of German-American Concepts of Property and Inheritance," *Perspectives in American History*, New Series, 3 (1986): 115–71; A. G. Roeber, "'The Origin of Whatever Is Not English among Us': The Dutch-speaking and German-speaking Peoples of Colonial British America," in *Strangers Within the Realm: Cultural Margins of the First British Empire*, ed. Bernard Bailyn and Philip D. Morgan (Chapel Hill: Univ. of North Carolina Press, 1991), 220–83; A. G. Roeber, *Palatines, Liberty, and Property: German Lutheranism in Colonial British America* (Baltimore: Johns Hopkins Univ. Press, 1993); Elizabeth A. Kessel, "'A Mighty Fortress is Our God': German Religious and Educational Organizations on the Maryland Frontier, 1734–1800," *Maryland Historical Magazine* 77 (1982): 370–87; Elizabeth A. Kessel, "Germans in the Making of Frederick County, Maryland, 1730–1800," in *Appalachian Frontiers: Settlement, Society, and Development in the Preindustrial Era*, ed. Robert D. Mitchell (Lexington: Univ. Press of Kentucky, 1991), 87–104.

3. I will use the term "Rhinelander" in this chapter to designate the German-speaking immigrants to colonial America. Germany did not exist as a nation in the seventeenth and eighteenth centuries, but was divided into hundreds of principalities, dukedoms, and territories governed by princes and electors, some of whom were German. The settlers who immigrated to America came from the Rhineland in modern Germany, Alsace in France, the lower Rhine in Holland, and from the headwaters of the Rhine in Switzerland.

4. Robert D. Mitchell, *Commercialism and Frontier: Perspectives on the Early Shenandoah Valley* (Charlottesville: Univ. Press of Virginia, 1977). Klaus Wust, *The Virginia Germans* (Charlottesville: Univ. Press of Virginia, 1969), is a solid study, but uses the approach of formal, traditional narrative history. See also John W. Wayland, *The German Element of the Shenandoah Valley* (1907; reprint, Harrisonburg, Va.: C. J. Carrier Co., 1978).

5. Albert H. Tillson Jr., *Gentry and Common Folk: Political Culture on the Virginia Frontier, 1740–1789* (Lexington: Univ. Press of Kentucky, 1991); Rhys Isaac, *The Transformation of Virginia, 1740–1790* (Chapel Hill: Univ. of North Carolina Press, 1982).

6. Warren M. Billings, John E. Selby, Thad W. Tate, *Colonial Virginia: A History* (White Plains, N.Y.: KTO Press, 1986).

7. Elmer Lewis Smith, John G. Stewart, and M. Ellsworth Kyger, *The Pennsylvania Germans of the Shenandoah Valley* (Allentown: The Pennsylvania German Folklore Society, 1964).

8. A. G. Roeber called for such an approach in "In German Ways? Problems and Potentials of Eighteenth Century German Social and Emigration History," *William and Mary Quarterly* 3d ser., 44 (1987): 750–74.

9. My understanding of peasant economic behavior in transforming markets is based upon Frank Ellis, *Peasant Economics* (Cambridge: Cambridge Univ. Press, 1988), 63–140, 234.

10. Wilhelm Abel, *Geschichte der deutschen Landwirtschaft vom fruehen Mittelalter bis zum 19. Jahrhundert* (Stuttgart: Verlag Eugen Ulmer, 1962), 251–57, 280–301; Ludwig Haeusser, *Geschichte der Rheinischen Pfalz nach ihren politischen, kirchlichen und literarischen Verhaeltnissen*, Zweiter Band (Pirmasens: Buchhandlung Johann Richter, 1970), 923–25; Gotthilf Nicolas Lutyens, *Etwas ueber den gegenwaertigen Zustand der Auswanderungen und Ansiedlungen im Staate vom Pennsylvanien in Nord-Amerika, besonders in Ansehung der Deutschen* (Ham-

burg: Carl Ernst Bohn, 1796), 7–12; Alan Mayhew, *Rural Settlement and Farming in Germany* (London: B. T. Batsford Ltd., 1973), 121–35, 161–77; B. H. Slicher van Bath, *The Agrarian History of Western Europe, a.d. 500–1850* (New York: St. Martin's Press Inc., 1963), 220–43; Marianne Sophia Wokeck, "A Tide of Alien Tongues: The Flow and Ebb of German Immigration to Pennsylvania, 1683–1776," (Ph.D. diss.: Temple Univ., 1983), 26, 47, 314; James J. Sheehan, *German History, 1770–1866*, The Oxford History of Modern Europe Series (Oxford: Clarendon Press, 1989), 73, 82, 90–91, 104–5.

11. Benjamin Rush, "An Account of the Manners of the German Inhabitants of Pennsylvania in 1789," *The Pennsylvania German* 10 (1909): 209; Samuel Kercheval, *A History of the Valley of Virginia* (Harrisonburg, Va.: C. J. Carrier Co., 1983), 152.

12. Mayhew, *Rural Settlement and Farming*, 130–35; Wolfgang Koellmann and Peter Marschalck, "German Emigration to the United States," in *Perspectives in American History* 7 (1974): 514; Wilhelm Heinrich Riehl, *Die Pfaelzer—Ein rheinisches Volksbild*, 3d ed. (Stuttgart: J. G. Cotta'sche Buchhandlung, Nachfolger, 1907), 678. Riehl, a pioneer observer of German folklife, said that Palatinate peasants living near the villages adjacent to the Haardt Mountains were half townspeople. They were not bound to the soil in traditional patterns of agriculture.

13. Kercheval, *History of the Valley*, 149; Klaus Wust, "Folklore, Customs, and Crafts of the Valley Settlers," *Historic Preservation* 20 (1968): 32. Farley Grubb speculates that the German immigrants to eighteenth-century America may have been more craft-oriented than emigrants who migrated from the Rhineland to eastern Europe after 1760. See Farley Grubb, "German Immigration to Pennsylvania, 1709 to 1820," *Journal of Interdisciplinary History* 28 (1990): 431–33. Lee Soltow and Kenneth Keller found high percentages of persons with craft occupations in Berks County, Pennsylvania, in the center of German settlement. See Lee Soltow and Kenneth W. Keller, "Rural Pennsylvania in 1800: A Portrait from the Septennial Census," *Pennsylvania History* 49 (1982): 35–38. Ambrose Henkel urged the Valley Germans to grow hemp, flax, and wool, as there was great demand for products made from these fiber crops. *Virginische Volksberichter*, Newmarket, Va., Jan. 11, 1809. Peter Heiskell advertised the sale of a mill in a German neighborhood of Shenandoah County. The business of the mill continue to thrive because the neighboring population was "principally made up of Germans, whose attachment to Domestic manufactures will not probably soon abate." See *Farmers Register*, Charles Town, Va., Oct. 1, 1817.

14. My calculations of Augusta County inheritance practices were taken from abstracts of the wills appearing in Lyman Chalkley, *Chronicles of the Scotch-Irish Settlement of Virginia, Extracted from the Original Court Records of Augusta County, 1745–1800*, 3 vols. (1912; reprint, Baltimore: Genealogical Publishing Co., Inc., 1980), vol. 3: 9–250. See also Kenneth E. Koons, "Families and Farms in the Lower-Cumberland Valley of Southcentral Pennsylvania, 1850–1880," (D.A. diss.: Carnegie-Mellon Univ., 1986), 217–60.

15. On Pietism and its impact on German Reformed, Lutheran, Mennonite, Moravian, and Church of the Brethen religiosity, see F. Ernest Stoeffler, *Continental Pietism and Early American Christianity* (Grand Rapids, Mich.: William B. Eerdmans Publishing Co., 1976), 8–162.

16. Riehl, *Die Pfaelzer,* 301–12; F. Ernest Stoeffler, *Continental Pietism and Early Christianity* (Grand Rapids, Mich.: William B. Eerdmanns Publishing Co., 1976); Stephen Lewis Longenecker, "Religion and Egalitarianism among Early Pennsylvania Germans," (Ph.D. diss.: Johns Hopkins Univ., 1990), 1–58; Charles H. Glatfelter, *Pastors and People: German Lutheran and Reformed Churches in the Pennsylvania Field, 1717–1793,* vol. 2, *The History,* in Publications of the Pennsylvania German Society, vol. 13 (Breinigsville, Pa.: The Pennsylvania German Society, 1981), 9–19.

17. Samuel S. Hough, ed., *Christian Newcomer—His Life Journal and Achievements* (Dayton, Ohio: Board of Administration—Church of the United Brethren in Christ, 1941), 19–20, 24–25, 35, 45–47, 55, 62–63, 66–67, 73–74, 85–86, 109–10, 125, 138, 166–67, 213. See also Wesley M. Gewehr, *The Great Awakening in Virginia, 1740–1790* (Durham: Duke Univ. Press, 1930), 25–27.

18. Wokeck, "Alien Tongues," 168–69, 310–18; Marianne Sophia Wokeck, "Promoters and Passengers: The German Immigrant Trade, 1683–1775," in *The World of William Penn,* ed. Richard S. Dunn and Mary Maples Dunn (Philadelphia: Univ. of Pennsylvania Press, 1986), 259–78; Lowell Colton Bennion, "Flight from the Reich: A Geographic Exposition of Southwest German Emigration, 1683–1815," (Ph.D. diss., Syracuse Univ., 1971); Grubb, "German Immigration to Pennsylvania," 417–30; Farley Grubb, "The Incidence of Servitude in Transatlantic Migration, 1771–1804," *Explorations in Economic History* 22 (1985): 316–39; Grubb, "Redemptioner Immigration to Pennsylvania: Evidence on Contract Choice and Profitability," *Journal of Economic History* 16 (1986); Hans Fenske, "International Migration in Germany in the Eighteenth Century," *Central European History* 13 (1980): 344; Werner Hacker, *Auswanderungen aus Rheinpfalz und Saarland im 18. Jahrhundert* (Stuttgart: Konrad Theiss Verlag, 1987), 9–97; Guenter Moltmann, "The Migration of German Redemptioners to North America, 1720–1820," in *Colonialism and Migration; Indentured Labor before and after Slavery,* ed. P. C. Emmer (Dordrecht, the Netherlands: Martinus Nijhoff Publishers, 1986), 105–22; Fritz Trautz, "Die Pfaelzische Auswanderung nach Nordamerika im 18. Jahrhundert," in *Heidelberger Veroffentlichungen zur Landesgeschichte und Landeskunde* 4 (1959): 5–30; Eva Schuenzel, "Die deutsche Auswanderung nach Nordamerika im 17. und 18. Jahrhundert," (Inaugural diss., Julius-Maximilians Universitaet zu Wuerzburg, 1959), 2, 143, 154, 173; Oscar Handlin and John Clive, eds., *Journey to Pennsylvania by Gottlieb Mittelberger* (Cambridge: The Belknap Press of Harvard Univ. Press, 1960), 17–18, 26.

19. Sharon Salinger, *"To Serve Well and Faithfully"—Labor and Indentured Servants in Pennsylvania, 1682–1800* (New York: Cambridge Univ. Press, 1987), 68.

20. Lutyens, *Etwas ueber den gegenwaertigen,* 16–17.

21. Grubb, "German Immigration to Pennsylvania," 429–33.

22. Lutyens, *Etwas ueber den gegenwaertigen,* 16–18; Christoph Daniel Ebeling, *Erdbeschreibung und Geschichte von Amerika—Die Vereinten Staaten von Nordamerika,* vol. 4, *Der Staat Pennsylvania* (Hamburg: Carl Ernst Bohn, 1797), 40, 276; Lemon, *Best Poor Man's Country,* 121.

23. Smith, Stewart, and Kyger, *Pennsylvania Germans of the Shenandoah Valley,* 11, 16–17, 21, 29, 41, 52–53.

24. One of the earliest scholarly discussions of the cultural impact of the Germans on the Middle Colonies was Thomas Jefferson Wertenbaker's classic, *The*

Founding of American Civilization, the Middle Colonies (New York: Cooper Square Publishers, Inc., 1938), 256–345. Wertenbaker, a native Virginian, familiar with the material culture of the Rhineland as no other American historian was, sees the migration up the Valley as a "vital" source of renewal of Germanic culture, even though what he calls the "melting-pot" was at work. Ibid., 25.

25. From the earliest days of their settlements, these Rhinelanders moved on their own. See Klaus Wust, "Palatines and Switzers for Virginia, 1705–1738: Costly Lessons for Promoters and Emigrants," *Yearbook of German-American Studies* 19 (1984): 43–54.

26. Aaron Fogleman, "Migrations to the Thirteen British North American Colonies, 1700–1775: New Estimates," *Journal of Interdisciplinary History* 22 (1992): 139–61.

27. The Shenandoah River watershed comprises about 3,054 square miles.

28. See Chalkley's abstracts from the Augusta County Order Books. Chalkley, *Chronicles of Scotch-Irish Settlement*, vol. 1: 58–248.

29. Ibid., vol. 2: 466–81. Klaus Wust suggests that the number of Germans in Augusta County was larger than previously thought. See Klaus G. Wust, "Settlement and Acculturation of Germans in Western Virginia," *American Philosophical Society, Yearbook* (1966): 561.

30. Christoph Daniel Ebeling, *Erdbeschreibung*, vol. 7, *Der Staat Virginien* (Hamburg: Carl Ernst Bohn, 1816), 276. Ebeling reported that few new settlers came to Virginia from Germany by the time his remarkable volume on Virginia was published. One of Ebeling's many informants was Henry St. George Tucker, sometime resident of Winchester. Tucker was one of three persons to whom the volume was dedicated and the only Virginian to be so honored. Ebeling repeatedly describes the Shenandoah Valley as the "German Valley."

31. J. R. Hildebrand, comp., *The Beverley Patent, 1736—Including Original Grantees, 1738–1815 in Orange & Augusta Counties, Va.* [map] (1954).

32. Grubb, "German Immigration to Pennsylvania," 419–27. See also Wokeck, "Alien Tongues," 314.

33. Richard M. Bernard, *The Melting Pot and the Altar: Marital Assimilation in Early Twentieth Century Wisconsin* (Minneapolis: Univ. of Minnesota Press, 1980), 53.

34. Charlene D. Hutcheson, "Evidence of Early Disruption of Ethnic Marriage Patterns in Rural Communities of Roanoke County, 1770–1850," paper presented at conference "After the Backcountry: Rural Life and Society in the Nineteenth-Century Valley of Virginia," Lexington, Va., 1995.

35. Sheehan, *German History*, 80.

36. Some of the Rhinelanders were familiar with the custom of sharing church buildings because it was done in Germany. In the Palatinate Protestants and Roman Catholics shared churches in small villages. See Riehl, *Die Pfaelzer*, 296. Mennonites and Amish worshiped in homes.

37. Church Record Book, St. Peter's Lutheran Church, Churchville, Va., Manuscript, Library of Virginia, Richmond.

38. Glatfelter, *Pastors and People*, vol. 1: 45, 61, 78, 92, 114, 133, 151, 166, 498.

39. Ibid., 15, 25–27, 133, 498, 499.

40. Martin E. Lodge, "The Crisis of the Churches in the Middle Colonies, 1720–1750," *Pennsylvania Magazine of History and Biography* 95 (1971): 197–98.

41. See Adolf Spaeth, Henry Eyster Jacobs, G. F. Spieker, eds., *Documentary History of the Evangelical Lutheran Ministerium of Pennsylvania and Adjacent States* (Philadelphia: Board of Publication of the General Council of the Evangelical

Lutheran Church in North America, 1898), 136–37, 214–15, 261, 264, 283–84, 308, 319, 350, 365, 376, 389.

42. Eastern Synod of the Reformed Church in the United States, *Minutes and Letters of the Coetus of the German Reformed Congregations in Pennsylvania, 1747–1792* (Philadelphia: Reformed Church Publication Board, 1903), 37, 158, 238, 253, 276, 331, 337, 445; H. M. J. Klein, *The History of the Eastern Synod of the Reformed Church in the United States* (Lancaster, Pa.: Eastern Synod of the Reformed Church in the United States, 1943), 91, 112, 117; J. Silor Garrison, *The History of the Reformed Church in Virginia, 1714–1940* (Winston-Salem, N.C.: The Clay Printing Company, 1948), 18–19, 30, 39–42.

43. William Edward Eisenberg, *The Lutheran Church in Virginia, 1717–1962* (Roanoke, Va.: Trustees of the Virginia Synod, Lutheran Church in America, 1962), 79–82. Four Virginia pastors attended with lay delegates from Virginia congregations. The conference met fairly regularly until the establishment of the Virginia Synod of the Lutheran Church in 1820. See also Klein, *History of the Eastern Synod*, 135–41. In 1823 the Reformed Church established a Classis composed of Virginia, the Carolinas, Kentucky, and Tennessee.

44. Christopher L. Dolmetsch, *The German Press of the Shenandoah Valley*, Studies in German Literature Linguistics, and Culture, vol. 4 (Columbia, S.C.: Camden House, 1984), 124–42.

45. Spaeth, Jacobs, and Spieker, eds., *Evangelical Lutheran Ministerium*, 13–20. The Lutheran Agenda was not printed, but transcribed by hand by each pastor. The copy used by John Peter Gabriel Muhlenberg, who was a theologically educated and ordained Lutheran pastor at Woodstock, Virginia, from 1769 to 1776, is reprinted in Spaeth. Congregations at Woodstock, Winchester, Strasburg, Rude's Hill and Powell's Fort (Shenandoah County), Fort Run (Rockingham County), and Hawksbill (Page County) were in Muhlenberg's pastoral charge. See Glatfelter, *Pastors and People*, vol. 1: 97–99.

46. See church registers of St. Paul's Lutheran Church, Strasburg, Virginia, 1854–1859, Manuscript, Library of Virginia, Richmond; St. Peter's Lutheran Church, Churchville, Va., 1843. For an announcement of a protracted meeting in a Valley Lutheran Church, see the *Martinsburg Gazette*, Martinsburg, Va., Sept. 7, 1843.

47. I have used the microfilmed and photostatic manuscript church registers for St. Paul's Lutheran Church, Strasburg, St. Peter's Lutheran Church, Churchville, Friedens Lutheran and Reformed Church, Rockingham Co., St. Michael's Reformed Church, Rockingham Co., Zion Lutheran and Reformed Church, Shenandoah Co., Library of Virginia, Richmond. See also William Edward Eisenberg, *This Heritage—The Story of Lutheran Beginnings in the Lower Shenandoah Valley, and of Grace Church, Winchester* (Winchester, Va.: Trustees of Grace Evangelical Lutheran Church, 1954), 72.

48. By 1776 nearly twenty Pennsylvania German Reformed and Lutheran Churches had pipe organs. See Glatfelter, *Pastors and People*, vol. 2: 181.

49. Dolmetsch, *German Press*, 1–3.

50. David A. Rawson, "News in the Valley: A Study of Newspaper Circulation through the New Market Post Office, 1797–1842," paper delivered at conference "After the Backcountry: Rural Life and Society in the Nineteenth Century Valley of Virginia," Lexington, Va., 1995.

51. Dolmetsch, *German Press*, 9–28.

52. The Apr. 19, 1809, edition of the *Virginische Volksberichter* advertised the sale in

the Henkel bookstore of a number of works the Pietists admired. They included Justus Heinrich Christian Helmuth's *Betrachtung der evangelischen Lehre von der Heiligen Schrift und Taufe*, Joachim Neander's *Harfenspiel*, Johann Friederich Starck's *Taegliches Handbuch*; more rationalistic imprints, like Georg Joachim Zollikofer's *Gebetbuch* and Johann Heinrich Jung-Stilling's *Geschichte der Florentin von Falkentorn*; works by earlier writers the Pietists loved, like Johann Arndt's orthodox Lutheran *Vier Buecher vom wahren Christenthum* and Johann Habermann's *Das Grosse Gebetbuch*; devotional works, like Gerhard Teerstegen's *Geistliches Blumengartlein*; and Johannes Huebner's biblical study aid, *Zweimal zwei und funfzig biblische Historien*. Most of these works had been published by Pennsylvania printers, not by the Henkels. The authors represented produced their works from the sixteenth to the eighteenth centuries. See Oswald Seidenstricker, *The First Century of German Printing in America, 1728–1830* (reprint, Millwood, N.Y.: Kraus, 1980).

53. Dolmetsch, *German Press*, 74.
54. *Martinsburg Gazette*, Apr. 7, 1825.
55. John Wise Ledger, Special Collections Dept., Univ. of Virginia Library, Charlottesville.
56. *Der Neue Nord-Americanische Stadt und Land Calendar, auf das Jahr unsers Heilandes Jesu Christi . . .* (Winchester, Va.: 1805, 1806).
57. I have compared Dietrich's almanac with Richard Bowen's English-language *Virginia Almanac* (Winchester, Va., 1795).
58. *Virginische Volksberichter*, Oct. 19, 1808.
59. Kurt Kehr, "'Deutsche' Dialekte in Virginia und West Virginia (U.S.A.). Zur Typologie virginiadeutscher Sprachinseln," *Zeitschrift fuer Dialektologie und Linguistik*, Heft 3, Jahrgang 46 (1979): 289–319.
60. *Deutsche Virginier Adler*, Nov. 18, 1809. Richard Hamrick of the Augusta County Historical Society allowed me to see the *Adler*. See issues of the *Volksberichter*, Jan. 6, 20, Feb. 3, 10, 1808.
61. *Deutsche Virginische Adler*, Nov. 18, 1809; *Virginische Volksberichter*, Feb. 1, 1809.
62. *Virginische Volksberichter*, Nov. 23, 1808.
63. In the presidential election of 1800, Virginia Republicans seeking to win votes for Jefferson had to write to Philadelphia for German-language political propaganda. Norman K. Risjord, *Chesapeake Politics, 1781–1800* (New York: Columbia Univ. Press, 1978), 557.
64. Roeber, *Palatines, Liberty, and Property*, 155. For minor officeholding by persons with German surnames in Augusta County, 1745–1790, see Chalkley, *Chronicles of Scotch-Irish Settlement*, vol. 1: 13–14, 17–19, 22–24, 45, 48, 107, 157, 229, 481.
65. Charles Sellers, *The Market Revolution: Jacksonian America, 1815–1846* (New York: Oxford Univ. Press, 1991), 5–25, 35–51, 151–55.
66. See issues of the *Virginische Volksberichter* for 1807 and the *Deutsche Virginische Adler*, Nov. 18, 1809. Jacob Dietrich advertised that he would publish the prices in Richmond, Fredericksburg, Baltimore, and Philadelphia on a weekly basis. Only one issue of his paper is known to exist, so it is impossible to say whether he kept his promise.
67. I have surveyed advertisements by persons with German surnames in the Winchester *Virginia Gazette*, the *Martinsburg Gazette*, the Staunton *Political Censor*

and *Spirit of the Press*, the Charles Town *Farmers Register* for issues from the 1780s to the 1830s.

68. For example, Hogmire and Boyd of Martinsburg, Heiskell and Sowers of Staunton, Mayberry and Kring, and Straher and Kauffmann at New Market.

69. *Virginische Volksberichter*, May 11, 1808.

70. Ibid., June 22, 29, 1808; Oct. 26, 1808.

71. See account books of Abraham Shepherd (1790–1803), Josiah Raymond (1793–97), Ann Frame (1798–1812), Philip Williams (1801–26), William Brown (1803–8), James Brown (1812–28), and Henry Shepherd (1815–62) in the Thornton Tayloe Perry Collection, Virginia Historical Society, and the Ledger of John Wise (1796–1816), Special Collections Dept., Univ. of Virginia Library, Charlottesville.

72. Kercheval, *History of the Valley*, 149.

73. *Virginische Volksberichter*, May 10, 1809.

74. Ambrose Henkel und Co., *Ein Verzeichniss der Deutschen und Englischen Bucher . . . (August 10, 1813)* Virginia Historical Society, Richmond.

75. Edward A. Chappell, "Acculturation in the Shenandoah Valley: Rhenish Houses of the Massanutten Settlement," *Proceedings of the American Philosophical Society* 124 (1980): 55–89. See also Klaus Wust, *Folk Art in Stone: Southwest Virginia* (Edinburg, Va.: Shenandoah History Publishers, 1970); Klaus Wust, *Virginia Fraktur: Penmanship as Folk Art* (Edinburg, Va.: Shenandoah History Publishers, 1975); Robert P. Turner, ed., *Lewis Miller, Sketches and Chronicles: The Reflections of a Nineteenth Century Pennsylvania German Folk Artist* (York, Pa.: The Historical Society of York County, 1966); Theodora Rezba, ed., *Valley Pioneer Artists and Those Who Continue: The Decorative and Fine Arts of the Lower Shenandoah Valley, 1760–1986* (Winchester, Va.: Shenandoah College and Conservatory, 1986); Elmer L. Smith, comp., *Arts and Crafts of the Shenandoah Valley* (Lebanon, Pa.: Applied Arts Publishers, 1968).

Works Cited

Abel, Wilhelm. *Geschichte der deutschen Landwirtschaft vom fruehen Mittelalter bis zum 19. Jahrhundert.* Stuttgart: Verlag Eugen Ulmer, 1962.

Bailyn, Bernard and Philip D. Morgan, editors. *Strangers Within the Realm: Cultural Margins of the First British Empire.* Chapel Hill: Univ. of North Carolina Press, 1985.

Bennion, Lowell Colton. "Flight from the Reich: A Geographic Exposition of Southwest German Emigration, 1683–1815." Ph.D. diss., Syracuse Univ., 1971.

Chalkley, Lyman. *Chronicles of the Scotch-Irish Settlement of Virginia, Extracted from the Original Court Records of Augusta County, 1745–1800.* 3 vols. 1912. Reprint, Baltimore: Genealogical Publishing Co., Inc., 1980.

Chappell, Edward A. "Acculturation in the Shenandoah Valley: Rhenish Houses of the Massanutten Settlement." *Proceedings of the American Philosophical Society* 124 (1980): 55–89.

Dolmetsch, Christopher. *The German Press of the Shenandoah Valley.* Camden, S.C.: Camden House, 1984.

Eisenberg, William Edward. *The Lutheran Church in Virginia, 1717–1962.* Roanoke, Va.: Trustees of the Virginia Synod, Lutheran Church in America, 1962.

Ellis, Frank. *Peasant Economics.* Cambridge: Cambridge Univ. Press, 1988.

Fogelman, Aaron. "Migrations to the Thirteen British North American Colonies, 1700–1775: New Estimates." *Journal of Interdisciplinary History* 22 (1992): 139–61.

Garrison, J. Silor. *The History of the Reformed Church in Virginia, 1714–1940.* Winston-Salem, N.C.: The Clay Printing Company, 1948.

Glatfelter, Charles. *Pastors and People: German Lutheran and Reformed Churches in the Pennsylvania Field, 1717–1793.* 2 vols. Breinigsville, Pa.: The Pennsylvania German Society, 1981.

Grubb, Farley. "German Immigration to Pennsylvania, 1709 to 1820." *Journal of Interdisciplinary History* 28 (1990): 417–30.

Hacker, Werner. *Auswanderungen aus Rheinpfalz und Saarland im 18. Jahrhundert.* Stuttgart: Konrad Theiss Verlag, 1987.

Haeusser, Ludwig. *Geschichte der Rheinischen Pfalz nach ihren politischen, kirchlichen und literarischen Verhaeltnissen.* Zweiter Band. Pirmasens, Germany: Buchhandlung Johann Richter, 1970.

Henretta, James A. "Families and Farms: *Mentalité* in Pre-Industrial America." *William and Mary Quarterly* 3d ser., 35 (1978): 3–32.

Kehr, Kurt. "'Deutsche' Dialekte in Virginia und West Virginia (U.S.A.). Zur Typologie virginiadeutscher Sprachinseln." *Zeitschrift fuer Dialektologie und Linguistik* 3 (1979): 289–319.

Kercheval, Samuel. *A History of the Valley of Virginia.* Harrisonburg, Va.: C. J. Carrier Co., 1983.

Kessel, Elizabeth A. "'A Mighty Fortress Is Our God': German Religious and Educational Organizations on the Maryland Frontier, 1734–1800." *Maryland Historical Magazine* 77 (1982): 370–87.

———. "Germans in the Making of Frederick County, Maryland, 1730–1800." In *Appalachian Frontiers: Settlement, Society, and Development in the Preindustrial Era,* edited by Robert D. Mitchell, 87–104. Lexington: Univ. Press of Kentucky, 1991.

Klein, H. M. J. *The History of the Eastern Synod of the Reformed Church in the United States.* Lancaster, Pa.: Eastern Synod of the Reformed Church in the United States, 1943.

Koellmann, Wolfgang, and Peter Marshalck. "German Emigration to the United States." In *Perspectives in American History* 7 (1973).

Lemon, James T. *The Best Poor Man's Country: A Geographical Study of Early Southeastern Pennsylvania.* Baltimore: Johns Hopkins Univ. Press, 1972.

Longenecker, Stephen Lewis. "Religion and Egalitarianism among Early Pennsylvania Germans." Ph.D. diss., Johns Hopkins Univ., 1990.

Mayhew, Alan. *Rural Settlement and Farming in Germany.* London: B. T. Batsford, Ltd., 1973.

Mitchell, Robert D. *Commercialism and Frontier: Perspectives on the Early Shenandoah Valley.* Charlottesville: Univ. Press of Virginia, 1977.

Moltmann, Guenter. "The Migration of German Redemptioners to North America, 1720–1820." In *Colonialism and Migration: Indentured Labor before and after Slavery.* Edited by P. C. Emmer. Dordrecht, the Netherlands: Martinus Nijhoff Publishers, 1986.

Riehl, Wilhelm Heinrich. *Die Pfaelzer—Ein rheinisches Volksbild.* Stuttgart: J. G. Cotta'sche buchhandlung, Nachfolger, 1907.

Roeber, A. G. *Palatines, Liberty, and Property: German Lutherans in Colonial British America.* Baltimore: Johns Hopkins Univ. Press, 1993.

———. "In German Ways? Problems and Potentials of Eighteenth Century German Social and Emigration History." William and Mary Quarterly 44 (1987): 750–74.

Schuenzel, Eva, "Die deutsche Auswanderung nach Nordamerika im 17. und 18. Jahrhundert." Inaugural diss., Julius-Maximilians Universitaet zu Wuerzburg, 1959.

Seidenstricker, Oswald. *The First Century of German Printing in America: 1728–1830.* Reprint, Millwood, N.Y.: Kraus, 1980.

Sheehan, James J. *German History, 1770–1866.* Oxford: Oxford Univ. Press, 1989.

Slicher van Bath, B. H. *The Agrarian History of Western Europe, a.d. 500–1850.* New York: St. Martin's Press, Inc., 1963.

Smith, Elmer Lewis, John G. Stewart, and M. Ellsworth. Kyger. *The Pennsylvania Germans of the Shenandoah Valley.* Allentown: The Pennsylvania German Folklore Society, 1964.

Stoeffler, F. Ernest. *Continental Pietism and Early American Christianity.* Grand Rapids, Mich.: William B. Eerdmans Publishing Co., 1976.

Trautz, Fritz. "Die Pfaelzische Auswanderung nach Nordamerika im 17. und 18. Jahrhundert." In *Heidelberger Veroffentlichungen zur Landesgeschichte und Landeskunde* 4 (1959): 5–30.

Wayland, John W. *The German Element of the Shenandoah Valley.* 1907. Reprint, Harrisonburg, Va.: C. J. Carrier Co., 1978.

Wertenbaker, Thomas Jefferson. *The Founding of American Civilization, the Middle Colonies.* New York: Cooper Square Publishers, 1938.

Wokeck, Marianne. "A Tide of Aliien Tongues: The Flow and Ebb of German Immigration to Pennsylvania, 1683–1776." Ph.D. diss., Temple Univ., 1983.

———. "Promoters and Passengers: The German Immigrant Trade, 1683–1775." In *The World of William Penn.* Edited by Richard S. Dunn and Mary Maples Dunn. Philadelphia: Univ. of Pennsylvania Press, 1986.

Wust, Klaus. "The Settlement and Acculturation of Germans in Western Virginia." *American Philosophical Society Yearbook* (1966): 561.

———. *The Virginia Germans.* Charlottesville: Univ. Press of Virginia, 1969.

Part III

Native Americans and African Americans on the Frontier

Settlement of the Virginia frontier traditionally has been viewed as an entirely European experience, with the only questions of a multicultural nature revolving around how Scotch-Irish settlers got along with their German counterparts, and how both of them reacted to the system of English administration. Early histories gave very limited recognition to the roles—or even the presence—of Native Americans and African Americans on the early frontier. And yet, both groups contributed to the development of the backcountry. Their influence cannot be ignored in coming to a holistic understanding of the Virginia backcountry environment.

Long before Europeans occupied the Virginia frontier, of course, Native Americans shaped the landscape. By the time that Scotch-Irish or German settlers began making their marks on the region, however, the native inhabitants were largely gone, due to contagions that preceded sustained physical contact between the cultures or the Indians' own economic motivations. And by the time of the American Revolution—and beyond in the literature of the frontier—the general image of Indians in the region was one associated with hostility and combat and reflected the various degrees of anger and fear that went along with the popular notion. In the absence of resident natives, eighteenth-century Virginia pioneers' only direct experience with Indians came from Cherokee or Catawba raiding parties passing through to attack their long-standing aboriginal enemies to the north, feared Iroquois warriors journeying south likewise to snipe at their foes, and Shawnee bands that jealously guarded their control over the western fringes of the colonial backcountry. Since the behavior of these natives was often precipitated by forces outside the control of the actual settlers—by the actions of imperial diplomats or colonial legislators, or by the excesses of often unscrupulous traders or land speculators— and since the settlers developed a mistrust of these foreign natives, the environment was ripe for conflict. Very few cooler heads prevailed.[1]

The roots of this uneasy relationship between the natives and settlers on the frontier go back to the earliest encounters between explorers from Virginia and the aboriginal inhabitants of the backcountry in the 1660s and 1670s. Accounts of these expeditions left the image of "a beautiful country peopled by suspicious and hostile natives who pretended friendship while plotting to destroy intruders."[2] As Gary Nash pointed out over twenty years ago, English impressions and attitudes concerning Indians, regardless of their accuracy, linked closely with intentions and desires, dictating the course of behavior and policy. If the actions which resulted from the colonists' attitudes provoked negative responses from the natives, the initial images were only reinforced.[3] If from their earliest probes, Virginians generally adopted a fear of natives on the frontier, it was very unlikely that this perception would change, particularly given the nature of relations by the mid-eighteenth century.

Hostility was not the only dynamic at work, however, in spite of the representation in the literature. Trade relationships also existed, and, especially early on, the natives' initial approach was not so much hostile as it was calculating. Focusing on a small assemblage of archaeological sites at the headwaters of the Roanoke River, Michael Barber and Eugene Barfield point out that the initial—and only—interaction between Europeans and the aboriginal inhabitants of the Valley of Virginia was of an indirect nature and the result of an already established native trade network. The paucity of European trade items found at these sites indicates to Barber and his team that the Occaneechis in the Southside, east of the mountains, tightly guarded their profitable position as middlemen in the colonial trade and strictly regulated the flow of both goods and people into the interior. That would explain the scarcity of European items in seventeenth-century sites, as well as the lack of ethnographic records from beyond the mountains during the period. Barber and Barfield paint a picture of "European concepts, ideas and artifacts" intruding into an established native system, but, as they portray it, that intrusion was limited and periodic; by the time a true European presence was realized, the natives no longer occupied the region, for whatever reasons. This fact leads to speculation about what might have happened had the Indians stayed in the Roanoke Valley. The fear of an Indian presence pervaded life on the southwest Virginia frontier during the eighteenth century, and, likewise, the anticipation of hostilities pervaded the early historiography; if an actual presence had persisted, would the European perspective have been different? No one can say. But, in any case, as the authors assert, European control of the backcountry west of the mountains was "won by default" from the departed natives.

Europeans, of course, were not the only newcomers who intruded, as Barber and Barfield phrase it, onto the Virginia frontier. Contrary to traditional assumptions, African Americans—both free and enslaved—were also part of the migration, if not always willingly, and they too contributed to the reconfiguration of the landscape of the region. Unfortunately, writers have not traditionally recognized this fact, as information on blacks has been sadly lacking from the literature. Very little research has been done on slavery—much less on free blacks—in the Shenandoah Valley, so many questions remain unanswered. In the absence of hard research, the accepted dogma has been that the early settlers of the backcountry were hardy subsistence farmers to whom the concept of slavery was foreign in the moral context and unattractive in the economic context. Only relatively recently has research indicated the presence of significant numbers of African American slaves in the region during the colonial period.[4]

Slightly more attention has been cast toward the institution in the more distant reaches of the Virginia backcountry. Eastern Kentucky and the Ohio Valley were, during most of the period covered by this volume, administratively an actual frontier of Virginia and were viewed as such by contemporaries. Settlement and development of those areas, including the institution of slavery and the dynamics of race relations, were direct extensions of the Virginia frontier experience. Naturally, because of the chronological order of settlement, ethnic relations in these regions cannot be addressed until the late eighteenth and into the nineteenth century. There were, obviously, clear links between slavery in eastern Kentucky and the Ohio Valley and its antecedents elsewhere on the Virginia frontier. Differences, however, also were apparent, due to the different motives of the slaveowners, the environments of the regions, and the pace of development; slavery on the fringes of the backcountry was, in many ways, distinct from the institution in the Valley or even east of the mountains, and, in some ways, relations between the races became ever more complex. Each of the following essays help to dispel the myth that slaveholding was absent or of minimal interest to settlers of the Virginia frontier, and, collectively, the authors portray the variety of challenges faced by African Americans in coping with the new environment—human and natural—into which they were thrust.

As early as 1727, runaway slaves sought refuge beyond the Blue Ridge, and, therefore, Susanne Simmons maintains, the backcountry initially had the potential to become a place of escape and opportunity for blacks, as well as whites. Of course, the vast majority of African Americans on the frontier were not runaways. While Simmons suggests that the famed frontier equality may have extended to blacks—in the forms of fairly standardized contracts of indenture regardless of race and in isolated indications of opportunity for free black landowners or craftsmen[5]—she concedes that Scotch-Irish settlers, before their German neighbors, became attracted to the institution of slavery, even if attitudes associated with plantation tobacco agriculture did not spread to the Upper Valley. Simmons correctly points out that African Americans were part of the fabric of backcountry society, even as opportunities became limited and the institution of slavery more widespread. What is more difficult to determine is the pace and nature of everyday life for blacks on the frontier. It is important to remember that most of them were not there of their own volition. In the end, the initial promise of opportunity that the frontier seemed to hold for African Americans proved to be an empty one.

By the time that settlers and their slaves reached the further extent of the trans-Appalachian frontier, any hint of opportunity for blacks in the migration process had disappeared. Ellen Eslinger seriously challenges the stereotypical assumption that slavery in that particular time and place was "the mildest that existed anywhere in the world."[6] That it was different she does not deny; in fact, she contends that, in some ways, slavery in the remote backcountry was more difficult for the slaves themselves than was the institution at the same time for their cousins back east.

Again challenging traditional beliefs, Eslinger maintains that "frontier conditions were extremely conducive to unfree labor" due to the combination of the demands of bringing the wilderness under cultivation and the absence of an adequate and willing free labor pool. African Americans suffered the same hardships of a difficult and dangerous journey, separation from family, and deprivations of frontier life as did their white masters, but their trials were compounded by their slave status. Because the slave population on the frontier was relatively small and dispersed compared to that of eastern Virginia, socialization and family formation were disrupted in a manner similar to the situation that had existed in the Tidewater region during the infancy of the institution there.[7] Living in close proximity to their masters, in the absence of formal slave quarters found on larger plantations in the east, slaves' position as inferior members of the household was sharply reinforced. How blacks coped with this situation is a question Eslinger cannot definitively answer, but indications exist that suggest they consciously favored their initial neighborhoods of more intense slavery but better-established African American social patterns over the new order on the frontier. Much work remains to be done concerning the daily life of slaves and master-slave relations in the region, but one conclusion seems clear: African Americans played a definite role in creating the frontier, and, in doing so, they suffered as much as did white settlers, but they stood to gain little from the enterprise.

Marilyn Davis-DeEulis expands on the theme that slavery in the trans-Appalachian frontier region was different from its counterparts back east, terming it "one of the least understood, most complicated slave relationships in the West." Slavery in the early years of the far western Virginia frontier, along the Ohio Valley, was characterized by small concentrations of blacks, periodic movement of slaves between work sites, and frequent lack of direct supervision, resulting in greater responsibilities being placed on the laborers. Davis-DeEulis credits all of these factors with combining to bring about a surprisingly high incidence of slave literacy and basic factoring skills, resulting, she maintains, in the "literate sophistication of anti-slavery enclaves on the other side of the river" later in the nineteenth century. The exact mechanisms by which these slaves learned to read are unclear, but that literacy arose out of the peculiar circumstances of the institution on the remote frontier seems evident.

Davis-DeEulis characterizes the relationship between slaves and masters or overseers in the region as one of "simultaneous cruelty and dependence." Masters needed the usual amount of labor from their slaves, but they also needed to depend upon them to act independently in the absence of supervision. Conversely, the discomforts and dangers incumbent with life on the frontier, along with conditions caused by the masters' own resource limitations and demands, made slave life particularly cruel. None of the hope nor promise suggested by Simmons in the early Shenandoah Valley frontier remained by the time slavery reached the Ohio Valley; rather, as Davis-DeEulis eloquently concludes, the opportunity for literacy skills represented a necessary survival mechanism against "the waking nightmare of vast wilderness spaces, endless, undefined, disorganized tasks, and remote, senseless authority." All settlers who ventured onto the frontier were subject to the forces of isolation, separation, insecurity, and hard work, to some degree, but for blacks caught in the additional "nightmare" of slavery, the forces were compounded by the intricacies of the system. Even free blacks on the frontier faced challenges above and beyond those which awaited European pioneers. African Americans were not absent from the Virginia frontier, and their contributions were shaped by the ways in which they responded to the varied, yet distinct, situations which confronted them.

However transplanted Europeans came to control the Virginia backcountry, whether "by default" or otherwise, they did not do so alone. While Native Americans no longer actually inhabited the portion of the Valley claimed by the settlers, all Europeans brought with them expectations of what they would find on the frontier, including their preconceptions about native society. These preconceptions continued to influence perspectives in the backcountry, particularly as actual contact with Native Americans was, relatively speaking, sparse. On the other hand, the presence of African Americans was not nearly as sparse as was traditionally assumed. Slaves and, to a lesser extent, free blacks contributed in very tangible ways to the physical, social, and economic landscape of the region, and they suffered the hardships of frontier life without reaping any of its rewards. No longer, as the following essays illustrate, can the story of the Virginia frontier be one which includes only European actors.

Notes

1. For examples of relations between natives and settlers on the Virginia frontier, see Nathaniel Turk McCleskey, "Across the First Divide: Frontiers of Settlement and Culture in Augusta County, Virginia, 1738–1770," (Ph.D. diss.: College of William and Mary, 1990). For particular examples of differences of opinion regarding Indians among residents of the frontier, see ibid., 285–302.
2. Alan V. Briceland, *Westward from Virginia: The Exploration of the Virginia–Carolina Frontier, 1650–1710* (Charlottesville: Univ. Press of Virginia, 1987), 5.
3. Gary Nash, "The Image of the Indian in the Southern Colonial Mind," *William and Mary Quarterly* 3d ser., 29 (1972): 197–98.
4. For example, see, McCleskey, "Across the First Divide," 115–16, 146–59.
5. See ibid., 160–71. Simmons cites the case of Augusta County resident Edward Tarr.
6. J. Winston Coleman Jr., *Slavery Times in Kentucky* (Chapel Hill: Univ. of North Carolina Press, 1940), 15.
7. See Russell Menard, "The Maryland Slave Population, 1658–1730: A Demographic Profile of Blacks in Four Counties," *William and Mary Quarterly* 3d ser., 32 (1975): 29–54; Alan Kulikoff, "The Origins of Afro-American Society in Tidewater Maryland and Virginia, 1700–1790," *William and Mary Quarterly* 3d ser., 35 (1978): 226–59.

Chapter 5

Native Americans on the Virginia Frontier in the Seventeenth Century

Archaeological Investigations along the Interior Roanoke River Drainage

Michael B. Barber and Eugene B. Barfield

In part due to the nature of early American history, New World anthropologists have always viewed the study of culture change and culture interaction as productive research themes. A prime example of the intensive interaction of cultures in direct and indirect competition for the same and limited resources can be seen in the interface between the early colonial settlers of the Chesapeake and the original Native American occupants. A period extensively studied by anthropologists, ethnohistorians, and historians,[1] the momentous events associated with the mingling of the Powhatan Chiefdom and the Jamestown colonials played out on the river banks of the James, York, Rappahannock, and Potomac Rivers. New World chiefdom versus Old World nation-state provided a combination of cooperation, blending, subjugation, and final dominance of superior technology and firepower heavily aided by voracious microbes.

Later periods of interaction are less well documented. As Jones points out, within a week of selecting the Jamestown site for settlement, the English recorded first contacts with Indians of the interior Piedmont.[2] The next historic record occurred only after a fifty-three-year hiatus when John Lederer, the German doctor, was commissioned to travel beyond the edge of civilization into the unknown wilds of Virginia.[3] While other Europeans undoubtedly ventured into the Piedmont and beyond prior to Lederer's adventure, there exists no historic documentation. Even with this limited number of primary sources, Merrell has gained some insight into the contact period and cultural interaction with the southern Piedmont where aboriginal trade networks and hunting patterns complemented the needs of the European skin traders.[4] Although there exists the limited historic documentation provided by explorations into the unknown west by such adventurers as Batts and Fallam, John Lederer,[5] and William Bartram,[6] the ethnographic record wanes as one moves toward and beyond the Blue Ridge.

As such, it falls to the archaeological study of material cultural remains to provide for an understanding of this period in Virginia's history. Three recent archaeological discoveries along the Roanoke (Staunton) River can provide the basis for an understanding of this period within a southern Piedmont and Ridge and Valley context. This chapter will focus on the archaeological implications of these sites. Regional perspectives will be supplied in order to provide a broader understanding of cultural events. The time period for the study is generally confined to the seventeenth century, although chronology spills over slightly into both the sixteenth and eighteenth centuries. Finally, the concept of frontier that is developed is one of aboriginal occupation and perspective with European concepts, ideas, and artifacts intrusion into an established cultural system.

Cultural Background

The southern portion of Virginia has been occupied for at least 11,500 years.[7] As small bands of Asians moved across the Bering Strait land bridge at the end of the last Pleistocene advances of the Wisconsin glaciation, these Paleoindian "Big Game Hunters" raced with amazing speed over the North American continent. In essence arriving on the first Virginia "frontier" at 9500–9200 B.C.,[8] the hunting of large herd animals may have continued in the eastern United States,[9] although current evidence may favor a more dispersed economy possibly devoid of a megafaunal contribution.[10] More likely a balance of hunting and generalized foraging for plant food prevailed with the subsistence pattern of a generalized omnivore.[11]

In any case, with the end of the Ice Age and the warming trends of the Holocene at ca. 8000 B.C., the Archaic Period pattern of hunting and gathering evolved in which animals and plants were harvested when ready on a seasonal round basis. Hunting likely focused on white-tailed deer, turkey, and box turtle,[12] with gathering oriented toward the ever-increasing numbers of deciduous forest species (nut and acorn crops) and seed crops. Social organization remained at the egalitarian band level where twenty-five to thirty-five individuals formed the operative social structure. Toward the end of the period at ca. 1000 B.C., the more stable environment, and the aboriginal population's understanding of that environment, allowed for an increased sedentism with a primary focus on riverine systems.[13]

At about 1000 B.C., two innovations were adopted into what is now the Woodland Period repertoire: fired clay ceramics and the bow and arrow. The first allowed for improved cooking and storage and the second for more effective hunting. Population increased with a concomitant increase in social complexity as demonstrated in the tribal level of social organization. Still egalitarian with achieved status, the social structure integrated the needs of hundreds of people. In some cases, chiefdoms[14] or ranked societies[15] developed, which integrated larger numbers of individuals through a paramount chief. Such societies were based on ascribed status into various social levels.

As population rose and territories became more circumscribed, added risk reduction techniques were included in the subsistence repertoire. Primary among these was the advent of horticulture. Although known in Archaic times, the raising of crops did not reach its apex until the Late Woodland time period from ca. A.D. 900 to 1700 when corn became the dominant subsistence item.[16] When combined with the earlier domesticated squash and the later tamed bean, these three formed the American domesticated triad. Swidden, or slash-and-burn, gardening became the primary subsistence activity, although it was always augmented by hunting and gathering.

An increased complexity of the settlement system was seen in the development of villages, both nucleated and dispersed. These settlements were very similar to those depicted by John White in his Roanoke Island water-color paintings.[17] Nucleated villages were circular in plan with an outer palisade of vertically set logs. Houses, storage pits, activity areas, and, sometimes, burial sites were arranged in concentric patterns around an open central plaza. Palisaded villages were from two hundred feet to four hundred feet in diameter, with a resident population of one hundred to four hundred individuals.

Dispersed villages lacked a palisade and circular configuration. Individual houses were occupied by nuclear or extended families and were distributed along a river terrace edge with a looser continuity of community. Population clusterings of houses could be identified as villages and this type of settlement pattern is suggested as a later type of organization just prior to contact.[18]

Regionalism and cultural differentiation became readily apparent in southwestern Virginia during late prehistoric times. In general terms, social complexity was highest in the far southwest corner of Virginia and tended to less complexity to the east in the southern Ridge and Valley.

In part due to proximity to the Southeast and Mississippian developments, unique cultural developments in Lee and Scott Counties included the construction of temple mounds by populations identified culturally as Dallas peoples.[19] This development is tied directly to eastern Tennessee, and the Virginia phenomenon can be seen as the extreme periphery of a complex chiefdom. Three Virginia mound complexes are known and are interpreted as indicative of the foci of paramount chiefs, at least in a local context. Such a chiefdom is usually characterized by a paramount leader and a hierarchy of settlements, with small units under the control of larger villages in a pyramidal system.[20] The larger settlements exact tribute from the smaller ones, and, in the western corner of Virginia, such donations were likely in the form of horticultural produce and deer skins. As the sites in Virginia are found along a fairly narrow creek bottom, the villages are atypical of usual Mississippian settlement systems, which emphasize large river bottoms in order to provide adequate food for high population densities with a fair number of artisans, elitists, etc., divorced from the food quest.

A second cultural development that exhibits a Mississippian flavor is the possible evolution of a petty chiefdom in the Chilhowie/Saltville area. First intimated by Gardner[21] and Turner,[22] the higher level than tribal complexity was suggested by high population density, a hierarchy of settlements, and a richness and supposed differential distribution of exotic grave goods. Barber and Barfield have taken the hypothesis one step further and have proposed the chiefdom development found its base in the salt trade.[23] Pointing to the clustering of elitist wealth items such as shell gorgets in the area, the distribution of Late Woodland settlements in a pattern protecting trade routes, the high concentration and ready availability of salt in Saltville, "hearsay" reporting of differential grave good inclusions, the location of Chilhowie along the Ridge and Valley trade route, and historic references that might relate to the area[24] have used this circumstantial evidence to propose that the added complexity of extensive trade led to an added complexity of social control.

Moving further to the east and into the Roanoke Valley at the headwaters of the Roanoke River and the Piedmont beyond, excavations and analyses to date point to a less complex, tribal level of social organization.[25]

Villages were of both the dispersed and nucleated varieties during the Late Woodland based on a horticultural base of corn, beans, and, likely, squash. Hunting and gathering activities continued with white-tailed deer, turkey, bear, and box turtle the focus of faunal harvesting[26] and nuts and seeds the plant products foraged.[27] Social organization was of an egalitarian level organized under the rubric of tribe. Within such a structure, leadership is ephemeral based on different situations where different individuals or groups of individuals acquire achieved status. The populations organized are in the hundreds of individuals with a number of villages recognized as having a communality based on language, culture, mate exchange, risk reduction, and kinship.

The Sites

Over the past two decades in Virginia archaeology, improved recovery techniques have led to an increased understanding of prehistoric lifeways. Foremost in this methodological revolution is the wet screening and flotation of midden and feature soils through fine mesh cloth. While usually discussed in terms of an increased recovery of ethnozoological and ethnobotanical material, such methodologies have led to the identification of a plethora of other artifact categories. Among these are the glass beads and small bits of copper which can lead to the placement of a site within the protohistoric or European contact period. At the very minimum, such recovery can vastly increase the numbers of trade goods identified to a meaningful and representative level.

This is precisely what has occurred on three Native American village sites on the middle and upper Roanoke (Staunton) River. The first site to be identified as containing European artifacts was the Ridge and Valley Thomas-Sawyer Site (44RN39) within the city of Salem. In the early winter of 1987, a number of Native American refuse-filled pits were noted by members of the Roanoke Chapter of the Archaeological Society of Virginia. Having recorded the site in 1979, the chapter had salvaged several features through the early 1980s and monitored the site whenever earth-moving equipment lumbered onto and into the general area. In this case, salvage efforts began and intensified when the first piece of copper was recovered. Although the discovery of copper and a single glass bead was made through visual inspection of fill, iron artifacts were noted only during wet-screening.[28]

The Thomas-Sawyer Site represents a long term occupation with at least two palisaded villages, a localized hamlet, and two seemingly independent foci of dispersed occupations stretched along almost a quarter mile of river terrace edge. The Archaeological Society of Virginia Roanoke Chapter began emergency excavations at the site as early as 1980. This phase of excavations dealt with a dispersed settlement in the western portion of the site. Nineteen features were excavated including straight-sided, flat-bottomed pits, roasting hearths, and one feature interpreted as a pit kiln for ceramic firing with carbon dates averaging A.D. 1585 (±60 years). The dominance of Dan River sand-tempered ceramics and small triangular arrow points substantiate the Late Woodland chronology.[29] Later excavations toward the central portion of the site uncovered two remnant portions of two village palisade lines with associated barbecue, refuse-filled pits, and a six-foot diameter storage pit. In an examination of the westernmost area of occupation, an additional dispersed occupation was examined and large eight-foot-diameter, four-foot-deep, refuse-filled pits were excavated, along with numerous smaller pits, a refuse-filled ditch, and numerous post molds. Based on artifact data including Dan River ceramics and small triangular points, the village is also of Late Woodland chronology.

Of particular interest here is an isolated area to the east of the palisades and directly along the terrace edge. Uncovered by plow zone removal for topsoil sale, ten pit features and a line of post molds were uncovered. The line of post molds isolated the hamlet from other nearby occupations. This line of 21 posts was located to the west and north of the pit-denoted occupation area. Set at 5-foot intervals, spacing is much wider than the normal ca. 1 to 1.5-foot placement found in Late Woodland palisade walls. No evidence of this wider spacing was noted to the east or south. Although mechanical soil removal may have destroyed the evidence of additional posts, this is unlikely as the topsoil was removed in a level fashion. The current hypothesis is that the series of posts mark a break necessary in fall and winter to protect the site occupants from the harsh winds from the west and the north. Such a wind break would have consisted of major posts set at 5-foot intervals with branches and brush woven between them in order to block the wind.

Three types of pits were recorded: 1) relatively shallow 2- to 3-foot-diameter, basin-shaped pits, 2) 2- to 3-foot-diameter, straight-sided 2- to 2.5-foot deep pits, and 3) 2- to 3-foot-diameter, 2.5-foot deep, bell-shaped pits. Most pits were filled with refuse, which contained copious animal bone, Dan River ceramics, riverine shell, and lithic debris including triangular arrow points. Several of these arrow points had serrated blades, an attribute noted in the Ohio/West Virginia area during the Late Prehistoric Fort Ancient cultures. The high frequency of Dan River ceramics, on the other hand, demonstrated close ties to the Piedmont peoples along the Roanoke (Staunton) and Dan Rivers.

The second Roanoke River site is also found within the city of Salem. Although recorded earlier, the Graham-White Site (44RN21) boundaries were determined by a Phase I survey for the construction of a massive softball complex.[30] As construction began, no Phase II or III was implemented, and numerous Native American features were impacted. The Roanoke Regional Preservation Office intervened and salvage excavations were implemented.[31] Soils were bagged for later water screening and flotation. During the salvage excavations in the spring and summer of 1990, a number of European trade goods were identified, and the site was identified as a Contact Period site.

Thirty-eight features were excavated and pits were found to be of the shallow, basin-shaped, straight-sided, and bell-shaped types. No palisade lines were recorded, and the suggestion is that the settlement was dispersed. As a late period Native American settlement, the artifact assemblage included the expected Dan River sand-tempered ceramics and small, triangular projectile points. Along with the Native American artifacts, European trade goods of copper alloy, iron, and glass were found.

The third Native American site containing European goods was located in the southern Piedmont province of Virginia near the town of Altavista. Recorded during Phase I survey for the possible construction of an electricity-generating facility in Pittsylvania County,[32] the Hurt Power Plant Village Site (44PY144) lies on the southern bank of the Roanoke River, approximately forty-two miles southeast of the two Salem villages. As the plans for plant construction coalesced, Phase III mitigation excavations were implemented in areas of impact, including a pump house facility and pipeline trenches. The excavations at the site uncovered an intact midden, as well as ca. one hundred features, including refuse-filled pits, hearths, natural flood chutes, and human burials. Ceramics were primarily of the quartz-tempered Dan River series with triangular Madison and Clarksville projectile points. Copper and glass beads were directly associated with Native American artifacts and demonstrated that the site could be dated to the Contact Period.

Based on radiocarbon dates and artifacts recovered, it would appear that the one component of the Thomas-Sawyer Site was the earliest occupied at ca. A.D. 1615, the Hurt Power Plant site slightly later at between A.D. 1620 and 1650, and the final occupation of the Graham-White Site likely took place in the late third or early fourth quarter of the seventeenth century.

The Artifacts

Four categories of artifacts will be discussed here: glass, copper, iron, and marine shell (and, to a lesser degree, bone). While glass and iron are indisputable indicators of European origins, the importation of copper and marine shell is not so clear-cut. However, the copper at all three sites has been demonstrated chemically to be of European manufacture. The marine shell is a more problematic indicator, but its continued recovery in contexts relating to European goods suggests a like time frame, and it is suggested here that the presence of copper, too, was a result of European intervention.

Glass

In the early context of the Thomas-Sawyer Site, a single white glass "seed" bead (3.70 percent of the trade goods total) was recovered from a sealed pit context.[33] In contrast, at the Hurt Power Plant Site, the most abundant evidence of European interaction were the glass artifacts.[34] In all, excavations produced 209 beads (or 59.04 percent of the total): 115 (55.02 percent) white beads, 67 (32.06 percent) blue, 15 (7.18 percent) aqua, 5 (4.78 percent) red or redwood, and 7 (7.18 percent) unidentifiable due to breakage or glass erosion. Typed following Kidd and Kidd,[35] the most frequently recovered group was a small (2 to 4 mm diameter), circular (diameter larger than length) clear, light-gray-core bead with a translucent, light gray exterior; 74 specimens were recovered. This group was followed by 22 small circular beads with a translucent, bright navy exterior with a clear, light gray core. Sixteen beads were small and circular with a translucent, bright navy blue exterior and a bright navy blue core; 14 were white, small circular beads with a translucent, light gray exterior and a clear, apple-green core. Simple blue, round (diameter equals length) beads followed: 13 were medium in size (4 to 6 mm), and 11 were small. Other categories numbered 8 or fewer. Glass beads were recovered from 19 in situ features at the Hurt Site, with a distribution in proximity to the riverbank. These may be interpreted as 3 isolated clusters and likely represent households.

Eighty glass seed beads (24.39 percent of trade goods) were recovered from the Graham-White Site: 54 were white, and rose-brown, black, blue, and yellow beads were also recovered.[36]

Copper

The copper artifacts recovered at the Ridge and Valley Sawyer Site were made up of 7 fragments. Of these pieces, 6 were made of sheet copper with 1 perforated for tag use. The remaining copper artifact was an amorphic chunk of the material. The single piece submitted for an electron micro probe contained lead and zinc, indicators of European origin.

Excavations at the Hurt Power Plant Site produced 55 copper or copper alloy artifacts. From a midden context 17 pieces were recovered, 36 from refuse-filled pits, and 2 were associated with burial fill. None were recovered as deliberately placed grave goods.

All copper artifacts were thin sheet copper fragments and likely of European origin. Surface patina coloration varies from a blue-green tinge to typical copper green and to a polished brown-green. Thickness varies from 28 mm to 82 mm, but most (31 of 41 which could be measured) fell between 30 and 49 mm. The thickness of rolled beads could not be ascertained.

Eight copper artifacts were analyzed under a scanning electron microscope in order to ascertain elemental makeup, which in turn would determine artifact origin. If the copper was found to be an alloy (including tin, zinc, lead, and/or antimony), the artifact would have been of European origin. The analyzed copper fell into two compositional patterns.[37] Six of the copper pieces proved to be composed of 95 percent to 97 percent pure copper. Zinc is the second most frequent element at between 1 percent and 2 percent. Particle inclusions were scanned with a heavy percentage of antimony (63 percent to 66 percent). Antimony is an additive that aids in the temperature expansion and contraction process. Two of the analyzed pieces were of brass alloy. Copper made up 65 percent of the material with zinc at ca. 33 percent. Inclusions scanned were lead in the range of 24 percent to 44 percent. Hence, the copper at the Hurt Power Plant Site was of a purer copper and brass, both of European origin.

Three analytical categories for copper were identified: tags, rolled beads, and manufacture waste or scrap. Four tags were recovered and were defined as regular geometric pieces that were perforated from suspension or for sewing onto clothing. Four examples of these were recovered with one square, one rectangle, one triangular, and one "claw" noted. All four pieces were perforated by punching a hole through the object from one side, resulting in lipping on the opposite side. Holes ranged from 94 mm to 168 mm in diameter.

The second category comprised rolled copper beads. Fourteen rolled beads or bead fragments were recovered; 13 were cylindrical and 1 was cone shaped. Cylinder lengths ranged from 14.28 cm to 26.42 cm. Diameters varied greatly, ranging from 1.58 cm to 4.67 cm.

By far the most numerous copper pieces were identified as manufacturing waste or scrap material. The result of sheet cutting into desired shapes, the waste material evinces the on-site manufacture of the artifacts from sheet copper obtained elsewhere. In all, 37 waste pieces were recovered. Varying widely in size and shape, elongated triangles, small, irregular-edged rectangles, and amorphic irregular polygons were recorded.

The Hurt Power Plant's Feature 28B contained the heaviest concentration of copper with 13 pieces recovered. Although 2 rolled bead fragments were present, the remaining copper was scrap material. If this refuse-filled pit is accepted as indicative of behavior associated with copper working, the copper resource can be seen as meager and marked by parsimonious use of rare materials. Possibly representing a single production episode, only the smallest of waste pieces of irregular shape were discarded here.

Copper from the later Graham-White Site showed a relatively similar pattern. Ten copper fragments were recovered, including 1 rolled bead (reminiscent of the Hurt Site), 2 sheet copper pieces perforated for suspension (similar to those found at the Sawyer and Hurt Sites), an L-shaped piece, and 6 sheet waste pieces. Chemical analyses demonstrated a high zinc content and a European origin. In addition, 1 thick brass object was recovered, as well as 5 iron pieces, including a seventeenth-century snaphaunce trigger.

Iron

A limited number of iron artifacts were recovered from the three sites in question. At the early-seventeenth-century Thomas-Sawyer Site, 7 pieces of iron were recovered: 6 small pieces of iron wire and 1 iron needle. At the Hurt Power Plant Site, a single fragment of an edged tool, likely a knife blade, was recovered in a sealed context. At the Graham-White Site, 5 pieces of iron were collected: 3 unidentifiable scraps, a possible nail, and one seventeenth-century snaphaunce rifle trigger.

Marine Shell and Bone Disc Beads

The protohistoric assemblage from the Thomas-Sawyer Site produced 6 marine shell and 6 bone disc beads. If the assumption is made that straight-sided suspension holes are the result of European iron tools and the hourglass holes the result of aboriginal stone tool manufacture, the distribution is evenly divided by manufacturing tool with both shell and bone included in both categories.

At the Hurt Power Plant Site, the distribution is completely different. Of the 92 disc beads recovered, 89 were manufactured from marine shell with only 3 bone beads identified. Sixty-three (68.48 percent) beads were drilled straight through, while 29 (31.52 percent) were shaped like an hourglass. While both methods were used, the presence of iron tool manufacture (off-site) appears to have been more popular.

The Graham-White Site also produced bone and shell disc beads.

In all, 232 were recovered, with both hourglass and straight-bore hole types present.

Interpreting the Artifacts

If the assumption is made that the three sites discussed above are representative of the contact period, patterns of diachronic change can be seen. The changes within the trade good assemblage can be interpreted as follows:

Glass beads were not a frequent item in the early Sawyer occupation, although shell disc beads were present in relatively large numbers. The popularity of glass beads increased during the mid-seventeenth-century occupation of the Hurt Power Plant site with a roughly two to one ratio with regard to shell/bone beads. The relationship reversed during the later seventeenth-century occupation at the Graham-White site with more than a two to one preference for shell/bone beads.

The use of copper remains fairly constant through time and space with a focus on ornamental use and no attempts at tool production or use beyond social function. Although Potter makes a case for copper artifacts functioning as indicators of a wealthy elite on Virginia's coastal plain,[38] the small size and numbers of copper artifacts and the egalitarian nature of tribal society would argue for a lower level, more traditional and achieved level of social symbols. It is likely that copper identified an individual as having access to rare commodities but, by the same token, involved few if any associated privileges.

Due to the presence of scrap material at all three sites, sheet copper was sought after, with tag and bead production taking place on-site. Tags were produced throughout the time period considered, but rolled copper beads were produced only in the latter two contexts. The presence of iron is of interest in all three occupations. Unlike copper, it appears to be a functional item and represents a technological progression from needles to knives to guns.

Shell beads have been a long noted and frequent trade item throughout late prehistoric times. Beads of this material continued to be a sought-after category. The type of shell, however, appears to have evolved beyond the marine marginellas to the disk "seed" beads. While available in prehistoric times, the popularity of discs and their accessibility increased geometrically at contact. At the Ridge and Valley Thomas-Sawyer site, shell disks do not appear until the protohistoric period. With around one hundred features identified and roughly fifty sampled, it is only at the ca. A.D. 1615 component that these beads are recovered, and recovered in association with other European artifacts. A similar pattern is found at the Hurt Power Plant Site; with the exception of a single shell disc bead, all ninety-two were recovered in association with other European trade artifacts. As noted above, the popularity of shell/bone disc beads in relation to glass beads increased at the later Graham-White Site.

The seventeenth-century settlements at the Thomas-Sawyer and the Graham-White Sites mark the first European intrusions into the upper Roanoke River Valley. While the trade goods at the southern Piedmont Hurt Power Plant Site were undoubtedly of English origin, the possibilities can be hypothesized for the source of the European goods at the Salem sites:

1. Trade networks from the west originating with the Spanish explorations and settlements.
2. Trade networks from the coastal plain originating with sixteenth-century contacts with European explorers and settlement, particularly with the Roanoke Island experiment.
3. Trade networks established from the east with permanent English settlement beginning with Jamestown.

The Spanish connection finds validity in the exchange of prehistoric status items, such as conch shell ornamental artifacts, from the Gulf of Mexico into Eastern Tennessee[39] and into western Virginia.[40] Two areas of Virginia have been noted to be the loci of typical Southeast artifacts within the Commonwealth: the extreme southwest portion of the state in Lee County, and the Washington/Smyth Counties area, where conch shell artifacts were traded. Waselkov has suggested that the presence of a brass gorget at the relatively nearby Trigg site in Radford, Virginia, was the result of Spanish trading networks.[41] For the Roanoke area, however, no conch shell or brass gorgets have been recovered from a reliable context.[42] There is currently no archaeological evidence that might connect the Roanoke Valley to trade with the Southeast.

Ties with the English colonists are more likely. Although the temporal occupation of the Thomas-Sawyer site would allow for interaction with Roanoke Island immigrants, the artifact assemblage there more closely mirrors the later "trading" assemblage of the colonials made up of glass and shell beads, copper artifacts, and, as John Smith so eloquently put it, other "trashe."[43] The time period for the Graham-White site, a late-seventeenth-century context, is definitely associated with the Jamestown residents and their expanding populations. It is likely that all three Roanoke River sites received European goods from the English on the coast.

The southern Piedmont and the Roanoke Valley Native Americans of the seventeenth century remained in the secondary role of "remoter Indians." By the end of the first quarter of the seventeenth century and the beginnings of the European settlement of the Roanoke area, the Native Americans were gone.[44] Their expatriation from the frontier and possible demise likely had multiple causes.

One major factor may have been European disease such as measles and small pox. Fausz, in a discussion of force brought to bear against the coastal Indians stated that "an even greater threat to Indian lives and cultural stability came in the form of killing epidemics transmitted by alien invaders. Virgin-soil epidemics decimated whole villages in the coastal plain soon after contact with the English."[45] Interior Indians had no better resistance to foreign microbes, and it may be that the depopulation of the Ridge and Valley was at least partially brought about by disease. Although this is a viable competing hypothesis, the evidence recovered from the Hurt Power Plant Site does not support it. The analyses of human skeletal material from the site suggests normal population demographics with no increase of the very young and very old as would be the expected result of an epidemic.[46]

The position of "remote Indian" may also have contributed to their demise. As Merrell relates, "Before long, despite the efforts of the more experienced native traders to screen the 'remote Indians' from direct contact with the Europeans and their ways, word still spread to distant towns regarding the range of products available from the English and the accepted means of procuring them."[47]

The recovery of the snaphaunce rifle part from the Graham-White site is indicative of the acquisition of highly desirable English goods within the Valley. It may be that more such goods were desired but appropriation was prohibited by distance. Although the absolute ethnicity of the peoples of the Roanoke Valley is difficult to establish, a strong case can be made that they were of the Siouan-speaking Tutelo tribe.[48] As related by the diary of the Batts and Fallam expedition in 1671, the town of Totero of the Tutelo Indians was visited near the end of the journey. Whether in the Roanoke Valley or along the New River in Radford, the Tutelo tribal group was located in proximity to the Roanoke Valley. If one accepts that the Tutelo were the occupants of the Salem sites, a portion of that group reported moved to the juncture of the Staunton and the Dan Rivers in the late seventeenth century and to the headwaters of the Yadkin by 1701.[49] In 1714, the Tutelo were reported to be associated with the Saponi, Occaneechi, and several other groups at Fort Christanna on the Meherrin River; later they were moved north and in 1753 became part of the Iroquois Confederacy.[50] The early movement may have been an attempt to occupy a location better suited for the acquisition of European trade goods. In any case, the Roanoke Valley was devoid of Native Americans early in the eighteenth century.

In a consideration of the sites discussed, it would seem that the early-seventeenth-century Sawyer Site represents an initial, noncontact experience with European trade goods. At this time, the potential of the deer skin trade had not been realized, and the goods conveyed were not particularly regularized; hence, the presence of the unimpressive yet functional iron wire and needle plus a small number of decorative items of copper, marine shell and, barely, glass. By the second quarter of the seventeenth century, a more standardized list of appropriate trade items had been developed by the Jamestown traders, consisting almost exclusively of ornamental items of glass, copper, and shell. By the late seventeenth century at the Graham-White Site, decorative items still carried the day, although impressive functional items, such as guns, were present. In addition, shell disc beads proved more popular than glass. Explanations for this preference may lie in the quantity of European glass produced and colonial access, Native American preferences for more traditional materials, differential access caused by the deer skin trade controlling Occaneechi, or some combination of these factors.

In viewing a Roanoke River context for the Late Woodland plus that of the southern Piedmont (similar for Ridge and Valley, although a time lag is expected, particularly in earlier periods), the following chronology can be proposed:

Late Prehistoric	A.D. 1200–1607
Protohistoric	A.D. 1607–1650
Early Contact	A.D. 1650–1664
Susquehannock Trade	A.D. 1664–1670
Occaneechi Trade	A.D. 1670–1676
Disintegration Period	A.D. 1676–1701
Multicultural Period	A.D. 1701–present.

For the lower Piedmont area of Virginia, it is indicated that the Late Woodland developments began at ca. A.D. 1200[51] and likely ca. 300 years earlier in the Ridge and Valley.[52] Within a Virginia context, the protohistoric period for the lower Piedmont began soon after the settlement at Jamestown in 1607. This period of limited contacts but exchange of trade goods likely continued into the 1650s. Although not directly documented, it is apparent that a few colonials were slipping into the interior, whether for trading purposes or for acquiring land.

The trade of skins began early in Virginia's history, although it was continually overshadowed by the tobacco industry. By 1620, the fur trade was well established in the colony, with more than twenty entrepreneurs plying the Chesapeake Bay on the "unexplored tidewater streams and rivers to find the villages of unpredictable savages, hazarding their very lives to learn the ways and languages of the aborigines and to trade with them."[53] According to Phillips, it was not until 1643 that the first serious effort was made to control the fur trade with the Native Americans.[54] The general assembly granted "all Profitt" to numerous individuals for exploration and trade. Although competition and political intrigue marked the process, the trade continued and increased through the third quarter of the seventeenth century.

In 1664, the English captured New Netherlands from the Dutch. This opened the Hudson River and Mohawk River Valleys to the beaver pelt quest. Deer skins were also sought but were of better quality to the south. The Susquehannock became the middlemen on the Potomac, bartering skins for English trade items.[55] Farther to the south, in an attempt to control a broader exploitation area, the Susquehannock encouraged the involvement of the Occaneechi on the Roanoke River as secondary middlemen to control the deer skin trade on routes to the south parallel to the Appalachians and through the mountain gaps to the west. Negative interaction between the Susquehannock and the Iroquois led to the demise of the Susquehannock trading network in 1670.

Subsequently, in the early 1670s, the Occaneechi become the major players within the Virginian and North Carolinian Piedmont and mountains.[56] Davis and Ward have suggested that the control of the deer skin trade by the powerful Occaneechi most likely filtered out European trade goods into the western Piedmont and mountains.[57] Due to the habit of this group to retain desired trade goods, few articles escaped their trading filter.

Alvord and Bidgood indicate that the fur-trading route passed by the village of the "Occaneechi" and that the path was named the "Occaneechi or Trading Path."[58] The village was located on an island just downstream from the confluence of the Dan and Staunton Rivers, and, according to Alvord and Bidgood, the temperament of this relatively small Siouan group was unique among the aboriginals of the area.[59] They are described as "fierce and treacherous" and intimidated surrounding tribes into secondary roles in the exchange of skins for European goods. When threats of direct European contact with interior tribes presented themselves, the Occaneechi reacted with attempts to protect their monopoly, and it has been suggested that they took an active role in preventing the first Needham and Arthur expedition from crossing the mountains.[60] Captain William Byrd indicated that five of his traders were killed by Indians "near Occaneechi" in 1684. In an earlier reference, Lederer reported in 1670 that the Occaneechi murdered six Cherokee upon learning of their plans to establish direct trade with the Europeans.[61] The expatriation of the Occaneechi from their homeland came in 1676, when, after aiding Nathaniel Bacon in defeating a band of Susquehannocks, Bacon attacked and decimated the Occaneechi.[62] Retreating from the Roanoke River to the Eno River to the south, Lawson, having visited the new Occaneechi village, remarked on the adequacy of "provisions," which indicates the Occaneechi continued to have a role in the exchange system.[63]

Although the majority of the trade turned south to the Carolinas and Georgia, it seems unlikely that the southern Piedmont and Ridge and Valley province went untapped.[64] Similar material culture, such as ceramic types, language, and other societal nuances, suggests a close continuity between the Indians of the Piedmont and their western neighbors. Earlier prehistoric exchange brought shell artifacts, such as marginellas, into the Ridge and Valley, and such trade most likely continued. It is likely that the early trade goods at the Thomas-Sawyer Site and the slightly later goods at the Hurt Power Plant Site were the result of low level, more traditional trade networks; the lack of European goods at the Graham-White may relate to a European goods trade embargo by the Occaneechi.

In 1676, notwithstanding the Occaneechi role in their victory over the invading Iroquois, Bacon's soldiers turned their guns on the Occaneechi. Reduced to radically smaller numbers, the Occaneechi retreated to the Eno River in North Carolina, where they continued their trading role.[65]

The Occaneechi defeat did, however, begin a period of cultural disintegration during which tribal groups suffered from the indignities of Europeans, possibly European disease, continued negative interaction with other Native American groups, and the effects of rum. The role of the Occaneechi traders was likely short-lived, and the colonials turned to the Catawba and Cherokee for the skin trade, and the trading network moved to the southwest as opposed to the west. By 1701, independent tribal groups within the lower Piedmont and Ridge and Valley of Virginia had joined forces into multicultural groups usually far from their original homelands. Although Batts and Fallam encountered the Occaneechi, the Saponi, and the Tutelo in their 1671 expedition to find the western waters,[66] the western Piedmont and the Ridge and Valley areas along the Roanoke River were abandoned as the first settlers arrived in the early eighteenth century.

The Native American frontier of the southern Piedmont and Ridge and Valley of Virginia was quite different from the earlier frontiers that suffered the intrusion of European society. On the coastal plain, the invaders eventually sought the annihilation of the aboriginal populations. Interaction was heavy and heavily favored the English nation state over the aboriginal chiefdom.

    The effects of European interaction along the interior Roanoke River drainage during most of the seventeenth century were negligible. In viewing the material culture of the Thomas-Sawyer Site and the Hurt Power Plant Site, little cultural change can be detected. With the exception of a meager number of beads, copper bangles, and rare functional iron goods, no alterations to settlement patterns, artifact assemblages, burial traditions, or demographics are apparent. At the third-quarter-seventeenth-century Graham-White Site, changes are equally difficult to determine. During this period, however, major changes took place with much cultural change and movement.

    Within the later frontier context of the southern Piedmont, the reactions had evolved and the Native Americans were seen as "partners" in trade. As Merrell suggests, the aboriginal populations continued to carry out aboriginal activities.[67] Certain activities, such as the hunting of white-tailed deer and other furbearers, were encouraged by the English as profit-making ventures, and interaction was on a more equal footing. In the end, however, a multitude of factors led to the deterioration of the Piedmont groups. The Indians of the southern Piedmont moved east in order to better coexist with the colonials. The Native American frontier on the Roanoke Valley front was mostly a case of indirect interaction. By the time the English moved west into the Valley, the Native Americans had also moved east out of the Valley. The European settlement on the edge of "civilization" was won by default.

Notes

1. J. Frederick Fausz, "Patterns of Anglo-Indian Aggression and Accommodation along the Mid-Atlantic, 1584–1634," in *Cultures in Contact*, ed. W. W. Fitzhugh (Anthropological Society of Washington Series, Washington, D.C.: Smithsonian Institution

Press, 1985), vol. 15; E. Randolph Turner, "An Archaeological and Ethnological Study on the Rank Societies in the Virginia Coastal Plain," (Ph.D. diss., Pennsylvania State Univ., 1976); E. Randolph Turner, "A Reexamination of Powhatan Territorial Boundaries and Population, ca. A.D. 1607," *Quarterly Bulletin: Archaeological Society of Virginia* 37 (1982): 45–64; E. Randolph Turner, "Socio-Political Organization within the Powhatan Chiefdom and the Effect of European Contact, A.D. 1607–1646," in *Cultures in Contact,* ed. Fitzhugh, 193–224; Stephen R. Potter, "An Analysis of Chicacoan Settlement Patterns," (Ph.D. diss., Univ. of North Carolina, Chapel Hill, 1982); Potter, "Early English Effects on Virginia Algonkian Exchange and Tribute in the Tidewater Province," in *Powhatan's Mantle: Indians of the Coastal Southeast,* ed. P. H. Wood, G. A. Waselkov, and T. M. Hatley (Lincoln: Univ. of Nebraska Press, 1990), 151–72; Christian F. Feest, "Virginia Algonquians," *Handbook of North American Indians: Northeast,* ed. B. G. Trigger (Washington, D.C.: Smithsonian Institution, 1967), vol. 15; Helen C. Rountree, *The Powhatan Indians of Virginia: Their Traditional Cultures* (Norman: Univ. of Oklahoma Press, 1989); Rountree, *Pocahantas's People: The Powhatan Indians of Virginia Through Four Centuries* (Norman: Univ. of Oklahoma Press, 1990).

2. Joe B. Jones, "Anglo-Siouan Relations on Virginia's Piedmont Frontier: 1607–1732," (M.A. thesis, College of William and Mary, 1989).

3. Clarence W. Alvord and Lee Bidgood, *The First Explorations of the Trans-Allegheny Region by the Virginians* (Cleveland: Arthur H. Clark Co., 1912).

4. James H. Merrell, "'This Western World': The Evolution of the Piedmont," in *The Siouan Project: Seasons I and II,* ed. R. S. Dickens, H. T. Ward, and R. P. S. Davis, Research Laboratories of Anthropology, Univ. of North Carolina, Chapel Hill, 1987; James H. Merrell, "'Our Bond of Peace': Patterns of Intercultural Exchange in the Carolina Piedmont," in *Powhatan's Mantle,* ed. Wood, Waselkov, and Hatley.

5. Alvord and Bidgood, *First Explorations.*

6. Mark van Doran, *Travels of William Bartram* (New York: Dover Publications, Inc., 1928).

7. C. G. Holland, *An Archaeological Survey of Southwest Virginia,* Washington, D.C.: Smithsonian Contributions to Archaeology, 1970, No. 12; Michael B. Barber and E. B. Barfield, "Paleoindian Chronology in Virginia," in *Paleoindian Research in Virginia: A Synthesis,* ed. J. M. Wittkofski and T. R. Reinhart, Richmond: Archaeological Society of Virginia Special Publication No. 19 (1989): 53–71.

8. Barber and Barfield, "Paleoindian Chronology"; William R. Gardner, "An Examination of Cultural Change in the Late Pleistocene and Early Holocene (circa 9200–6800 B.C.)," in *Paleoindian Research in Virginia,* ed. Wittkofski and Reinhart.

9. Clifford C. Boyd, "Paleoindian Paleoecology and Subsistence in Virginia," in *Paleoindian Research in Virginia,* ed. Wittkofski and Reinhart, 139–56.

10. Eugene B. Barfield, "The Paleoindian Period in the Environs of Saltville, Virginia," paper presented at Upland Archaeology in the East: Fifth Symposium, Appalachian State Univ., Boone, N.C., 1991.

11. Gardner, "Cultural Change."

12. Michael B. Barber, "Vertebrate Faunal Utilization Systems during the Late Woodland in Southwest Virginia: Changes through Time," paper presented at the Eastern States Archaeological Federation annual conference, Williamsburg, Va., 1991.

13. L. Daniel Mouer, "The Formative Transition in Virginia," in *Late Archaic and Early Woodland Research in Virginia: A Synthesis,* ed. T. R. Reinhart and M. E. N. Hodges, Richmond: Archaeological Society of Virginia Special Publication No. 23 (1991): 1–88.
14. Elman Service, *Primitive Social Organization* (New York: Random House, 1960).
15. Morton H. Fried, *The Evolution of Political Society* (New York: Random House, 1967).
16. Jefferson Chapman and A. B. Shea, "The Archeobotanical Record: Early Archaic Period to Contact in the Lower Little Tennessee River Valley," *Tennessee Anthropologist* 4 (1) (1981): 61–84.
17. British Museum, Dept. of Prints and Drawings, 1906.
18. Michael B. Barber, "The Thomas-Sawyer Site: A Proto-Historic Site in the Roanoke Valley," Manuscript, Virginia Dept. of Historic Resources, Richmond (1988).
19. Keith T. Egloff, *Ceramic Study of Woodland Occupation Along the Clinch and Powell Rivers in Southwest Virginia,* Dept. of Historic Resources, Richmond, Virginia, Research Report Series No. 3 (1987); Michael B. Barber and E. B. Barfield, "A New Perspective on the Development of Chiefdoms in Southwest Virginia: Is It Worth Its Salt?" paper presented at the annual Middle Atlantic Archaeological Conference, Ocean City, Md., 1991.
20. Service, *Primitive Social Organization;* Fried, *Evolution of Political Society;* Allen W. Johnson and T. Earle, *The Evolution of Human Societies: From Foraging Group to Agrarian State* (Stanford: Stanford Univ. Press, 1987).
21. William R. Gardner, "A Phase I Archaeological Resources Reconnaissance of the Proposed Appalachian Power Company Hydroelectric Project in Poor Valley, Washington County, Virginia," Manuscript, Virginia Dept. of Historic Resources, Richmond (1979).
22. E. Randolph Turner, "The Archaeological Identification of Chiefdom Societies in Southwest Virginia," in *Upland Archaeology in the Easy: A Symposium,* ed. C. A. Geier, M. B. Barber, and G. A. Tolley, USDA-Forest Service, Atlanta, Region 8 Cultural Resources Report No. 2 (1983).
23. Barber and Barfield, "Development of Chiefdoms in Southwest Virginia"; Michael B. Barber and E. B. Barfield, "The Woodland Period in the Environs of Saltville, Virginia," paper presented at the Upland Archaeology in the East: Fifth Symposium, Appalachian State Univ., Boone, N.C., 1991.
24. Alvord and Bidgood, *First Explorations;* Barber and Barfield "Development of Chiefdoms in Southwest Virginia"; Barber and Barfield, "Woodland Period in Saltville."
25. Wayne E. Clark, "A Preliminary Report on the 1977 Excavations of the Buzzard Rock Site (44RN2)," Manuscript, Virginia Dept. of Historic Resources, Richmond (1978); William T. Buchanan, "The Hall Site, Montgomery County, Virginia," *Quarterly Bulletin: Archaeological Society of Virginia* 35 (2) (1980); Barber, "Thomas-Sawyer Site"; Michael B. Barber, "A Preliminary Report on the Salvage Excavations at the Thomas/Sawyer Site (44RN39) Area D, Roanoke County, Virginia–February 1992," Manuscript, Virginia Dept. of Historic Resources, Richmond, 1992; David Rotenizer, "1985 Salvage Excavations at the Hall Site, Montgomery County, Virginia," paper presented at the annual Archaeological Society of Virginia meeting, Roanoke, 1991; Thomas S. Klatka, "Preliminary Report on the Graham-White Site: A Contact Period Site on the

Roanoke River, Virginia," paper presented at the Upland Archaeology in the East: Fifth Symposium, Appalachian State Univ., Boone, N.C., 1991.

26. Barber, "Vertebrate Faunal Utilized Systems."
27. Barber, "Thomas-Sawyer Site."
28. Ibid.
29. Holland, *Archaeological Survey*; Clifford Evans, *A Ceramic Study of Virginia Archaeology*, Smithsonian Bureau of Ethnology, Washington, D.C., Bulletin 160 (1950); William J. Hranicky, *Projectile Point Typology and Nomenclature for Maryland, Virginia, and North/South Carolina*, Archaeological Society of Virginia, Richmond, Special Publication No. 26 (1991).
30. Calvert McIlhaney, "The Phase I Inventory of the Proposed Moyer Softball Complex, Salem, Virginia," Manuscript, Virginia Dept. of Historic Resources, Richmond (1990).
31. Klatka, "Graham-White Site."
32. Michael B. Barber, "The Contact Period within the Lower Piedmont and Ridge and Valley of Virginia," paper presented at the annual Southeastern Archaeological Conference, Raleigh, N.C., 1993.
33. Barber, "Thomas-Sawyer Site."
34. Michael B. Barber, "Excavations at the Hurt Power Plant Site (44PY144), Pittsylvania County, Virginia: A Protohistoric Saponi Village on the Middle Staunton (Roanoke) River," paper presented at the annual Southeastern Archaeological Conference, Raleigh, N.C., 1993.
35. Kenneth E. Kidd and M.A. Kidd, "A Classification System for Glass Beads for the Use of Field Archaeologists," in *Proceedings of the 1982 Glass Bead Conference*, ed. C. F. Hayes, III, Rochester, N.Y.: Research Records no. 16 (1983): 219–57.
36. Klatka, "Graham-White Site."
37. Michael B. Barber, "The Compositional Analysis for Copper Recovered from Contact Native American Sites in the Lower Piedmont and Ridge and Valley of Virginia," paper presented at the annual Virginia Academy of Sciences meeting, Harrisonburg, 1993.
38. Stephen R. Potter, "Early English Effects on Virginia Algonkian Exchange and Tribute in the Tidewater Province," in *Powhatan's Mantle*, ed. Wood, Waselkov, and Hatley, 151–72.
39. Roy Dickens, *Cherokee Prehistory* (Knoxville: Univ. of Tennessee Press, 1976); Howard Earnest, personal communication.
40. Holland, *Archaeological Survey*; Egloff, *Ceramic Study of Woodland Occupation*; Turner, "Chiefdom Societies in Southwest Virginia"; Barber and Barfield, "Development of Chiefdoms in Southwest Virginia"; Barber and Barfield, "Woodland Period in Saltville."
41. Gregory Waselkov, "Seventeenth Century Trade in the Colonial Southeast," *Southeastern Archaeology* 8 (2) (1989).
42. Clark, "Buzzard Rock Site"; Barber, "Thomas-Sawyer Site"; Barber, "Salvage Excavations at the Thomas-Sawyer Site"; Klatka, "Graham-White Site."
43. Philip L. Barbour, *The Complete Works of Captain John Smith*, 3 vols. (Chapel Hill: Univ. of North Carolina Press, 1987).
44. F. B. Kegley, *Kegley's Virginia Frontier* (Roanoke, Va.: Southwest Virginia Historical Society, 1938); Deedie Kagey, *When Past Is Prologue: A History of Roanoke County* (Roanoke, Va.: Roanoke County Sesquicentennial Committee, 1988);

Clare White, *Roanoke 1740–1982* (Roanoke, Va.: Roanoke Valley Historical Society, 1982).

45. Fausz, "Anglo-Indian Aggression and Accommodation," 233.
46. C. Clifford Boyd and Donna C. Boyd, "The Skeletal Biology of the Native Americans from the Hurt Power Plant Site, Pittsylvania County, Virginia," in "Phase III Excavations at the Hurt Power Plant Site, Pittsylvania County, Virginia," ed. M. B. Barber, M. F. Barber, and C. Bowen, Manuscript, Virginia Dept. of Historic Resources, Richmond (1995).
47. Merrell, "Our Bond of Peace," 204.
48. Alvord and Bidgood, *First Explorations*; Briceland, *Westward from Virginia.*
49. John R. Swanton, *The Indians of the Southeastern United States* (Washington, D.C.: Smithsonian Institution, Bureau of American Ethnology Bulletin, 1946), 137.
50. Ibid., 201.
51. Roy S. Dickens, *Cherokee Prehistory: The Pisgah Phase in the Appalachian Summit Region* (Knoxville: Univ. of Tennessee Press 1976); Bennie C. Keel, *Cherokee Archaeology: A Study of the Appalachian Summit* (Knoxville: Univ. of Tennessee Press, 1976); Trawick Ward, "A Review of Archaeology in the North Carolina Piedmont: A Study of Change," in *Prehistory of North Carolina*, ed. M. A. Mathis and J. J. Crow (Raleigh: North Carolina Division of Archives and History, 1983); Lawrence E. Abbot, E. E. Sanborn, M. N. Vaca, D. C. Crass, and E. Dull, "The Archaeology of Charity Lake, Virginia: Phase I," Ms., U.S. Corps of Engineers, Wilmington, N.C. (1985).
52. Michael B. Barber, "Human Prehistory Beyond the Blue Ridge," paper presented at The Blue Ridge Symposium, Roanoke, Va., 1980, updated 1994.
53. Nathaniel C. Hale, *Pelts and Palisades* (Richmond: Dietz Press, Inc., 1959).
54. Paul C. Phillips, *The Fur Trade* (Norman: Univ. of Oklahoma Press, 1961), 1: 166.
55. Jones, "Anglo-Siouan Relations," 43.
56. Alvord and Bidgood, *First Explorations.*
57. R. P. Davis and T. Ward, "The Occaneechi and Their Role as Middlemen in the 17th Century Virginia–North Carolina Trade Network," paper presented at the annual meeting of the Society for Historic Archaeology, Richmond, Va., 1991.
58. Alvord and Bidgood, *First Explorations*, 80.
59. Ibid., 80.
60. Ibid.; Davis and Ward, "The Occaneechi and Their Role as Middlemen."
61. William P. Cumming, ed., *The Discoveries of John Lederer* (Charlottesville: Univ. Press of Virginia, 1958).
62. Warren Billings, *The Old Dominion in the Seventeenth Century: A Documentary History of Virginia, 1606–1689* (Chapel Hill: Univ. of North Carolina Press, 1975); Dickens, Ward, and Davis, *The Siouan Project.*
63. Hugh T. Leflar, ed., *A New Voyage of Carolina* (Chapel Hill: Univ. of North Carolina Press, 1967).
64. Phillips, *The Fur Trade.*
65. Lefler, *A New Voyage of Carolina.*
66. Alvord and Bidgood, *First Explorations.*
67. Merrell, "Our Bond of Peace."

Works Cited

Abbot, Lawrence E., E. E. Sanborn, M. N. Vacca, D. C. Crass, and E. Dull. "The Archaeology of Charity Lake, Virginia: Phase I." Manuscript. On file with U.S. Corps of Engineers, Wilmington, N.C. (1985).

Alvord, Clarence W., and Lee Bidgood. *The First Explorations of the Trans-Allegheny Region by the Virginians.* Cleveland: Arthur H. Clark Co., 1912.

Barber, Michael B. "The Thomas-Sawyer Site: A Proto-Historic Site in the Roanoke Valley." Manuscript. Virginia Dept. of Historic Resources, Richmond (1988).

———. "Vertebrate Faunal Utilized Systems in the Late Woodland in Southwest Virginia: Changes through Time." Paper presented at the Eastern States Archaeological Federation annual conference. Williamsburg, Va., 1991.

———. "A Preliminary Report on the Salvage Excavations at the Thomas/Sawyer Site (44RN39) Area D, Roanoke County, Virginia—February 1992." Manuscript. Virginia Dept. of Historic Resources, Richmond (1992).

———. "The Contact Period within the Lower Piedmont and Ridge and Valley of Virginia." Paper presented at the annual Southeastern Archaeological Conference. Raleigh, N.C., 1993.

———. "The Compositional Analysis for Copper Recovered from Contact Native American Sites in the Lower Piedmont and Ridge and Valley of Virginia." Paper presented at the annual Virginia Academy of Science meeting, Archaeology Section. Harrisonburg, 1993.

———. "Excavations at the Hurt Power Plant Site (44PY144), Pittsylvania County, Virginia: A Protohistoric Saponi Village on the Middle Staunton (Roanoke) River." Paper presented at the annual Southeastern Archaeological Conference. Raleigh, N.C., 1993.

———. "Human Prehistory Beyond the Blue Ridge." Paper presented at The Blue Ridge Symposium. Roanoke, Va., 1980. Recently updated, 1994.

Barber, Michael B., and Eugene B. Barfield. "Paleoindian Chronology for Virginia." In *Paleoindian Research in Virginia: A Synthesis,* edited by J. M. Wittkofski and T. R. Reinhart, 53–71. Archaeological Society of Virginia, Richmond, Special Publication No. 19 (1989).

———. "A New Perspective on the Development of Chiefdoms in Southwest Virginia: Is It Worth Its Salt?" Paper presented at the annual Middle Atlantic Archaeological Conference. Ocean City, Md., 1991.

———. "The Woodland Period in the Environs of Saltville, Virginia." Paper presented at the Upland Archaeology in the East: Fifth Symposium, Boone, N.C., 1992.

Barbour, Philip L. *The Complete Works of Captain John Smith.* 3 vols. Chapel Hill: Univ. of North Carolina Press, 1987.

Barfield, Eugene B. "The Paleoindian Period in the Environs of Saltville, Virginia." Paper presented at the Upland Archaeology in the East: Fifth Symposium, Boone, N.C., 1992.

Barfield, Eugene B., and M. B. Barber. "Late Woodland Subsistence Patterns in Virginia." Paper presented at the Council of Virginia Archaeologists Symposium No. 4—The Middle and Late Woodland Periods in Virginia, Roanoke, 1991.

Billings, Warren. *The Old Dominion in the Seventeenth Century: A Documentary History of Virginia, 1606–1689.* Chapel Hill: Univ. of North Carolina Press, 1975.

Boyd, C. Clifford. "Paleoindian Paleoecology and Subsistence in Virginia." In *Paleoindian Research in Virginia: A Synthesis,* edited by J. M. Wittkofski and T. R. Reinhart, 139–56. Archaeological Society of Virginia, Richmond, Special Publication No. 19 (1989).

Boyd, C. Clifford, and D. M. Boyd. "The Skeletal Biology of the Native Americans from the Hurt Power Plant Site, Pittsylvania County, Virginia." In "Phase III Excavations at the Hurt Power Plant Site, Pittsylvania County, Virginia." Edited by M. B. Barber, M. F. Barber and C. Bowen. Manuscript. Virginia Dept. of Historic Resources, Richmond (1995).

Briceland, Alan V. *Westward from Virginia: The Exploration of the Virginia–Carolina Frontier 1610–1710.* Charlottesville: Univ. Press of Virginia, 1987.

Buchanan, William T. "The Hall Site, Montgomery County, Virginia." *Quarterly Bulletin: Archaeological Society of Virginia* 35 (2) (1980).

Chapman, Jefferson, and A. B. Shea. "The Ethnobotanical Record: Early Archaic Period to Contact in the Lower Little Tennessee River Valley." *Tennessee Anthropologist* 6 (1981): 61–84.

Clark, Wayne E. "A Preliminary Report on the 1977 Excavations of the Buzzard Rock Site (44RN2)." Manuscript. Virginia Dept. of Historic Resources, Richmond (1978).

Cumming, William P., editor. *The Discoveries of John Lederer.* Charlottesville: Univ. Press of Virginia, 1958.

Davis, R. P., and T. Ward. "The Occaneechi and Their Role as Middlemen in the 17th Century Virginia–North Carolina Trade Network." Paper presented at the annual meeting of Society for Historic Archaeology, Richmond, Va., 1991.

Dickens, Roy S. *Cherokee Prehistory.* Knoxville: Univ. of Tennessee Press, 1976.

Dickens, Roy S., H. T. Ward, and R. P. S. Davis. *The Siouan Project: Seasons I and II.* Chapel Hill: Research Laboratories of Anthropology, Univ. of North Carolina, Monograph No. 1 (1987).

Egloff, Keith T. *Ceramic Study of Woodland Occupation Along the Clinch and Powell Rivers in Southwest Virginia.* Richmond: Virginia Dept. of Historic Resources, Research Report Series No. 3 (1987).

Evans, Clifford. *A Ceramic Study of Virginia Archaeology.* Washington, D.C.: Smithsonian Institution Bureau of Ethnography Bulletin 160 (1955).

Fausz, J. Fredrick. "Patterns of Anglo-Indian Aggression and Accommodation Along the Mid-Atlantic Coast, 1584–1634." In *Cultures in Contact.* Edited by W. W. Fitzhugh. Washington, D.C.: Anthropological Society of Washington Series, Smithsonian Institution Press, vol. 15, 1985.

Feest, Christian F. "The Virginia Indian in Pictures." *Smithsonian Journal of History* 2 (1967): 1–30.

Fried, Morton H. *The Evolution of Political Society.* New York: Random House, 1967.

Gardner, William M. "A Phase I Archaeological Resources Reconnaissance of the Proposed Appalachian Power Company Hydroelectric Project in Poor Valley and Hidden Valley, Washington County, Virginia." Manuscript. Virginia Dept. of Historic Resources, Richmond (1979).

———. "An Examination of Cultural Change in the Late Pleistocene and Early Holocene (circa 9200–6800 B.C.)." In *Paleoindian Research in Virginia: A Synthesis.*

Edited by J. M. Wittkofski and T. R. Reinhart. Archaeological Society of Virginia, Richmond, Special Publication No. 19 (1989).

Hale, Nathaniel C. *Pelts and Palisades.* Richmond, Va.: Dietz Press, Inc., 1959.

Holland, C. G. *An Archaeological Survey of Southwest Virginia.* Washington, D.C.: Smithsonian Contributions to Archaeology No. 12 (1970).

Hranicky, William J. *Projectile Point Typology and Nomenclature for Maryland, Virginia, and North/South Carolina.* Archaeological Society of Virginia, Richmond, Special Publication No. 26 (1991).

Johnson, Allen W., and Timothy Earle. *The Evolution of Human Societies: From Foraging Group to Agrarian State.* Stanford: Stanford Univ. Press, 1987.

Jones, Joe B. "Anglo-Siouan Relations on Virginia's Piedmont Frontier: 1607–1732." M.A. thesis, College of William and Mary, 1989.

Kagey, Deedie. *When Past Is Prologue: A History of Roanoke County.* Roanoke, Va.: Roanoke County Sesquicentennial Committee, 1988.

Keel, Bennie C. *Cherokee Archaeology.* Knoxville: Univ. of Tennessee Press, 1976.

Kegley, F. B. *Kegley's Virginia Frontier.* Roanoke, Va.: Southwest Virginia Historical Society, 1938.

Kidd, Kenneth E., and M. A. Kidd. "A Classification System for Glass Beads for the Use of Field Archaeologists." In *Proceedings of the 1982 Glass Trade Beads Conference.* Edited by C. F. Hayes, III. Rochester Museum and Science Center, Rochester, N.Y., Research Records No. 16 (1983).

Klatka, Thomas S. "Preliminary Report on the Graham-White Site: A Contact Period Site on the Roanoke River, Virginia." Paper presented at the Upland Archaeology in the East: Fifth Symposium, Boone, N.C., 1992.

Lefler, Hugh T., editor. *A New Voyage of Carolina.* Chapel Hill: Univ. of North Carolina Press, 1967.

McIlhaney, Calvert. "The Phase I Inventory of the Moyer Softball Complex, Salem, Virginia." Manuscript. Virginia Dept. of Historic Resources, Richmond, 1990.

Merrell, James H. "'This Western World': The Evolution of the Piedmont." In *The Siouan Project: Seasons I and II.* Edited by R. S. Dickens, H. T. Ward, and R. P. S. Davis. Chapel Hill: Research Laboratories of Anthropology, Univ. of North Carolina, Monograph Series No. 1 (1987).

———. "'Our Bond of Peace': Patterns of Intercultural Exchange in the Carolina Piedmont, 1650–1750." In *Powhatan's Mantle: Indians of the Coastal Southeast.* Edited by P. H. Wood, G. A. Waselkov, and T. M. Hatley. Lincoln: Univ. of Nebraska Press, 1989.

Mouer, L. Daniel. "The Formative Transition in Virginia." In *Late Archaic and Early Woodland Research in Virginia: A Synthesis.* Edited by T. R. Reinhart and M. E. N. Hodges. Archaeological Society of Virginia, Richmond, Special Publication No. 23 (1991).

Phillips, Paul C. *The Fur Trade.* Norman: Univ. of Oklahoma Press, 1961.

Potter, Stephen R. "An Analysis of Chicacoan Settlement Patterns." Ph.D. diss., Univ. of North Carolina, Chapel Hill, 1982.

———. "Early English Effects on Virginia Algonkian Exchange and Tribute in the Tidewater Province." In *Powhatan's Mantle: Indians of the Coastal Southeast.* Edited by P. H. Wood, G. A. Waselkov, and T. M. Hatley. Lincoln: Univ. of Nebraska Press, 1990.

Rotenizer, David. "1985 Salvage Excavations at the Hall Site, Montgomery County,

Virginia." Paper presented at the annual meeting of the Archaeological Society of Virginia, Roanoke, 1991.

Rountree, Helen C. *The Powhatan Indians of Virginia: Their Traditional Cultures.* Norman: Univ. of Oklahoma Press, 1989.

———. *Pocahontas's People: The Powhatan Indians of Virginia Through the Four Centuries.* Norman: Univ. of Oklahoma Press, 1990.

Service, Elman. *Primitive Social Organization.* New York: Random House, 1962.

Swanton, John R. *The Indians of the Southeastern United States.* Washington, D.C.: Smithsonian Institution Press, Bureau of American Ethnology Bulletin, 1946.

Turner, E. Randolph. "An Archaeological and Ethnohistorical Study on the Rank Societies in the Virginia Coastal Plain." Ph.D. diss., Pennsylvania State Univ., 1976.

———. "A Reexamination of Powhatan Territorial Boundaries and Population, Ca. A.D. 1607." *Quarterly Bulletin: Archaeological Society of Virginia* 37 (1982):45–64.

———. "The Archaeological Identification of Chiefdom Societies in Southwest Virginia." In *Upland Archaeology in the East: A Symposium.* Edited by C. A. Geier, M. B. Barber, G. A. Tolley. Atlanta: USDA-Forest Service, Region 8 Cultural Resources Report No. 2 (1983).

———. "Socio-Political Organization within the Powhatan Chiefdom and the Effect of European Contact, A.D. 1607–1646." In *Cultures in Contact.* Edited by W. W. Fitzhugh. Washington, D.C.: Anthropological Society of Washington Series, Smithsonian Institution Press, vol. 15, 1985.

Van Doran, Mark. *Travels of William Bartram.* New York: Dover Publications, Inc., 1928.

Ward, Trawick. "A Review of Archaeology in the North Carolina Piedmont: A Study of Change." In *Prehistory of North Carolina.* Edited by M.A. Mathis and J. J. Crow. Raleigh: North Carolina Division of Archives and History, 1983.

Waselkov, Gregory. "Seventeenth-Century Trade in the Colonial Southeast." *Southeastern Archaeology* 8 (2) (1989).

Chapter 6

Augusta County's Other Pioneers

The African American Presence in Frontier Augusta County

J. Susanne Schramm Simmons

From the Potomac River south to the headwaters of the James River, the Shenandoah Valley stretches for two hundred miles between the Blue Ridge Mountains on the east and the Allegheny Mountains on the west. Its north-south direction, its abundant land, water, timber, and game spread, and its scarcity of permanent Indian settlement turned what was simply a route to somewhere else into a cultural milieu called the frontier.[1]

Unblemished by contested land titles, Augusta County beckoned to the pioneer.[2] Beginning in 1736, Scotch-Irish, German, and English pioneers carved out small family farms in Augusta County. Indeed, some historians maintain this area represented the largest assemblage of Scotch-Irish in America;[3] it is important, however, not to disregard the German and English cultural influences. The area soon acquired characteristics that set it apart from the rest of Virginia. It is equally important not to ignore the emerging African American presence in frontier Augusta County. It was a presence that helped advance the evolving commercialism of the frontier and one that provided the context of slavery in the antebellum period.

It is tempting, albeit specious, to think of the frontier as a clean slate, a place, unlike the Tidewater or Piedmont, that was immune to the institution of slavery. A few African Americans arrived on the frontier of their own volition; the rest, however, were brought as chattel. There was, perhaps, a short period during which the frontier could have maintained its immunity, could have been a land of promise and opportunity to all. As the frontier evolved into a permanent society, however, the scales tipped toward a slave society. Indeed, by the antebellum period, slavery was firmly established. Slavery's presence, and its eventual dominance, perhaps more than any other factor, manifested the growing commercial tendencies present at the beginning of frontier settlement.[4] This chapter endeavors to demonstrate that the foundation of Augusta County's slave society was irreversibly laid in the frontier period.

It is impossible to report the number of African Americans living in Augusta County prior to the first federal census taken in 1790. Estimates of the colonial population generally are made on the basis of incomplete parish records and lists of tithables contained therein. The enumeration of tithables provides the only clue,[5] and an inconclusive one at that, to the composition of the early colonial population. It is fair to say, however, that even if the exact numbers are not known, the extant enumeration gives a relatively accurate accounting.

The first black tithes appear in 1755. Based on the return of 2,313 tithables in 1755, of which 40 were black tithes, and using a multiplier of 2, scholars estimate 80 African Americans lived in Augusta County at that time. The 1,196 tithables reported in 1745 and the 1,421 reported in 1748 indicate nothing about the black population, even though court records indicate that a small mix of both free and slave African Americans did indeed exist.[6]

The most familiar account of a colonial African American west of the Blue Ridge, but by no means the first, is that of a Moravian missionary's diary entry telling of an encounter with a free Negro living in Augusta County in 1753.

Bro. Gottlob had preceded up half a mile to a free negro, who is the only blacksmith in the district. He had his horse shod. The negro and his wife, who was born in Scotland, were very friendly towards Bro. Gottlob and related to him that not long ago they had removed hitherto from Lancaster County. They had often heard Bro. Nyberg preach and also the brethren in Philadelphia, and now they are reading the Berlin Address [of Zinzendorf]. They were very glad to see us and very willing to serve us. The woman

baked several loaves of bread for us and invited Bro. Gottlob and Nathanael
to breakfast. The negro also understands German very well.[7]

This brief narrative not only tells us of a skilled, literate, bilingual, free,
black man, it implies that he was a partner in an interracial marriage. Unfortunately, the good brother did not even bother to record the man's
name, much less how and why he had come to settle in Augusta County.
We could, until recently, only guess that this man, perhaps like other landless, land-hungry settlers from the East, saw opportunity on the frontier.
Recent scholarship has identified the free Negro as Edward Tarr, about
whom more will follow.[8]
    The earliest mention of an African American is one who was a slave.
At the second court held in Augusta County, on February 19, 1745/46,
the court upheld Patrick Martin's claim for "taking up a slave" who belonged to Dr. Hopkins.[9] A year later, on June 17, 1747, the court acquitted John Johnson of being a runaway slave,[10] although Johnson is not identified by race. Two accounts of free Negroes also predate the Moravian
narrative, one by several years. Christopher Roarrey, "a Mulattoe child
age one year three months," was bound out to Thomas Milsap on February 16, 1748.[11] In August 1753, just a few months before the Moravians
visited the blacksmith, Nicholas Smith, a free mulatto, "absconded from
the county." The record teases us with the information that his five abandoned children were bound out, lest they become a burden to society, and
never refers to them again.[12]
    The existence of a free Negro people caused the Augusta commu-
nity social problems and created moral dilemmas. As often happens,
people used government and the law as tools to maintain social order.
Relationships inevitably developed between the races, and children were
born. As in other regions, Augusta County's frontier society frowned
upon interracial relationships and actively discouraged miscegenation.
Traditionally, children born to slave mothers assumed the social status
of their mothers. However, the mulatto offspring of a black father and
white mother were not so easily accommodated or tolerated.[13] Indeed,
depending on the circumstances of the mother, both mother and child
were punished for their social indiscretion in Virginia. "If any English
woman being free have a bastard by a negro she shall pay £15 within a
month to the Church Wardens and if failing to be disposed of for five
years ye fine or wht. she shall be sold for disposed 1/3 of their [?], 1/3
to yer parish & 1/3 to ye informer & ye child bound out by ye Ward for
30 years & if ye woman be a servant she shall be sold for 5 years after
her time is expired."[14]

Christopher Roarrey's contract of indenture differs significantly from that of the other black or mulatto children who would follow. In 1748 Christopher Roarrey was bound out "until he shall attain the age of thirty-one," the destiny of a free yet impoverished, illegitimate, mulatto child. If he survived his indenture, Christopher received no tangible "freedom dues" for his labor, a return due white indentured servants.

The great majority of white and black people bound out for the purpose of labor in the first two decades of Augusta County settlement were children under the age of sixteen. On her deathbed, Elizabeth Hodge, described as "a woman of no means," bound out her six children to six different families.[15] Perhaps because she was white, she was able to exercise more control over the terms of their indenture. Each child's return for his or her years of labor, which typically ended at the age of twenty-one, as it did for all white indentured servants, included sustenance, a smattering of education, and knowledge of a trade. Hannah Hurley, the bastard mulatto child of a white woman, and, like the Hodge children, a burden to society, was also bound out; yet, the terms of her indenture were quite different from those of her white counterpart.[16] Beginning at the age of three, Hannah's indenture was to last until she reached the age of thirty-one, a veritable lifetime. Still, she fared somewhat better than her predecessor, Christopher Roarrey, in that the law directed Hannah's master, William Bethel, to teach her to read the Bible; to provide her with meat, drink, washing, lodging, and apparel; and to pay her freedom dues.

Just five months after Hannah Hurley was indentured for twenty-nine years, the Smith children, whose father had abandoned them and left the county, were bound out under the same terms as any white children in the same position. Why did these terms become more equitable? Did the contracts negotiated on behalf of the Smith children reflect a fundamental frontier attitude, an acceptance of the mulatto presence, or did the Smith children receive special treatment? It would appear that, because the contracts of indenture had become more standardized and less discriminating of race, opportunities for free blacks had improved. This interpretation, however, may be far too simplistic, given the dearth of extant material.

Joseph Bell Jr., who was "the mulattoe, natural son of Joseph Bell, begat upon a white woman," found himself bound out to William Wilson in 1759 because he had "no other relation in this colony."[17] The inventory made of Joseph Bell Sr.'s estate suggests that a free black could succeed modestly well on the frontier and achieve literacy. While by no means a wealthy man, Bell possessed at his death a sorrel horse, a white mare, a pair of buckles, razor, one old coat and a jacket, a Bible and a small history, an old saddle and a bridle, an old shirt and a pair of stockings, a piece of "blew woolling cloath, blew sarge," a short rifle gun and shot pouch, an old tin cup, and sundry other things. His estate, valued at £10, included cash from his pocketbook and cash received from Captain Preston. John Tate, William Wilson, and Samuel Steele settled the estate, which amounted to £7.[18] By the time they paid fees, satisfied debts, and reimbursed themselves liberally for their trouble, a balance of £3 remained: a sum equal to the payment allowed bound children upon reaching their majority at the age of twenty-one. The infant son and namesake of Joseph Bell was subsequently bound to William Wilson, one of the estate's administrators.[19] Whether motivated by racial bigotry, class prejudice, or simple greed, Messrs. Tate, Wilson, and Steele kept the orphaned mulatto Joseph Bell Jr. in his place.

Still, the frontier offered opportunity even to free Negroes. The story of Edward Tarr, the only known free black property owner in frontier Augusta County, is instructive. It would appear that, despite his race, this former slave represented the quintessential frontier man: landowner, businessman, church member, and taxpayer. The Great Wagon Road passed through his landholding southwest of Staunton near Lexington, in present-day Rockbridge County. Local people and travelers alike patronized his blacksmith shop. Tarr's membership in the Timber Ridge Presbyterian Church, located a few miles from his home, and his thriving trade caused his shop to become a popular meeting place for other free Negroes, whites of the "middlin' sort," and neighboring slaves.

By the end of the colonial period, however, Edward Tarr's situation changed. A malcontent neighbor and eventually the vestry came to view Tarr as a nuisance or a threat to the public order. The court must have been sending a message to Edward Tarr and to those who congregated at his forge, when, in 1763, it ordered an executed slave's severed head placed on a pike and posted on the road that led to Tarr's forge, nearly fifty miles from the murder scene. The changing attitudes toward Tarr also perhaps explain the morals charge brought against Ann Moore, his wife, the sale of his land at a loss in 1772, and his subsequent move to Staunton. Forsaking the rural life for the anonymity of a city was a pattern consistent with the free black experience in Virginia at the time.[20]

Although comparatively few African Americans lived in Augusta County before 1745, the growth of the slave population outpaced that of free blacks.[21] The early part of the decade of the 1760s saw the greatest importation of slaves into Augusta County. Thirty-two African child registrations were made in 1761 and fifteen in 1762. Only one child was registered in 1766, four in 1767, and none in 1768 and 1769.[22]

Notoriously ambitious to own slaves, the Scotch-Irish eagerly adopted the institution.[23] Germans, who favored farms only as large as a family could cultivate efficiently, were less inclined to buy slaves. While some Germans probably felt a certain antipathy toward Negroes,[24] others voiced a sectarian objection to the institution of slavery. It has been suggested that perhaps some Germans, fleeing oppression, empathized with enslaved blacks. Indeed, it seems that first-generation Germans felt little compulsion to copy the English style. After the French and Indian War and the advent of the second generation, however, Germans did begin to acquire slaves. In time the institution became very broad-based.[25]

While tobacco did not dominate the agriculture of Augusta County as it did in the Tidewater, hemp emerged as the first cash crop in the upper Valley in the 1760s. Dominated by the Scotch-Irish and English, this labor-intensive crop decimated all available labor sources. Expanding hemp production coincided with the first significant importation of Negro slaves in 1761–62. An increased wartime demand for hemp a decade later only accelerated the demand for labor to grow the crop.[26] Paradoxically, the proportion of slaveholders producing hemp in Augusta County apparently shrank throughout the 1760s. In 1769 11 percent of the individuals certifying hemp were known to be slaveholders.

Slaveholdings in Augusta County were comparatively small. Most households did not own slaves. As would become the case in the antebellum period, those who did own slaves owned only one slave. Interestingly, forty-eight of the seventy-two identified owners owned little or no land.[27] This begs the question for what were these slaves used?

"Plantation" attitudes associated with tobacco agriculture did not find their way into the Upper Valley. A typical Tidewater view that "A man, unless he was willing to take up the hoe or ax, had to buy a slave"[28] was not the norm in Augusta County. Travelers to the area reported seeing slaves working side-by-side with their masters. Samuel McCune expressed it best when he pointed out that his slave "could work as well as himself at grubbing thrashing or the like."[29] Clearly, a man's status was not determined by the separation of his labor from that of his slave.

Ownership of slaves did offer what today would be called upward mobility. Cost rather than ethics impeded the investment in slaves. Slaves were expensive to buy and could be costly to maintain, but they offered a great return as a long-term investment with only a modicum of risk. Before 1760, the price of a slave was prohibitive at between twenty-five pounds and thirty-five pounds, or twenty-five pounds sterling. That price could buy a substantial amount of land on the frontier where land sold for shillings per acre.

The purchase price plus an annual upkeep made a slave the single most valuable item in personal inventories.[30] Slave values did not depreciate under ordinary circumstances. Even after the depression of the early 1780s, when labor for hire was more plentiful, the value of a slave remained stable. Two Negroes inventoried along with one pair of pot racks and five tongs were all valued at £114, a sum that constituted nearly half the value of George Rankin's estate.[31] By 1770 a prime field hand brought £80–85 and a domestic servant £75. After 1782, males were rarely sold for less than £100. Nothing in society had a comparable worth; even horses were valued less.

Some of Augusta County's first wills indicate not only the value of slaves, but also their uses as a legacy. The appraisal of James Coburn's estate in 1749 places a value of £33 for a "negro woman" and £20 for "one negro man named Louis."[32] Another estate, totaling £194 in value listed "for a negro Wench £35; for a Negro girl £25; for a Negro boy £15; for another Negro girl £10."[33] John Hays's last will and testament left to his wife, Rebecca, "my negro women to abide with you during your lifetime and at your decease the negroes wench [sic] to be sold and divided between my three sons equally."[34] In his will, Samuel Scott specified that his wife bring up his children in a "Christian manner and make them good English Scholars for which she is to have use of the negroos [sic]."[35]

Money—hard cash—was scarce on the frontier. John Dawson's urgent letter to a friend, probably written around 1788, illustrates this scarcity and how slaves could generate cash flow: "By an unlucky mistake you did not receive a letter sent you this morning by Mr. John Benson Jr. Abraham Lymons set out [?] morning for Augusta County with Negroes for sale so I have prevailed on him to take ours—they go by Abraham Lymons—you will therefore please have Lat and Sam brought to Lymons by [?] two hours by [?]—where I will be—pray do not fail as this is a most excellent opportunity and you as well as myself am pushed for cash v.-J Dawson."[36] The opportunity to sell a slave, therefore, could prove to be advantageous.

While slave ownership provided status, labor, and investment to any given individual, it often created problems for society generally. Indeed, slaves were so valuable that individuals tried illegally to enslave free men. In 1763 John Anderson sued the Reverend John Craig for detaining him as a slave. The court summoned Craig and directed him to allow Anderson permission to go to Brunswick County to summon his own witnesses. Four months later, Anderson presented the deposition of Joel Baker, taken in Brunswick County, attesting to the fact that "Said Anderson is the son of a free white woman and was bound by the Church Wardens of the Parish of Saint Andrews in Brunswick County, to serve till age 21, and he is now that age. It is the Judgement of the Court that he be released."[37] Nat, "an Indian Boy," complained to the court in 1777 of "being held in slavery by Mary Greenlee" who was subsequently ordered to release the boy.[38] Mary Greenlee found herself back in court in 1778 when a slave petitioned her to show why she had held him in servitude. Mary's bill of sale did not satisfy the court as sufficient proof of ownership, and the slave was subsequently freed.[39]

Litigation against criminal slaves further institutionalized slavery in Augusta County. Slaves involved in criminal activity were severely and quickly punished by a variety of methods borrowed from the English judicial system.[40] An Augusta slave named Hampton was sentenced to be hanged for house breaking and larceny in 1757.[41] On two other occasions in Augusta County, hanging alone was neither punishment enough nor thought to set a sufficient example. In 1763 the court convicted the slave Tom for shooting John Harrison in the back. Following the hanging, Tom's head was severed and "affixed on a pole on the top of the hill that leads from this Court House to Edward Tarr's."[42] Tried as an accomplice, the victim's Negro slave, Fanner, was acquitted.

Two other slaves suffered the same gruesome fate ten years later for murdering Thomas Marmeon.[43] That piked heads served as object lessons to blacks there is no argument. This grisly spectacle, however, also served to reassure whites, slaveholders as well as others, that blacks were "under control" and that they need not fear insurrection or for their safety.

Because counties were compelled to compensate an owner for "condemned" property, executing a slave was not a favorite or common punishment. Public whipping and mutilation served as a far more acceptable alternative punishment for criminal slaves.[44] Tom received thirty-nine lashes and had his ear cropped for the crime of house breaking and horse stealing.[45] The court found Jacob innocent of house breaking, but guilty of shooting at the children of Alexander Moore,[46] a malfeasance for which he received thirty-nine lashes. George and Poll, slaves belonging to George Rice of North Carolina, who had apparently abandoned them in Augusta County, were found guilty of house breaking. The court recommended leniency for the two slaves, who were, it was said, unduly influenced by one George Hendricks. Instead of execution, George and Poll each received thirty-nine lashes, had their ears cropped, and were jailed. When their owner failed to claim his property, the court directed the jailer to fit them with iron collars stamped with the letters "A G" and to hire them out until their master arrived and proved proprietorship.[47]

Not everyone on the frontier embraced slavery. A sizable community of German Baptist Brethren, whose opposition to slavery was based on Biblical interpretation, made their home in northern Augusta County. While they lived apolitical lives in closed communities apart from the secular world, they were unable to isolate themselves from the institution. The Brethren permitted marriages outside of the denomination on the condition that non-Brethren spouses join the church. Inevitably, marriages to slaveholders brought slaves into the cloistered Brethren community, and the growing ownership of slaves among the brothers and sisters eventually forced the issue.

In 1782, the church recorded its opposition to slavery: "It has been unanimously considered that it cannot be permitted in any wise by the church, that a member should or could purchase negroes, or keep them as slaves."[48] Slavery appeared to be a significant topic of concern at the Annual Meeting held in 1797 in Franklin County, the first such meeting held in the South. Attended by Brethren from all over the new nation, the Church resolved that slaveholding members should emancipate their slaves. This resolution not withstanding, the issue of slave ownership and hire, as well as the church response to a slave society, continued to plague Brethren into the next century.

The Brethren were not alone in their objection to slavery. In the aftermath of the American Revolution, the paradox of slavery in a free society became apparent to some. Breaking the colonial precedent, where the governor alone had the power to manumit a slave, slaveowners began to exercise that right themselves. The rhetoric of liberty, coupled with a stagnant slave economy, led to a wave of manumissions and a revision of views concerning slavery. A backlash ensued, however, as slaveholders reacted to this threat to their property.

A 1785 law temporarily settled the slavery question by establishing limited manumission while maintaining the institution of slavery. Manumission of a slave could be accomplished by will or affidavit witnessed by two persons and certified in county court. It further prohibited slaveowners from emancipating slaves simply to free themselves of financial obligation, especially in a time of recession, former owners had to support manumitted slaves who were underage or superannuated.

The first federal census taken in 1790 coincides with the closing of the frontier in the Shenandoah Valley. The census reported a total population for Augusta County of 10,886 people, of whom 1,567 were slaves and 59 were free Negroes. In the years that the frontier was settled, the population of African Americans grew at a greater rate than their European American counterparts.

The Scotch-Irish, German, and English who settled frontier Augusta County forged a unique society. Manifestations of that society have been closely examined in everything from government to material culture. The African American presence on the frontier demands further examination. Social and economic opportunities became increasingly limited for free blacks as the frontier developed commercially and the number of slaves grew. Slaves supplied labor. Slave ownership also represented an investment and accorded status—the means for a struggling immigrant to appear "less woodsy." Clearly, with the disappearance of the frontier, Augusta County, like the rest of Virginia, had evolved from "a society with slaves to a slave society." This frontier slave society thus became the model for slavery as it continued to develop within the context of the grain economy in antebellum Augusta County.

Notes

1. Robert Mitchell, *Commercialism and Frontier: Perspectives on the Early Shenandoah Valley* (Charlottesville: Univ. Press of Virginia, 1977), 16.
2. Keep in mind that Augusta County was vast, stretching all the way to the Mississippi River. The county did not reach its present size until the formation of Botetourt County in 1770 and Rockingham and Rockbridge Counties in 1778.
3. James G. Leyburn, *The Scotch-Irish: A Social History* (Chapel Hill: Univ. of North Carolina Press, 1962), 200.
4. Mitchell, *Commercialism and Frontier*, 4. In fact, the usefulness of slavery as labor and as means of income fits Mitchell's concept of a commercial frontier from the onset of settlement.
5. A head count made periodically by the vestry for tax purposes included all males over the age of sixteen and all Negro, Mulatto, and Indian women not free.
6. Augusta County Order Book, 1745–1778, 1: 65 (hereafter cited as AOB).
7. The Reverend William J. Hinke and Charles E. Kemper, eds. "Moravian Diaries of Travels through Virginia," *Virginia Magazine of History and Biography* 7 (1904): 148.
8. Nathaniel Turk McCleskey, "Across the First Divide: Frontiers of Settlement and Culture in Augusta County, Virginia, 1738–1770," (Ph.D. diss.: College of William and Mary, 1990), 161–72. The compelling story of Edward Tarr has

yet to be told in its entirety. McCleskey's use of cadastral maps of colonial Augusta County, however, identifies Edward Tarr as the free Negro blacksmith mentioned in the 1753 Moravian account.

9. AOB 1: 18.
10. Ibid., 1: 216.
11. Augusta County Vestry Book, 1746–1753, 49 (hereafter cited as AVB).
12. AOB 3: 328.
13. James Oakes, *Slavery and Freedom: An Interpretation of the Old South* (New York: Alfred K. Knopf, 1990), 157. Legally, the term "Negro" meant mulatto or Negro. The law deemed anyone a mulatto with one-quarter or more Negro blood, that is one Negro parent or grandparent.
14. William W. Hening, comp., *The Statutes at Large: Being a Collection of All the Laws of Virginia from the First Session of the Legislature in 1619*, 13 vols. (Richmond, New York, and Philadelphia, 1819–23), 10: 565.
15. Augusta County Will Book 1: 424–25 (hereafter cited as AWB).
16. AVB, 118. The term "fit for a servant" often followed the standard contract clause, "meat, drink, washing, and apparel," or was implied if not actually recorded. That which was judged fit for a servant was an extremely coarse existence.
17. AOB 4: 276. Parish and court records, the largest source of information about black men and women on the frontier, too often give an incomplete and skewed account. Running afoul of the law or becoming a burden to the community are the most frequent reasons free Negroes appear in the court record.
18. "Inventory of Joseph Bell, 26 Mar 1760," Bell Family Papers, 1790–1880, Microfilm, formerly held by Special Collections Dept., Univ. of Virginia Library, Charlottesville.
19. AOB 6: 276.
20. Turk McCleskey, "The Mystery of Edward Tarr," paper presented at Virginia Foundation for the Humanities Colloquium, Charlottesville, 1993.
21. It should be noted that slaves made up 96 percent of the African American population of Augusta County by 1790.
22. McCleskey, "Across the First Divide," 152, 155.
23. Frederick Law Olmstead, *A Journey into the Seaboard Slave States* (New York: C. G. Putnam, 1856), 356.
24. John Wayland, "The Germans of the Valley," *Virginia Magazine of History and Biography* 10 (1902): 120.
25. Mitchell, *Commercialism and Frontier*, 129.
26. The Revolution interrupted the supply of indentured servants who were needed to fill the Continental Army's ranks. Slave labor appeared to be the logical alternative to a diminished labor pool.
27. McCleskey, "Across the First Divide," 155.
28. Robert E. Brown and Katharine Brown, *Virginia 1705–1786: Democracy or Aristocracy?* (East Lansing: Michigan State Univ. Press, 1964), 48.
29. AOB 4: 141.
30. Compared to a slave's annual upkeep of just over a pound, indentured servants cost more to maintain annually, at approximately three pounds, but were cheaper to acquire. The legal obligation to provide certain necessities, to teach a trade and certain educational skill, and to pay freedom dues at the end of the indenture combined to make indentured labor the least attractive alternative. Augusta County

inventories show that many indentured servants also expected some sort of goods, such as a horse or saddle, at the end of their employ.

31. AWB 2: 433.
32. Ibid., 1: 165.
33. Ibid., 1: 261.
34. Ibid., 1: 292.
35. Ibid., 1: 140.
36. John Dawson, Letter, Manuscript, Virginia Historical Society, Richmond.
37. AOB 6: 462, 7: 122.
38. Augusta County Minute Book, Aug. 19, 1777, n.p.
39. Freeman H. Hart, *The Valley of Virginia in the American Revolution: 1763–1789* (Chapel Hill: Univ. of North Carolina Press, 1942), 16.
40. Philip J. Schwarz, *Twice Condemned: Slaves and the Criminal Laws of Virginia, 1705–1865* (Baton Rouge: Louisiana State Univ. Press, 1988), 6.
41. AOB 6: 35.
42. Ibid., 8: 324.
43. Ibid., 14: 362.
44. It is interesting to note that a number of shooting deaths caused by white men between 1745 and 1790 were consistently ruled accidental. It appears that the only murder case transferred to Williamsburg involved a group of female suspects.
45. AOB 12: 123.
46. Ibid., 14: 59.
47. Ibid., 13: 72, 109. The meaning of the letters "A" and "G" is unknown. It appears that the two letter were used together to mark each slave.
48. Roger E. Sappington, *The Brethren in Virginia: A History of the Church of the Brethren in Virginia* (Harrisonburg, Va.: The Committee for Brethren History in Virginia, 1973), 61. Although the Brethren framed the question after the American Revolution at a time when many Americans questioned the existence of slavery, it is safe to say that their concern was independent of the public debate.

Works Cited

Augusta County Minute Book, 1750–1777. Augusta County Courthouse, Staunton, Va.

Augusta County Miscellaneous Papers. Augusta County Courthouse, Staunton, Va.

Augusta County Order Book, 1745–1778. Augusta County Courthouse, Staunton, Va.

Augusta County Parish Vestry Book, 1746–1753. Augusta County Courthouse, Staunton, Va.

Augusta County Will Book, 1745–1753. Augusta County Courthouse, Staunton, Va.

Bell Family Papers, 1790–1880. Microfilm. Formerly held by Special Collections Dept.. Univ. of Virginia Library, Charlottesville.

Brown, Robert E., and B. Katharine. *Virginia 1705–1786: Democracy or Aristocracy?* East Lansing: Michigan State Univ. Press, 1964.

Dawson, John. Letter. Manuscript. Virginia Historical Society, Richmond.

Hart, Freeman H. *The Valley of Virginia in the American Revolution: 1763–1789.* Chapel Hill: Univ. of North Carolina Press, 1942.

Hening, William W., compiler. *The Statutes at Large: Being a Collection of All the Laws of Virginia from the First Session of the Legislature in 1619.* 13 vols. Richmond, New York, and Philadelphia, 1819–1823.

Hinke, The Reverend William J., and Charles E. Kemper, editors. "Moravian Diaries of Travels through Virginia." *Virginia Magazine of History and Biography* 7 (1904): 134–53.

Leyburn, James G. *The Scotch-Irish: A Social History.* Chapel Hill: Univ. of North Carolina Press, 1962.

McCleskey, Nathaniel Turk. "Across the First Divide: Frontiers of Settlement and Culture in Augusta County, Virginia." Ph.D. diss., College of William and Mary, 1990.

———. "The Mystery of Edward Tarr." Paper presented at Virginia Foundation for the Humanities and Public Policy, Charlottesville, 1993.

Mitchell, Robert D. *Commercialism and Frontier: Perspectives on the Early Shenandoah Valley.* Charlottesville: Univ. Press of Virginia, 1977.

Oakes, James. *Slavery and Freedom: An Interpretation of the Old South.* New York: Alfred K. Knopf, 1990.

Olmstead, Frederick Law. *A Journey into the Seaboard Slave States.* New York: C. G. Putnam, 1856.

Sappington, Roger E. *The History of the Church of the Brethren in Virginia.* Harrisonburg, Va.: The Committee for Brethren History in Virginia, 1973.

Schwarz, Philip J. *Twice Condemned: Slaves and the Criminal Laws of Virginia, 1705–1865.* Baton Rouge: Louisiana State Univ. Press, 1988.

Wayland, John W. "The Germans of the Valley." *Virginia Magazine of History and Biography* 10 (1902): 120–42.

Chapter 7

The Shape of Slavery on Virginia's Kentucky Frontier, 1775–1800

Ellen Eslinger

In 1778, the Virginia General Assembly received a petition from Kentuckian Nathaniel Henderson requesting recompense for one of his bondsmen. This slave, whose name was London, had been killed when a British-led force of more than four hundred Indians besieged Boonesborough for nine days earlier that year. With fewer than forty men in the fort, the commanding officer of the militia had ordered Henderson's slave to a sentry post in a log building used as a kitchen, near an embankment where the enemy was trying to tunnel under the fort's timber walls. In the nighttime stillness, the inhabitants of Boonesborough could hear the digging beneath them. London took several shots at the enemy, until the bright flash from his gun betrayed his location to sharpshooters. He was one of two American casualties.[1]

What was London doing at Boonesborough? Was his death mourned by a wife and children? Does his participation in the community's defense indicate that slaves on the frontier held a closer status with whites—a greater equality wrought by conditions of extreme danger? Did the ability to use a gun and proximity to expanses of wilderness facilitate making a bid for freedom? Did the frontier create special conditions for slaves, and, if so, how were these conditions regarded by the slaves themselves?

Most studies of slavery in Kentucky address the antebellum years, merely noting the arrival of blacks during the settlement period.[2] Given the much greater abundance of source material for the nineteenth century, this emphasis is understandable. But it encourages a tendency to project antebellum patterns of slavery back to an earlier period. In some settings the distinction between frontier and later periods might not be too problematic, but Virginia's Kentucky frontier involved extraordinary isolation and danger. Historians have shown that these conditions affected every aspect of daily life for white settlers. It therefore seems reasonable to consider that the frontier also created a special situation for black pioneers, different from slavery as it existed elsewhere in the late eighteenth century and from slavery as it later existed in nineteenth-century Kentucky.

Blacks figured among the very earliest of the trans-Appalachian settlers. The first effort to establish a permanent settlement in Kentucky, led by Daniel Boone in 1773, was aborted after Boone's eldest son and another young man were killed by Indians. How many blacks accompanied the Boone party is unknown, but surviving the ambush was a slave named Shadrach who led Boone to the bodies.[3] At Harrodsburg, established in 1774 and the first permanent Anglo-American settlement in Kentucky, a tally of the inhabitants in early 1777 revealed that, in addition to the eighty-five adult white males and twenty-six white women, there were twelve slaves over age ten and seven black children. Similarly, St. Asaph's, another of the important early settlements, had twenty-five men, seventy-four women and children, and twenty blacks in 1780.[4] Slaves thus constituted a significant portion of the frontier population long before the appearance of staple agriculture. By 1790, Kentucky slaves numbered more than twelve thousand, with another three thousand in Tennessee. By the end of the century, Kentucky alone had more than forty thousand slaves (18.3 percent of the total population). Moreover, western slavery was broadly based. More than thirty-two thousand Kentuckians owned slaves in 1800, roughly one-quarter of all householders, a level comparable to much of the seaboard South.[5]

Western slavery appeared early and grew rapidly because frontier conditions were extremely conducive to unfree labor. Bringing wilderness land under cultivation required large quantities of unskilled labor, but few free laborers would work for wages when land was readily available for sale or rent on easy terms. Western employers complained that "White servants are difficult to be had, and indifferent when procured, and expect at all times to be [seated] at the same table with their masters." With free labor in short supply, slavery presented a very attractive alternative. Those westerners who could not afford to purchase a prime adult male for eighty to one hundred pounds might choose to hire one for ten to eighteen pounds annually, plus clothing and taxes.[6] These rates were considerably higher than those in other parts of the United States. Nonetheless, "Negroes hire very well in this country," reported a Kentuckian to a prospective immigrant.[7] Thus, the proportion of westerners with an interest in slavery extended beyond the number of actual owners. When Kentucky became a state in 1792, there existed enough support for slavery to overcome a strong church-based emancipation movement. Indeed, Kentucky was the first state to grant slavery constitutional protection.[8]

The prospect of a trans-Appalachian migration was probably regarded with dread by most slaves. The trip itself presented untold miseries. The primary route during the early years was the famous Wilderness Road, a steep pathway too narrow for anything wider than packhorses. Land speculator John May, traveling in 1780 without the burden of a family and household belongings, made the passage in only ten days but reported that it had been "through an uninhabited Country the most rugged and dismal I ever passed through, there being thousands of dead Horses & Cattle on the Road Side which occasioned a continual Stench; and one Half the way there were no Springs." The worst part for May and for most other travelers was the "continual apprehension we were under, of an Attack from the Indians, there not being one Day after we left Holston, but News was brought us of some Murders being committed by those Savages."[9]

Descent down the Ohio River was also unsafe and unpleasant. In addition to treacherous sections of water, the Indian territory along the northern shore posed great danger, and major parts of the journey were still overland. When nineteen of John Breckinridge's slaves left for Kentucky in March 1792, they encountered snow or rain every day. The cart carrying their belongings and supplies broke down before reaching the designated point of departure on the Ohio River. The overseer reported that the slaves were "Every day out of heart & Sick." He kept them moving on only by providing hourly doses of whiskey.[10] Whatever route was chosen, the westward journey was usually harder for slaves because, in contrast to many white migrants, slaves usually walked the overland sections. A boy living on the main road between the Ohio River and Lexington during the 1790s, for instance, noted the passing of "great wagons, laden with merchandise for the interior; the caravans of travelers, mounted on horseback; and the gangs of negroes on foot—all moving south."[11]

But much more painful than the journey was the prospect of separation from friends and relations. Most slaves were probably unwilling pioneers, brought to the frontier by their owner's initiative rather than their own. They were not, however, necessarily passive migrants. Perhaps because of the enormity of the separation involved, some slaves were able to influence migration decisions made by their masters. For example, a Williamsburg man in 1780 refused an excellent price for a black woman and her two children because the prospective buyer "was going to settle in Cantuckey and she beg'd off—otherwise I believe I shu'd have taken it."[12] In another instance, Henry Bedinger of Berkeley County, Virginia, wrote his brother in Kentucky, "You request me to send out your Negro Woman Sarah[.] I will attempt it but this cannot be done instantly for the inclement weather will not permit the taking her Two youngest Children and without them I suppose she would not go."[13] When John Breckinridge had a party of slaves in Fincastle County preparing to embark for Kentucky, his mother-in-law, Mary Cabell, attempted to send some others with the group. Wrote Cabell, "I did my best to send little Sarah there to go with them but Violet would not agree to part with her so I proposed for her to go with her daughter." Violet was "as good a slave as Ever was born," wrote Cabell, "how ever she said she would not go to Cantuckey nor let Sarah untill I deye'd unless Stephen her Husband could go with them." Negotiations were therefore undertaken to purchase Stephen from a neighboring planter and kinsman.[14] Even masters less caring of their slaves' happiness probably attempted to win their cooperation, if only in the interest of discipline.

When persuasion failed, some slaves made desperate attempts to avoid separation. For example, a western Virginia newspaper included an advertisement in 1794 for the return of a slave named Tom whose owner had given him permission to visit his wife, the property of a man named Botts, living in another county. But as Tom's master later discovered, Botts had already departed for Kentucky. Tom's owner declared in a newspaper advertisement: "I very much suspect that he intends pursuing his rout [sic] to Kentucky, where the abovementioned Botts is about to carry his wife."[15] Two years later, also in the same newspaper, appeared the tragic story of "old Negro Sam," a slave estimated to be about seventy years old and the property of Colonel John Sinkers in Fauquier County. Sinkers described Sam as a gardener, "well dressed, a great talker," who, on account of old age, "stoops much in walking." Sinkers had given Old Sam a pass to visit his wife, the property of a Major Read living near Winchester. Only later did Sinkers discover that Read had moved to Kentucky. In the advertisement, Sinkers stated his belief that Old Sam had followed, "imprudent enough to pursue her as far as his strength will permit."[16] Similarly, in 1789, a slave whose owner had moved to Kentucky was hired to ironmaster Henry Miller in the Shenandoah Valley, but was captured on the mouth of the Kanawha River by none other than Daniel Boone.[17] Even after the migration to Kentucky, a few slaves persisted in attempting to reunite with loved ones. A notice published in the *Kentucky Gazette* in 1788 described some runaway slaves and mentioned that they had recently come to Kentucky from Cumberland County, Virginia. A newspaper in Staunton alerted Virginians that a slave named Aaron had run away from a Colonel Barbee and was probably headed for Fredericksburg.[18]

Slaves in larger holdings did not necessarily escape the pain of separation from family and friends. The undeveloped character of the trans-Appalachian economy during the frontier period could not support large agricultural operations. Although the Bluegrass region of central Kentucky and adjacent areas held excellent prospects for staple agriculture, until 1795 the Spanish authorities at New Orleans effectively prevented western Americans from exporting produce down the Mississippi River. In the meantime, large slaveowners could engage only a portion of their slaves in frontier agriculture. One method for dealing with this problem was to hire out slaves to settlers in need of extra labor. Though not permanently separating slave kin, the hiring agreement was often on an annual basis and negotiated by the master. Other large slaveholders apparently sold slaves off before embarking for the western settlements. Virginian Hubbard Taylor of Orange County, for example, owned nine adult slaves and fourteen between age twelve and sixteen in 1788. The following year, on the eve of departure for Kentucky, his holdings had shrunk to only five adults and one slave between twelve and sixteen years old. With extremely few exceptions, trans-Appalachian migration meant major separations for slaves.[19]

Safe arrival in Kentucky provided no guarantee that surviving slave relationships would remain intact. On the contrary, tax records for western counties suggest a lively intraregional slave market. The most readily apparent evidence may be found in the number of white pioneers who did not become slaveholders until after their arrival in Kentucky. In Madison County, where settlement commenced with Boonesborough in 1775, at least 13.4 percent of the slaveholders listed in 1792 had not owned slaves five years earlier. In Woodford County, the proportion was 10 percent.[20]

Other Kentucky central counties, typically characterized by lush Bluegrass soils, probably experienced similar rates of increase.

In addition to new slaveowners were the pioneers who had brought slaves and later added further to their holdings. Tax records reveal that numerous individual slaveholdings increased in ways which cannot be reasonably accounted for by natural increase. For example, the slave holdings of William Miller Sr. of Madison County increased from one adult slave in 1787 to three adults and one slave below age sixteen by 1792. Similarly, Aaron Lewis had two adults and one young slave in 1787; five years later he had four adults and two young slaves. The many new slaveholders and the number of slaveholders whose slaves abruptly increased points to an active frontier slave trade. Of 247 Madison County slaveowners in 1792, 101 had resided there in 1787. Of these, 48 (47.5 percent) had apparently bought slaves in the intervening years. Other counties reveal a similar pattern. Woodford County, an area where staple agriculture was already beginning, marks the higher end of the scale. Of 348 slaveholders in 1792, 104 had resided there since 1787, 60 (57.5 percent) of whom showed a pattern of change indicating slave purchases. Tracing a small, randomly selected sample of individual slaveholders annually through this five-year period suggests that most of the slave purchases occurred after around 1790, as the Kentucky economy entered a period of prosperity.[21]

Moreover, these figures represent a minimum level of activity. Some slave purchases are disguised by patterns of growth possibly caused by natural increase. A holding which changed from one adult slave and two children to two adults and one child, for example, could have been due to the purchase of an adult and the death of a child, but it can also be explained by the passage of time and the natural life course. Such cases were therefore excluded from the analysis. Secondly, the tax records from which these figures were derived do not begin until 1787, after more than a decade of western settlement. Some Kentuckians had already bought slaves by then, obscuring the actual extent of western slave trading. For example, Pressley Anderson came to Kentucky with next to nothing, described by a fellow pioneer as arriving at Strode's Station sometime around 1780 barefooted, with his young wife and young child. Yet, by 1787 Anderson owned two young slaves. How many other pioneers bought slaves during this early period is impossible to determine. Nonetheless, that settlers of modest means like Anderson lost little time in purchasing slaves underscores the importance of slavery in newly settled areas.[22]

To what extent did western slavery grow as a result of an interregional slave trade with the seaboard states? During the eighteenth century, most slaves probably came with their owners rather than with dealers, as Allan Kulikoff has argued. Still, the strong frontier demand for labor was a matter of general public knowledge.[23] During the constitutional debates at Philadelphia in 1787, George Mason pointed out, "The western people are already calling for slaves for their new lands."[24] Other scattered references also raise the possibility that the internal slave trade operated from an early date. In 1792, for example, Knoxville merchant James Miller advertised goods recently brought from Philadelphia and Richmond, including "a few young, likely Virginia born Negroes." And an inhabitant of Williamsburg in 1780 wrote of a man in town who was "daily expected to purchase Young Negros for the Gent men whos going to Cantuckey." Whether this incident involved slave purchases for personal use or for resale is impossible to tell, but the opportunities for profit make the latter possibility all the more likely. Particularly suggestive is a letter from Kentuckian Richard Woolfolk to his brother in Virginia. Woolfolk introduced the carrier of the letter, Ambrose Young, and explained, "he comes in to p[ur]chase negroes."[25]

The strong western demand for slave labor boosted price levels significantly. By the early 1790s, an adult male slave that might sell for seventy pounds in Virginia, sold for a hundred pounds in Kentucky.[26] The ready market for slaves encouraged at least some prospective migrants to bring surplus slaves for western sale. William Christian, for instance, warned his mother, who was preparing to leave her home in Virginia's Botetourt County and join him in Kentucky, that the western economy was so utterly devoid of cash that it was difficult to make any kind of purchase. The only items readily accepted in lieu of cash were slaves. Christian advised, "Unless you can sell in Botetourt to get some good working Negroes & money to bring with you you had better remain where you are." Kentucky lawyer John Breckinridge likewise advised a prospective settler, "Negroes would exchange well for lands, or sell for cash."[27] Slaves were among the most liquid of western assets.

If an organized interregional slave trade dates to the late eighteenth century, as Steven Deyle suggested in his study of its origins, the weak western economy kept the volume low.[28] As long as the trans-Appalachian West lacked ready access to export markets, the region's economic growth remained severely restricted. Traders of imported goods needed to receive payment in a form acceptable to their eastern creditors. Without cash or an export market where produce could be readily converted to cash, an interregional slave trade could not thrive. Even prosperous westerners, such as William Christian, found it difficult to meet the cash terms required for long-distance trade. The pressure on western money reserves diminished

somewhat during the early 1790s because the flood of immigration remained high and the federal government's purchasing of supplies for western military campaigns brought cash into the region. Unfortunately, this
spell of relative prosperity proved temporary. Only with the opening of
New Orleans to American trade did Kentuckians finally gain an adequate
circulation of currency.

Other factors also discouraged the development of an interregional
slave trade, though probably less severely. As part of Virginia, Kentucky
was subject after 1778 to slave import restrictions, which were reinforced a decade later with a second law specifically pertaining to the
District of Kentucky. Immigrants from outside Virginia were required
to take an oath that slaves brought into the Commonwealth were intended for personal use and not for resale.[29] The oath was duly administered, although whether such laws proved an effective deterrent is hard
to say. In any case, the restriction did not apply to internal migration
from Virginia, the primary source of western slaves. The uncertain legal future of western slavery also worked as a deterrent. In contrast to
other states, Kentucky's religious culture was dominated by evangelical
denominations that were sympathetic toward emancipation, creating a
political atmosphere that gave some prospective settlers who owned
slaves reason for pause. While making plans to migrate in 1792, John
Breckinridge confessed, "I am somewhat afraid of the Kentucky politi-
cians with respect to negroes." Similarly, in 1798, a new settler named
David Meade believed that western support of emancipation was strong
enough that "I would not advise Slaveholders to come here immediately." Emancipation stood as Kentucky's most controversial political
issue, dominating the state constitutional debates in 1792 and 1799.[30]

With opposing sets of conditions in the West, the development of
an interregional slave trade may ultimately prove to have had as much
to do with conditions in the seaboard states as in the West. Agricultural change and high rates of natural increase among Virginia slaves
were important factors in the expansion of the slave trade in the nineteenth century, but how early did they begin to exert an effect? "Push"
factors have usually been overshadowed by the "pull" of frontier opportunity. Yet, they should not be dismissed without a fuller understanding of the conditions facing slaveowners in the older settlements during
the post-Revolutionary decades.[31]

Most western immigrants were people of modest means who probably
took with them whatever slaves they had or found readily available, but
scattered evidence suggests a preference for slaves in their mid-teens or

twenties. Slaves of this age presumably appealed to western masters because they offered a nearly adult capacity for labor with a minimum of disruption in child care and family life. Kentuckian James Davis of Lincoln County, for example, sought to purchase slaves in 1789 through his friend Zachariah Johnson, then representing Rockbridge County in the Virginia Assembly. Davis sent cash and requested that, when Johnston next went to Richmond, he "purchase a young Negroe fellow between Sixteen & twenty & a girl between twelve & Eighteen if you can procure them." If money was left over, Johnston was asked also to buy a "Small One."[32] Another Kentuckian requested his brother in Virginia to send grass seed, a still, and "a Negro boy likely as Common Between the age of 15 and 25."[33] Similarly, a 1794 newspaper advertisement in Winchester, Virginia, offered "A very likely, lively and healthy NEGRO MAN not more than twenty years old. He has been used to plantation work only . . . I believe he would suit a person moving to the Western Country, as well as any Negro whatever."[34] When a British immigrant named Harry Toulmin met several members of Virginia's prominent Taylor family, one of these wealthy men told of having started a second plantation near Louisville where he had sent twenty-one "children of his slaves."[35] Other studies of slave migration to newly settled areas, both before and after the trans-Appalachian settlement, likewise reveal a general preference for younger slaves.[36]

Also in keeping with findings for other slave frontiers, trans-Appalachian masters demonstrated no discernible preference for male over female slaves. Probate inventories in two sample counties reveal balanced sex ratios. Woodford County inventories recorded between 1787 and 1800 include thirty adult males and thirty-one adult females. In Madison County, the figures were thirty-one males and thirty-four females. In Bourbon County probate inventories for roughly the same period, the number of adult men and women stood even at forty-seven each.[37] Clearing land for agriculture placed the greatest pressure on unskilled labor, and its arduous nature made male slaves especially valuable. Yet, female slaves also could serve as field workers, plus they usually cost less. The value of an adult female slave in Kentucky probate inventories ranged between sixty-five and eighty-five pounds, compared to from eighty-five to one hundred pounds for a male.[38] Late-eighteenth-century masters probably also valued female slaves for their reproductive capabilities, but in newly settled areas such as Kentucky immediate labor requirements probably overshadowed long-term concerns.

Since most slaves arrived in Kentucky as they were entering their childbearing years, the youthful character of western slavery fostered by the selective migration process persisted as the pioneer generation began bearing children.[39] In Fayette County, one of the earliest counties to make the transition from frontier outpost to staple agriculture, 53.2 percent of the slaves recorded on the 1787 tax lists were below age sixteen. By 1800, the proportion had edged upward to 54.2 percent. Neighboring Bourbon County experienced a similar trend. There, 53.1 percent of the slaves were below age sixteen in 1787; fifteen years later the proportion was 55.6 percent. In Madison County, the change was slightly more pronounced, increasing from 52.1 percent to 57.7 percent in 1800. The rapid growth of the western slave population resulting from the skewed age structure of the pioneer generation, combined with the balanced sex ratio, may partially explain why an interregional slave trade is not more evident during the eighteenth century. In any case, it certainly helped provide slaves for subsequent frontiers, as Kentucky's labor requirements declined in the years following the War of 1812.

Slavery on Virginia's trans-Appalachian frontier was shaped not only by the selective migration process, but also by a second factor: the hostile relationship between Anglo-Americans and native people. Whereas later settlement expansion would be carefully supervised by the federal government, the first trans-Appalachian settlements coincided with the Revolutionary War and the weak Confederation government. Also, the northern Amerindian peoples during this period were well armed and supplied by the British in the Great Lakes region, as were the southern Indians by the Spanish. The prolonged Indian wars dominated western life for nearly two decades, until General Wayne's victory at Fallen Timbers in 1794. The danger affected western slaves in three basic ways: personal survival, material conditions, and social organization.

The racial attitudes of Amerindians toward blacks is insufficiently understood. Compared to whites, blacks in early Kentucky may have been less likely to be killed, probably due to their unarmed condition rather than skin color.[40] Clearly black casualties occurred. Settler Samuel Shepherd of Georgetown, for example, noted in his diary several local incidents involving slaves. On June 1, 1788, Shepard noted that "a Young Man named George Gibson was killed and a Negro taken by the Indians about one mile from where I was at work in the woods." A year later, on August 9, 1789, "The Indians killed two Negro children this day near the Crossings meeting house . . . and wounded two large ones who survived." On August 29, 1792, Shepard commented on "considerable mischief" by Indians in the last two days. Four men were dead, five slaves captured, and one Indian had been killed by a white woman. A pursuit party retook the slaves and killed one more Indian.[41] Shepard's journal indicates that slaves had just as much cause for fear as did their white owners.

One response to the danger was training in the use of firearms. An inhabitant stated that during the siege of Boonesborough in 1778, when London was killed, "arms & ammunition were given to the negroe men."[42] The absence of any additional explanation suggests that this was not an extraordinary practice during crisis situations and, further, that black men had experience with firearms even if they did not normally possess them. At least some frontier slaves handled guns routinely. An early white pioneer named William McBride, for example, told of "Old" Joseph Gray, an early settler near modern Nashville. Gray made his settlement "with his negroes alone, whom he armed." According to this informant, Gray was attacked once and the slaves "made good soldiers." One of them, a slave named Chick, was described as a "good woodsman."[43]

The extent to which such individuals shared in the general defense is impossible to gauge, but frontier narratives preserve at least a few episodes of heroic action. One instance occurred when a cabin was attacked by a small group of Indians in early 1783 near a place called the Crab Orchard. The only adults home at the time were the mistress and an ailing male slave. They quickly moved to secure the door, but one Indian managed to squeeze in. The slave "presented his gun at the Indian," who grabbed it. The two grappled until the slave stunned the intruder with sharp blows to the head. He then rushed to help with the door, telling his mistress to dispatch the prone Indian with the broad ax, which she did. Meanwhile, the other Indians were using their tomahawks against the door and hacking at the cabin's crude wooden chimney in order to shoot in. The slave boldly proposed that they be let in one at a time. He would wrestle them to the ground and hold them until the mistress could kill them with the ax. Fortunately, however, help arrived from neighbors.[44]

In a few instances, heroic action brought freedom. The most famous case involved a slave named Monk, the property of Captain James Estill. In early 1782, a group of Wyandot Indians approached Estill's fortified settlement, killing a white girl and capturing Monk. They intended to attack the fort and could have easily succeeded but withdrew instead, largely because Monk exaggerated the number of defenders. As soon as possible, Estill organized a militia party to pursue the would-be attackers. When they closed, Monk helped again by shouting assurances that the Wyandots did not outnumber the whites. A vicious battle ensued, during which Estill was killed, and Monk used the confusion to escape. He also saved one of Estill's wounded men, carrying him some forty miles back to the settlement. Monk's new owner, Wallace Estill, freed him as a reward for his loyalty and valor.[45]

Surprisingly seldom did western blacks use their proximity to wilderness as a means of achieving freedom. One of the few recorded instances occurred in 1780 and involved a slave belonging to a prominent land speculator named John May. When May went away on business he left his slave at Louisville, where he "fell in with some worthless Negroes who persuaded him to run away & attempt to get with the Indians." After thrashing about in the woods for ten days, May's slave returned to Louisville. Although not the kind of outcome that would encourage emulation, the incident led May to believe that Kentucky "would be a bad place to bring Slaves to, being so near . . . Indians that they will frequently find their way to them."[46] May's concern, however, proved without much foundation. Opportunities for escape certainly existed and were sometimes taken, but the generally hostile relations with Native Americans made such initiatives risky. Black assimilation to Euro-American culture may have also played a part, as suggested by the following incident. During Indian negotiations at Fort Greenville, Colonel John Grant encountered a slave woman whom he recognized as having been captured some years earlier from his neighborhood and he tried to gain her release. Whether her Indian captors were amenable is not related, but she refused to abandon the four children she had given birth to since her capture. If her children were allowed to go with her, she told Grant, "She wo'd rather live w[ith] white people."[47]

Kentucky settlement involved numerous hardships and dangers, and this was especially true for slaves. Masters often sent their slaves ahead to build a cabin and prepare land for farming so that when white family members arrived they would not have to begin from scratch. For example, when Colonel Abram Bowman returned to Virginia in 1778, he left behind a male slave at Harrodsburg to tend the crops. Such practices often exposed slaves to extreme danger. In 1780 Nathaniel Hart, a prominent member of Boonesborough, left for the Nashville area, at that time a dangerous frontier. Hart took along slaves belonging to his brother Thomas, apparently to clear land belonging to them both. Thomas Hart soon wrote to Nathaniel, "I apprehend Our people at your Station [are] in eminent danger of being all cut off as it is So very weak and Such Numbers of Indians in the Country[.] [W]ere they free people I dont know that it would give me Any uneasiness, but to Send a parcel of poor Slaves where I dare not go myself [should anything happen] I fear it would prove a great drawback on my future happiness in this Life." The eagerness to open new land nonetheless prevailed. Other sources also make mention of slaves living on their own in exposed locations. An early Kentuckian named John Bruce, for example, erected a small cabin in Bourbon County and left a man and woman slave there to open the land for cultivation, arranging for hunters to occasionally supply them with meat. How long they remained there is unknown, but one day the man was discovered scalped and tomahawked, and the woman was missing and supposed taken prisoner.[48]

Slaves also endured harsher conditions because of their inferior status in the frontier household, as illustrated by the fate of Bob, the property of a prominent early settler named John Floyd. In November of 1779, Bob slipped and severely wounded himself in the foot with an ax while erecting a cabin for Floyd. Throughout one of the harshest winters, Bob languished in a temporary shelter, perhaps the same shelter previously used by Floyd and his family. Frostbite led to gangrene, and, "reduced to a mere skeleton," Bob finally died three months after receiving his injury. Floyd and his young family, meanwhile, spent the winter huddled in the cabin. No doubt conditions were miserable, as they were for all westerners that particular winter, but the suffering experienced by the Floyds can hardly compare to what Bob endured before he finally expired.[49]

Frontier conditions also affected slave life by reducing opportunities for black socializing and family formation. Because the majority of slaves lived in holdings of five or fewer, most western blacks had to look beyond their master's household for a spouse. In some parts of Kentucky slaves were extremely dispersed. In Madison County, where Boonesborough was located, for example, forty-two (44 percent) slaveowners owned only one slave in 1787; 83 percent owned five or less. The average slaveholding unit remained small throughout the eighteenth century, measuring only 4.39 statewide in 1800. Moreover, approximately one-fifth of western slaveowners had only a single slave. By this time the emergence of staple crop production, particularly hemp and tobacco, was beginning to have an effect in some areas, but most slave masters still owned only a single slave, or perhaps two.[50] The dispersed pattern of slaveowning meant that many western slaves lived in relative social isolation from other blacks. Those residing in outlying settlements still vulnerable to Indian attack were particularly isolated.

How western blacks coped with this situation remains largely a mystery, but the journal of a young Kentucky settler named James Taylor, the son of a prominent Virginia planter, provides a rare glimpse of its importance for western slaves. After a brief stay with his brother, Hubbard Taylor, who had settled in Clark County three years earlier, James Taylor retraced part of his route to reach lands given to him by his father on the Kentucky shore of the Ohio River near modern Newport. With him were his body servant, Adam (aged seventeen), and two adult male slaves, Moses and Humphrey. That first year, 1793, Taylor and his slaves cleared roughly fifteen acres and planted it in corn. One day, Moses approached his master and said that he and his fellow servants could not remain in Newport because "there are no colored people here, we have no women to wash for us, on Sundays we stalk about without being able to talk to any one." Moses urged Taylor to sell his land and move to the densely settled area where Hubbard Taylor lived. Taylor replied, "Moses, I am a stranger as well as you and my servants. I have good land here on a fine river. I have no land there and you will in time have many black people here for neighbors." Moses found it hard to believe that such an isolated place would ever be better. Taylor urged patience. "Depend on it we will reap the advantages in due time," he told Moses, "We can raise four times as much corn and every kind of produce as we could in Virginia, on those poor worn out lands we have left." Taylor's future may have looked promising, but Moses and his fellow bondsmen had less to look forward to. They ran away a short time later when Taylor went to spend a weekend with neighbors. Although Taylor's land lay on the southern banks of the Ohio River, his slaves ran toward slavery rather than away from it, retracing their way to Hubbard Taylor's large plantation. Their destination being readily surmised, they were soon caught. No women joined Taylor's men for at least another four years.[51]

The material presented here sketches a few ways in which slavery on Virginia's Kentucky frontier differed from slavery elsewhere during this period. The two most important factors shaping western slavery were the selective migration process and the danger of Indian attack. Much more work remains to be done before the effect of these and other influencing factors can be fully understood. Yet, a few broad conclusions may be drawn. First and foremost, instead of regarding slavery as contrary to the norm in newly settled areas, the reverse is probably more accurate. Slavery thrived on American frontiers wherever it was not prohibited by national law because of the virtually insatiable demand for the unskilled labor needed in opening new land for agriculture. Virginia's trans-Appalachian frontier was no exception; slavery appeared early in Kentucky and grew rapidly. Second, slaves regarded movement to frontier places very differently than did their white owners. Slaves had little to gain yet shared all the risks and discomfort of western life. They exercised limited influence in making the decision to migrate and were subject to a much greater degree of social up-heaval—at the point of departure, from resale in the West, and as a result of geographic dispersal in small slaveholdings. Third, due to the migration process, the frontier slave population was characterized by a skewed age structure (as was the white population). This, and the balanced sex ratios, enabled the frontier generation of slaves to reproduce rapidly. Whether re-production occurred in a family setting seems doubtful, however, consid-ering the typically small size of western slaveholdings and the active re-gional slave trade.

Much remains to be learned about slavery on the early national fron-tier, especially regarding matters such as daily living conditions and mas-ter-slave relationships. Most intriguing of all, though far beyond the scope of this brief essay, is the possibility that the frontier experience left a lasting imprint among black pioneers commensurate with that left among whites. Just as Virginia's trans-Appalachian frontier was an important episode in subsequent American settlement, it could eventually prove to have been equally important for understanding the course of American slavery, espe-cially in Kentucky. At the very least, the material presented here seriously challenges J. Winston Coleman's classic statement that slavery during Kentucky's frontier period was "the mildest that existed anywhere in the world."[52]

Notes

This work was supported in part by grants from the Virginia Center for the Hu-manities and Public Policy and from the James Madison University Program of Grants for Faculty Assistance. Earlier versions were presented at the University of Chicago Economic History Workshop and published in the Winter 1994 issue of the *Register of the Kentucky Historical Society*, where it received the Rich-ard H. Collins Award for best article.

1. James Rood Robertson, *Petitions of the Early Inhabitants of Kentucky to the Gen-eral Assembly of Virginia, 1769 to 1792*, Filson Club Publication 27 (Louisville: John P. Morton and Co., 1914), 44–45. The siege is depicted in numerous his-tories of Kentucky, but see John Mack Faragher, *Daniel Boone, The Life and Leg-end of an American Pioneer* (New York: Henry Holt and Co., 1992), 183–90. Pompey, who served as a translator for the Shawnee, also played a key role in this event. He too died during the siege. Ted Franklin Belen, "Did Daniel Boone Kill Pompey, the Black Shawnee, at the 1778 Siege of Boonesborough?" *Filson Club History Quarterly* 67 (1993): 5–22.

2. The classic work is J. Winston Coleman Jr., *Slavery Times in Kentucky* (Chapel Hill: Univ. of North Carolina Press, 1940). See also Ivan E. McDougle, *Slavery in Kentucky 1792–1865* (Lancaster, Pa.: Press of the New Era Printing Co., 1918); Marion B. Lucas and George C. Wright, *A History of Blacks in Kentucky*, 2 vols. (Frankfort: Kentucky Historical Society, 1992). The situation is similar

for Tennessee, but the frontier has been treated as a distinctive phase in the following two works: Anita S. Goodstein, "Black History on the Nashville Frontier, 1780–1810," *Tennessee Historical Quarterly* 38 (1979): 401–20; Edward Michael McCormack, *Slavery on the Tennessee Frontier* (Nashville: Tennessee American Revolution Bicentennial Commission, 1977).

3. William Stewart Lester, *The Transylvania Colony* (Spencer, Ind.: Samuel R. Guard and Co., 1935), 46.

4. "Col. William Fleming's Journal in Kentucky from Nov. 10, 1779 to May 27th 1780," in *Travels in the American Colonies*, ed. Newton D. Mereness (New York: The MacMillan Co., 1916), 654.

5. Joan Wells Coward, *Kentucky in the New Republic: The Process of Constitution Making* (Lexington: Univ. Press of Kentucky, 1979), 63.

6. Harry Toulmin, *The Western Country in 1793, Reports on Kentucky and Virginia*, ed. Marion Tinling and Godfrey Davis (San Marino, Calif.: Henry E. Huntington Library, 1948), 65. All prices are given in Virginia currency.

7. Samuel Meredith to John Breckinridge, May 17, 1792, Breckinridge Family Papers, Library of Congress, Washington, D.C.

8. Coward, *Kentucky in the New Republic*, 36–45.

9. John May, Kentucky County, to Samuel Beall, Williamsburg, Apr. 15, 1780. Beall-Booth Family Papers, The Filson Club Historical Society, Louisville, Ky.

10. George Thompson to John Breckinridge, June 14, 1792, Breckinridge Family Papers.

11. Daniel Drake, *Pioneer Life in Kentucky* (New York: Henry Schuman, 1948), 176.

12. A. Drummond, Williamsburg, to John Coles, Petersburg, Mar. 13, 1780, Carter-Smith Family Papers (no. 1729), Special Collections Dept., Univ. of Virginia Library, Charlottesville.

13. Henry Bedinger to George Michael Bedinger, Feb. 1792, in Danske Dandridge, *George Michael Bedinger, A Kentucky Pioneer* (Charlottesville: The Michie Co., 1909), 155.

14. Mary Cabell to Mary ("Polly") H. Breckinridge, Apr. 6, 1799, Breckinridge Family Papers.

15. *Virginia Centinel and Gazette Or, the Winchester Repository*, Winchester, Va., Nov. 3, 1794.

16. Ibid., May 6, 1796.

17. *Kentucky Gazette*, Lexington, Ky., June 14, 1790.

18. Ibid., July 5, 1788. *The Staunton Spy*, Staunton, Va., Feb. 1, 1794. Additional information concerning these two runaways may be found in a letter written by James Wilson (Cumberland County) to Benjamin Wilson (near Danville), Aug. 25, 1788, Benjamin Wilson Papers, Univ. of Kentucky Library, Lexington.

19. Orange County, Virginia, Personal Property Tax Lists, Library of Virginia, Richmond. On slave efforts to maintain contact with separated kin, see the fascinating study by Gail S. Terry, "Sustaining the Bonds of Kinship in a Trans-Appalachian Migration, 1790–1811: The Cabell-Breckinridge Slaves Move West," *Virginia Magazine of History and Biography* 102 (1994): 456–76.

20. These figures were derived from county tax lists on microfilm at the Kentucky Historical Society in Frankfort. Northern Madison County, where the preponderance of inhabitants concentrated, and Woodford County both lay within the fertile Bluegrass region. The Woodford area was settled more slowly due to

188   Ellen Eslinger

greater exposure to danger from Indians. Regional variation was quite pronounced during the early settlement period and future research will have to include a greater distribution of counties.

21. Ellen T. Eslinger, "The Great Revival in Bourbon County, Kentucky," (Ph.D.
    diss.: Univ. of Chicago, 1988), 130–36.
22. Lucien Beckner, ed., "Reverend John D. Shane's Interview with Pioneer Will-
    iam Clinkenbeard," *Filson Club Historical Quarterly* 2 (1928): 98.
23. Allan Kulikoff, "Uprooted Peoples: Black Migrants in the Age of the American
    Revolution," in *Slavery and Freedom in the Age of the American Revolution*, ed. Ira
    Berlin and Ronald Hoffman (Urbana: Univ. of Illinois Press, 1983), 148.
24. Jonathan Elliot, ed., *Debates on the Adoption of the Federal Constitution in the
    Convention Held at Philadelphia in 1787 with a Diary of the Debates of the Con-
    gress of the Confederation as Reported by James Madison* (New York: Burt Franklin
    Reprints, 1974), vol. 5: 458.
25. *Knoxville Gazette*, Knoxville, Tenn., Feb. 11, 1792; A. Drummond to John
    Coles, Apr. 5, 1780; Richard Woolfolk to John George Woolfolk, July 16,
    1794, Woolfolk Family Papers, Virginia Historical Society, Richmond. See also
    McCormack, *Slavery on the Tennessee Frontier*, 18–19.
26. Toulmin, *The Western County in 1793*, 108. Part of the price difference, of
    course, is attributable to transport costs. If a professional interregional trade ex-
    isted at this time, qualitative differences may also have been a factor. On the
    latter point, see Jonathan B. Pritchett and Herman Freudenberger, "A Peculiar
    Sample: The Selection of Slaves for the New Orleans Market," *Journal of Eco-
    nomic History* 52 (1992): 109–27.
27. William Christian letter, dated Dec. 12, 1785, Hugh Blair Grigsby Papers, Vir-
    ginia Historical Society, Richmond; John Breckinridge to Samuel Hopkins,
    Sept. 15, 1794, Breckinridge Family Papers.
28. Steven Deyle, "The Irony of Liberty: Origins of the Domestic Slave Trade,"
    Journal of the Early Republic 12 (1992): 37–62.
29. William W. Hening, comp., *The Statutes at Large: Being a Collection of all the
    Laws of Virginia from the First Session of the Legislature in 1619*, 13 vols. (Rich-
    mond, New York, and Philadelphia, 1819–23), 12: 713–14.
30. John Breckinridge to Letticia Breckinridge, Mar. 18, 1792, Breckinridge Family
    Papers; David Meade to William Bolling, May 6, 1798, William Bolling Pa-
    pers, Duke Univ. Library, Durham, N.C. On emancipation, see Coward, *Ken-
    tucky in the New Republic*.
31. For a statewide study, see Peter Joseph Albert, "The Protean Institution: The
    Geography, Economy, and Ideology of Slavery in Post-Revolutionary Virginia,"
    (Ph.D. diss.: Univ. of Maryland, College Park, 1976). For a more local exami-
    nation, see John Thomas Schlotterbeck, "Plantation and Farm: Social and Eco-
    nomic Change in Orange and Greene Counties, Virginia, 1716 to 1860,"
    (Ph.D. diss.: Johns Hopkins Univ., 1980).
32. James Davis, Lincoln County, to Zachariah Johnston, Rockbridge County, Aug.
    10, 1789, Zachariah Johnston Papers, Special Collections, Leyburn Library,
    Washington and Lee Univ., Lexington, Va.
33. Robert Johnson to Benjamin Johnson, Feb. 9, 1783, Barbour Family Papers (no.
    38–144), Special Collections Dept., Univ. of Virginia Library, Charlottesville.

34. *Virginia Centinel and Gazette Or, the Winchester Repository,* Winchester, Va., Jan. 27, 1794.
35. Toulmin, *The Western Country in 1793,* 22.
36. Peter H. Wood, *Black Majority: Negroes in Colonial South Carolina from 1670 through the Stono Rebellion* (New York: Knopf, 1974); Philip Morgan and Michael L. Nicholls, "Slaves in Piedmont Virginia, 1720–1790," *William and Mary Quarterly* 3d ser., 66 (1989): 211–51; Brady Hughes, "Migration of Virginia Slaves Based on the Census of 1820," *Virginia Social Science Journal* 20 (1985): 86–92.
37. Woodford County Will Book A; Madison County Will Book A; Bourbon County Will Book A, microfilm copies at the Kentucky Historical Society. Woodford and Bourbon Counties lay in the core slaveholding region and their probate records begin early, but a few inventories were omitted because they were too faded to read.
38. Based on probate records for Madison, Woodford, and Bourbon Counties, 1786–95, microfilm copies at the Kentucky Historical Society, Frankfort.
39. See Morgan and Nicholls, "Slavery in Piedmont Virginia," for a similar pattern in that region.
40. Most of the historical literature covering the late eighteenth century concerns southern Amerindians, whereas early Kentuckians had more contact with the Shawnee and their allies. Nonetheless, scattered evidence, such as the role played by Pompey at the siege of Boonesborough, suggests an equally complicated set of relations. Key works on early Indian-black relations include Kenneth W. Porter, "Relations between Negroes and Indians within the Present Limits of the United States," *Journal of Negro History* 17 (1932): 287–369; Theda Perdue, *Slavery and the Evolution of Cherokee Society, 1540–1866* (Knoxville: Univ. of Tennessee Press, 1979); Daniel H. Usner Jr., *Indians, Settlers, and Slaves in a Frontier Exchange Economy* (Chapel Hill: Univ. of North Carolina Press, 1992); Kathryn E. Holland Braund, "The Creek Indians, Blacks, and Slavery," *Journal of Southern History* 57 (1991): 601–36; William Loren Katz, *Black Indians: Hidden Heritage* (New York: Macmillan, 1986). That blacks often received different treatment in violent encounters is also noted by McCormack, *Slavery on the Tennessee Frontier,* 17.
41. Samuel Shepard, "Extracts from the Journal of Samuel Shepard, April 10, 1787–December 3, 1796," Microfilm, Univ. of Kentucky Library, Lexington, entries for June 1, 1788, Aug. 9, 1789, and Apr. 28–29, 1792. Many similar examples may be found scattered through personal narratives left by the pioneer generation.
42. Deposition of W. Buchanan, Nov. 28, 1778, Robertson, *Petitions,* 45.
43. William McBride Interview, Lyman C. Draper Collection, Microfilm 11CC262St, Historical Society of Wisconsin, Madison.
44. This story quickly gained wide circulation. See Isaac Hite to Abraham Hite, Apr. 26, 1783, The Filson Club Historical Society, Louisville, Ky.; "Col. William Fleming's Journal in Kentucky," in Mereness, *Travels in the American Colonies,* 672–73. A version drawn from the William Whitley Papers in the Draper Collection is found in Coleman, *Slavery Times in Kentucky,* 10–11.
45. Zachariah F. Smith, *History of Kentucky from Its Earliest Description and Settlement to the Present Date* (Louisville: The Prentice Press, 1895), 189–96. Monk

also contributed to Kentucky's defense through his knowledge of gunpowder manufacture. One of his sons was the first child of color to be born at Boonesborough.

46. John May to Samuel Beall, Dec. 9, 1780, Beall-Booth Family Papers.
47. John Graves Interview, Draper Collection, 11CC122.
48. Lucien Beckner, ed., "Reverend John D. Shane's Notes on an Interview with Elijah Foley of Fayette County," *Filson Club Historical Quarterly* 11 (1937): 259; Thomas Hart to Nathaniel Hart, Aug. 3, 1780, in Hart Family Papers, Presbyterian Church (U.S.A.) Dept. of History and Records Management Services, Philadelphia; Jesse Kennedy Interview, Draper Collection, 11CC37. See also Elizabeth Ann Perkins, "Border Life: Experience and Perception in the Revolutionary Ohio Valley," (Ph.D. diss., Northwestern Univ., 1992), 124–25. The slave perspective on such arrangements is unclear, but the lack of supervision for extended periods of time suggests a degree of acquiescence.
49. Neal Hammon and James Russell Harris, eds., "'In a Dangerous situation': The Letters of Col. John Floyd, 1774–1783," *Register of the Kentucky Historical Society* 83 (1985): 217, 220.
50. Coward, *Kentucky in the New Republic*, 63.
51. James Taylor, Autobiography of General James Taylor of Newport, Kentucky, Codex 181, typescript copy, Reuben T. Durrett Collection, Dept. of Special Collections, Univ. of Chicago Library, 4, 7, 24–26. When Taylor visited Virginia in 1797 his father was ready to give him a woman slave. James Taylor Sr. to Hubbard Taylor, Oct. 26, 1797, Hubbard Taylor Papers, Univ. of Kentucky Library, Lexington.
52. Coleman, *Slavery Times in Kentucky*, 15.

Works Cited

Albert, Peter Joseph. "The Protean Institution: The Geography, Economy, and Ideology of Slavery in Post-Revolutionary Virginia." Ph.D. diss., Univ. of Maryland, College Park, 1976.

Barbour Family Papers (no. 38–144). Special Collections Dept., Univ. of Virginia Library, Charlottesville.

Beall-Booth Family Papers. The Filson Club Historical Society, Louisville, Ky.

Beckner, Lucien, editor. "Reverend John D. Shane's Interview with Pioneer William Clinkenbeard." *Filson Club History Quarterly* 2 (1928): 95–128.

———. "Reverend John D. Shane's Notes on an Interview with Elijah Foley of Fayette County." *Filson Club History Quarterly* 11 (1937): 252–59.

Belen, Ted Franklin. "Did Daniel Boone Kill Pompey, the Black Shawnee, at the 1778 Siege of Boonesborough?" *Filson Club History Quarterly* 67 (1993): 5–22.

Bolling, William. Papers. Manuscript Division, Duke Univ. Library, Durham, N.C.

Bourbon County, Kentucky, Will Book A. Microfilm. Kentucky Historical Society, Frankfort.

Braund, Kathryn E. Holland. "The Creek Indians, Blacks, and Slavery." *Journal of Southern History* 57 (1991): 601–36.

Breckinridge Family Papers. Manuscripts Division, Library of Congress, Washington, D.C.

Carter-Smith Family Papers (no. 1729). Special Collections Dept., Univ. of Virginia Library, Charlottesville.

Coleman, J. Winston. *Slavery Times in Kentucky*. Chapel Hill: Univ. of North Carolina Press, 1940.

Coward, Joan Wells. *Kentucky in the New Republic: The Process of Constitution Making*. Lexington: Univ. Press of Kentucky, 1979.

Dandrige, Danske. *George Michael Bedinger, A Kentucky Pioneer*. Charlottesville: The Michie Co., 1909.

Deyle, Steven. "The Irony of Liberty: Origins of the Domestic Slave Trade." *Journal of the Early Republic* 12 (1992): 37–62.

Drake, Daniel. *Pioneer Life in Kentucky*. New York: Henry Schuman, 1948.

Draper, Lyman C. Collection. Microfilm. State Historical Society of Wisconsin, Madison.

Elliot, Jonathan, editor. *Debates on the Adoption of the Federal Constitution in the Convention Held at Philadelphia in 1787 with a Diary of the Debates of the Congress of the Confederation as Reported by James Madison*. Vol. 5. New York: Burt Franklin Reprints, 1974.

Eslinger, Ellen T. "The Great Revival in Bourbon County, Kentucky." Ph.D. diss., Univ. of Chicago, 1988.

Faragher, John Mack. *Daniel Boone, The Life and Legend of an American Pioneer*. New York: Henry Holt and Co., 1992.

Fleming, William, "Col. William Fleming's Journal in Kentucky from Nov. 10, 1779 to May 27th 1780." *Travels in the American Colonies*. Edited by Newton D. Mereness. New York: The Macmillan Co., 1916.

Goodstein, Anita S. "Black History on the Nashville Frontier, 1780–1810." *Tennessee Historical Quarterly* 38 (1979): 401–20.

Grigsby, Hugh Blair. Papers. Virginia Historical Society, Richmond.

Hammon, Neal, and James Russell Harris, editors. "'In a Dangerous Situation': The Letters of Col. John Floyd, 1774–1783." *Register of the Kentucky Historical Society* 83 (1985): 202–36.

Hart Family Papers. Presbyterian Church (U.S.A.) Dept. of History and Records Management Services, Philadelphia.

Hening, William W., compiler. *The Statutes at Large: Being a Collection of all the Laws of Virginia from the first Session of the Legislature in 1619*. 13 vols. Richmond, New York, and Philadelphia, 1819–23.

Hughes, Brady. "Migration of Virginia Slaves Based on the Census of 1820." *Virginia Social Science Journal* 20 (1985): 86–92.

Johnston, Zachariah. Papers. Special Collections, Leyburn Library, Washington and Lee Univ., Lexington, Va.

Katz, William Loren. *Black Indians: Hidden Heritage*. New York: Macmillan, 1986.

Kentucky Gazette. Lexington, Ky., 1788–90.

Knoxville Gazette. Knoxville, Tenn., Feb. 11, 1792.

Kulikoff, Allan. "Uprooted Peoples: Black Migrants in the Age of the American Revolution." *Slavery and Freedom in the Age of the American Revolution*. Edited by Ira Berlin and Ronald Hoffman. Urbana: Univ. of Illinois Press, 1983.

Lester, William Stewart. *The Transylvania Colony*. Spencer, Ind.: Samuel R. Guard and Co., 1935.

Lucas, Marion B., and George C. Wright. *A History of Blacks in Kentucky*. 2 vols. Frankfort: Kentucky Historical Society, 1992.

Madison County, Kentucky, Tax Lists. Microfilm. Kentucky Historical Society, Frankfort.

Madison County, Kentucky, Will Book A. Microfilm. Kentucky Historical Society, Frankfort.

McCormack, Edward Michael. *Slavery on the Tennessee Frontier.* Nashville: Tennessee American Revolution Bicentennial Commission, 1977.

McDougle, Ivan E. *Slavery in Kentucky, 1792–1865.* Lancaster, Pa.: Press of the New Era Printing Co., 1918.

Miscellaneous Manuscripts. The Filson Club Historical Society, Louisville, Ky.

Morgan, Philip, and Michael L. Nicholls. "Slaves in Piedmont Virginia, 1720–1790." *William and Mary Quarterly* 3d ser., 66 (1989): 211–51.

Orange County, Virginia, Personal Property Tax Lists. Library of Virginia, Richmond.

Perkins, Elizabeth Ann. "Border Life: Experience and Perception in the Revolutionary Ohio Valley." Ph.D. diss., Northwestern Univ., 1992.

Pritchett, Jonathan B., and Herman Freudenberger. "A Peculiar Sample: The Selection of Slaves for the New Orleans Market." *Journal of Economic History* 52 (1992): 109–27.

Perdue, Theda. *Slavery and the Evolution of Cherokee Society, 1540–1866.* Knoxville: Univ. of Tennessee Press, 1979.

Robertson, James Rood. *Petitions of the Early Inhabitants of Kentucky to the General Assembly of Virginia, 1769 to 1792.* Filson Club Publications 27. Louisville: John P. Morton and Co., 1914.

Schlotterbeck, John Thomas. "Plantation and Farm: Social and Economic Change in Orange and Greene Counties, Virginia, 1716 to 1860." Ph.D. diss., Johns Hopkins Univ., 1980.

Shepard, Samuel. "Extracts from the Journal of Samuel Shepard, April 10, 1787–December 3, 1796." Microfilm. Univ. of Kentucky Library, Lexington.

Smith, Zachariah F. *The History of Kentucky from its Earliest Description and Settlement to the Present Date.* Louisville: The Prentice Press, 1895.

The Staunton Spy. Staunton, Va., Feb. 1, 1794.

Taylor, Hubbard. Papers. Margaret I. King Library, Univ. of Kentucky, Lexington.

Taylor, James. Autobiography of General James Taylor of Newport, Kentucky. Codex 181, Typescript. Reuben T. Durrett Collection, Univ. of Chicago Library.

Terry, Gail S. "Sustaining the Bonds of Kinship in a Trans-Appalachian Migration, 1790–1811: The Cabell-Breckinridge Slaves Move West." *Virginia Magazine of History and Biography* 102 (1994): 456–76.

Toulmin, Harry. *The Western County in 1793, Reports on Kentucky and Virginia.* Edited by Marion Tinling and Godfrey Davis. San Marino, Calif.: Henry E. Huntington Library, 1948.

Usner, Daniel H., Jr. *Indians, Settlers, and Slaves in a Frontier Exchange Economy.* Chapel Hill: Univ. of North Carolina Press, 1991.

Virginia Centinel and Gazette Or, the Winchester Repository. Winchester, Va., Jan. 27, 1794, and Nov. 3, 1794.

Wilson, Benjamin. Papers. Univ. of Kentucky Library, Lexington.

Wood, Peter H. *Black Majority: Negroes in Colonial South Carolina from 1670 through the Stono Rebellion.* New York: Knopf, 1974.

Woodford County, Kentucky, Tax Lists. Microfilm. Kentucky Historical Society, Frankfort.
Woodford County, Kentucky, Will Book A. Microfilm. Kentucky Historical Society, Frankfort.
Woolfolk Family Papers. Virginia Historical Society, Richmond.

Chapter 8

Slavery on the Margins of the Virginia Frontier

African American Literacy in Western Kanawha and Cabell Counties, 1795–1840

Marilyn Davis-DeEulis

In 1813 a young African American slave whose name appears to have been D'lea was whipped on a frontier farm called Gardner's Bend, one of Wilson Cary Nicholas's Tug River holdings in the Ohio Valley. The overseer there, who prided himself on his tight control of the farm, had caught her reading a religious tract, an activity he frowned upon. D'lea usually resided at Greenbottom, Virginia, about twenty miles up the Ohio River from Gardner's Bend, where she bundled hay, wove coarse cloth, and assisted when hemp bundles were tallied and transported downriver. However, on the day she was whipped, she and approximately twenty other slaves from Greenbottom were sitting, more or less idle, out of sight in Kentucky, while a tax assessor visited Wilson Cary Nicholas's westernmost Virginia property. Had this young woman—a slave on what is conventionally seen as a classic, sprawling, "Appalachian overseer plantation"—picked up that tract at Greenbottom instead of Gardner's Bend, the chances are that she would not have been punished for reading it. Interestingly, members of the slave community in which she lived and the disorganized, disagreeable overseer of Greenbottom all *knew* she had reading skills, as well as rudimentary factoring skills; indeed, the overseer had made occasional, grudging use of them. In fact, both D'lea's abilities and her master's unhappy dependence on her follow a pattern not uncommon on this post-Revolutionary western Virginia border.

The rise of African American life on the early Ohio Valley/Virginia frontier (1790–1820) and its complex relationship to local church and plantation literacy demographics in the 1820s through the 1840s are important elements in understanding why this area assumed its cultural, social, and labor structure in the nineteenth century. The dynamics of this connection also suggest the forces that shaped attitudes about reading and writing among enslaved blacks, which Valley of Virginia settlers encountered when they recolonized the large land-grant holdings of the Ohio and Virginia frontier into smaller farms in the 1820s. Finally, these dynamics help account for the literate sophistication of antislavery enclaves on opposite sides of the Ohio River during the late antebellum period. Ohio communities such as Burlington, Federal Creek–Traceport, and Black Fork had a much longer, and functionally complex, literacy history than has been generally assumed.

As literacy scholars such as David Cressy and Harvey Graff have emphasized, the dominant cultural myth of the evolving West has been that literacy was a precondition for economic growth.[1] This mythography was never stronger than in post-Revolutionary America. Yet the economic motivation for learning literacy skills remained relatively low among captive slave-labor populations, as it did among most masters (although not necessarily their mistresses).[2] The rationale for why so many African Americans acquired reading and writing facility so well, whatever the risk, has been intensely studied; literacy as identity in the quest for freedom lies at the root of perhaps the major strain of slave narratives in America (those in the Douglass autobiographical mode). A writer such as Henry Louis Gates might argue that acquiring rudimentary English literacy was more than a way of declaring one's psychic freedom; it was a cultural building block in the system of creating meaning that some critics call "fusional accommodation"—a non-assimilatory means of acculturation that African Americans brought with them to the New World. Learning to "read and write" was an aesthetic, as well as pragmatic necessity, which allowed one to make it through life with a sense of historical being and "presence."[3]

Such analysis of African American literacy's heritage is important; I teach both American book culture and literacy historiography, and deal with their implication constantly in my classroom. To a certain extent, they also inform how I think about the relationship of occupational literacy and so-called "slave-labor relations," particularly on the frontier. David Vincent has observed in *Literacy and Popular Culture* that understanding a specific period's "occupational literacy"—the allocation of a literate task in history—requires a hard look at how labor relations functioned in a particular time and place.[4] Looking at the relationship of literacy and task allocation *in* history requires stripping away the progressive myths with which we have entangled early-nineteenth-century literate cultures. Only then can we learn how diverse laboring populations occupied time in a way that required forms of literacy to be shared with ruling elites.[5]

On the Ohio Valley frontier, irregular laboring circumstances gave rise to a grudging "multicultural" sharing of reading, writing, and factoring skills. This happened very early, as early as 1786.[6] By the time William Jenkins and tanner John Hannan purchased Governor Cabell's lands and many of his slaves in September 1825,[7] they were buying into several generations of "occupational literacy" forged in very confusing circumstances that were backbreaking, ruthless, yet often collaborative. It is little wonder that the African American heritage of the Ohio Valley basin has been called one of the least understood, most complicated slave relationships in the West.

The basin formed by the Kanawha, Ohio, and Sandys Rivers, although surveyed in the late 1760s, was not occupied significantly by white settlers until after 1795; the large plantation operations at Gardner's Bend and the Levisa Fork of the Big Sandy River go back a little further, to the late 1780s. Thus, area slaves participated in both the irregular, often cruel nature of early frontier authority relations, as well as the schizophrenia about slave literacy common to the late Federal, early antebellum Old South. The existence these people endured was singularly difficult. Yet, even though most Virginia frontier slaves on the Ohio River lived hard, labor-intensive, disorganized existences, a surprising number (0.032 to 0.037/sample of 75 studied)[8] could both sign their names and factor, or sign their names and orally recite portions of Methodist or Baptist devotional tracts. A number (five to six of them) could do all three.[9] These figures were taken from a tannery and logging operation of greater than two thousand acres in Mason County, a small farm at Lesage of greater than eight hundred acres in Cabell County, and two large farming populations of nearly eight thousand acres, one at Greenbottom, Cabell County, and the other at Gardner's/Louisa Bend (now Lawrence County, Kentucky). A close examination of the nature of labor life on these plantations suggests that slave conditions and literacy rates were related, often in unexpected ways, on the margins of the Virginia frontier. Furthermore, the relative stability of core African American populations in the area left literacy with a confused functional identity for Ohio Valley African Americans.

Diversity of land use, disorganized task delegation, and class and age

diversity of white laboring partners did provide some unusual early opportunities for slaves to learn English or simple factoring skills. One of the first
settlers in the Kanawha and Ohio River basin was Thomas Hannan, who
was granted nearly a thousand acres on October 11, 1796.[10] He also owned
approximately 3,420 acres of timber and farmland in Cabell and Mason
counties.[11] He later conveyed most of it to John Hannan, believed to be his
brother. Although the 1810 census does not mention that John Hannan
owned a slave, the record indicates that he inherited two slaves with his
property transfers, one of whom was named Essa: Essa shows up, along
with six other slaves, in the 1830 tax assessments.[12] Hannan had an unusual household; he was both a farmer and a tanner, and his gross income
from both occupations exceeded twenty-six hundred dollars per year. Four
of the ten white members of his household were non-English-speaking
German citizens who worked in "manufacture" (leather production).[13]
Family documents suggest that Essa had not only learned to factor when
he was one of two slaves working under Thomas Hannan, but also that he
served as an informal teacher in the tannery to his German-speaking co-
workers, several of whom were quite young.[14] John Hannan increasingly
employed young indentured whites or neighborhood children as "hide
chewers" and is reported to have bought them a "little chappie set" to make
up for their lost schooling.[15] If this was in fact the case, the presence of
chapbooks would explain the unusual nature of Essa's "relation of experience" in church in 1839, in which he sounded a little like a Welsh Episco-
pal rather than a Baptist.[16] John Hannan, who was appointed Superior
Court Judge in 1809, grudgingly admitted in 1812 that he had been "forced
. . . to teach him [Essa] back some time, to count and read, when he was
our only man."[17]

The complex interrelation of slavery, spoken language, and functional literacy is underscored in another small but very intriguing setting, one which suggests the unexpected linguistic diversity of the
Guyandotte and Sandys River basin as early as 1800. It also delineates
the unexpected avenues by which African Americans learned English.
The Ancells were one of several French families who originally settled
a small hamlet called Lesage, Virginia, a swamp tract to the south of
Joshua Frye's 4,441-acre Greenbottom plantation. The Ancell and
Crawford families appear to have acquired the land through a treasury
warrant rather than a grant of simple deed.[18] The families saw the Ohio
frontier as a seasonal investment. Revenue assize records at the Port of
New Orleans (as well as family narrative) suggest that the Ancells took
their crops down the river to market every year for seven years (1805–
12), remaining in Portulac Parish to log in the winter.[19] They left be-

hind an overseer and an elderly African/Caribbean slave couple. In the beginning, none of them spoke English. The unnamed slave couple learned enough English to get by, while the overseer, "Mr. Elbrein," refused to learn "this Virginie English."[20] His two slaves, who were true polyglots, gradually took over both oral and simple written transactions for the plantation; the husband signed himself "D. Ancell Man."[21] When the Ancells and Crawfords eventually split into permanent communities in Louisiana and Virginia (now West Virginia), the Virginians sent the overseer—"a limp man"—home. In this case, disorganized task delegation and the stubborn pride of an authority figure abetted a complex oral and written literacy acquisition already in progress. Thus, writing, a tool of authority and control, was acquired along with oral English. How this was accomplished by the French slave couple is unclear, but as neither the Methodist Hannans, Baptist Waughs, nor any other early settler in the area had French-speaking Catholic slaves, neighborhood religious instruction probably played a minimal part. Certainly, the entire communal, labor, and literacy dynamic of early non-English communities on the frontier is worthy of further investigation. Lesage, Virginia, emphatically underscores the fluidity of cultures that contributed to "slavery on the margins" of the frontier.

The debt problems of an absentee owner seem also to have been conducive to raising the level of slave literacy on the Ohio, even at what should have been relatively large and strictly organized plantations. Wilson Cary Nicholas, one of two governors of Virginia to own large tracts of property in this area, appears only in the 1820 Cabell County population census;[22] Louisa Bend (elsewhere Sandys or Gardner's Bend in his documents) was already held in the name of a trustee by this date. The property Nicholas owned on the south side of the Ohio River had originally been granted to Joshua Frye. Nicholas acquired the upper 1,941 acres from Frye sometime before 1811; the other 2,500 acres were purchased from Peyton Short, a logger and farmer from Woodford County, Kentucky, who had bought the property from Frye in 1805.[23] It appears that Nicholas acquired Short's slaves, along with some of those which Frye's brother supervised for him at Greenbottom, when he bought his property. Further, he added several families of known slaves to this group from his other plantations.[24] Indeed, by 1820 his property listing included fifty-three slaves, thirty-seven of them employed in agriculture. However, his 1815 Cabell County tax listing recorded only eighteen slaves, twenty-three horses, and one hundred cattle.[25] As Wilson Cary Nicholas was deeply in debt in 1820, one wonders why he would have acquired thirty-five slaves. The answer is provided by the tax and census records for Louisa Bend, where the numerical ratio is nearly reversed. In both cases, Nicholas listed nearly the same number of slaves in the tax assize, which was taken at different times. He simply moved people around from farm to farm. Indeed, Nicholas's letters to his overseer at Louisa Bend emphasized that he wanted "my [his] people moved," to avoid "detection."[26] The first overseer at Greenbottom, David Cobbs, and his agent in eastern Kentucky, Sam McWilliam, poured significant amounts of Wilson Cary Nicholas's money into capitalizing Greenbottom.[27] It is clear that Nicholas planned to offset some of these expenses and to pay off his property investment note on Greenbottom by rotating a static number of slaves at financially strategic moments. Thus, he could stretch his human "resources" as thinly as possible, and cut his tax bill to boot.

What this strategy has to do with African American literacy in the Ohio/Sandys valley is grimly interesting. Continual long-distance travel, erratic supervision, and labor-intensive regimens made slave life very harsh on these overseer farms. Nicholas recorded the deaths of some twenty-two slaves, between the ages of twenty-four and forty, in the two-year period from 1812 to 1814. Although fewer died at Louisa Bend because the overseer routinely called in "doctors" when slaves were dangerously ill, neither farm was a very healthy place to work.[28]

Yet, Greenbottom, according to both Nicholas and one of his trustees, was far the worse of the two—chronically disorganized, undermanned, and occasionally completely unsupervised. Mr. Cobbs seems to have kept careful records of his successes at market, but he was gone far too often.[29] When Cobbs returned to Greenbottom, problems ensued, sometimes very violent ones. The subsequent overseer at Greenbottom was, even in John Hannan's estimation, "harsh to a fault and unpredictable."[30] Yet it was the slaves at Greenbottom, rather than Louisa Bend, who knew how to "factor." Some, such as Nicholas's "Old Julius," could both count and do simple ledgers.[31] The overseer at Louisa Bend did not *need* that kind of assistance; as has been previously stated, he whipped one of the "Bottom girls" when he caught her reading a tract while she was on "tax furlough" in Kentucky.[32]

By the time the second overseer, Mr. Gough, came to Greenbottom, Nicholas's slaves had begun to use their skills for other purposes. The Cabell County courthouse records list at least three missing slaves from Greenbottom for the years 1817 and 1818.[33] All are listed as "having escaped through Millersport with pass." One of these missing slaves is advertised as having "writ himself a pass." Nicholas and his overseers spent considerable time and money bringing back two of these slaves, Joshua and

Joe; Gough even employed a "slavebreaker" to change Joshua's ways.[34] Yet someone in the slave community kept writing these passes, and Gough was forced to ship a number of slaves to Kentucky in 1819 for what he called "safety." Indeed, when Governor Cabell bought Greenbottom at public sale in Richmond in 1821, his bargain included, explicitly, "twenty-two slaves, and one named Moses, 'fled *with a note* into the wilderness of Ohio.'"[35] Wilson Cary Nicholas's 1815 Slave Tax Records indicate that he began buying slaves from his neighbors in 1815 or so, rather than transferring them from other properties.[36] Thus, Moses may have been acquired from one of the religious families newly removed to the Ohio from the Valley of Virginia, where slave reading was encouraged, at least in the churches. But so many of the Greenbottom slaves seem to have been task functionally literate that the overseers' erraticness may have been in large part responsible for their facilities in reading and writing. This model accounts for motivation through occupational self-organization rather than through religion. Although it is appropriate to doubt that loyalty to Mr. Nicholas motivated anyone, evidence exists that his slaves learned to read and factor *in the absence of supervision.* In 1819, "Old Julius" and another veteran slave, Silas, worked on the Greenbottom wharf, without an overseer, marking bales as they were loaded for market and projecting their markup.[37]

Nicholas soon discovered that Greenbottom and his own finances were in too much of a "state" for anyone to save them. Even Cabell's adroit move to assist Nicholas and himself by paying thirteen thousand dollars for Greenbottom and its twenty-two slaves and Moses, when, in point of fact, Nicholas should have paid Cabell, only brought trouble down on Cabell's head and that of one of his trustees, Robert Gamble. Eventually, the "property and people intact" were conveyed on March 1, 1821, by William Wirte and Robert Gamble to John Coaltes and John Cocke, who resold it in 1825 to William A. Jenkins and John Hannan.[38] The legacy of Greenbottom's mismanagement even dogged Thomas Jefferson Randolph through his bankruptcy proceedings in 1831. He had served as "security" for Wilson Cary Nicholas in another matter, and the Bank of the United States tried to seize Greenbottom through him, in apparent ignorance that Nicholas had sold his property to Cabell in 1821.[39] Interestingly, the figures they used in their writ were taken from the 1819 report to Nicholas that a "ghost" overseer presented to him through Mr. Wirte. This single ledger from Greenbottom is signed with a large "S" and is very badly printed, though *accurately accounted.* When William Jenkins bought Greenbottom in 1825, the oldest slave on the farm was named Silas, and he could count, according to Janetta. Silas joined the Greenbottom Baptist Church the first year it opened its doors to black members. He was by then John Hannan's slave.[40]

Greenbottom was not an anomaly on the Ohio River. The mechanism by which frontier slaves came to read is not completely clear, but the circumstances under which they learned are. Isolation, responsibility for huge land area, and "irregular management" seem to have been common factors. Greenbottom's overseers evidenced a propensity for simultaneous cruelty and dependence in their relationships with their slaves. Such confusing treatment seems to have provided a fertile seedbed for black literacy and active reading and writing communities on these plantations.

In the case of Greenbottom, William Jenkins inherited thirty slaves from Cabell's overseers; neither his bill of sale nor records of public slave auctions in the area suggest that he sold any of them. This was a community in continuity with Governor Nicholas's 1811 purchases. Jenkins's Greenbottom household more or less recapitulated the twenty-two-slave community Cabell had purchased in 1821. In one of her first letters to a sibling, Janetta Jenkins observed that "the older people on this place can read and write. Some can figure."[41] Janetta, who was the nineteen-year-old bride of a rather stern older husband, seems to have become involved in her extended "family's" reading. Two factors combined to bring this event about. Janetta was a member of the Grigsby-McNutt family, of very different parentage from her new husband. Her oldest brother, Alexander McNutt, was the first governor of Mississippi; her childhood sweetheart was her older cousin, famous antebellum diarist Hugh Blair Grigsby. She and her sister Fanny—the babies in a very large, fatherless family—wrote sophomoric love letters to Blair Grigsby right up to the time of Janetta's marriage to William Jenkins.[42] However, to her mother's brother Reuben Grigsby, wheat factor and shipper William Jenkins's relative fortune offset wide differences in age and social upbringing. Mr. Grigsby saw to it that Mr. Jenkins paid the marriage bond, and Janetta brought no dowry to the marriage.[43] But she brought her name, her fitness for bearing children, and her education—she was trained in a small Presbyterian female academy near Falling Springs Presbyterian church in Glasgow, Virginia. The small "parcel of books" that her mother gave her westward-migrating daughter included, at least, a well-worn copy of Milton, Ainsworth's Dictionary, several primers, and a battered copy of Gibbon.[44] She and the young tutors she brought from Rockbridge County to Greenbottom in the 1830s and 1840s discussed literature and theology quite openly, before children and servants alike.

Indeed, Falling Springs Presbyterian would have brought her up in a tradition of tolerance for a family slave's right to read and engage in discussion about the Bible. Falling Springs contained a significant number of slave members (21 out of 187),[45] and the minister, Reverend James Ewing, subjected his black parishioners to full church discipline and active participation in most church functions. On two occasions, one documented in Hugh Blair Grigsby's diary, he turned his pulpit over to a black preacher, who "espoused . . . with the Bible in his hand."[46] No prohibition against slave literacy, unless it was imposed by a slave's owners, was articulated in church policy. Literate slaves could sign their name to the church roll book, although few chose to do so. When Janetta came to Cabell County in 1825, the Greenbottom Baptist Church would not open its doors for another ten years. According to her letters to her sister and the comments of the family tutor in 1829, Janetta conducted a sort of weekly service (she called them "sharings") in which she read devotional and religious poetry, spoke "simply" from the Bible to her slaves, occasionally let "one or two older ones" read, and then asked for testimony of the week's spiritual events.[47] Whether she taught literacy skills to those who did not already know how to read is not clear from the record, but she definitely exposed ten to twelve of her slaves to an ongoing, rather high level of oral and written religious experience. Ironically, she was probably unaware of the complex foundation concerning reading and writing's function in the world upon which she was building.

Indeed, circumstantial evidence suggests that younger slaves employed more conventional stratagems to expose themselves to letters, which suggests that Janetta was not openly teaching reading. In one widely circulated family narrative about Albert Gallatin Jenkins, his black nurse brought him daily to sit under the trees with his sister and two brothers as they were tutored. She carried him, pasha-style, on a huge feather pillow so he might hold his favorite cat. His nurse is recorded as having "sat with him to mind the cat."[48] However, Janetta's small devotional "sharings" bore specific identifiable fruit in the two or three years before her death in 1841. When pastor Hezekiah Chilton took over the pastorate of the newly formed Greenbottom Baptist Church in 1839, he announced a series of revivals. For the first time since its incipience in 1835, Greenbottom Baptist opened its doors officially to black members; they were baptized, chastised, and given letters of membership on the rare occasions they were sold with some propriety. Four women from Jenkins's plantation immediately joined, as well as Jenkins's former slave, Silas. Interestingly, in April of 1840, a corrected version of the church roster was issued by church recorder Ezekiel Waugh in which at least one of Jenkins's slaves (Nelly, who was fifty-seven) signed her name prominently. April through July was a period in which black women often joined with their masters or mistresses; church registers from these months in 1839–40 note, for examples, that "Frances Hannan . . . and her black woman Mariah," "Sarah Waugh and a black woman named Miliah," and "John Hannan and his colored woman Elizabeth" had joined. Black men generally joined alone; an example was Bright, a servant of Thomas Chauppen's, who, like Silas, was a former slave of Jenkins's.[49] When Jenkins's slaves "presented a note from their master giving leave . . . that they might become members of this church," their public recitations of experience (a prerequisite of membership and baptism) bore definite marks of Janetta's "sharings." In fact, they were *so* different from the testimonies of other neighborhood slaves that the difference was noted in the record: "these four each proceeded to tell of the increase of their mind through Bible study and professed their faith very satisfactorily to the Church, so that each was baptized by elder Hezekiah Shelton, pastor, that evening."[50] As the next few weeks' minutes suggest, not all of the members of the church approved of this change. Given what we know about the confused heritage of African American literacy on the Ohio River and Virginia frontier, this should come as no surprise. An evangelical Christianity that encouraged black reading did not fit comfortably over the still prevailing harsh frontier ethos of slave relations. Although Old Nelly's name stands out boldly on Mr. Waugh's revised 1840 roll, Hezekiah Chilton was made to pay dearly for its presence by his neighbors. He is recorded as having said, the day before Old Nelly was baptized, that he was "willing to give offense and take it and if reprimanded, to bear it with meekness," but he also reminded the church "the love of God will cause us to love the Church and each other, and if so, we will love our pastor also. . . . We will not only be careful of his reputation but his comfort and welfare . . . we will defend his character, at all times and in all places as far as truth and ability will present and Christian duty require."[51]

Hezekiah Chilton was able to avoid the censure of his congregation at this time, but, several weeks later, he gave in to a call for increased meetings "for the purpose of examining into the secular concerns of the church and her various parts."[52] The records that follow from 1840 through 1842 suggest that a significant number of African American parishioners (although perhaps not a disproportionate number, given the size of the congregation) came under church discipline for sexual misconduct and laxity of attendance. The number of "colored" members dwindled significantly throughout the 1840s (Janetta Jenkins, her maid Nelly, and Mrs. Hannan's Mariah all died in 1841); the Greenbottom slaves attended very erratically thereafter. Three were excluded in 1841. By 1843, the church's slaves had lost their individual identities; they were simply listed as "four colored members." In 1844, when Mr. Hannan died, four more blacks joined the church—two of Elizabeth Hannan's servants and Nelly's children, Betsy and Peggy.[53] There is some evidence that Elizabeth Hannan hoped to find protection for favored servants by raising their profiles as church members. By 1845, the last year of Hezekiah Chilton's pastorate, the roster did include six black members. One died in 1846; the rest remained with the church until 1855, when it dissolved.

When William Jenkins died in 1859, he left a bequest that a church be built on Greenbottom for the use of the "household and neighborhood."[54] Jenkins had never been a Baptist, and with the Baptist church gone, he may have felt the need for a source of household worship closer to his beliefs; he had been a Presbyterian at Falling Springs, owning a pew as far back as 1811.[55] However, William Jenkins had not been known for his religious fervor since he moved to Greenbottom; this was probably a deathbed request for the benefit of his son, who had a very real problem to deal with. At least ten of Jenkins's slaves had become temporary church members across the Ohio River in one of two "sanctuary communities."[56] If William Jenkins's slaves lived to get out of Greenbottom, they generally did not have to run too far into Ohio for structured assistance after 1850.

Ultimately, the stories of these communities and others—Burlington and Federal Creek, Black Fork, Wilgus, and Berlin Crossing, Ohio—are fodder for another essay; all had striking numbers of black teachers and literate farmers after the Civil War. This is a story, however, that by 1850 carried nearly a half-century's heritage, one that Frederick Douglass understood strikingly to be a mixed blessing. As often as not, so-called plantation literacy in the Kanawha Valley of the Ohio River was not baptized in hope; it was born of the waking nightmare of vast wilderness spaces, endless undefined, disorganized tasks, and remote, senseless authority that showed up without warning, ready to strike at the handiest target of its anger about unrealistic production expectations. In more than one instance, that target was the slave who had tallied figures and labeled crops the day before. Occasionally, the result of African American literacy on the Ohio and Virginia frontier was ironic and spirit affirming; most often, both on farms and in plantation churches, it was not.

Notes

1. David Cressy, *Literacy and the Social Order* (New York: Cambridge Univ. Press, 1980). See particularly chap. 2. Harvey J. Graff, *The Labyrinths of Literacy* (London: Falmer Press, 1986), 162–86.

2. Janet Cornelius, *When I Can Read My Title Clear* (Columbia: Univ. of South Carolina Press, 1991), 20–27.

3. Henry Louis Gates, *The Signifying Monkey* (Cornell: Cornell Univ. Press, 1988), chap. 3.

4. David Vincent, *Literacy and Popular Culture: England, 1750–1914* (New York: Cambridge Univ. Press, 1990), 96–104.

5. Ibid., 134–35.

6. At this time slaves were first used for "counting hay bundles" at Gardner's Bend. Wilson Cary Nicholas Papers (no. 2343), Accounts 1786, Box 6, Special Collections Dept., Univ. of Virginia Library, Charlottesville. Earlier instances exist in nonfarming contexts.

7. Cabell County, Virginia, Deed Book 4: 55, 107 (hereafter cited as CDB).

8. I consulted a combination of Cabell County Tax Records; Cabell County Census Data; Wilson Cary Nicholas's 1815 Slave Tax Book, Oversize Mss: 2343, Folio 2, Wilson Cary Nicholas Papers; Greenbottom correspondence and accounts in the Wilson Cary Nicholas Papers; Hannan Family Papers, Elizabeth Hannan Papers, 1807–12, Special Collections, Univ. of Kentucky Library, Lexington; various county indexes to slaves and owners before 1860 in Western Virginia; and Crawford Family Papers, Southwestern Louisiana State Univ. Library, Shreveport, and West Virginia Univ. Library, Morgantown, to conduct my survey.

9. This is probably a conservative estimate, as some (e.g., "Old Julius") could factor, sign his name, and write short, coherent notes. Oral recitation in church may or may not point to actual reading capacity, as numerous literacy scholars have mentioned. One of the best discussions on this issue for black and white women is Jean Friedman, *The Enclosed Garden* (Chapel Hill: Univ. of North Carolina Press, 1986), 37.

10. For a review of these transactions, see Robert Sawrey, *A National Register Evaluation of Selected Archeological Sites in the Gallipolis Mitigation Site at Greenbottom* (Lexington, Ky.: Cultural Resources Analysis, 1990), 219; See also Kanawha County, Virginia, Book of Record (Index) to Federal Patents, West Virginia State Archives, Charleston, 11.

11. CDB 4: 150–51.

12. Ibid., 1: 147; Elizabeth Hannan Papers; *Union Tax List Based on the 1830 Census,* Cabell County, Virginia, cited in Sawrey, *National Register,* 221.

13. U.S. Bureau of the Census, *Fifth Census of the United States, 1830,* Mason County, Virginia [West Virginia], 4; Sawrey, *National Register,* 219.

14. Elizabeth Hannan Papers.

15. George Selden Wallace, *Cabell County Annals and Families* (Richmond: Garrett and Massie, 1935), 221; Elizabeth Hannan Papers.

16. Greenbottom Baptist Church, Register and Minutes, 1834–55 (June 27, 1840), quoted courtesy of the American Baptist Historical Society, Rochester, N.Y.

17. Elizabeth Hannan Papers; Cabell County, Virginia, Circuit Court Records, "Notes," 1809–11.

18. Kanawha County, Book of Record (Index), Federal Patent to Col. Joshua Frye, Feb. 25, 1754, June 2, 1795. Very little information is currently available about Lesage, Virginia. The best source remains Wallace, *Cabell County Annals.* See also Mason County, Virginia, Deed Book 1 (hereafter cited as MCD); "Index to

Land Grants and Patents," Sept. 14, 1787, "Edward Crawford, 2670"; Mason County, Virginia, Chancery Record Book, chap. 1, 353 (hereafter cited as MCCR); MCD, Book B, "Rev. Edw. Crawford to James Crawford," Sept. 20, 1815, 53. Dr. Robert Kearns, a Crawford descendant who is an emeritus professor at Marshall University, attended a bistate reunion of the Crawfords and the Ancells in Louisiana in 1986. Telephone interview with author, Oct. 1992.

19. *Annual Collections of the Port of New Orleans, 1800–1830* (New Orleans), vol. 2: 221; Crawford and Ancell Family Papers, miscellaneous documents, 1802–15, Southwestern Louisiana State Univ. Library, Shreveport.

20. Crawford Family Papers, Mr. Elbrien to [?], Nov. 1809, Special Collections, West Virginia Univ. Library, Morgantown. See also William Beer, "Early Census Tables of Louisiana," *Louisiana Historical Society Publications* (1911): 82.

21. Ancell and Crawford Family Papers.

22. U.S. Bureau of the Census, *Fourth Census of the United States, 1820,* Cabell County, Virginia [West Virginia], Appendix, 17.

23. CDB, I: 36, 437–38; See also, Mercer County, Kentucky, *Records of Deeds and Land Holdings,* 1805–6, (n.p., 1911), 29.

24. Joshua Frye to Wilson Cary Nicholas, Apr. 2, 1802, Wilson Cary Nicholas Papers, Box 9; "Farming Notes, January 1812," Ibid.

25. Cabell County, Virginia, Tax Assessment, 1815, C-7.

26. Wilson Cary Nicholas to M. R. McAllister, Aug. 10, 1813, Wilson Cary Nicholas Papers, Box 9. Nicholas spelled out this stratagem even further in "Farming Notes, January 1812," ibid.

27. For examples of this practice, see "Sam McWilliam's Book, Aug. 22, 1812," ibid.; "List of Expenses on Hogs from Kentucky paid by David Cobbs," ibid., Box 10.

28. "Col. Wilson C. Nicholas In Amount with David Cobbs," Feb. 15, 1814, ibid., Box 10; "Accounts to William Charles Everdle," Louisa Bend, Apr. 1, 1813, ibid., Box 9.

29. For what it is worth, he was referred to as "Mrs. Wilson's overseer" by Sam McWilliam. "Sam McWilliam's Book," Dec. 12, 1812, ibid., Box 9. The ledger book is filed under Aug. 22, 1812.

30. John Hannan as reported by Elizabeth Hannan, Elizabeth Hannan Papers.

31. See note 9 above.

32. Sam McWilliam to William Powers, Jan. 22, 1815, Wilson Cary Nicholas Papers, Box 11.

33. Cabell County, Virginia, "Writs of Lost Property, 1815–1825." See John Hannan's "Invoice for printing posters regarding a missing slave, Jacob, July 17, 1817," Wilson Cary Nicholas Papers, Box 11.

34. Receipt of Sam Pursell to William Gough "in full account [of] that worke I done fore W. C. Nicholas," Apr. 13, 1817, and James Wilson's receipt for the second capture of Joshua, "Received 24 June 1817 of Mr. Gough two dollars for drawing a power of attorney from him to John Hannan . . . to proceed into the state of Ohio and use all lawful means to get possession of a negro slave named Joshua. . . ." Wilson Cary Nicholas Papers, Box 11. Millersport was a small Ohio flatboat terminus across the river from Greenbottom.

35. July 20, 1821, CDB 3: 104. The italics are mine.

36. 1815 Slave Tax Book, Wilson Cary Nicholas Papers.

37. William Wirte to Wilson Cary Nicholas, Apr. 9, 1819, Wilson Cary Nicholas Papers, Box 11.
38. Trustees William Wirte and Robert Gamble placed the property on sale in Richmond on July 20, 1821, and Cabell bought it. However, between Mar. 1, 1821, and Sept. 20, 1825, he slowly conveyed it to John Coaltes and John Wilke. Since they were trustees of Governor Cabell, the property came in the form of a "trustee deed," as it had with W. C. Nicholas. However, Cabell County records show that the property was deeded to William Jenkins and John Hannan free of all encumbrances. This little "misrepresentation" may explain why the Bank of the United States came after Thomas Jefferson Randolph to seize Greenbottom. See Thomas Jefferson Randolph Papers, 1819–1839, MS2R1574b, Virginia Historical Society, Richmond.
39. See Note 38.
40. Greenbottom Baptist Church, Register and Minutes, June 20, 1840.
41. Janetta Jenkins to Laura Simms, Oct. 1829, Simms Family Papers, Natchez Historical Preservation Archives, Natchez, Miss. The Virginia Historical Society also contains letters from Laura and Janetta's sister in which she is mentioned (particularly Fannie to Hugh Blair Grigsby, where Janetta's marriage is discussed), but few letters back from her. Hugh Blair Grigsby Papers, 1745–1944, MSSIG 8782b 2049, Virginia Historical Society, Richmond. In all, about five exist, scattered across the country.
42. For example, Janetta's letter of Apr. 1824, Hugh Blair Grigsby Papers, MSSIG 8782b 1933.
43. See Rockbridge County, Marriage Bonds, 1823–28, Reel 64, Oct. 5, 1824, Library of Virginia, Richmond.
44. See Frances McNutt McChesney to Sally Hamilton, Hugh Blair Grigsby Papers, MSSIG 8782b 2057. All of these were preserved in Albert Gallatin Jenkins's library, which contained over 580 volumes and was inventoried by Cabell County after the Civil War. Cabell County, West Virginia, Probate Records, Estate of A. G. Jenkins (Deceased) Appraisement Bill, Apr. 1866.
45. Falling Springs Presbyterian Church Register, 1793–1899, VM Reel 20-A, Union Theological Seminary, Richmond, Va.
46. The itinerant minister's name was Irskine. Hugh Blair Grigsby Diary, July 27, 1829, Hugh Blair Grigsby Papers, MSSIG 8782b 71.
47. Janetta Jenkins to Laura Simms, Oct. 1829; Joseph Grigsby to Rachel Grigsby McNutt, n.d., Reuben Grigsby Papers, Special Collections, Washington and Lee Univ. Library, Lexington, Va.
48. Jack Dickinson, The Jenkins of Greenbottom: A Civil War Saga (Charleston, W.Va.: Pictorial Historic Publishing, 1988), 27.
49. Greenbottom Baptist Church, Register and Minutes, July–Oct. 1839, June 27, 1840; Aug. 1840.
50. Ibid., June 28, 1840.
51. See Hezekiah Chilton's June 17, 1840, statement and special session, ibid., Sept. 27, 1840.
52. Ibid.
53. Ibid., Jan. 1843, Aug. 1844.
54. Dickinson, The Jenkins of Greenbottom.
55. Falling Springs Presbyterian Church Register.

56. See Jenkins's speech to Eli Thayer at Ceredo, Virginia, Aug. 1857, discussed in Dickinson, *The Jenkins of Greenbottom.*

Works Cited

Annual Collections of the Port of New Orleans, 1800–1830. Vol. 2. New Orleans, La.

Beer, William. "Early Census Tables of Louisiana." *Louisiana Historical Society Publications* 2 (1911).

Cabell County, Virginia [West Virginia], Circuit Court Records, 1809–11. Cabell County Courthouse, Huntington, W.Va.

Cabell County, Virginia [West Virginia], Deed Books 1 and 4. Cabell County Courthouse, Huntington, W.Va.

Cabell County, Virginia [West Virginia], Probate Records. Cabell County Courthouse, Huntington, W.Va.

Cabell County, Virginia [West Virginia], Tax Assessments 1812, 1815. Cabell County Courthouse, Huntington, W.Va.

Cabell County, Virginia [West Virginia], *Union Tax List Based on the 1830 Census.*

Cabell County, Virginia [West Virginia], "Writs of Lost Property, 1815–1825." Cabell County Courthouse, Huntington, W.Va.

Cornelius, Janet. *When I Can Read My Title Clear: Literacy, Slavery and Religion in the Antebellum South.* Columbia: Univ. of South Carolina Press, 1991.

Crawford Family Papers. Special Collections, West Virginia Univ. Library, Morgantown.

Crawford and Ancell Family Papers. Miscellaneous 1802–15, Southwestern Louisiana State Univ. Library, Shreveport.

Cressy, David. *Literacy and the Social Order: Reading and Writing in Tudor and Stuart England.* New York: Cambridge Univ. Press, 1980.

Dickinson, Jack. *The Jenkins of Greenbottom: A Civil War Saga.* Charleston, W.Va.: Pictorial Historic Publishing, 1988.

Falling Springs Presbyterian Church, Register, 1793–1899. VM Reel 20-A. Union Theological Seminary, Richmond, Va.

Friedman, Jean. *The Enclosed Garden: Women and Community in the Evangelical South, 1830–1900.* Chapel Hill: Univ. of North Carolina Press, 1986.

Gates, Henry Louis. *The Signifying Monkey.* Ithaca: Cornell Univ. Press, 1988.

Graff, Harvey J. *The Labyrinths of Literacy.* London: Falmer Press, 1986.

Greenbottom Baptist Church, Register and Minutes, 1834–55. Quoted courtesy of the American Baptist Historical Society, Rochester, N.Y.

Hannan Family Papers. Elizabeth Hannan Papers, 1807–12. Special Collections, Univ. of Kentucky Library, Lexington.

Grigsby, Hugh Blair. Papers, 1745–1944. Virginia Historical Society, Richmond.

Grigsby, Reuben. Papers. Elisha Paxton, 1792–1856. Special Collections, Washington and Lee Univ. Library, Lexington, Va.

———. Papers. McNutt Family Papers, 1823–1910. Special Collections, Washington and Lee Univ. Library, Lexington, Va.

Kanawha County, Virginia [West Virginia], Book of Record (Index) to Federal Patents. West Virginia State Archives, Charleston.

Kearns, Robert. Telephone interview with author, Oct. 1992.

Mason County, Virginia [West Virginia], Chancery Record Book. Mason County Courthouse, Point Pleasant, W.Va.

Mason County, Virginia [West Virginia], Deed Book 1: "Index to Land Grants and Patents." Mason County Courthouse, Point Pleasant, W.Va.

Mason County, Virginia [West Virginia], Deed Book B. Mason County Courthouse, Point Pleasant, W.Va.

Mercer County, Kentucky. *Records of Deed and Land Holdings.* N.p., 1911.

Wilson Cary Nicholas Papers (no. 2343). Special Collections Dept., Univ. of Virginia Library, Charlottesville.

Wilson Cary Nicholas Papers (no. 2343). 1815 Slave Tax Book. Oversize Manuscript 2343, Folio 2. Special Collections Dept., Univ. of Virginia Library, Charlottesville.

Randolph, Thomas Jefferson. Papers, 1819–1839. Virginia Historical Society, Richmond.

Rockbridge County, Virginia. Marriage Bonds, 1823–28. Library of Virginia, Richmond.

Sawrey, Robert. *A National Register Evaluating Selected Archeological Sites in the Gallipolis Mitigation Site at Greenbottom.* Lexington, Ky.: Cultural Resources Analysis, 1990.

Simms Family Papers. Janetta Jenkins to Laura McNutt Simms, Oct. 1829. Natchez Historical Preservation Archives, Natchez, Miss.

United States Bureau of the Census. *Fourth Census of the United States, 1820.* Washington, D.C.

———. *Fifth Census of the United States, 1830.* Washington, D.C.

Vincent, David. *Literacy and Popular Culture: England, 1750–1914.* New York: Cambridge Univ. Press, 1990.

Wallace, George Selden. *Cabell County Annals and Families.* Richmond: Garrett and Massie, 1935.

Part IV

Community Ties in Southwest Virginia

As settlement progressed southward along Virginia's backcountry, many of the old dynamics involving contact and relationships between cultures remained current, but new dimensions were added as well. For those settlers who followed the main migration route through the Great Valley, or whose parents and grandparents had initiated the trek before them, the path became somewhat more tenuous and ties back East became problematic as they pressed farther into the remote wilderness. At the same time, they were met by new situations, as Virginia's administrative structure raced to catch up with settlement during the middle decades of the eighteenth century; later, by the time of the American Revolution and beyond, the region became a focus of state—and even national—political and economic issues, as the Appalachian frontier became a pivotal area in the evolution taking place.

The forces of the relative isolation of the southwest Virginia frontier and the pressures of the colonial administration may have led to a pragmatic approach to cultural relations in the region, helping to break down at least the official distinctions that remained. Political participation in southwest Virginia is the topic of Turk McCleskey's essay, though his analysis has more to do with ethnic relationships than with campaigns or elections. It is well known that British imperial policy restricted non-English, non-Anglican church members from holding public office, but that occasionally German immigrants on the Virginia frontier received appointments to local positions. McCleskey's focus is not on the fact that Germans held office only relatively infrequently, but rather that they held office at all.

In his comparison of two communities in Augusta County—the predominantly German Toms Creek neighborhood and the predominantly English settlement along Reed Creek—McCleskey finds that the same considerations went into the choice of local officials in each, regardless of ethnic prescription in the law. On the frontier, at least, colonial authorities judged potential leaders not on the language they spoke or the country of their origin, but rather applied standards such as material and economic substance, local prominence, an understanding of power and status, adherence to mainstream Protestantism, and a demonstrated loyalty to the principles and procedures of Virginia political culture. Therefore, political participation, like economic activity, tended to work against the existence of strict boundaries between ethnic groups and toward the opening of opportunity for persons of substance and initiative, making accommodation one of the very real dynamics of social development in the backcountry.

Settlers who migrated to southwest Virginia faced the troubling degree of separation that went along with frontier existence. If they had moved on from families who had previously settled farther north and east on the migration route, they likely left more behind—in terms of familiarity, material resources, and stability—than had earlier generations who had made their moves when backcountry society was less well established, in general. And for many who ventured into the rougher terrain beyond the Shenandoah drainage basin, the road back may have seemed even longer. As Gail Terry portrays, however, for elite families, at least, life on the frontier did not necessarily break the close bonds of family ties. She maintains that the oligarchic character of Virginia society, based on intertwined webs of elite families, survived both the Revolution and migration beyond the mountains. In addition, however, Terry addresses the level to which national political trends made their way into local backcountry contests in the decades after the Revolution, concluding that the conflict brought the seeds of change in the political culture of the region, including a recognition even among elite candidates that their run of rarely contested political dominance had ended, and that they had to appeal, to a greater degree, to the wishes of their constituents. Focusing on the Congressional elections of 1793, 1795, and 1797 in southwest Virginia, Terry examines the concerted efforts of the Preston clan to boost the political career of Francis Preston. Kinship remained a strong force at this level of society, and the actions of the Prestons suggest that the members of elite families recognized the continued importance of mutual support and loyalty.

The following essays support the thematic perspective that there was not just one, universal frontier experience. Obviously, the forces of life in the backcountry differed for Native American, African American, and European settlers, but as these chapters and those of the previous section illustrate, geographical and chronological setting also made a difference, within the cultural groups. Just as the challenges faced by black slaves in the Ohio Valley differed from those encountered in the Shenandoah Valley, Scotch-Irish, German, and English settlers experienced an environment and dynamics in southwest Virginia that in many ways differed from what they had left behind. Frederick Jackson Turner was correct in at least one respect: the frontier caused constant renewal as pioneers faced new situations. Whereas he emphasized conquest as the solution, the following chapters suggest the importance of perseverance and accommodation in coping with the challenges of the frontier.

Chapter 9

The Price of Conformity

Class, Ethnicity, and Local Authority on the Colonial Virginia Frontier

Turk McCleskey

From the beginning, interpreters of American settlement have been of two minds about the acculturation of foreign immigrants. Thomas Jefferson once lauded the docile orderliness of Germans settlers, claiming for them a social quiescence based on their distinctive culture; unable to speak English, "they confine themselves to their farms and their families, compare their present state to what it was in Europe, and find great reason to be contented." Later, though, Jefferson lost his certainty that cultural isolation produced biddable subjects. Eventually he argued that "It's better to discourage the settlement of foreigners in large masses, wherein, as in our German settlements, they preserve for a long time their own languages, habits, and principles of government."[1] Virginia's experience seemingly demonstrated that enclaves of alien culture could only threaten the American body politic.

Modern scholars of colonial Virginia have had no more success than Jefferson in reconciling issues of ethnic distinction and political participation. Historians like Thomas Perkins Abernethy followed Jefferson's early lead. "The Germans were the best farmers that the colonies ever had," Abernethy asserted about frontier families west of the Blue Ridge, "but they took little interest in politics and were not inclined to leave the farms which they had established."[2] Klaus Wust read the evidence quite differently, charging that in Virginia, "the determination of the colonial authorities to bring the West under effective control and the handicap of language conspired to deny the Germans the share they deserved in public offices."[3]

Abernethy's broad vision and Wust's deep research both produced images of Virginia Germans that are inconsistent with subsequent investigations of other colonies. In polyglot Pennsylvania, German speakers often held the balance of power in both provincial and local politics, and in Rowan County, North Carolina, and its successor, Surry County, Moravian magistrates supervised the legal interests of Germans and non-Germans alike.[4] Abernethy took no notice of comparable political activity in Virginia, and Wust dismissed Germans in government as cultural turncoats who shed their identity to curry favor with the Anglo-Virginian elite.[5] There matters remained stalled until recent work by A. G. Roeber at last moved the investigation of German roles in Virginia politics past the increasingly irrelevant issue of German exclusion. As part of his larger study of how German immigrants adopted an Anglo-American philosophy of property, Roeber found that the Germans of Hebron, Virginia, took to politics in very much the same way as their counterparts in North Carolina or Pennsylvania had.[6] Hebron residents did indeed express an interest in the county court system when their property was at stake, and both the county oligarchy and the Virginia Council were willing to vest German leaders with power and authority. The Hebron community produced few county officials by comparison to the more robust German communities west of the Blue Ridge—Roeber mentions one German justice of the peace and two militia lieutenants appointed from the community—but the possibility for German political ascension clearly existed even in eastern Virginia.[7]

Roeber's investigations advanced the study of Virginia Germans to a point comparable to other colonies, but, even so, important questions remain about the social significance of ethnicity, politics, and acculturation. Three issues in particular stand out. Most obviously, it is neither a myth nor a revelation that Germans settled together, creating predominantly German-speaking neighborhoods.[8] When they did so in Virginia west of the Blue Ridge Mountains, how did local political activity in those neighborhoods compare with county norms? It is also clear that German participation in public life required would-be leaders to make some sort of accommodation to the dominant Anglo-Virginian culture: Wust's assessment that "such men were hardly representative of the

German element" surely overstated the case, but it contains an important insight.[9] To play an effective political role in colonial Virginia,
German leaders had to learn more rules than just those pertaining to
government. Beyond politics, what other aspects of German life were
affected by the decision to participate in Virginia-style structures of local or colonial authority? And, finally, broad cultural accommodations
such as those demanded by the Virginia political process necessarily require a recalibration of cultural values. This change, or acculturation,
affected not just the individuals who elected to change, but also the
communities whom they represented. Is it possible to estimate the emotional cost of German acculturation?

    Two early Augusta County settlements in the New River valley—one
on Reed Creek and the other on Toms Creek—offer the opportunity to
compare ethnic aspects of local authority structures. Both communities
were established at about the same time—during the 1740s—and both
were remotely located in southwest Virginia. Spaced only a day's journey
apart, the two settlements were approximately equal in population, com-
parably endowed with good water and soil, equally distant from colonial
markets—and ultimately just as vulnerable to hostile Indians.[10]

    Their principal difference, of course, was in the European origins of
their population. The community of Anglo-American settlers was located
along the Reed Creek Valley in modern Wythe County, and it included a
total of sixteen resident landowners by 1754. The German American
community was centered around Toms Creek in modern Montgomery
County. It contained nineteen resident landowners by 1754 (table 9.1).

    Both the Reed Creek and Toms Creek settlements were developed in
parts of a one-hundred-thousand-acre grant issued by the Virginia Council to Col. James Patton and others in 1745.[11] This grant lay on the New
and Holston rivers, within Augusta County—of which Colonel Patton was
senior magistrate, senior militia officer, and premier land speculator.[12]
Patton may have recruited these settlers, British and German alike, during
his visit to southeastern Pennsylvania in the summer of 1744.[13] We certainly know that he advertised Augusta County land for sale in the *Pennsylvania Gazette* the following winter, clear evidence that Patton saw a potential market to the north.[14]

    In any event, by 1746 the two creek valleys were sufficiently well popu-
lated to require official regulation. During the earliest period of settlement
in the Reed Creek community, one inhabitant acted simultaneously as senior militia officer and magistrate, while another held concurrently the offices of constable and road overseer. With time, some of these functions

Table 9.1.
Initial Acquisitions of Toms Creek Land as of 1754

Name	Price in £	Acreage
Adams, John	25	210
Barrier, Casper	50	507
Byers, William	20	160
Cook, John	24	190
Draper, John	25:5:0	315
Draper, John, & Wm Ingles	35	440
Harman, Adam	?	500
Harman, Jacob, Jr.	75	625
Harpe, Harness	40	320
Ingles, William	20:70:0	255
Kinder, Conrad	35	290
Leppard, William	70	620
Lingle, Jacob	32	280
Lorton, Jacob	79	560
Loy, Martin	30	230
Price: Augustine, Daniel, Henry	80	1,130
Sharp, George	35	285
Wood James	?	650

NOTES: Adam Harman's 500 acres was a patent. James Wood's 650 acres was a survey. The remaining transactions were all purchases of a portion of James Patton's 7,500-acre patent on Toms Creek. James Wood was not actually a resident in the Toms Creek neighborhood.

were distributed among other settlers. In 1750, the Augusta County court appointed a separate militia captain and a separate road overseer. Two years later, a pair of Reed Creek residents became junior officers—a lieutenant and an ensign—in the Reed Creek militia company (table 9.2). All the while, Reed Creek settlers participated in Augusta County public life as actively as their relatively remote locations would permit. Between 1745 and 1755, inhabitants of Reed Creek appeared occasionally but with increasing frequency as members of juries, witnesses to court documents, and appraisers of neighborhood estates.[15]

The development of officeholding in Toms Creek differed little from that in Reed Creek (table 9.3). The earliest official in Toms Creek was, like his counterpart in Reed Creek, appointed to serve both as road

Table 9.2.
Officeholding by Reed Creek Residents through 1755

Date	Office	Name	Source
9/21/1744	militia colonel	Buchanan, John	Draper Mss 1QQ26
12/9/1745	undersheriff	Buchanan, John	AOB 1:2
12/9/1745	magistrate	Buchanan, John	AOB 1:2
7/16/1746	coroner	Buchanan, John	AOB 1:71
11/19/1746	road overseer	Calhoun, James	AOB 1:130
1746	constable	Calhoun, James	AOB 1:198
4/6/1747	vestryman	Buchanan, John	Aug Parish VB. p 1
5/23/1750	road overseer	Crockett, Joseph	AOB 2:371
5/23/1750	road overseer	McFarland, John	AOB 2:371
11/29/1750	militia captain	Calhoun, James	AOB 2:501
1751	constable	McFarland, John	
8/20/1752	militia captain	Sayers, Alexander	AOB 3:318
11/16/1752	militia captain	Crockett, Joseph	AOB 3:366
11/16/1752	militia captain	McFarland, John	AOB 3:366
11/16/1752	militia lieutenant	McFarland, Robert	AOB 3:366
3/25/1754	road overseer	McCall, James	AOB 4:142
3/25/1754	road overseer	Miller, James	AOB 4:142
3/20/1755	magistrate	Sayers, Alexander	AOB 4:382

overseer and militia captain.[16] This new official, Adam Harman, was a German Lutheran.[17] His combined duties involved the oversight not only of fourteen of his German neighbors but of four British neighbors as well. Harman's responsibilities increased still further when the Augusta County court appointed him as constable for the Toms Creek vicinity after the death of the area's Anglo-Virginian constable in 1749.[18] Like Reed Creek, Toms Creek continued to grow in the early 1750s.

Table 9.3.
Officeholding by Toms Creek Residents through 1755 (Germans Italicized)

Date	Office	Name	Source
11/19/1746	road overseer	*Harman, Adam*	AOB 1:130
2/18/1746/7	militia captain	*Harman, Adam*	AOB 1:152
5/21/1747	constable	Draper, George[a]	AOB 1:198
6/14/1749	magistrate	Ingles, Thomas	EJC 5:290
10/27/1749	magistrate	Ingles, Thomas	EJC 5:303
5/25/1750	tithable taker	Ingles, Thomas	AOB 2:380
1750	constable	Ingles, Thomas	Chalkley 1:436
5/30/1751	tithable taker	Ingles, Thomas	AOB 2:586
6/11/1751	magistrate	Ingles, Thomas	AOB 3:176
1752 or before	constable	*Harman, Adam*	AOB 4:9
8/19/1752	militia captain	*Harman, Adam*	AOB 3:313
8/19/1752	militia cornet	*Harman, Jacob, Jr.*	AOB 3:313
8/19/1752	militia lieutenant	*Price, Augustine*	AOB 3:313
8/16/1753	road overseer	*Leppard, William*[b]	AOB 4:9
8/16/1753	constable	*Leppard, William*[b]	AOB 4:9
3/25/1754	road overseer	*Leppard, William*	AOB 4:142
8/24/1754	militia captain	Ingles, William	AOB 4:289

NOTES: [a]Died by May 1749. August County Will Book 1:127 (microfilm, VSLA). [b]Replaced Adam Harman.

By 1752, some further differentiation of local officeholding proved necessary, and the Augusta County court appointed two additional German colonists—Augustine Price and Jacob Harman—to serve as junior officers in the local militia.[19] And in 1753, Adam Harman relinquished two of his three public duties—constable and road overseer—to his German neighbor William Leppard.[20] During these years, Toms Creek residents also participated in more intermittent forms of community service as jurymen, witnesses to documents, or court-appointed appraisers in actions that affected Anglo as well as German members of their community. In short, the British settlers of Reed Creek and the predominantly German settlers of Toms Creek shared similar experiences in the establishment and succession of local officeholding.

The only significant distinction between Reed Creek and Toms Creek lies in the office of magistrate—and for colonial Virginians, of course, that distinction was no small matter. Both communities included a justice of the peace among their resident landowners, and in both communities that magistrate was British. On Toms Creek, the magistrate's office was occupied from the spring of 1749 to the spring of 1752 by Thomas Ingles, even though by that time Germans outnumbered British settlers by a ratio of about six to one.[21]

Excluding Germans from the office of magistrate does not necessarily indicate a discriminatory limit on upward mobility for Germans—after all, they were still legally excluded from *any* authority.[22] County officials cannot be said to have discriminated if a higher power prevented them from promoting Germans. Moreover, Augusta County officials did pick German magistrates in other neighborhoods: two Germans, Peter Scholl and Mathias Selzer, served as justices of the peace in the northern end of the county during the latter 1740s and early 1750s.[23] The appointment of these German magistrates suggests a tolerance for German officeholders far exceeding the imperial limits—and a tolerance that extended well beyond the improvisations of a frontier county.

Arguably, low-level German officials like Adam Harman, Augustine Price, and William Leppard were expedient appointments, designated by county officials who knew that such junior militia officers, constables, and road overseers need never come to the attention of colonial authorities, let alone agents of the king. But higher officers, magistrates such as Peter Scholl and Mathias Selzer or militia captains like Scholl and Adam Harman, could not be concealed. Their nominations necessarily required approval by the governor and council of Virginia, which implicated the colony's highest officers in the appointment of Germans to the Augusta County bench.

The best way to account for this colonial complicity is to recognize that county leaders and colonial leaders alike appraised Germans for their potential to regulate and govern. The members of the Virginia elite who controlled the early settlement of Augusta County cared less about ethnicity than about creating the sort of hierarchical society that was well established back East. Colonial and county leaders therefore manipulated access to land and officeholding in order to insure that those who achieved wealth and power along the Virginia frontier would be very like themselves in social sensibility.[24] The standards were identical to those imposed on Anglo-Americans, and if Germans passed the test, they could serve.[25]

Peter Scholl and Mathias Selzer clearly measured up. Scholl, a leader of the Peaked Mountain Presbyterian congregation, owned a 420-acre farm on the North Fork of the Shenandoah and, in addition to a decade's service as justice of the peace, also held office in Augusta County as a militia captain, tithable taker, and coroner.[26] Selzer, an affluent Lutheran with ties to the German communities in Lancaster, Pennsylvania, and Hebron, Virginia, owned 250 acres in the vicinity of Peaked Mountain (Massanutten Mountain) during his tenure as an Augusta County magistrate; before his appointment to that office, Selzer served as a road overseer and processioner.[27]

Their visible success as frontier entrepreneurs, county officials, mainstream Protestants, and leaders within their own communities enabled Germans like Scholl and Selzer to transcend much of the stigma that might otherwise have attached to their ethnic origins. Class counted for more than ethnicity, so Germans and elite Anglo-Virginians alike at first ignored the formality of naturalization. Naturalization ceremonies thus were rare in early Augusta County, and no Toms Creek Germans took part in them before 1758. Instead, Toms Creek Germans received authority long before they acquired citizenship: militia cornet Jacob Harman Jr. was naturalized in 1758, six years after his appointment to that position, and militia lieutenant Augustine Price was naturalized thirteen years after his promotion to that office.[28] In the high-stakes game of Virginia authority, behavior trumped nationality.

Beyond behavior, though, it is also possible to recognize something of the interior perspectives of German officials and the citizens they governed. Outwardly, Germans who aspired to authority had to convince Virginia elites of their loyalty not just to the British crown, but to the hierarchically organized society over which the monarch ruled. Inwardly, Germans who aspired to public authority had to accept and implement the deferential nuances of Virginia society. Three pieces of evidence from Augusta County give some insights into how this acculturation worked and what it cost.

The first evidence comes from the Peaked Mountain neighborhood, in what today is Rockingham County. Local magistrate Peter Scholl, a Calvinist, worshiped not with other Germans in a Reformed congregation, but instead attended a Presbyterian meeting house.[29] Scholl's membership in a Scotch-Irish, rather than German, congregation presumably accomplished both a spiritual and a secular goal. Individually, Scholl practiced his

faith while collectively identifying with the majority Scotch-Irish population. Scholl's actions are comparable to actions of Germans in Pennsylvania, who responded to Anglo-Pennsylvanian ethnic suspicions by demon-
strating respectability.[30] The example tells us that Scholl modified his
behavior, but he left no record of what he or his neighbors thought about
the change.

A second example, this one involving the Toms Creek community,
suggests that accepting Anglo-Virginian norms sometimes generated considerable heat within German communities. In 1749, Captain Adam Harman levied treason charges against fellow German Jacob
Cassell for allegedly threatening to move to the Mississippi River and live
among the French settlements there. Harman attempted to forestall
Cassell's departure by attaching, or confiscating, some of Cassell's personal property. To the militia captain, Cassell's nationality made
no difference; the key issue was Cassell's willingness to switch loyalties away from the British crown.[31]

Captain Harman's probable motives seem relatively clear, but Cassell's
purpose is less certain: did he threaten to defect in order to escape Anglo-
American government, or just that government's local representative? In
Augusta County this was precisely the sort of disrespect that contemporary elites treated as antisocial behavior. As usual in such cases, frontier
magistrates preferred ritual atonement to stiffer punishment, thus
drawing the offender back into his properly deferential role in the social hierarchy.[32] Cassell escaped lightly; the county court acquitted him
of Harman's charge.[33] Indeed, Cassell not only defended himself successfully, but also retaliated for the attachment of his property by having
Harman and his assistant jailed for violent robbery.[34] The two men almost
certainly disliked each other, but any further attribution of a motive for
Cassell's rebellion can only be speculative. As in the case of Peter Scholl's
Presbyterianism, the surviving documentary evidence describes an external
conformity but cannot explain individual motives or psychic costs.

The Anglophonic documentary record may be silent on these matters,
but other German artifacts are not. Evidence about the internal aspects of
German conformity takes tangible shape in an assemblage of eighteenth-
and early-nineteenth-century German houses near Peaked Mountain,
known today as Massanutten Mountain. The older houses conform to a
traditional German *Flurküchenhaus* design, but later buildings, such as
Fort Stover (1760), reflect changes in how Germans thought about
their houses. From the outside, Fort Stover looks like a traditional
Anglo-American hall-parlor house of the colonial period, but this fa-

cade covers a *Flurküchenhaus* interior.[35] The result is a powerful metaphor for German acculturation in the Great Valley.

From a distance, Fort Stover's German occupants looked like good Virginians, using architecture to demonstrate fealty to Anglo-Virginian culture. Beneath the surface presentation, though, they hid a valued part of their traditional culture, camouflaging a German dwelling as a Virginia house. Fort Stover and other buildings in the vicinity of Massanutten Mountain thus caution modern historians that German acculturation as church members, county officials, or property owners cannot be taken simply as part of a relatively benign and naturally inevitable process of becoming American.

Once we define political participation to include local as well as colonial government, the willingness of German officials to champion the principles of Virginia political culture stands out as a prominent feature in the history of the colonial frontier. At first glance the Germans look both separate and equal: in the Toms Creek neighborhood of southwest Virginia, an essentially German community defined itself with an almost exclusive geography from the earliest days of settlement, but, having acquired land, the Toms Creek Germans organized themselves *politically* after the British colonial pattern.

The Toms Creek residents and their German peers throughout colonial Virginia found a reception commensurate with their status as men of property. Like Anglo-American men of substance, German frontier leaders continuously reshaped themselves and their communities in an ever more exact approximation of eastern Virginia. They were not all separatists, and they were not all excluded; instead, German officials participated willingly in the fabrication of a deferential, hierarchical frontier society. Beneath the surface, though, ran a powerful tension. The same pressure to conform that found expression as Fort Stover's Anglicized facade also offers the best explanation for the angry clash two hundred miles away between Jacob Cassell and Adam Harman. German society paid a stiff price for its American liberty and property.

Notes

1. Boyd, *Papers of Jefferson*, vol. 12: 6, and Lipscomb, et al., eds., *The Writings of Thomas Jefferson*, vol. 15: 140, as quoted in Wust, *The Virginia Germans* (Charlottesville: Univ. Press of Virginia, 1969), 107.
2. Thomas Perkins Abernethy, "The Southern Frontier: An Interpretation," in *The Frontier in Perspective*, ed. Walker D. Wyman and Clifton B. Kroeber (Madison: Univ. of Wisconsin Press, 1957), 134.
3. Klaus Wust, *Virginia Germans*, 43.

4. John J. Zimmerman, "Benjamin Franklin and the Quaker Party, 1755–1756," *William and Mary Quarterly* 3d ser., 17 (1960): 292–93; J. Philip Gleason, "A Scurrilous Colonial Election and Franklin's Reputation," *William and Mary Quarterly* 3d ser., 18 (1961): 78–81; Benjamin H. Newcomb, "Effects of the Stamp Act on Colonial Pennsylvania Politics," *William and Mary Quarterly* 3d ser., 23 (1966): 258–60; Jerome H. Wood Jr., *Conestoga Crossroads: Lancaster, Pennsylvania, 1730–1790* (Harrisburg: Pennsylvania Historical and Museum Commission, 1979), 27–31; Daniel B. Thorp, *The Moravian Community in Colonial North Carolina* (Knoxville: Univ. of Tennessee Press, 1989), 164–68.

5. Wust, *Virginia Germans,* 109–11.

6. In his earlier work, Roeber leaned toward the Abernethy interpretation, arguing that German immigrants were more interested in maintaining their distinctive private lives than they were in joining the ranks of colonial British officialdom. He stated that "German-speakers' relations with British political institutions were overwhelmingly positive," implying somewhat paradoxically that Germans liked British-style authority so well that they saw no need to acquire any for themselves. "'The Origin of Whatever Is Not English among Us': The Dutch-speaking and the German-speaking Peoples of Colonial British America," in *Strangers Within the Realm: Cultural Margins of the First British Empire,* ed. Bernard Bailyn and Philip D. Morgan (Chapel Hill: Univ. of North Carolina Press, 1991), 241. For the Virginia portion of this transformation, see A. G. Roeber, *Palatines, Liberty, and Property: German Lutherans in Colonial British America* (Baltimore: Johns Hopkins Univ. Press, 1993), 135–58.

7. The magistrate, Jost Hite, soon removed to the Shenandoah Valley; Roeber identifies a second justice of the peace, Benjamin Borden, as a German, but this is almost certainly an error. Roeber, *Palatines, Liberty, and Property,* 141–42. Borden, an immigrant to the Valley by way of New Jersey, sold none of his 92,100-acre grant to Germans. For sources of my colonial Augusta County land database, see Turk McCleskey, "Rich Land, Poor Prospects: Real Estate and the Formation of a Social Elite in Augusta County, Virginia, 1738–1770," *Virginia Magazine of History and Biography* 98 (1990): 449n. 2.

8. James A. Henretta, "Families and Farms: *Mentalité* in Pre-Industrial America," *William and Mary Quarterly* 3d ser., 35 (1978): 4.

9. Wust, *Virginia Germans,* 109.

10. The sole early distinction may lie in the relative affluence of the settlers: initial German investments in real estate substantially outweighed the investments of Reed Creek purchasers (see n. 26 below).

11. Patton was listed as the senior partner in the council's order, dated Apr. 26, 1745. Wilmer L. Hall, ed., *Executive Journals of the Council of Colonial Virginia,* (Richmond: Virginia State Library, 1967), 5: 173 (hereafter cited as EJC).

12. Patton was listed as the most senior magistrate in every commission of the peace for Augusta County between 1749 and 1755, when he was killed by Indians at Toms Creek. For the first 1749 commission, see EJC 5: 191; for the last in Patton's lifetime, see Augusta County Court Order Book 4: 382, Microfilm, Library of Virginia, Richmond (hereafter cited as AOB). For Patton's commission as county lieutenant, or senior militia officer, see AOB 3: 310.

13. "William Black Journal," *Pennsylvania Magazine of History and Biography* 1 (1887): 413 (June 4, 1744), and 418 (June 6, 1744).

14. *Pennsylvania Gazette,* Feb. 12, 1745/46.

15. Mary B. Kegley, *Wythe County, Virginia: A Bicentennial History* (Wytheville, Va.: Wythe County Board of Supervisors, 1989), 35.
16. AOB 1: 152.
17. "Agreement between the Reformed and Lutheran Congregations," *William and Mary Quarterly* 1st ser., 13 (1905): 249–50.
18. The constable, George Draper, was appointed May 21, 1747, and died by May 1749. AOB 1: 198; Augusta County Will Book 1, Microfilm, Library of Virginia, Richmond, 127. Harman's appointment was not recorded, but the county court replaced him on Aug. 16, 1753. AOB 4: 9.
19. AOB 3: 313.
20. AOB 4: 9; 4: 142.
21. According to the antebellum family tradition, Thomas Ingles came from Dublin, Ireland, to southwest Virginia via Wales and Pennsylvania. F. B. Kegley, *Kegley's Virginia Frontier: The Beginning of the Southwest, The Roanoke of Colonial Days, 1740–1783* (Roanoke, Va.: Southwest Virginia Historical Society, 1938), 194. The six-to-one ratio compares resident German landowners (seventeen) to resident British landowners (two), plus Thomas Ingles.
22. Under British law, naturalized citizens could not hold office in the colonies until the eve of the American Revolution. Roeber, "Origin of Whatever Is Not English among Us," 265n. 87.
23. Peter Scholl was first commissioned on Oct. 30, 1745, and was absent from the commission presented in court on Mar. 20, 1755, probably because a boundary change between Augusta and Frederick Counties shifted his residence to the latter polity. Mathias Selzer was appointed in the commission of Oct. 27, 1749, and dropped from Gov. Dinwiddie's "reform" commission on Apr. 30, 1752. EJC 5: 191, 303, 389; AOB 4: 382. I am indebted to John M. Hemphill II for explaining Dinwiddie's efforts to increase the governor's control over county commissions of the peace, an ambition that seemingly cost Selzer his place on the Augusta County bench. Dinwiddie retained Scholl, who ranked third in the commission of Apr. 30, 1752.
24. McCleskey, "Rich Land, Poor Prospects," 449–86.
25. Toms Creek Germans, especially the larger landowners, in part demonstrated their financial resources through their purchase of real estate. With the exception of a tract bought by Augustine, Daniel, and Henry Price for 1 shilling, 5 pence per acre, developer James Patton charged each of the Toms Creek German purchasers at least 2 shillings per acre, or 10 pounds per hundred acres. Omitting the Price family, the highest charge was 2 shillings, 10 pence per acre and the median charge was 2 shillings, 5 pence (table 9.1). By comparison, unimproved land elsewhere in Augusta County sold for £3:6:6 per hundred acres in the late 1740s. Robert D. Mitchell, *Commercialism and Frontier: Perspectives on the Early Shenandoah Valley* (Charlottesville: Univ. Press of Virginia, 1977), 76.
26. Scholl's denomination is listed in the lease for the Peaked Mountain joint Presbyterian/Lutheran meeting house, May 20, 1765. Augusta County Deed Book 19: 227, Microfilm, Library of Virginia, Richmond (hereafter cited as ADB). Peaked Mountain today is known as Massanutten Mountain. For his landholding, see Northern Neck Grants, Book G, p. 229, Library of Virginia, Richmond. For officeholding, see Proceedings of Augusta County Militia Courtmartial, Sept. 21, 1744, and Jan. 15, 1744/45, Draper Mss. 1QQ26 and 1QQ28, Microfilm, State Historical Society of Wisconsin, Madison; AOB 1: 47, 3: 312.

27. For Selzer's affluence, denomination, and connections, see Roeber, *Palatines, Liberty, and Property,* 139. For his landholding, see Orange County Deed Books 5:42, 5:195, Library of Virginia, Richmond, and Patent Book 35: 290, Library of Virginia. For early officeholding, see AOB 1:51, and Augusta Parish Vestry Book, 4–10, Manuscript, Library of Virginia, Richmond.

28. Two of the first Toms Creek purchasers and one relative of an original settler eventually performed the required acts—took the sacrament, swore an oath to the king's person and government, subscribed the abjuration and test, and received their certification from the county government. These were Jacob Harman, Aug. 16, 1758, Stephen Loy, May 24, 1765, and Augustine Price, Oct. 16, 1765. AOB 6: 180, 9: 368, 10: 8. For a complete list of naturalizations in colonial Augusta County, see Katherine Gentry Bushman, ed., *Naturalization Records: Augusta County, Virginia, 1753–1902* (Verona, Va.: Mid-Valley Press, 1992), 1.

29. ADB 19: 227.

30. Roeber, *Palatines, Liberty, and Property,* 244.

31. AOB 2: 105, and Lyman Chalkley, *Chronicles of the Scotch-Irish Settlement of Virginia, Extracted from the Original Court Records of Augusta County, 1745–1800,* 3 vols., (1912; reprint, Baltimore: Genealogical Publishing Co., Inc., 1980), 1: 434. Cassell was an early landowner on the South Shenandoah, purchasing two hundred acres on the South Shenandoah River from Jacob Stoever in 1740; he subdivided his property and sold the remainder in 1742. Orange County Deed Book 4: 47, 52, and 8: 228. For Cassell's subsequent move to the New River valley, see road petition in Chalkley, *Chronicles of Scotch-Irish Settlement,* 1: 434.

32. For example, when one James Akry was arraigned in 1752 "for Mispreson [*sic*] of Treason in speaking disrespectfully of the King," the Augusta County magistrates accepted Akry's apology and let him off with only a token fine and a modest bond for future good behavior. The fine was five shillings, and the bond was ten pounds (AOB 3: 260). Akry owned no land and held no office in Augusta County before this incident.

33. A called court acquitted Cassell on May 22, 1749. AOB 2: 130.

34. Chalkley, *Chronicles of Scotch-Irish Settlement,* 1: 432, 433.

35. Edward A. Chappell, "Acculturation in the Shenandoah Valley: Rhenish Houses of the Massanutten Settlement," in *Common Places: Readings in American Vernacular Architecture,* ed. Dell Upton and John Michael Vlach (Athens: Univ. of Georgia Press, 1986), 27–57.

Works Cited

Abernethy, Thomas Perkins. "The Southern Frontier: An Interpretation." In *The Frontier in Perspective.* Edited by Walker D. Wyman and Clifton B. Kroeber. Madison: Univ. of Wisconsin Press, 1957.

"Agreement between the Reformed and Lutheran Congregations." *William and Mary Quarterly* 1st ser., 13 (1905): 249–50.

Augusta County Court Order Books. Microfilm. Library of Virginia, Richmond.

Augusta County Vestry Books. Microfilm. Library of Virginia, Richmond.

Augusta County Will Books. Microfilm. Library of Virginia, Richmond.

[Black, William.] "William Black Journal." *Pennsylvania Magazine of History and Biography* I (1887): 117–32, 233–49, 404–19; II (1888): 40–49.

Bushman, Katherine Gentry, editor. *Naturalization Records: Augusta County, Virginia, 1753–1902*. Verona, Va.: Mid-Valley Press, 1992.

Chalkley, Lyman. *Chronicles of the Scotch-Irish Settlement of Virginia*. 3 vols. 1912. Reprint, Baltimore: Genealogical Publishing Co., Inc., 1980.

Chappell, Edward A. "Acculturation in the Shenandoah Valley, Rhenish Houses of the Massanutten Settlement." In *Common Places: Readings in American Vernacular Architecture*, edited by Dell Upton and John Michael Vlach, 27–57. Athens: Univ. of Georgia Press, 1986.

Draper, Lyman C. Collection. Microfilm. State Historical Society of Wisconsin, Madison.

Gleason, J. Philip. "A Scurrilous Colonial Election and Franklin's Reputation." *William and Mary Quarterly* 3d ser., 18 (1961): 68–84.

McIlwaine, H. R., et al., editors. *Executive Journals of the Council of Colonial Virginia*. 6 vols. Richmond: Virginia State Library, 1925–67.

Henretta, James A. "Families and Farms: *Mentalité* in Pre-Industrial America." *William and Mary Quarterly* 3d ser., 35 (1978): 3–32.

Kegley, F. B. *Kegley's Virginia Frontier: The Beginning of the Southwest, The Roanoke of Colonial Days, 1740–1783*. Roanoke: Southwest Virginia Historical Society, 1938.

Kegley, Mary B. *Wythe County, Virginia: A Bicentennial History*. Wytheville, Va.: Wythe County Board of Supervisors, 1989.

McCleskey, Turk. "Rich Land, Poor Prospects: Real Estate and the Formation of a Social Elite in Augusta County, Virginia, 1738–1770." *Virginia Magazine of History and Biography* 98 (1990): 449–86.

Mitchell, Robert D. *Commercialism and Frontier: Perspectives on the Early Shenandoah Valley*. Charlottesville: Univ. Press of Virginia, 1977.

Newcomb, Benjamin H. "Effects of the Stamp Act on Colonial Pennsylvania Politics." *William and Mary Quarterly* 3d ser., 23 (1966): 257–72.

Orange County Deed Books. Microfilm. Library of Virginia, Richmond.

Pennsylvania Gazette, 1728–76.

Roeber, A. G. "'The Origin of Whatever Is Not English among Us': The Dutch-speaking and the German-speaking Peoples of Colonial British America," In *Strangers Within the Realm: Cultural Margins of the First British Empire*, edited by Bernard Bailyn and Philip D. Morgan, 220–83. Chapel Hill: Univ. of North Carolina Press, 1991.

———. *Palatines, Liberty, and Property: German Lutherans in Colonial British America*. Baltimore: Johns Hopkins Univ. Press, 1993.

Thorp, Daniel B. *The Moravian Community in Colonial North Carolina*. Knoxville: Univ. of Tennessee Press, 1989.

Wood, Jerome H., Jr. *Conestoga Crossroads: Lancaster, Pennsylvania, 1730–1790*. Harrisburg: Pennsylvania Historical and Museum Commission, 1979.

Wust, Klaus. *The Virginia Germans*. Charlottesville: Univ. Press of Virginia, 1969.

Zimmerman, John J. "Benjamin Franklin and the Quaker Party, 1755–1756." *William and Mary Quarterly* 3d ser., 17 (1960): 291–313.

Chapter 10

An Old Family Confronts the New Politics

The Preston-Trigg Congressional Contests of the 1790s

Gail S. Terry

In 1793 Francis Preston and Abram Trigg vied to represent the far western counties of Virginia in the United States House of Representatives; both came from prominent western Virginia families and both were, at least nominally, Republicans. Preston won the election, but Trigg contested the results, citing irregularities in the polling in Montgomery County. Preston's brother, a captain in the United States Army, had paraded about seventy soldiers around the courthouse, blocked the door, and prevented several Trigg supporters from voting. Captain Preston then demanded that his soldiers be allowed to vote. Some scuffling occurred, a county magistrate was knocked to the ground, and a riot broke out. In 1794 the House Committee on elections reviewed and supported Trigg's case, but the House as a whole decided that Preston should retain his seat.[1]

The Preston-Trigg encounter remains one of the more colorful examples of contested elections in the scholarly literature on political development in the early republic, and historians usually cite the fact that Preston retained his seat to illustrate how little the practice of politics actually changed in the South or in western Virginia following the American Revolution.[2] That contest and two subsequent ones between

Francis Preston and Abram Trigg are re-examined here to illuminate the ways that individuals grappled with and eventually adjusted to the political and social changes accompanying the American Revolution, the ratification of the Constitution, and the creation of the nation. Analysis of the rich personal correspondence among members of the Preston family as well as the published debates between Francis Preston and his adversaries make possible this reconstruction of events as they unfolded. In addition to Preston and Trigg, two other pivotal figures emerge from these documents: Preston's sister, Eliza Madison, and Alexander Smyth, an ambitious young man and comparatively recent immigrant to Virginia.

A close examination of all three Preston-Trigg elections reveals the extent to which the family remained a significant force in politics, even as the first American party system took shape. Preston family members, including Eliza Madison, actively worked to promote the election of their kinsman, family connections continued to contribute to the definition of one's place in the social and political order, and family honor figured in the published debates and influenced the behavior of individual family members. At the same time, an increasingly polarized debate between Federalists and Republicans in the 1790s provided well-educated newcomers like Alexander Smyth with opportunities to challenge longer-established governing families like the Prestons, to enter the regional elite, and to attain national office.

Historians of the family in eighteenth-century Virginia have tended to focus their inquiries on the eastern gentry and generally concluded that family life in the last half of the century was characterized by a growing privatism. Daniel Blake Smith emphasized the emergence of the child-centered nuclear family in this period, while Jan Lewis stressed the eastern gentry's retreat from public life into an emotional, family-centered lifestyle.[3] The experience of the Preston family did not follow this pattern. Political historians have offered a less uniform interpretation of the same period. Charles Sydnor provided the classic description of a political system where family oligarchies passed power from one generation to the next with the tacit support of the lesser orders. Most historians writing about the relationship between politics and society since Sydnor have concluded that the era of the American Revolution marked a shift away from an older system of politics and government based on kinship, patronage, and influence to a newer one resting on merit and sociability. There is considerable disagreement on the timing of the transition, however, and on the relationship between political theory and practice.[4] This analysis of the Preston-Trigg elections reminds scholars of

the continuing public significance of the family in the early national period and beyond and refines their understanding of the evolving relationship
between politics and society in the early republic.

Members of the Preston family had been among the governing elite
of Virginia since their arrival in 1738, when Francis Preston's father, William, emigrated from Ireland as a child with his parents, sisters, and uncle,
James Patton. Patton, who entered the colony with connections to the eastern Virginia gentry, immediately held important positions in government
on the Virginia frontier.[5] After William Preston's father died in 1748 or
1749, his only son became Patton's protégé. William served in the House of
Burgesses, commanded the Montgomery County militia during the War for
Independence, and held the position of surveyor for that county, at a time
when it included most of western Virginia as well as the state of Kentucky.
Francis was too young to benefit directly from his father's patronage
before his death in 1783, but William aided several of his Breckinridge
nephews by making them his deputy and assistant surveyors. When twenty-
two-year-old Francis Preston began his political career in 1787, he appeared to stand securely within a system under which family oligarchies transferred power from one generation to the next.[6]

By the late 1780s, however, both Francis and his older brother John
had accepted popular sovereignty as the basis for government and recognized the importance of a representative's role as advocate for his
constituents, although neither expressed much confidence in the ability
of the voters to choose those best qualified to govern. Instead, a sense
of family solidarity and of their own right to hold office characterized
the Preston family's correspondence. When Francis ran for election to
the Virginia House of Delegates from Montgomery County, his brother
John suggested that he temporarily abandon his legal studies at the College of William and Mary to be present for the polling at the opposite
end of the state. John also outlined for Francis what the people expected
from a candidate:

> You ought to prepare a political speech & deliver it to them: if it should
> consist of froath only it will please but let it touch on the principals of Gov-
> ernment, the office of a representative, his duty &c. & how amenable he is
> to the people for his conduct & submit yourself to them alone: The division
> of the county is the main object among them therefore tho it should be contrary to
> your opinion you must be for it. Many other things you will be obliged to
> do to make yourself agreeable [to them] tho not pleasing to you. I'll inform
> you what they are when you arrive which will be time enough.

Perhaps Francis failed to heed his brother's advice; when the House of Delegates met in Richmond eight months later, Francis was not among them.[7]

Both brothers proved more successful in the 1790s; in 1792, John Preston was elected to the Virginia State Senate. He asked his cousin, James Breckinridge, a Federalist and an attorney who resided in Botetourt County, to attend the polling there and to see that, if appropriate, an "instrument of writing purporting my intentions should be made public at your Court House" drawn up in the "electioneering stile." He also asked John Smith, probably not a relative, to write to the most "respectable" Germans in the county and solicit their support. Despite his fear that "the passions & whims of the people (on whom we must depend) ebbs and flows very frequently: [and] it may be the tide of their passions are at ebb on the day of the election with me," John Preston won his election. After it was over, his brothers represented him at the meeting of the county sheriffs to certify the returns.[8]

In the following year Francis Preston and Abram Trigg opposed each other in the contest to represent western Virginia in the U.S. Congress. Like Preston, Trigg also came from a prominent family. He had represented Montgomery County at the Virginia Ratifying Convention in 1788, where he had opposed the new Constitution, and two of his brothers had served in the Virginia House of Delegates during the 1780s. According to Preston, Trigg "industriously engaged in promoting his popularity," and Francis appealed to his brother in the state senate for help. When the creation of the separate state of Kentucky prompted a reconfiguration of Congressional districts in Virginia, Francis asked John to see that Greenbriar County, in present-day West Virginia, was included in his district. Greenbriar's representatives, along with those from other northwestern and Shenandoah Valley counties, had supported the new Constitution at the Virginia Ratifying Convention, while delegates from the southwestern counties had not, and Preston believed that he would be advantaged by a larger district. Greenbriar was added to the district, and Francis Preston won the election by a narrow margin.[9]

Preston's success at the polls signaled the beginning, not the end, of a bitter political rivalry. In June 1793 Trigg contested the election in Montgomery County on the grounds that Francis's brother William Preston, a captain in the U.S. Army, "did interfere and influence the said election . . . by insisting that his soldiers should be polled and evincing a determination to enforce the receipt of their votes . . . [and] By Causing his soldiers during the time of taking the poll . . . repeatedly to march to the Court house

Map 10.1. Francis Preston's Congressional district, 1793.

and manoeuvre before and around the same . . . with intent to intimidate those who were in favor of your petitioner . . . [and] by permitting his soldiers to mix with the voters . . . among whom they conducted themselves in an assuming, turbulent, insolent and riotous manner." Trigg also charged that residents of Kentucky, now a separate state, had voted for Preston in the Washington County election but that his own supporters had been prevented from voting there by an early closing of the polls.[10]

Trigg's intention to contest the election galvanized the Preston family network. Francis Preston, who learned of Trigg's plan before he filed his petition, immediately asked his brother, Captain William Preston, to arrange for the taking of depositions among soldiers and civilians who had been present. He instructed Billy to bring out in his own deposition that he had not asked his brother to influence the election and that Billy had never intended to interfere, but had kept his soldiers in ranks *to prevent* a confrontation between soldiers and civilians. Francis, who was by this time sitting in the House of Representatives in Philadelphia, also appealed to his cousin, James Breckinridge, to attend to the taking of depositions in Botetourt county and asked his brother John to oversee the questioning of Billy's soldiers.[11]

Billy's conduct quickly emerged as the focal point of the investigation of Francis's election. Three Montgomery County magistrates, who had already tried to remove Captain Preston from his position as Montgomery County surveyor on grounds of nonresidency, now appealed to President Washington and asked that Billy be declared unfit for command by a military tribunal because of "his attempt to use a Military force to prescribe to Freemen who they *shall* choose to represent them." Trigg sent a copy of the charges to James Madison, along with a request for advice on how to have the election voided.[12] The Preston family rallied around Billy. While spearheading his own defense, Francis cautioned his brother to hold his temper and added, "If you will do your part with respect to the riot where you are; [and] leave the Balance here to me, no trouble shall be spared nor no expence shall alarm me." Their cousin, John Breckinridge, who would later become attorney general of the United States under President Thomas Jefferson, wrote from Kentucky to assure Billy that he was being used by those who dared not make a direct attack on Francis. Younger brother James Patton Preston, who would eventually become governor of Virginia, carried the depositions of Billy's supporters as far as Richmond to insure that they reached Philadelphia before those of the opposition.[13]

On April 17, 1794, after reading "voluminous and . . . contradictory" testimony, the House committee on elections concluded that William Preston's actions were "inconsistent with that freedom and fairness that ought ever to prevail at elections." While the committee upheld the right of the soldiers to vote as long as they met property and residential qualifications for suffrage and conceded that no evidence "other than hearsay" indicated "that any voter was actually prevented from voting," they reasoned that some voters had been intimidated and "the election was unduly biased by the turbulent and menacing conduct of the military." They recommended that Francis Preston be ejected from his seat. In the debate of the full House of Representatives that followed, however, two of Preston's colleagues, one from Pennsylvania and another from North Carolina, defended Billy Preston's behavior, and Congressmen from Maryland and South Carolina maintained that the election was typical of southern practices. The House rejected Trigg's petition and the committee's recommendation by a significant majority; Francis Preston retained his seat.[14]

In December 1794 Francis's sister, Eliza Preston Madison, wrote to their brother Billy to inform him that the district court for Montgomery County had upheld his right to the surveyorship of the county. She noted that this had been done in spite of the "violent defense" of the county magistrates' position by a local attorney, Alexander Smyth.

Smyth also represented Trigg at the taking of depositions concerning the contested election, where his presence had prompted Francis to caution his own attorney that "cunning is such as ought to be counteracted with the strictest attention." In the two decades following the election of 1793, Alexander Smyth, not Abram Trigg, emerged as the principal antagonist of the Preston family.[15]

On first consideration, the Preston-Trigg election of 1793 and its immediate aftermath appear to support the contention that little changed in the actual practice of government during the eighteenth century. Certainly the contest can be cited as evidence that old-style, personal politics persisted beyond the War for Independence in the South and in western Virginia. But, by 1787, the Prestons had clearly acknowledged popular sovereignty as the basis for government and the importance of a representative's role as advocate for the people,[16] if only because both were essential for gaining and retaining pubic office. In this spirit John courted German voters in 1792. Yet, neither John nor Francis trusted the voters to choose the best qualified leaders. They relied on kin and manipulated the electoral system through gerrymandering. There is no evidence that Francis knew ahead of time about his brother Billy's plans for the polling place in Montgomery County, but they were in keeping with Francis and John's lack of faith in the electorate. Preston retained his seat in the U.S. House of Representatives and his brother Billy held on to his surveyorship, but as subsequent events revealed, the Preston family recognized a real challenge to their authority and mobilized to resist it.

At first glance, little also appears to have distinguished candidates Preston and Trigg from each other. Both came from prominent, well-to-do families in the region, and, by 1793, both expressed Republican sentiments, although the nation's first party system had not fully taken shape.[17] Trigg and delegates from the neighboring southwestern Virginia counties of Washington and Russell had opposed the Constitution, however, while the Prestons and members of their extended kin network tended to support it. Support for the Constitution had been strong in the Shenandoah Valley and in Kanawha and Greenbriar Counties, where the Prestons had historic ties and economic interests, and Francis Preston believed that Greenbriar County was essential to his victory in 1793.[18]

The entrance of Eliza Preston Madison and Alexander Smyth into the dispute between Francis Preston and Abram Trigg in 1793 mark two of the more significant developments in the practice of politics in the Virginia backcountry. Eliza, eldest sister of Francis, William, and

John, had been educated with her brothers by tutors until her marriage in 1779. The sixteen-year-old bride was widowed three years later, after having given birth to two daughters. Madison never remarried but continued to live on her farm in Montgomery County until her death at the age of seventy-five. Alexander Smyth had left Ireland as a young boy in 1775 to join his father in Virginia. The elder Smyth had served as an Anglican curate and rector in the Virginia backcountry. Disadvantaged in the predominantly Presbyterian parishes of August and Botetourt, his salary remained unpaid after his death in 1785 for nearly ten years before his son finally recovered it. Alexander Smyth served a political apprenticeship in local government as deputy clerk of Botetourt County before securing a license to practice law in 1789. In 1791 he married the daughter of a German immigrant, and in the following year the couple moved to her home in Wythe County. Smyth represented the county in the Virginia House of Delegates in 1792 and 1796.[19] Both Madison and Smyth became increasingly visible in Francis Preston's campaigns for re-election in 1795 and 1797. Smyth used his ties to the German community as well as his education and an expanding access to print to create a space for himself among the region's elite, while the political climate of the early republic and the challenge to her family's authority drew Madison into a public arena where Preston women had not previously gone, the realm of politics.

The geographical boundaries of the nation and the political base of the Prestons expanded together in the 1790s, and early December of 1794 found John Preston in the Virginia State Senate in Richmond, Francis in the U.S. House of Representatives in Philadelphia, Billy stationed at Fort Wayne in the Ohio country where he had participated in the Battle of Fallen Timbers, and Eliza in Montgomery County. Letters continued to enable family members to inform one another about political developments in these places. Eliza wrote to John about a cabal formed by several Montgomery County gentlemen to recruit a more effective opponent to run against Francis, noting that the "incendiary A[lexander]. S[myth]." hoped to get a commission as brigadier general in the militia out of the deal. Her assessment of Francis's chances for re-election was that they were not good. "Canvising [sic] runs high now in the District," she wrote, "and I am apprehensive the *Absent* [i.e., Francis] stands a ticklish chance—the people are thirsty for News and he is silent—however write to him to circulate his information & liberally—perhaps that may have some influence." Eliza closed by apologizing for presuming to advise her brothers on election strategy, but noted that she feared the bearer of her letter would prove "backward" in informing John of the state of affairs.[20]

Francis Preston's district stretched from the North Carolina line to the Ohio River and encompassed nearly one-quarter of Virginia's land mass. Two major transportation routes to the West, the Ohio River and the Wilderness Road, passed through the district, but within it mountainous terrain created isolated pockets of settlement and made travel difficult, especially during seasons of inclement weather, which often included the early Spring when Congressional elections were held. The size and geography of the district may have encouraged Preston to rely on printed circulars to communicate with his constituents, but even if they had not, the activities of Alexander Smyth would have pushed him in that direction. Smyth and Preston waged a continual war of words from shortly before Preston's second election in 1795 until his defeat in 1797.

As the positions of Federalists and Republicans diverged during the second Washington administration, Smyth used Republican rhetoric to undercut Preston. In 1794 westerners expressed their dissatisfactions with the national government through the Whiskey Rebellion in western Pennsylvania and a secession movement in Kentucky. Those two incidents, along with the signing of the Jay Treaty and the appearance of Democratic Republican Societies increasingly polarized the debate between Federalists and their Republican opponents. By the end of 1794, Abram Trigg had once again emerged as Francis Preston's opponent; but while both were nominally Republicans, Alexander Smyth, now head of the local Democratic Republican Society, published a series of pamphlets linking Preston with unpopular Federalist positions and circulated them in his overwhelmingly anti-Federalist and Republican district. The first one appeared in the form of a letter in 1794, and, although no copy of it has been located, Preston's subsequent point-by-point printed refutation suggests Smyth's approach. According to Preston, Smyth objected to the degree of Preston's wealth, claiming that the rich "have more weight at an election than the best informed amongst us." Preston countered by emphasizing Smyth's "short residence" among the people of Southwest Virginia, noting that he, Francis Preston, who had "lived amongst them since . . . infancy" had never seen any undue exertion of influence. Smyth also objected to the form of Preston's wealth, especially a large salt works that had come to Preston through his wife in 1793, and linked Preston's opposition to outfitting a national navy to his economic self-interest in keeping the price of salt high. Preston asserted that he opposed the navy because it would be ineffective against both British impressment and the Barbary pirates. The two differed on the issue of voting rights for soldiers in the U.S. Army as well, with Smyth maintaining that soldiers lacked sufficient independence to qualify for suffrage because they took orders, while Preston defended suffrage for soldiers who met the legal qualifications for voting and supported reserving bounty lands for them in the Northwest Territory. Smyth concluded by arguing that Preston and his family constituted an "aristocracy" by monopolizing the most powerful offices in the district, and Preston countered by claiming that the Trigg family might be accused of the same and that they were "doubly as numerous" as Francis's male kin. In February 1795, Preston sent five hundred copies of his response to Smyth's letter to his brother John in Montgomery County. He asked John to distribute them in the district and to accompany each with a short letter to the recipient. "Sister [Eliza]," he noted, "will help you if you think it necessary."[21]

In the following month, Smyth responded by reiterating his claims about wealth and Preston's lack of "disinterestedness." Smyth stopped just short of calling Preston a Federalist, charging that he had supported measures to protect American manufactures out of self-interest, and contrary to the interest of the people he represented. Smyth elaborated on the earlier charge that the Prestons represented an aristocracy by pointing out that Francis and two of his brothers held two brigadier generalships, a post as inspector of the revenue, the office of representative to the U.S. Congress, and the office of senator in the Virginia General Assembly. According to Smyth, five different men from five different families should have held those offices. The Triggs, in contrast, were only county officials, militia officers, and justices of the peace. Smyth returned to the issue of the army, stating his fear that a standing army might turn against the citizenry, a fear that he claimed the House of Representatives had recently justified by upholding the authority of the army to act against U.S. citizens in suppressing the Whiskey Rebellion. This issue may have had a special resonance among Trigg supporters who remembered the activities of Billy Preston's soldiers two years earlier.[22]

Preston arrived in southwestern Virginia shortly before the election in 1795, in which he narrowly defeated Trigg after a bitter campaign. During the course of it, one Robert Crockett also published a pamphlet critical of Francis; the Prestons believed Smyth was actually the author and had merely used Crockett's name. Shortly thereafter, John Preston encountered Alexander Smyth in the lobby of the Virginia House of Delegates and threatened to horsewhip him; Smyth responded with a challenge to a duel. The two met, with pistols, outside Richmond. Trigg stood second for Smyth. After the first round, Trigg intervened and established that Crockett had indeed written the document and that Smyth had only edited it for him before publication. Crockett was able to write but lacked the education to produce a polished piece. As early as 1788, Trigg had begun looking over letters and recopying them for him. After the duel John Preston boasted, "I hear no more of fighting since; the safest mode of warfare is the press; this he [Alexander Smyth] exercises. . . . Every attempt was made to prevent Frank's election to Congress but in vain; he rose superior to all their calumny, envy, rage & malice."[23]

John Preston's duel in defense of his brother's honor indicates the degree to which the Preston family felt besieged by published attacks against Francis. During the two years preceding the election of 1797 this sentiment intensified, as Smyth's publications contrasted Francis Preston's character and behavior unfavorably with the abstract standards of republican virtue, and the men and women of the Preston family reacted to defend the family's honor. In his second published letter, Smyth accused Preston of trying to bribe him to gain his support in the general assembly of 1792 for including Greenbriar in Preston's Congressional district. Preston struggled to sustain a dispassionate tone in his response and denied the bribery charge. The second in their series of public exchanges also revealed that Smyth had initially supported Preston in the Congressional election of 1793. Smyth claimed that he had only agreed to take depositions for Trigg concerning the contested election because all the other lawyers at the bar were in Preston's employ. According to Smyth, what he learned at the taking of depositions had led him to shift his support to Trigg.[24] Smyth's third pamphlet accused Preston of being attached "in principle to the anti-republican party." Any support by Preston of republican causes, according to Smyth, arose only from Preston's self-interest. Although Smyth never used the word "virtue," he clearly believed that Preston lacked the quality. He pointed out that Preston's vote in favor of western bounty lands for soldiers would benefit his uncle and brother William "to the amount of *one thousand dollars* each." Smyth again resurrected the bribery charge and included affidavits from six men who claimed to have overheard or observed the conversations between him and Preston.[25]

In early February 1797 Francis Preston wrote from Philadelphia that he intended to return home well before the next election, "For I hear Colo. Trigg opposes me again, if so I know my presence will be necessary indeed I do not know whether it will be sufficient as I expect he will be industrious . . . because there has been such a Contest between us I therefore would feel mortified at being refused, although I know it would be singularly to my pecuniary advantage." Shortly thereafter a friend sent Preston a copy of another published letter by Alexander Smyth. In it Smyth charged Preston with altering the commission naming the justices for Wythe County and attacked the Preston lineage by questioning the reputation of Preston's deceased father. Francis cautioned his brothers John and Billy against overreacting and then drafted a circular addressed to his constituents in which he denied the charges and defended his father's reputation. He maintained that the character of William Preston could not be "impaired by the envenomed shafts and corrupt pen of Alexander Smyth" and appealed to the "good sense of the people," trusting them to return an experienced public servant, who early in his career may have been "liable . . . to err" but had "become so acquainted with our political situation as to give opinions with less hazard of error."[26]

While Francis appealed to the judgment of the people, his family worried. Eliza Madison wrote to her brother John that both she and Francis's wife were "anxious to see you on your way to Russell or some of the back counties" to work for Francis's re-election. "It now appears that nothing should be left undone," she declared, "it is said our Enemies already exult in our downfall; already conceive they have the Rein in their own hands & triumphantly calumnate & degrade the whole family." She pointed out that officials in Washington County, now Francis's home county, had proclaimed a freehold election, i.e., one confined to voters who met the property qualifications for suffrage, in an attempt to limit his total number of votes. This conduct had "irritated the people much." Madison advised her brothers to adopt the same tactic in counties where Trigg's strength lay, but not to "make it known until the day of the election & as the example was set by the opposite party it could not be a subject of reproach to you." She concluded by hoping that her brother would "pardon my appearing so engaged in a business which I candidly acknowledge out of my sphere but I feel myself actuated by motives which I flatter myself will admit of excuse," namely, the warmth of her affections and her resentment at the opposition's attack on her father and brothers.[27]

Despite western Virginia's reputation as a backward region, Francis Preston, Alexander Smyth, and even the barely literate Robert Crockett all used the press as they jockeyed for position in the local political scene, relying on printers in Richmond or Philadelphia. During his first term in Congress, Preston was one of two members who spoke in favor of a petition submitted by the Virginia Germans, a significant component of his constituency, to have Federal laws published in German translation. The relative newcomer Smyth ultimately proved most adept in using the press, however. The rapid changes in political ideology and tactics during the 1790s left Francis Preston struggling to adjust. As rural Virginia became overwhelmingly Republican in the wake of the ratification of the Jay Treaty, Preston's economic investments, his support for the Constitution of 1787, and his family's elevated status in colonial backcountry Virginia left him vulnerable in the face of the Republican rhetoric that he claimed to endorse.[28]

Southern historians have long acknowledged the significance of family honor but usually have depicted it in exclusively masculine terms.[29] Eliza Madison's political activities are especially noteworthy when viewed in this light. Her perception of the threat to her family's honor posed by published attacks on her father and brother and the loss of power and status that could result from them moved her to self-consciously step outside the female sphere to participate in politics. Although the law denied her the right to vote, she demonstrated a grasp of local election practices sophisticated enough to enable her to offer her brothers a strategy for manipulating the outcome of the 1797 contest. Madison knew that although Virginia legally limited suffrage to white male freeholders who met a property requirement, that procedure was not routinely followed in western Virginia. Thus she advised her brothers to insist on freehold elections in counties where support for Trigg was strongest, but suggested that they keep the fact a secret until election day, when it would be too late for Trigg's supporters to counter the unpopular maneuver. While the evidence does not reveal whether her brothers took her advice in this instance, they probably had listened to her earlier, when she called attention to the fact that Francis needed to communicate with his constituents in print before the election of 1795. He responded by publishing an answer to Smyth's first printed letter and specifying that John or Eliza should write the covering notes for his circular.

Historians do not agree on the impact of the American Revolution on women's civic roles. Some maintain that as the theoretical rationale for government shifted away from a hierarchical system based on kinship, patronage, and influence, elite women lost some of the social authority formerly accorded them on the basis of their family's rank. Others emphasize that the public debate over what constituted citizenship in the early republic drew women and others who had previously been little concerned with formal politics into that realm. Most scholars agree that eventually civic participation took separate, gendered forms for men and women, largely as a consequence of the influence of the ideology of separate spheres on the process of redefining women's roles in the early republic. The Republican Mother, an ideal creation that married civic responsibility to domesticity and assigned mothers the duty of rearing republican sons, represented one gender-specific channel for women's political and patriotic participation in the life of the nation. Historians continue to disagree, however on the amount of influence that women actually wielded while being denied the full rights of citizenship.[30]

Eliza Madison stood on a cusp in the evolution of women's political participation. Concern for her family's honor and status moved her to use the knowledge of local politics that she had gained growing up in an elite household and living independently as a widow of means. She in no way resembled a Republican Mother, however, for she lacked sons and her interest in politics had a practical bent—manipulating and winning elections—not a moral one.

Election manipulations and pamphlet distribution were not enough to save Francis Preston's Congressional seat. Shortly before the polling in Greenbriar County, he wrote, "I am satisfied almost that I must loose the Election . . . & I am preparing my mind to meet the mortification."[31] His prediction proved accurate; failure to win the old Federalist stronghold of Greenbriar doomed Preston in the rest of his overwhelmingly Republican Congressional district. But in spite of their fears, the Preston family proved remarkably adept at holding on to political power. Although Francis lost the Congressional election in 1797 and never held national office again, he was elected to the Virginia House of Delegates in 1812 and afterward served in the state senate. Other members of his family continued to hold important positions in both state and national governments.[32] When Francis Preston died in 1836 he was visiting his son, a United States senator from South Carolina. The political career of Alexander Smyth also advanced. After leading an unsuccessful invasion of Canada during the War of 1812, he was elected to the United States Congress in 1817. He held office until 1825 and was re-elected in 1827. Smyth died in Washington, D.C., while Congress was in session and is buried there.[33]

Francis Preston represented the third generation of Preston family members to govern the Virginia backcountry, but the world of the 1790s was not the one that he had expected to inherit. When independence created a new tier of offices at the national level, Preston and his kin automatically assumed that they would fill them. During the creation of the Republican Party, republican rhetoric left the Prestons and the system of kinship, patronage, and influence on which their power was based exposed to criticism. That intensive scrutiny probably cost Francis Preston his Congressional seat, but it did not mark the end of the Preston family's political power, nor did it signal the departure of networks of kinship, patronage, and influence from American politics. Old families like the Prestons adjusted to the new politics of the nineties, and new men like Smyth used republican rhetoric to enter the regional elite. But family honor and individual character remained important in published debate, and ties of kinship and interest continued to shape political practices well beyond the period of the early republic.

Notes

The author would like to thank W. W. Abbot, Trevor Burnard, Robert Calhoon, Ann Marie Plane, and James P. Whittenburg for their comments on earlier versions of this essay.

1. The incident is described in Abram Trigg, Petition to the U.S. House of Representatives [June 1793], typescript, Preston Family Papers, Virginia Historical Society (hereafter cited as VHS), Richmond. See also Report of the Committee of Elections, U.S. House of Representatives, Apr. 17, 1794, ibid., and St. Claire Clarke and David A. Hall, *Cases of Contested Elections in Congress from the year 1789 to 1834, Inclusive* (Washington, D.C., 1834), 78–84. The contest was a rematch of the 1792 election, won by Preston, the results of which were invalidated by the creation of the separate state of Kentucky. William W. Hening, comp., *The Statutes at Large: Being a Collection of All the Laws of Virginia from the First Session of the Legislature in 1619*, 13 vols. (Richmond, New York, and Philadelphia, 1819–23), 13: 331–35, and W. P. Palmer, et al., eds., *Calendar of Virginia State Papers* (Richmond, 1875–93), 5: 450.

2. Edmund S. Morgan, *Inventing the People: The Rise of Popular Sovereignty in England and America* (New York: W. W. Norton, 1988), chap. 8; I am grateful to Kevin Hardwick for initially directing my attention to this reference. James Roger Sharp, *American Politics in the Early Republic: The New Nation in Crisis* (New Haven: Yale Univ. Press, 1993), 58–59; Richard R. Beeman, *The Old Dominion and the New Nation, 1788–1807* (Lexington: Univ. Press of Kentucky, 1972), 108–13; Daniel P. Jordan, *Political Leadership in Jefferson's Virginia* (Charlottesville: Univ. Press of Virginia, 1983), 154.

3. Daniel Blake Smith, *Inside the Great House: Planter Family Life in Eighteenth-Century Chesapeake Society* (Ithaca: Cornell Univ. Press, 1980), and Jan Lewis, *The Pursuit of Happiness: Family and Values in Jefferson's Virginia* (Cambridge: Cambridge Univ. Press, 1983). For an alternative interpretation concerning extended kin, see Joan Cashin, "The Structure of Planter Families: 'The Ties That Bound Us was Strong,'" *Journal of Southern History* 56 (1990): 55–70.

4. Charles Sydnor, *Gentlemen Freeholders* (Chapel Hill: Univ. of North Carolina Press, 1952). For a general statement regarding this transition, see Gordon S. Wood, *The Radicalism of the American Revolution* (New York: Alfred A. Knopf, 1992). Rhys Isaac, *The Transformation of Virginia, 1740–1790* (Chapel Hill: Univ.

of North Carolina Press, 1982), charted the decline of the system outlined by Sydnor, attributing it to a breakdown in deferential attitudes accompanying the Great Awakening. For a recent reconsideration of deference, including its coercive dimension, see Richard Beeman, "Deference, Republicanism, and the Emergence of Popular Politics in Eighteenth-Century America," *William and Mary Quarterly* 3d ser., 49 (1992): 401–30. No scholarly consensus exists on the extent to which Isaac's hierarchical/deferential model was replicated in the colonial Virginia backcountry. See Beeman, *The Evolution of the Southern Backcountry: A Case Study of Lunenburg County, Virginia, 1756–1832* (Philadelphia: Univ. of Pennsylvania Press, 1984); Emory G. Evans, "Trouble in the Backcountry: Disaffection in Southwest Virginia during the American Revolution," in *An Uncivil War: The Southern Backcountry during the American Revolution*, ed. Ronald Hoffman, Thad W. Tate, and Peter J. Albert (Charlottesville: Univ. Press of Virginia, 1984), 179–212; Turk McCleskey, "Rich Lands, Poor Prospects: Real Estate and the Formation of a Social Elite in Augusta County, Virginia, 1738–1770," *Virginia Magazine of History and Biography* 98 (1990): 469–77; and Albert J. Tillson Jr., *Gentry and Common Folk: Political Culture on a Virginia Frontier, 1740–1789* (Lexington: Univ. Press of Kentucky, 1991).

5. Patricia Givens Johnson, *James Patton and the Appalachian Colonists* (Verona, Va.: McClure Press, 1973); Robert D. Mitchell, *Commercialism and Frontier: Perspectives on the Early Shenandoah Valley* (Charlottesville: Univ. Press of Virginia, 1977), 82; and Gail S. Terry, "Family Empires: A Frontier Elite in Virginia and Kentucky, 1740–1815," (Ph.D. diss.: College of William and Mary, 1992), 25–37.

6. Patricia Givens Johnson, *William Preston and the Allegheny Patriots* (Pulaski, Va.: B. D. Smith and Bros., Printers, Inc., 1976); and Terry, "Family Empires," 49–50, 56–61, 67, 69–74. Ages calculated from information in John Frederick Dorman, *The Prestons of Smithfield and Greenfield in Virginia* (Louisville, Ky.: Filson Club, 1982).

7. Quotation from John Preston to Francis Preston, Feb. 17, 1787, Preston Family Papers, Swem Library, College of William and Mary (hereafter cited as W&M), Williamsburg, Va. See also Francis Preston to John Preston, Feb. 19, 1787, Preston Family Papers, VHS. Although he lost the election in 1787, Preston joined Daniel Trigg in representing Montgomery County in the House of Delegates in 1788; Preston also served in 1789. Cynthia Miller Leonard, *The General Assembly of Virginia* (Richmond: Virginia State Library, 1978), 165, 169, 176.

8. Quotations from John Preston to James Breckinridge, Feb. 8, 1792, James Breckinridge Papers (no. 2752), Special Collections Dept., Univ. of Virginia Library, Charlottesville; John Preston (misidentified as his younger brother J[ames] P. Preston by the transcriber) to John Smith, Feb. 11, 1792, typescript, Preston Family Papers, VHS; and John Preston to Francis Preston, May 5, 1792, Preston Family Papers, W&M.

9. Quotation from John Preston to James Breckinridge, Feb. 8, 1792, James Breckinridge Papers; John Preston to John Smith, Feb. 11, 1792, typescript, Preston Family Papers, W&M. On Trigg's brothers, see Leonard, *General Assembly*, 130, 138, 157, 165, and John Pendleton Kennedy, ed. *Journals of the House of Burgesses for Virginia 1773–1776* (Richmond: Virginia State Library, 1905), 13: 163. Support or opposition to the Constitution of 1787 is broken down by region in E. Lee Shepard, *Reluctant Ratifiers* (Richmond: Virginia Historical Society, 1988).

10. Abram Trigg, Petition to the U.S. House of Representatives [June 1793], Preston Family Papers, VHS.

11. Francis Preston to William Preston, Apr. 11, 1793, typescript, and Francis Preston to John Preston, May 14, 1793, Preston Family Papers, VHS; John Preston to James Breckinridge, Feb. 9, 1794, and Francis Preston to James Breckinridge, June 12, 1793, James Breckinridge Papers.

12. Memorial of James McCorkle, Daniel Howe, and James Craig to George Washington, Apr. 29, 1794, typescript, and Abram Trigg to James Madison, Oct. 1, 1793, Preston Family Papers, VHS. On the surveyorship, see also Francis Preston to William Preston, June 23, 1793, typescript, ibid.

13. Francis Preston to William Preston Jan. 1 [June], and June 22, 1793, typescripts; Francis Preston to John Preston, June 22, 1793; and John Breckinridge to William Preston, July 2, 1793; all in Preston Family Papers, VHS; Francis Preston to James Breckinridge, July 3, 1793, James Breckinridge Papers; John Preston to Francis Preston, Aug. 8, 1793, typescript, Preston Family Papers, W&M.

14. Report of the Committee of Elections, Apr. 17, 1794, Preston Family Papers, VHS; Francis Preston to James Breckinridge, Apr. 30, 1794, James Breckinridge Papers; and Clarke and Hall, *Cases of Contested Elections*, 78–84. The debate of the committee's report in the House is discussed in Morgan, *Inventing the People*, 187–89.

15. Eliza Madison to William Preston, Dec. 4, 1794, typescript, Preston Family Papers-Davie Collection, The Filson Club Historical Society, Louisville, Ky. See also Francis Preston to James Breckinridge, Feb. 17, 1794, Papers of James Breckinridge. In June 1793 the Montgomery County Court declared William Preston incapable of holding the county surveyor's office while absent in the service of the U.S. Army. See Palmer, et al., eds., *Calendar of State Papers*, 6: 400–401. The district court apparently reversed the decision, but only the deed books for that court survive.

16. Tillson also makes this point in *Gentry and Common Folk*, 134–35.

17. Norman K. Risjord, *Chesapeake Politics 1781–1800* (New York: Columbia Univ. Press, 1978), and Noble E. Cunningham Jr., *The Jeffersonian Republicans: The Formation of Party Organization 1789–1801* (Chapel Hill: Univ. of North Carolina Press, 1957), discuss the development of political parties from a national perspective.

18. John Breckinridge, James Breckinridge, and John Preston all supported the Constitution. See John P. Kaminski, et al., eds., *Documentary History of the Ratification of the Constitution: Virginia* (Madison: State Historical Society of Wisconsin, 1988), 8: 136–37, 361–62. Tillson, *Gentry and Common Folk*, 136–37, maintains that the controversy over ratification had little lasting effect on the Virginia backcountry, but on the Pennsylvania backcountry cf. Saul Cornell, "Aristocracy Assailed: The Ideology of Backcountry Anti-Federalism," *Journal of American History* 76 (1990): 1148–72.

19. On Madison, see Dorman, *Prestons*, 47–48. She held a life interest in the farm, which went to her daughters at her death. On Smyth, see F. B. Kegley, *Kegley's Virginia Frontier* (Roanoke, Va.: Southwest Virginia Historical Society, 1938), 394–96; Robert Douthat Stoner, *A Seed-Bed of the Republic* (Roanoke, Va.: Roanoke Valley Historical Society, 1962), 318–19, 328; Lewis Preston Summers, *Annals of Southwest Virginia 1769–1800* (Abingdon: by the author, 1929), 1: 401,

311, 416, 427–28, 432, 435, 832; 2: 1309; Lewis Preston Summers, *History of Southwest Virginia 1746–1786: Washington County 1777–1870* (Richmond: J. L. Hill Printing Co., 1903), 756–57; and W. R. Chitwood, "The Duels of General Alexander Smyth," *Smyth County Historical Review* 7 (July 1974): 7–15.

20. Quotation from Eliza Madison to John Preston, Dec. 8, 1794, Preston Family Papers, VHS.

21. *A Letter from Frances Preston to Alexander Smyth, Wythe Court-House, Virginia* (Philadelphia, 1795), in St. George Tucker pamphlets, VHS.

22. *Letter from Alex[ander] Smyth to Francis Preston* (Richmond, 1795), in *Early American Imprints*, ed. Clifford K. Shipton (Readex Microprint, Evans No. 29538).

23. Quotation from John Preston to James Breckinridge, Mar. 19, 1795, James Breckinridge Papers. See also Francis Preston to John Preston, Jan. 11, and Mar. 18, 1795; John Preston to William Preston, May 23, 1795, typescript; Abram Trigg to John Preston, 1788; and William Lewis and Abram Trigg, Affidavit, Dec. 22, 1794; all in Preston Family Papers, VHS.

24. *Letter from Alex[ander] Smyth to Francis Preston*; Francis Preston, *Address to the People of the Congressional District . . . of Wythe, Washington, Montgomery, Greenbrier, Kanhawa, Grayson, Russell, and Lee* (Philadelphia, 1796).

25. *The Third and Last Letter from Alexander Smyth to Francis Preston* (1796), (Readex Microprint, Evans No. 31215).

26. Quotations from Francis Preston to John Preston, Feb. 1, 1797, and Francis Preston, *To the People of the Congressional District Composed of . . .* (1797), typescript of printed circular, Preston Family Papers, VHS. See also Francis Preston to John Preston, Feb. 12, 1797, ibid.

27. Eliza Madison to John Preston, Feb. 27, 1797, typescript, Preston Family Papers–Davie Collection.

28. An extensive literature on republican ideology is reviewed in Robert E. Shallhope, "Toward a Republican Synthesis: The Emergence of an Understanding of Republicanism in American Historiography," *William and Mary Quarterly* 3d ser., 29 (1972): 49–80, and Robert E. Shallhope, "Republicanism and Early American Historiography," *William and Mary Quarterly* 3d ser., 39 (1982): 334–58. For a discussion of the relationship of Lockean liberalism to post-Revolutionary republicanism, see Joyce Appleby, *Capitalism and a New Social Order: The Republican Vision of the 1790s* (New York: New York Univ. Press, 1984), and Joyce Appleby, "Republicanism in Old and New Contexts," *William and Mary Quarterly* 3d ser., 43 (1986): 20–34. For an attempt to link anti-Federalism, Republicanism, and class consciousness in backcountry Pennsylvania, see Cornell, "Aristocracy Assailed." For a recent discussion of the relationship between political ideology and Thomas Jefferson's life, see Peter Onuf, "The Scholars' Jefferson," *William and Mary Quarterly* 3d ser., 50 (1993): 675–84. On the relationship between political ideology and practice in New York, see Alan Taylor, "'The Art of Hook & Snivey': Political Culture in Upstate New York During the 1790s," *Journal of American History* 79 (1993): 1371–96.

29. Bertram Wyatt-Brown, *Southern Honor: Ethics and Behavior in the Old South* (Oxford: Oxford Univ. Press, 1982).

30. For a view that suggests that women lost authority, see Mary Beth Norton, *Founding Mothers and Fathers: Gendered Power and the Forming of American Society* (New York: Alfred A. Knopf, 1996). On women being drawn into public debate, see Louise Belote Dawe and Sandra Gioia Treadway, "Hannah Lee Corbin: The For-

gotten Lee," *Virginia Cavalcade* 29 (1979): 70–77, and Edith B. Gelles, "The Abigail Industry," *William and Mary Quarterly* 3d ser., 45 (1988): 666–67. The classic work on Republican Motherhood is Linda K. Kerber, *Women of the Republic: Intellect and Ideology in Revolutionary America* (Chapel Hill: Univ. of North Carolina Press, 1980). On gender and politics, see also Paula Barker, "The Domestication of Politics: Women and American Political Society, 1780–1920," *American Historical Review* 89 (1984): 620–48; Elizabeth R. Varon, "Tippecanoe and the Ladies, Too: White Women and Party Politics in Antebellum Virginia," *Journal of American History* 82 (1995–96): 494–521; and Cynthia A. Kierner, "Genteel Balls and Republican Parades: Gender and Early Southern Civic Rituals, 1677–1826," *Virginia Magazine of History and Biography* 104 (1996): 185–210. On the relationship between women and the ideology of separate spheres, see Linda K. Kerber, "Separate Spheres, Female Worlds, Woman's Place: The Rhetoric of Women's History," *Journal of American History* 75 (1988): 9–39. Edmund Morgan interprets women's participation in electoral politics as indicative of the carnival aspect of elections, i.e., a ritualistic role reversal signaling acceptance of the existing social order. Morgan, *Inventing the People*, 190–208. Madison's correspondence belies this interpretation of her behavior.

31. Quotation from Francis Preston to John Preston, Mar. 21, 1797, Preston Family Papers, VHS.

32. Francis Preston's brother John became treasurer of Virginia; another brother, James Patton Preston, served as governor of the state. Their first cousin John Breckenridge represented Kentucky in the U.S. Senate and served as attorney general under President Thomas Jefferson. His brother James remained a Federalist and his career suffered accordingly.

33. Summers, *History of Southwest Virginia*, 755–57; Lawrence F. Kennedy, comp., *Biographical Directory of the American Congress 1774–1971* (Washington, D.C.: U. S. Government Printing Office, 1971), 1567, 1658, 1725.

Works Cited

Appleby, Joyce. *Capitalism and a New Social Order: The Republican Vision of the 1790s.* New York: New York Univ. Press, 1984.

———. "Republicanism in Old and New Contexts." *William and Mary Quarterly* 3d ser., 43 (1986): 20–34.

Barker, Paula. "The Domestication of Politics: Women and American Political Society, 1780–1920." *American Historical Review* 89 (1984): 620–48.

Beeman, Richard. *The Old Dominion and the New Nation, 1788–1807.* Lexington: Univ. Press of Kentucky, 1972.

———. *The Evolution of the Southern Backcountry: A Case Study of Lunenburg County, Virginia, 1746–1832.* Philadelphia: Univ. of Pennsylvania Press, 1984.

———. "Deference, Republicanism, and the Emergence of Popular Politics in Eighteenth-Century America." *William and Mary Quarterly* 3d ser., 49 (1992): 401–30.

Breckinridge, James. Papers (no. 2752). Special Collections Dept., Univ. of Virginia Library, Charlottesville.

Cashin, Joan. "The Structure of Planter Families: 'The Ties That Bound Us was Strong.'" *Journal of Southern History* 56 (1990): 55–70.

Chitwood, W. R. "The Duels of General Alexander Smyth." *Smyth County Historical Review* 7 (July 1974): 7–15.

Clarke, St. Claire, and David A. Hall. *Cases of Contested Elections in Congress from the year 1789 to 1834, Inclusive.* Washington, D.C., 1834.

Cornell, Saul. "Aristocracy Assailed: The Ideology of Backcountry Anti-Federalism." *Journal of American History* 76 (1990): 1148–72.

Cunningham, Noble E., Jr. *The Jeffersonian Republicans: The Formation of Party Organization 1789–1801.* Chapel Hill: Univ. of North Carolina Press, 1957.

Dawe, Louise Belote, and Sandra Gioia Treadway, "Hannah Lee Corbin: The Forgotten Lee." *Virginia Cavalcade* 29 (1979): 70–77.

Dorman, John Frederick. *The Prestons of Smithfield and Greenfield in Virginia.* Louisville, Ky.: Filson Club, 1982.

Evans, Emory G. "Trouble in the Backcountry: Disaffection in Southwest Virginia during the American Revolution." In *An Uncivil War: The Southern Backcountry during the American Revolution,* edited by Ronald Hoffman, Thad W. Tate, and Peter J. Albert, 179–212. Charlottesville: Univ. Press of Virginia, 1984.

Gelles, Edith B. "The Abigail Industry." *William and Mary Quarterly* 3d ser., 45 (1988): 666–67.

Hening, William W., compiler. *The Statutes at Large: Being a Collection of All the Laws of Virginia from the First Session of the Legislature in 1619.* 13 Vols. Richmond, New York, and Philadelphia, 1819–23.

Isaac, Rhys. *The Transformation of Virginia, 1740–1790.* Chapel Hill: Univ. of North Carolina Press, 1982.

Johnson, Patricia Givens. *James Patton and the Appalachian Colonists.* Verona, Va.: McClure Press, 1973.

———. *William Preston and the Allegheny Patriots.* Pulaski, Va.: B. D. Smith and Bros., Printers, Inc., 1976.

Jordan, Daniel P. *Political Leadership in Jefferson's Virginia.* Charlottesville: Univ. Press of Virginia, 1983.

Kaminski, John P., et al., editors. *Documentary History of the Ratification of the Constitution: Virginia,* vol. 8. Madison: State Historical Society of Wisconsin, 1988.

Kegley, F. B. *Kegley's Virginia Frontier.* Roanoke: Southwest Virginia Historical Society, 1938.

Kennedy, John Pendleton, editor. *Journals of the House of Burgesses for Virginia 1773–1776,* vol. 13. Richmond: Virginia State Library, 1905.

Kennedy, Lawrence F., compiler. *Biographical Directory of the American Congress 1774–1971.* Washington, D.C.: U.S. Government Printing Office, 1971.

Kerber, Linda K. *Women of the Republic: Intellect and Ideology in Revolutionary America.* Chapel Hill: Univ. of North Carolina Press, 1980.

———. "Separate Spheres, Female Worlds, Woman's Place: The Rhetoric of Women's History." *Journal of American History* 75 (1988): 9–39.

Kierner, Cynthia A. "Genteel Balls and Republican Parades: Gender and Early Southern Civic Rituals, 1677–1826." *Virginia Magazine of History and Biography* 104 (1996): 185–210.

Leonard, Cynthia Miller. *The General Assembly of Virginia.* Richmond: Virginia State Library, 1978.

Lewis, Jan. *The Pursuit of Happiness: Family and Values in Jefferson's Virginia.* Cambridge: Cambridge Univ. Press, 1983.

McCleskey, Turk. "Rich Lands, Poor Prospects: Real Estate and the Formation of a Social Elite in Augusta County, Virginia, 1738–1770." *Virginia Magazine of History and Biography* 98 (1990): 469–77.

Mitchell, Robert D. *Commercialism and Frontier: Perspectives on the Early Shenandoah Valley.* Charlottesville: Univ. Press of Virginia, 1977.

Morgan, Edmund S. *Inventing the People: The Rise of Popular Sovereignty in England and America.* New York: W. W. Norton and Co., 1988.

Norton, Mary Beth. *Founding Mothers and Fathers: Gendered Power and the Forming of American Society.* New York: Alfred A Knopf, 1996.

Onuf, Peter. "The Scholars' Jefferson." *William and Mary Quarterly* 3d ser., 50 (1993): 671–99.

Palmer, W. P., et al., editors. *Calendar of Virginia State Papers,* vols. 5–6. Richmond, 1875–1893.

Preston Family Papers. Earl Gregg Swem Library, College of William and Mary, Williamsburg, Va.

Preston Family Papers. Virginia Historical Society, Richmond.

Preston Family Papers–Davie Collection. Filson Club Historical Society, Louisville, Ken.

[Preston, Francis]. *A Letter from Frances Preston to Alexander Smyth, Wythe Court-House, Virginia.* Philadelphia, 1795.

Preston, Francis. *Address to the People of the Congressional District . . . of Wythe, Washington, Montgomery, Greenbrier, Kanhawa, Grayson, Russell, and Lee.* Philadelphia, 1796.

Risjord, Norman K. *Chesapeake Politics 1781–1800.* New York: Columbia Univ. Press, 1978.

Shallhope, Robert E. "Toward a Republican Synthesis: The Emergence of an Understanding of Republicanism in American Historiography." *William and Mary Quarterly* 3d ser., 29 (1972): 49–80.

———. "Republicanism and Early American Historiography." *William and Mary Quarterly* 3d ser., 39 (1982): 334–58.

Sharp, James Roger. *American Politics in the Early Republic: The New Nation in Crisis.* New Haven: Yale Univ. Press, 1993.

Shepard, E. Lee. *Reluctant Ratifiers.* Richmond: Virginia Historical Society, 1988.

Smith, Daniel Blake. *Inside the Great House: Planter Family Life in Eighteenth-Century Chesapeake Society.* Ithaca: Cornell Univ. Press, 1980.

[Smyth, Alexander]. *Letter from Alex[ander] Smyth to Francis Preston.* Richmond, 1795. In *Early American Imprints.* Edited by Clifford K. Shipton. Readex Microprint, Evans No. 29538.

———. *The Third and Last Letter from Alexander Smyth to Francis Preston.* 1796. In *Early American Imprints.* Edited by Clifford K. Shipton. Readex Microprint, Evans No. 31215.

Stoner, Robert Douthat. *A Seed-Bed of the Republic.* Roanoke, Va.: Roanoke Valley Historical Society, 1962.

Summers, Lewis Preston. *History of Southwest Virginia 1746–1786: Washington County 1777–1870.* Richmond: J. L. Hill Printing Co., 1903.

———. *Annals of Southwest Virginia 1769–1800.* Abingdon: by the author, 1929.

Sydnor, Charles. *Gentlemen Freeholders.* Chapel Hill: Univ. of North Carolina Press, 1952.

Taylor, Alan. "'The Art of Hook & Snivey': Political Culture in Upstate New York During the 1790s." *Journal of American History* 79 (1993): 1371–96.

Terry, Gail S. "Family Empires: A Frontier Elite in Virginia and Kentucky, 1740–1815." Ph.D. diss., College of William and Mary, 1992.

Tillson, Albert H., Jr. *Gentry and Common Folk: Political Culture on a Virginia Frontier, 1740–1789.* Lexington: Univ. Press of Kentucky, 1991.

Varon, Elizabeth R. "Tippecanoe and the Ladies, Too: White Women and Party Politics in Antebellum Virginia." *Journal of American History* 82 (1995–96): 494–521.

Wood, Gordon S. *The Radicalism of the American Revolution.* New York: Alfred A. Knopf, 1992.

Wyatt-Brown, Bertram. *Southern Honor: Ethics and Behavior in the Old South.* Oxford: Oxford Univ. Press, 1982.

Part V

Material Reflections of Culture

The experience of cultural blending reflected in social, political, and economic encounters was evident in material reflections of life on the frontier, particularly in such areas as architecture. Following the lead of Henry Glassie and his students in the 1960s, contemporary vernacular architecture studies concentrate on identifying ethnic influences apparent in houses, barns, and related domestic structures. Previously, historians of the Virginia backcountry tended to ignore vernacular buildings in favor of outstanding architecture, which perhaps supported the images that these writers drew of life in the region, but were not necessarily representative of the more numerous commonplace structures built and used by the mass of backcountry settlers. Fewer of the humbler buildings survived—or, at least, were preserved and maintained in their original form—of course, so researchers are challenged in their efforts to create a collective image of frontier life, particularly as existing structures succumb to age and neglect. This synthesis can only come through individual case research, relying on survey efforts, which provide data bases of raw material for analysis.

Rather than describing houses and other frontier buildings in their own right, current scholars have linked their research into the larger context of backcountry studies, addressing such topics as relationships and reflections of architectural plans on land use, settlement patterns, and indicators of cultural persistence and change. Ann McCleary undertakes a survey of architectural styles in the Shenandoah Valley, focusing on ethnic influences in the evolution of living spaces and particularly on the traditional assumption of a "German plan" structure, which provided a basic style for frontier architecture in the region. Noting from a larger context of research that there was a wide variety of housing styles within the native provinces of German immigrants and that most of them had experienced some acculturation after arriving in the colonies and migrating to the Virginia backcountry, she maintains that the view of a homogenous German American house pattern in the Shenandoah Valley is too simplistic. Of course, the first wave of impermanent structures that would have most directly reflected stylistic predispositions no longer exist, but, through a combination of historical and archaeological research, along with a recognition that early-nineteenth-century structures reflect an ongoing process of cultural interaction between the memories, experiences, and adaptations of Valley residents, architectural scholars can piece together the evolution of building styles. What resulted, according to McCleary, was a regional style, a composite of social and cultural influences, which appealed to a cross section of the population, regardless of ethnic origin.

McCleary addresses an issue of unique relevance to architectural study: the passage of time has brought about the rapid deterioration of the architectural record. Few early buildings survive, and those that do tend not to be representative of the majority of structures built by and for common people. To combat this inevitable trend, much more field survey work needs to be done to identify and describe existing structures before they vanish, so that their adaptations and additions can be deciphered from their origins. Unfortunately, the amount of survey work to be done and the logistical and budgetary pressures placed on the process effectively limit the effort to the col-

lection of data, with analysis and synthesis secondary. Fulfill-
ment of the process will allow backcountry scholars to incorpo-
rate architectural patterns into detailed studies of backcountry
society and culture.

One study that approaches this goal is John Morgan's analysis of barn construction in southwest Virginia as a reflection of
cultural diffusion resulting from migration in the backcountry.
Based upon intensive and extensive survey field work, he interprets the cantilever structures of Wythe, Smyth, and Washington Counties as a transition phase between the classical Pennsylvania forebay bank barns common in more northern regions
and the classical cantilever barns of eastern Tennessee. The
driving forces behind this evolution, according to Morgan, were
the dominant influence of the transfer of cultural patterns, tem-
pered by local adaptations. Like McCleary, however, Morgan
emphasizes that more field work and analysis are essential in
order to draw definitive links between cultural diffusion and social development on the frontier.

Both of these essays provide another perspective on the
theme that pervades the scholarship presented in this collection.
The myth of ethnic separation and exclusivity is far too simplistic and misleading an interpretation to explain the dynamic social development that occurred on the Virginia frontier. Accommodation and adaptation were both necessary and widely
evident. Of course, there were cultural differences and they influenced the whole; there never appeared a generic frontier culture. But backcountry forces did lead to the development of regional traits that represented the blending of influences from
the various cultures, as well as the environment they faced.
These traits became apparent in economic activities, political
organization, social systems, and, as these chapters portray, in
material manifestations such as architectural forms.

Chapter 11

Ethnic Influences on the Vernacular Architecture in the Shenandoah Valley

Ann E. McCleary

The diverse ethnic character of the eighteenth-century Shenandoah Valley has attracted the interest of many cultural historians, including students of vernacular architecture. Here, a diverse group of settlers from Ireland, Germany, England, and Africa shared a common land, blending old memories and new experiences to forge a distinctive culture that clearly reflected its ethnic roots. Much of the interest in Valley architecture has focused on identifying and assessing these ethnic influences, particularly as they are felt on the most personal of living spaces, the house and its related domestic and farm buildings. This chapter reviews research on vernacular architecture in the early Shenandoah Valley, examines questions that have arisen within this scholarship, and recommends directions for future research.

In its most general sense, the term "vernacular architecture" refers to "ordinary buildings." During the romantic movement of the nineteenth century, architectural theorists became intrigued by the rural buildings that dotted the preindustrial countryside, partly as source material for their work and partly due to their nostalgia for the past in an increasingly urbanizing society. The term "vernacular architecture" then referred largely to domestic buildings that reflected the honest, truthful character of country life.[1] Today, the field of vernacular architecture studies embraces a wide variety of buildings, typically those neglected by traditional art historians, from the earliest structures of a community to popular commercial architecture.

While contemporary accounts can occasionally provide a window into housing of the eighteenth century, finding these references and trying to delineate patterns in housing construction or plan types is difficult. By the early nineteenth century, however, some of the early historical writing about the Shenandoah Valley began to mention more about the character of local housing, although these descriptions are often romanticized. The description of "frontier" buildings in Samuel Kercheval's *History of the Valley of Virginia,* first published in 1833, characterizes the image of early dwellings popular in this historical literature. In his chapter entitled "Mode of Living of the Primitive Settlers," Kercheval described the "first houses erected by the primitive settlers" as being "log cabins, covered with split clapboard roofs" and "frequently seen with earthen floors." By the eve of the Revolution, Kercheval wrote, a few "framed and stone buildings" had been erected, corresponding with improvements in population and wealth. These new buildings were built of "hewn logs, shingle roofs, and plank floors." Like his contemporaries, who commented on the different lifestyles present in the Valley, Kercheval was also quick to distinguish between the housing of families from Germany and Switzerland and Scots-Irish settlers, noting that "there were none of our primitive immigrants more uniform in the form of their buildings than the Germans."[2] Still, contemporary descriptions like those Kercheval provides are not abundant nor entirely accurate, so cultural historians must rely on other types of documentation.

Nineteenth- and early-twentieth-century illustrations and photographic sources provide an opportunity to view at least selected parts of buildings and allow modern-day historians to do more of the analysis themselves. While useful, these sources, too, have their biases. The mid-nineteenth-century illustrations of travel writer and illustrator David Hunter Strother, known by his pen name of Porte Crayon in the *Harpers New Monthly Magazine,* depicted architecture in western Virginia, but recent studies have suggested that Strother often borrowed different drawings from his sketchbook to create the illustrations, so they may or may not be accurate for specific areas he described in his accounts.[3] Late-nineteenth-century atlases, like the 1885 *Atlas of Augusta County,* often include illustrations of local farms, although these

Fig. 11.1. "Locust Grove," drawing by Porte Crayon, included in Jim Comstock, *Porte Crayon Sampler* (Richwood, W.Va.: Jim Comstock Publisher, 1974).

are typically the finest or most historically significant examples.[4] Early photographs are also useful, and collections from local photographers can be found in many communities. In the Shenandoah Valley, historian John Wayland, a Bridgewater College history professor, devoted much of his professional career to researching and interpreting the history of this region. His *Historic Homes of Northern Virginia* includes a large collection of early-twentieth-century photographs of Valley architecture, including numerous buildings that are now gone.[5]

By the early twentieth century, the federal government had become involved in documenting historic buildings through the Historic American Buildings survey (HABS), organized in 1933. The Virginia survey began the following year. Between 1935 and 1941, with funds from the Works Progress Administration (WPA), HABS compiled records of numerous buildings, but largely the finer antebellum homes. The HABS reports included property histories, recorded from the owners or residents, which were often inaccurate; photographs; and some measured drawings. This HABS survey formed the basis for much of the Virginia Department of Historic Resources archives.[6] Like the work

Fig. 11.2. Jedediah Hotchkiss's illustration of the farm of H. J. Williams also incorporates a drawing of Doak's Fort, an older property which was still standing on this site in 1885. See Jedediah Hotchkiss, *Historical Atlas of Augusta County. Virginia*, (Chicago: Waterman, Watkins, and Co., 1885).

of John Wayland, one of the greatest values of the HABS record is its collection of photographs, which document many buildings that have long since disappeared.

At the same time as HABS was being established, cultural geographer Fred Kniffen embarked on one of the first scholarly studies of American vernacular architecture, tracing the diffusion of folk housing forms throughout the American landscape.[7] But it was Kniffen's student, Henry Glassie, who drew attention to the rich architectural heritage of the Shenandoah Valley through his field work and writing of the mid-1960s. Kniffen and Glassie moved the study of Shenandoah Valley architecture out of the antiquarian mode by proposing new perspectives for analyzing and interpreting the architecture of this important cultural region. Glassie's *Pattern in the Material Folk Culture of the Eastern United States* set the stage for scholarly work in the following two decades.[8]

The significance of the Shenandoah Valley in these broader patterns of diffusion is articulated in Glassie's proposal for the Museum of American Frontier Culture, written in 1978. Glassie posited the importance of the Appalachian frontier region to American identity. He argued that the nation needed a "major outdoor museum dedicated to the culture of the frontier, located naturally in the Appalachian region." In this "difficult environment" of the frontier, Glassie suggested, "people were forced out of accustomed habits into a willingness to engage in cultural trading." At the proposed museum, visitors should ask: "Is America but the natural extension of the world's other continents or did American culture spring freshly from the earth of the New World?"[9]

By the 1960s and 1970s, regional architecture had captured the interest of local historians and amateur writers, who began to produce books on local architecture. Most of these books provided photographs and brief histories of historic homes, but a few organized their discussion by references to the ethnic types outlined in Glassie's and Kniffen's early writings. Because these sources drew largely upon oral histories for documentation, they often perpetuated inaccurate dates and histories about these properties. Only a few more scholarly monographs were printed during this time; one of the most notable of these books is *The Architecture of Historic Lexington*, which provides good architectural analysis, but focuses on urban structures, many of which are quite stylish.[10]

For documentation on more ordinary buildings in the Shenandoah Valley, scholars have turned to the extensive body of literature on southeastern Pennsylvania architecture, which shares a similar ethnic mix and history. The rich scholarship provided by the Pennsylvania German Society, both in its annual publication and in *Pennsylvania Folklife*, have proved invaluable for comparative research. One of the most helpful studies for Shenandoah Valley farm buildings is Amos Long's *The Pennsylvania German Family Farm*, published by the Pennsylvania German Society. This volume incorporates descriptions and folklore relating to all types of buildings found on farms in southeastern Pennsylvania.[11]

With the passage of the National Historic Preservation Act in 1966, Virginia established its first historic preservation office. By the mid-1970s, the state office was funding summer surveys, which included several Valley counties. Although these projects did not permit time for intensive study or a thorough survey, they did suggest the richness of the Valley's resources. Dell Upton, survey director for the Virginia Historic Landmarks Commission (VHLC) at the time, spearheaded efforts to conduct intensive surveys that would examine all the historic resources in the county. In the late 1970s and early 1980s, the VHLC conducted intensive surveys of Bath, Allegheny, Augusta, Rockbridge, and part of Rockingham Counties. Changes to the state survey program over the past ten years have restructured survey projects from intensive to reconnaissance projects. Through this revised survey strategy, the Virginia Department of Historic Resources has continued to fund reconnaissance surveys in other Valley counties, including Clarke, Frederick, Botetourt, and Shenandoah.

While the surveys have produced more documentation about buildings, there have still been few serious efforts to analyze the data. In 1985, the Virginia Division of Historic Landmarks completed its first regional preservation plan for the Shenandoah Valley. The plan assessed the quality and quantity of survey and National Register recognition by county and town, but did not attempt any in-depth analysis of the surveyed structures.[12] As part of this plan, work began on developing overall historic contexts for the region, but these were never completed. Even on the county or community level, there are very few architectural studies that move beyond the realm of description. For rural buildings, the most notable recent studies are Edward Chappell's work on the Massanutten settlement, Warren Hofstra's study of the Opequon community in Frederick County, and the analysis of a three-year intensive survey of Augusta County.[13] With limited time and funding for survey grants and projects, there is little time for analysis; most "final" survey reports often plug the resources into an existing chronology of plan and style, rather than using the resources as a basis for developing or creating a framework.[14]

For those interested in studying the architecture of the Valley of Virginia frontier, survey results have shown that there are very few buildings remaining from the first generations of settlement. Like other frontiers, the Shenandoah Valley was first characterized by a wave of impermanent buildings. To what extent these reflected the ethnic forms of the native lands is difficult to determine. With very few surviving buildings from the early years of settlement, archaeological investigations and historical research are still needed to uncover this early layer of Valley building, in much the same manner as a recent study conducted concerning impermanent architecture in the Tidewater region.[15]

A comparison of standing structures with historical accounts clearly reveals that the surviving buildings are not the typical ones for their times, as students of vernacular architecture all too clearly know. For example, Samuel Kercheval described the German American houses as being most often one story in height, but the majority of the standing houses in the early Massanutten settlement of Page County are two full stories. Chappell suggests that one reason for the demolition of smaller German American houses—like the Andrew Keyser House, which was documented by the WPA survey but demolished by the 1970s—may be due to the owner's interest in having a larger, more modern house.[16] Historical records confirm that the humbler buildings usually do not survive. The majority of extant structures from the late eighteenth century are of masonry construction throughout the Valley, while historical records suggest that most houses were wooden buildings. The Clarke-Hite Survey of 1786 described 140 houses in Shenandoah and Warren Counties; of these, one was frame, one stone, and the remainder log.[17]

Drawing on the early work of Kniffen and Glassie, students of vernacular architecture have sought to document ethnic forms on the Virginia frontier. Taking the basic story from Glassie's work, scholars have attempted to flesh out the details of ethnicity and acculturation. These efforts reflect efforts in the field of vernacular architecture as a whole. The new wave of vernacular architecture studies in the past twenty years has focused heavily on the study of rural, ethnic forms and the regional architecture that developed from these ethnic influences. This interest sparked the National Trust, in 1986, to publish a volume in the "building watcher's series" entitled *America's Architectural Roots: Ethnic Groups That Built America.*

Of the ethnic groups in the Valley, the Germans and Swiss have received the most attention in architectural and material culture studies because their cultures appear most distinctive from the dominant Anglo lifestyles. The Shenandoah Valley Folklore Society pioneered early efforts to collect folklore and the description of material culture of the Valley's German heritage, led by Elmer Smith, John Stewart, and Klaus Wust. Much of this work by the Folklore Society focused on traditions, customs, and furnishings, but less occurred on the architecture of the region.

In the 1970s, Dell Upton initiated more serious investigation of German American architecture in the Valley. Upton identified and documented many German American houses in the Valley for nominations to the National Register of Historic Places.[18] He encouraged Edward Chappell to write his master's thesis in architectural history on a pocket of German settlement in the northwestern part of Augusta County. Completed in 1977, this thesis, "Cultural Change in the Shenandoah Valley: Northern Augusta County Houses Before 1861," presented one of the first

efforts to systematically survey and analyze a geographically confined collection of historic resources. Chappell explored the ways in which German
American settlers became "acculturated" into the dominant Anglo-American culture by the early nineteenth century.[19] Chappell's second and more
well-known study features the early houses of the Massanutten settlement
in Page County. This report, based on intensive recording of the surviving
German American dwellings and retrieval of any available information on
related demolished buildings, provided an opportunity to identify and examine some of the oldest surviving forms from this ethnic group in the
Valley and to define the distinctive characteristics of their houses. The in-
clusion of this study in a relatively recent anthology on vernacular architecture studies, entitled *Common Places* and edited by Dell Upton and John
Vlach, has brought this examination of Shenandoah Valley architecture to
a wide audience throughout the United States.[20]

The study of eighteenth-century German American architecture has
focused heavily on plan type, arrangement and use of space, and building
construction. While scholars have identified a common plan type, they
have differed on its label. In the 1960s, picking up on work by Alfred Shoemaker in Pennsylvania, Glassie and Robert Bucher identified a distinctive
German-inspired plan in Pennsylvania; this "Continental" plan featured a
central chimney house, with usually three (but sometimes two or four
rooms) clustered around the chimney. In their work in the Shenandoah
Valley, Upton and Chappell called this plan a *Flurküchenhaus*, or hall-
kitchen house. According to their use of the term, the plan could include
two, three, or four rooms. In recent years, Chappell has noted that this plan
should be more appropriately termed an *Ernhaus*. Edward Lay, from the
University of Virginia, has distinguished between the three- and four-room
Flur Küchenhaus and the four-room *Kreuzhaus*, a "cross house" organized
around an off-center chimney but with a fourth room used as a kitchen
pantry. In his recent contribution to the scholarship on German American
architecture, architectural historian William Woyes Weaver describes and
illustrates a four-room *Kreuzhaus*, but the room arrangement is different:
The kitchen is pushed toward the back, and the front door now opens upon
a rectangular-shaped *flur*, or hallway.[21]

With a growing interest in German American architecture, surveyors
in the Shenandoah Valley, as well as in other parts of the greater Appalachian region, have doggedly searched for more examples of the "German"
plan in their area. For most surveyors, this was the *Flurküchenhaus* that
Chappell identified, particularly since his work appeared to be most widespread of the scholarship on German American architecture. But closer

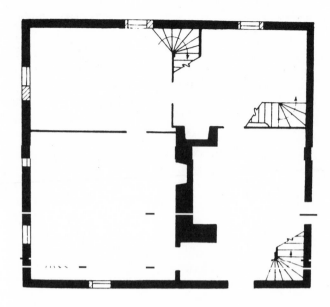

Fig. 11.3. Four-room floor plan of Fort Egypt, Page County, Virginia. From Edward A. Chappell, "Acculturation in the Shenandoah Valley: Rhenish Houses of the Massanutten Settlement," *Proceedings of the American Philosophical Society* 124 (1980).

reading into studies of German architecture and inspection of historic homes in Germany suggest a wider variety of plans found in southern and middle Germany and the neighboring Alsace region of France. Our interpretation of the German American house appeared much more homogenous than those contemporary dwellings in the homeland.

In his 1986 article "The Pennsylvania German House" in *Winterthur Portfolio*, William Woyes Weaver challenged us to rethink many of our interpretations of German American architecture. According to Weaver, there was considerable diversity among dwellings in southern and middle Germany at the time of eighteenth century emigration. As an example, Weaver described one such plan as a three-part, linear structure, combining a dwelling, threshing area, and stable under one roof. Documentary evidence suggests at least thirteen of these plans existed in the Philadelphia area. If one were to define the most common room arrangement in middle and southern Germany, Weaver suggests that this would be a two-room plan, containing a *Stube*, or "stove room,"

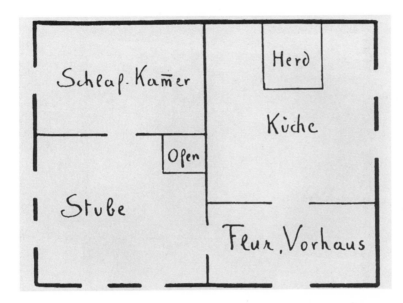

Fig. 11.4. A traditional four-room *Kreuzhaus* plan from southeastern Germany. From Rudolph Meringer, *Das deutsche Haus und sein Hausrat* (Leigpzig and Berlin: B. G. Teubner, 1906). Reprinted in William Wayes Weaver, "The Pennsylvania German House: European Antecedents and New World Forms," *Winterthur Portfolio* 21 (Winter 1986).

and *Küche*, or "hearth room." Beyond that two-room base, the plan could take many variations. The main distinction between this two-room German plan and the two-room, hall-parlor plan popular in contemporary England was the use of the rooms. The German *Stube* was quite different from either of the rooms in the English hall-parlor plan.[22]

Weaver concludes his article by calling for a "thorough reevaluation of the label 'Continental plan.'" While he has uncovered German prototypes of this plan, Weaver asserts that the plan had its "greatest expression in Pennsylvania rather than in Germany." In America, the plan "developed a character of its own" in what he calls a "complex evolution of Pennsylvania German culture into something American." Since German architecture was so regional in character, he questions, why would Germans from different regions all build the same type of house?[23]

All of this suggests the possibility that we have seen what we have wanted to see from the studies of German architecture, or *Hausforschung*.

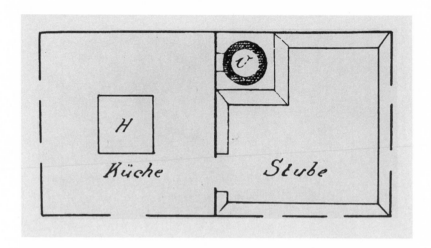

Fig. 11.5. A traditional two-room house plan from southeastern Germany. From Rudolph Meringer, *Das deutsche Haus und sein Hausrat* (Leigpzig and Berlin: B. G. Teubner, 1906). Reprinted in William Wayes Weaver, "The Pennsylvania German House: European Antecedents and New World Forms," *Winterthur Portfolio* 21 (1986).

According to Weaver, the German historians of *Hausforschung* were quite selective, choosing to document existing architecture to help the government make political statements about the character of German culture. During the Third Reich, a government-sponsored research bureau undertook projects to document the architecture of the border regions to prove through architecture that these regions were historically connected to Germany. American students of vernacular architecture often draw largely upon these historical studies, which echo Third Reich theories. Weaver warned us to be very careful in the use of this *Hausforschung*, as the examples and data has been subjectively collected.[24]

But beyond the bias of the authors and the existing scholarship, the language barrier also presents problems for American scholars in understanding the complex character of German architecture at the time of emigration. Unless American researchers are fluent in German, they may be missing important parts of the overall architectural context. We may be selectively choosing from the architectural literature the passages or examples that we need to make our arguments.

Weaver's article raised further questions beyond merely the plan type. The use of the rooms in this "Continental plan" in Germany appears different from that depicted in American scholarship. The German *Stube*, with its stove, provided a smoke-free living space that was the center of family life. The *Küche*, translated as the hearth room, was considered a work room for cooking and food preparation, but not a living area, as was the English kitchen. Many students of spatial arrangement in Pennsylvania and Virginia German-American houses interpret the *Küche* as comparable to the English hall, being used for both cooking and "informal living space." The *Stube* served more formal occasions, like the Anglo-American "parlor."[25] Have historians fully documented room use through contemporary records, or are we imposing familiar English room usages on German room names?

Some evidence does survive to document the traditional dining table in the corner of the *Stube*. This was an important "living center" in German and German American homes. In Virginia, Samuel Kercheval notes, "there was always a long pine table fixed in one corner of the stove room, with permanent benches on one side."[26] Weaver suggests that this traditional room usage was used in many of the older homes in Pennsylvania. Additional historical research is needed to reveal more documentation about the use of these rooms, how and when usages changed, and what relationship this may have had to the introduction of the central passage or the so-called acculturation of the domestic spaces.

There are other aspects of Germanic housing that we are only beginning to explore. In the past few years, Weaver's essay and an article by Steve Frieson in the 1991 *Pennsylvania Folklife* have identified the raised hearth as an important feature of the German home. The Germans preferred the raised hearth over the open hearth since it required less fuel, which was not free nor easily available. Backed up against the stove to the *Stube*, the hearth also provided a more efficient use of fuel. Were there any in America? Upon closer inspection, Steve Frieson has found evidence that the Hans Herr House in Lancaster had a raised hearth. Now that this feature has received more notice, no doubt owners and curators of other German American houses will inspect their kitchens for possible evidence of this hearth.[27]

The German *Küche* differed in other ways. German farm women preferred bake ovens in the kitchen, although some towns had regulations that required outdoor bake ovens to keep hot fires out of the house. It is not surprising to find that many houses in Germany did not have chimneys. Instead, as in contemporary Ireland, smoke left the house through a smoke

Fig. 11.6. Raised hearth illustrated in a ca. 1581 German cookbook. From *Pennsylvania Folklife* vol. 40, no. 3 (Spring 1991); courtesy of the Pennsylvania Folklife Society.

hole in the roof. In the early seventeenth century, some wealthy families began to add chimneys, but usually in association with more expensive tile roofs, which were less prone to fire than the traditional thatch ones. Weaver speculated that some of the more primitive dwellings in Pennsylvania may have lacked chimneys.[28] One wonders about whether such structures could have been built in Virginia as well.

All of this new research about German architecture muddies the waters of what had seemed a fairly simple, straightforward story. We have much more to learn from the German context before we can completely understand our buildings here. But the story in Virginia is more complicated. Since some settlers spent time in Pennsylvania before moving to Virginia, it is also important to look at cultural developments in that region; we must remember that Virginia is not the first region where these cultures interacted. Could the Continental plan have arrived as a more standardized template in Pennsylvania and, from there, was brought to Virginia? What impact did this stay in Pennsylvania

Fig. 11.7. German woodcut showing a raised hearth and jambed fireplace. From *Pennsylvania Folklife*, Vol. 40, No. 3 (Spring 1991). Courtesy of the Pennsylvania Folklife Society.

have on the development of architectural forms and cultural diversity? To better understand Valley houses, we need to do more research related to specific dwellings that do survive or that we can document, tracing the paths of the families before they came to Virginia. The research currently underway regarding the Opequon settlement suggests one such approach.

With the absence of extant structures representing the more typical homes of the eighteenth-century frontier, studies of Shenandoah Valley architecture must take an interdisciplinary approach. We need to locate and analyze more contemporary historical references and documentation regarding buildings to develop a better architectural context. Through archaeology, we can address different sets of questions regarding the house plans, dimensions, construction, and locations.

While German American architecture has certainly aroused the most attention in the Valley of Virginia, there has also been considerable interest in the Scots-Irish architecture of the region, particularly among college students in search of the quintessential "Scots-Irish" house in the Valley. This issue has come up numerous times in what was an annual symposium on the Ulster heritage in Staunton over the past seven years. Speakers who tried to pinpoint special Irish elements of the material culture often found few specific Valley examples that could be closely associated to Ulster precedents. At the 1986 Ulster symposium, Henry Glassie suggested that the Scots-Irish were more willing to accept new cultural features when they moved because they were more accustomed to moving and adjusting to new dominant cultures. Many of those coming to America were descended from Scotch Presbyterians who had come over to Ulster only a few generations before.[29]

Many of our present ideas about the Scotch-Irish influence on architecture come from what has become a well-known article by Henry Glassie on the "Types of the Southern Mountain Cabin." Glassie traced a two-room house plan from Ulster to the Appalachian region where many Scots-Irish settled. Meshed with log construction from Central Europe, a building tradition associated with the German or Swiss settlers, this "southern mountain cabin" became the prototype of the typical Appalachian farm.[30] Glassie proposed that this hall-parlor, log house be selected for the American farm at his proposed Museum of American Frontier Culture, since it illustrated the blend of ethnic traditions into a distinctive American form.[31]

The familiar story about the evolution of Valley architecture attributes this two-room plan to the Scots-Irish settlers. While the two-room plan is a popular one in Ulster, it is not by far the only plan. Alan Gailey's research in Ulster housing documents a one-room cottiers cottage that was popular at the time of emigration.[32] Recent research in the early Opequon settlement of Frederick County has identified one-room plans built by Scots-Irish settlers. The Mutual Assurance insurance records for Augusta County in 1804–5 include two one-room houses, one owned by a John McCutchan and one by James Ramsey.[33]

Nor is the two-room plan confined only to Ulster. Glassie notes in *America's Architectural Roots* that the two-room plan represented an ancient Celtic heritage, found in Scotland, Wales, and western England.[34] Certainly two-room plans cannot be easily interpreted as purely an Ulster component in the architectural context. The same type of intensive historical research and archaeology, linked with in-depth research of our existing or documented eighteenth-century resources, remains critical to understanding the ethnic links between Ulster and the Valley buildings.

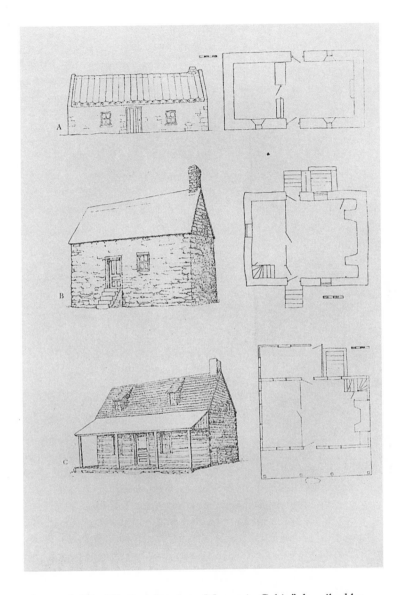

Fig. 11.8. The "Typical Southern Mountain Cabin" described by
Henry Glassie in "The Types of the Southern Mountain Cabin,"
from *The Study of American Folklore: An Introduction*, 3d ed., by Jan
Harold Brunvand. Copyright 1986, 1978, 1968 by W. W. Norton
& Company, Inc. Reprinted by permission of W. W. Norton &
Co., Inc.

Fig. 11.9. One-room fisherman's house from Northern Ireland dating to the early twentieth century illustrates the type of form found in the eighteenth century. From Alan Gailey, *Rural Houses of the North of Ireland.* Reproduced by permission of John Donald Publishers, Edinburgh.

While the first- or second-generation buildings may be noticeably absent from the landscape, we should not overlook the importance of studying the first generation of more permanent building construction that survives from the turn of the nineteenth century to understand the ethnic mix of the region. We may not find "pure" ethnic forms, but the period presents an excellent opportunity to explore a rich period of cultural interaction in material forms. During this period, regional architecture exhibited a tremendous diversity in house plan, construction, and decoration, reflecting the varied ideas, memories, and adaptations of the region's residents. Two examples illustrate this point.

Architectural surveys in Augusta and Rockbridge Counties have uncovered a popular three-room, central-passage plan found in larger houses, particularly stone dwellings, at the turn of the nineteenth century. These appear to be an important part of the first wave of permanent construction.[35] Some scholars have suggested that they might be Anglicized German forms, but several of these dwellings at least were

Fig. 11.10. Elaborate and heavily carved parlor mantel in the Seawright House, made by joiner James Rankin in 1827 in Augusta County, Virginia. Photographs by Ann McCleary, 1978, courtesy of Virginia Department of Historic Landmarks.

built for Scots-Irish families. A similar three-room, central-passage arrangement was also found in eighteenth-century Tidewater Virginia, but the Valley houses were most often two stories in height rather than one or one and one-half as in the Tidewater. What do these examples mean?

The second example focuses on interior decoration. Valley houses have a tradition of more elaborate—and often wild—decoration in the early nineteenth century, involving robust, heavily carved mantels and unusual decorative painting. In some cases, elements of German folk art are incorporated into the carving or painting of the woodwork. These rich interiors are often found within a more popular brick I-house shell dating to the 1820s and 1830s. Cultural historians associate this rich decoration, which represented a strong regional style, with the central European settlers, suggesting an outward acceptance of the new styles but an inward expression of their familiar art.[36]

The Seawright House, built ca. 1827 in Augusta County, exempli-

Fig. 11.11. The Plecker-Wise House, Augusta County, contains a brightly decorated interior. Photographs by Ken Gibbs, 1973, and Edward A. Chappell, 1978; courtesy of Virginia Department of Historic Landmarks.

fies the heavy, robust mantels of this regional tradition. But there were no known Germans connected with the construction of this house. According to his account book, joiner James Rankin, a third-generation Scots-Irish resident of Augusta County, made these mantels for a family of English descent. While this decorative spirit may have been inspired by central European tradition, it had clearly become a regional style, appealing to all ethnic groups.[37] Seen within the larger context of Pennsylvania, the Valley's decorative styles had clearly developed their own character. Several houses from the 1820s survive with elaborate sponge-type painting. A paint consultant from Pennsylvania, upon inspecting some of this work, remarked that it was both similar yet very distinct from the traditions in Pennsylvania.

While we have learned much about Valley architecture, we still have much more to learn. First, we need to deepen our architectural analysis by working first with survey data. We need to increase the data base of architectural survey, through covering more territory and through more intensive survey efforts; we need to continue our research into the historical documents to interpret Valley buildings; and we need to derive a better understanding of the old world forms, not depending solely on the published studies available. Further, we may need to re-evaluate our models of cultural interaction and to avoid trying to plug a new survey into existing models. Finally, architecture, like all forms of material culture, reflects the social and cultural history of the region. Future studies need to better integrate the study of the buildings into the social and cultural context that created them through more commu-nity and regional studies.

Notes

1. Dell Upton, "The Power of Things," in *Material Culture: A Research Guide*, ed. Thomas J. Schlereth (Lawrence: Univ. Press of Kansas, 1985), 57.
2. Samuel Kercheval, *A History of the Valley of Virginia* (Woodstock, Va.: J. Gatewood, 1850), 150–51.
3. Jessie Poesch, "David Hunter Strother, An Artist of the Valley of Virginia: His Paintings and Drawings of Friends and Neighbors, c. 1837–1876," paper pre-sented at the Shenandoah Valley Regional Studies Seminar, Harrisonburg, Va., 1995.
4. See the many illustrations scattered throughout Jedediah Hotchkiss, *Illustrated Historical Atlas of Augusta County, Virginia* (Chicago: Waterman, Watkins, and Co., 1885).
5. John Wayland, *Historic Homes of Northern Virginia* (Staunton, Va.: McClure Press, 1937).
6. For a recent study of HABS efforts in Virginia, see Allen Chambers, Jr., "HABS in Virginia: Fifty-two Years of Documenting the Commonwealth's Architecture," *Notes on Virginia* 26 (Spring 1985): 8–15.
7. Kniffen's work culminated in the seminal article, "Folk Housing: Key to Diffu-sion," *Annals of the Association of American Geographers* 55 (1965): 549–77.
8. Henry Glassie, *Pattern in the Material Folk Culture of the Eastern United States* (Philadelphia: Univ. of Pennsylvania Press, 1969).
9. Henry Glassie, "A Museum of American Frontier Culture—A Proposal," (Scotch-Irish Trust of Ulster, 1978), 10, 16.
10. Pamela Hemingway Simpson and Royster Lyle, *The Architecture of Historic Lex-ington* (Charlottesville: Univ. Press of Virginia, 1983).
11. Amos Long Jr., *The Pennsylvania German Family Farm* (Breinigsville, Pa.: The Pennsylvania German Society, 1972).
12. Virginia Division of Historic Landmarks, *Valley Regional Preservation Plan*, Vir-ginia Division of Historic Landmarks, Richmond (1985). This plan consists of separate volumes for each of the cities and counties in the region, from Frederick to Botetourt Counties.
13. For one of several articles on the Opequon settlement, see Warren R. Hofstra, "Land, Ethnicity, and Community at Opequon Settlement, Virginia, 1730–1800," *Virginia Magazine of History and Biography* 98 (1990): 423–48. For the

Massanutten settlement, see Edward A. Chappell, "Acculturation in the Shenandoah Valley: Rhenish Houses of the Massanutten Settlement," in *Common Places: Readings in American Vernacular Architecture*, ed. Dell Upton and John Michael Vlach (Athens: Univ. of Georgia Press, 1986), 27–57. For an analysis of Augusta County's architecture, see Ann E. McCleary, "Historic Resources in Augusta County, Virginia, Eighteenth Century to the Present," typescript, Virginia Division of Historic Resources, Richmond, 1983.

14. Ideally, each survey should end with an analysis of the survey findings. Some states publish this analysis, thus promoting the importance of the region's architecture and updating the dates and interpretations of the local resources for public consumption. These are also useful for architectural historians in other states for comparative use. Realistically, with declining preservation budgets, time and money are available only to identify and describe the buildings. The analysis gets placed on the back burner in preservationists' efforts to continue to describe a rapidly vanishing architectural record.

15. For the Tidewater region, see Cary Carson, Norman F. Barka, William M. Kelso, Garry Wheeler Stone and Dell Upton, "Impermanent Architecture in the Southern American Colonies," *Winterthur Portfolio* 16 (Summer–Autumn 1981): 135–96. The more one researches so-called eighteenth-century buildings, the later the dates often become. This is not a new phenomenon for those interested in vernacular architecture; seventeenth-century dates for several of the oldest houses in Tidewater Virginia have recently been disproved by closer architectural inspections and through dendrochronology.

16. Kercheval, *History of the Valley*, 151; Chappell, "Acculturation in the Shenandoah Valley," 47.

17. K. Edward Lay, "European Antecedents of Seventeenth and Eighteenth Century Germanic and Scots-Irish Architecture in America," *Pennsylvania Folklife* (Autumn 1983): 18.

18. For examples of Upton's writing on the German architecture of the Shenandoah Valley, see "Arts of the Virginia Germans," in *Notes on Virginia* 19 (Summer 1979): 2–7, and Upton, "British and German Interaction in the Blue Ridge," paper delivered at the Seminar on Blue Ridge Life and Culture, Blue Ridge Institute, Ferrum, Va., 1977.

19. Edward A. Chappell, "Cultural Change in the Shenandoah Valley: Northern Augusta County Houses Before 1861," (M.A. thesis: Univ. of Virginia, 1977).

20. See Edward A. Chappell, "Acculturation in the Shenandoah Valley," 27–57.

21. Chappell, "Acculturation in the Shenandoah Valley," 29–30; Lay, "European Antecedents," 19–23; William Woyes Weaver, "The Pennsylvania German House: European Antecedents and New World Forms," *Winterthur Portfolio* 21 (Winter 1986): 253.

22. Weaver, "Pennsylvania German House," 249–53.

23. Ibid., 264.

24. Ibid., 247.

25. Chappell, "Acculturation in the Shenandoah Valley," 29–30.

26. Kercheval, *History of the Valley*, 151.

27. Weaver, "Pennsylvania German House," 254–7; Steve Frieson, "Home Is Where the Hearth Is," *Pennsylvania Folklife* 40 (Spring 1991): 98–118.

28. Weaver, "Pennsylvania German House," 255.

29. Henry Glassie, "The Ulster Influence on American Vernacular Architecture," Ulster Heritage Symposium, Staunton, Va., 1986.
30. Henry Glassie, "The Types of the Southern Mountain Cabin," in *The Study of American Folklore: An Introduction*, ed. Jan Van Brunvand (New York: W. W. Norton, 1968), 338–70.
31. Glassie, "Museum of American Frontier Culture," 30–35.
32. The best study of Ulster architecture is Alan Gailey, *Rural Houses of the North of Ireland* (Edinburg: John Donald, 1984).
33. Warren R. Hofstra, "Folk Housing at Opequon: A Preliminary Report," paper delivered at the Ulster Heritage Symposium, Staunton, Va., 1987.
34. Henry Glassie, "Irish," in *America's Architectural Roots: Ethnic Groups That Built America*, ed. Dell Upton (Washington, D.C.: National Trust for Historic Preservation, 1986), 75–79.
35. Ann McCleary, "Old Homes of Augusta County: A Survey," *Augusta County Historical Bulletin* 19 (Spring 1983): 8–10.
36. Chappell, "Cultural Change in the Shenandoah Valley," 163.
37. Ann McCleary, "Doing the Carpenters and Joiners Work: A Study of the Account Book of James Rankin," *Augusta County Historical Bulletin* 19 (Fall 1983): 28–39.

Works Cited

Carson, Cary, Norman F. Barka, William M. Kelso, Garry Wheeler Stone, and Dell Upton. "Impermanent Architecture in the Southern American Colonies." *Winterthur Portfolio* 16 (Summer–Autumn 1981): 135–96.
Chambers, Allen, Jr. "HABS in Virginia: Fifty-Two Years of Documenting the Commonwealth's Architecture." *Notes on Virginia* 26 (Spring 1985): 8–15.
Chappell, Edward A. "Cultural Change in the Shenandoah Valley: Northern Augusta County Houses Before 1861." M.A. thesis, Univ. of Virginia, 1977.
———. "Acculturation in the Shenandoah Valley: Rhenish Houses of the Massanutten Settlement." *Proceedings of the American Philosophical Society* 124 (1980): 55–89.
———. "Acculturation in the Shenandoah Valley: Rhenish Houses of the Massanutten Settlement." In *Common Places: Readings in American Vernacular Architecture*, edited by Dell Upton and Michael Vlach, 27–57. Athens: Univ. of Georgia Press, 1986.
Comstock, Jim. *Port Crayon Sampler*. Richwood, W.Va.: Jim Comstock Publisher, 1974.
Frieson, Steve. "Home Is Where the Hearth Is." *Pennsylvania Folklife* 40 (Spring 1991): 98–118.
Gailey, Alan. *Rural Houses of the North of Ireland*. Edinburg: John Donald, 1984.
Glassie, Henry. "The Types of the Southern Mountain Cabin." In *The Study of American Folklore: An Introduction*, edited by Jan Van Brunvand, 338–70. New York: W. W. Norton, 1968.
———. *Pattern in the Material Folk Culture of the Eastern United States*. Philadelphia: Univ. of Pennsylvania Press, 1969.
———. "A Museum of American Frontier Culture—A Proposal." Scotch-Irish Trust of Ulster, 1978.
———. "The Ulster Influence on American Vernacular Architecture." Paper pre-

sented at Ulster Heritage Symposium, Woodrow Wilson Birthplace, Staunton, Va., 1986.

Hofstra, Warren R. "Folk Housing at Opequon: A Preliminary Report." Paper presented at the Ulster Heritage Symposium, Woodrow Wilson Birthplace, Staunton, Va., 1987.

———. "Land, Ethnicity, and Community at Opequon Settlement, Virginia, 1730–1800." *Virginia Magazine of History and Biography* 98 (1990): 423–48.

Hotchkiss, Jedediah. *Illustrated Historical Atlas of Augusta County, Virginia.* Chicago: Waterman, Watkins, and Co., 1885.

Kercheval, Samuel. *A History of the Valley of Virginia.* Woodstock, Va.: J. Gatewood, 1850.

Kniffen, Fred. "Folk Housing: Key to Diffusion." *Annals of the American Association of American Geographers* 55 (1965): 40–66.

Lay, K. Edward. "European Antecedents of Seventeenth and Eighteenth Century Germanic and Scots-Irish Architecture in America." *Pennsylvania Folklife* (1983): 2–43.

Long, Amos, Jr. *The Pennsylvania German Family Farm,* Breinigsville, Pa.: The Pennsylvania German Society, 1972.

McCleary, Ann E. "Doing the Carpenters and Joiners Work: A Study of the Account Book of James Rankin." *Augusta County Historical Bulletin* 19 (1983): 28–41.

———. "Historic Resources in Augusta County, Virginia, Eighteenth Century to the Present." Richmond: Virginia Division of Historic Resources, 1983.

———. "Old Homes of Augusta County: A Survey." *Augusta County Historical Bulletin* 19 (Spring 1983): 4–21.

Poesch, Jessie. "David Hunter Strother, An Artist of the Valley of Virginia: His Paintings and Drawings of Friends and Neighbors, c. 1837–1876." Paper presented at the Shenandoah Valley Regional Studies Seminar, Harrisonburg, Va., 1995.

Upton, Dell. "British and German Interaction in the Blue Ridge." Paper presented to the Seminar on Blue Ridge Life and Culture, Blue Ridge Institute, Ferrum College, Ferrum, Va., Sept. 1977.

———. "Arts of the Virginia Germans." *Notes on Virginia* 19 (Summer 1979): 2–7.

———. "The Power of Things." In Thomas J. Schlereth, ed. *Material Culture: A Research Guide.* Lawrence: Univ. of Kansas Press, 1985.

Upton, Dell, ed. *America's Architectural Roots: Ethnic Groups That Built America.* Washington, D.C.: National Trust for Historic Preservation, 1986.

Virginia Division of Historic Landmarks. *Valley Regional Preservation Plan.* Richmond: Virginia Division of Historic Landmarks, 1985.

Wayland, John. *Historic Homes of Northern Virginia.* Staunton Va.: McClure Press, 1937.

Weaver, William Woyes. "The Pennsylvania German House: European Antecedents and New World Forms." *Winterthur Portfolio* 21 (Winter 1986): 243–64.

Chapter 12

The Cantilever Barn in Southwest Virginia

John Morgan

Several scholars have described barn types and their general distribution in Appalachia, but detailed studies are needed to identify additional barn types and to improve our understanding of the distribution, origin, evolution, and diffusion of barn types in the region.[1] Because folk barns tend to exhibit greater variety of form than other folk buildings in Appalachia and the Upland South, maps of areal variations of barn types may provide a basis for refining maps of culture areas.[2]

This essay focuses on the "cantilever barn," an Appalachian folk structure that is the dominant barn in some parts of the region and yet noticeably absent in other sections of Appalachia.[3] The greatest concentration of cantilever barns has been observed near Knoxville, Tennessee, where the structure is the dominant folk barn in Blount and Sevier Counties (map 12.1). Nearly three hundred such structures remain on the landscape in those two counties.[4] Folklorist Henry Glassie's map of the cantilever barn in the 1960s indicated that most of the barns were found in the Great Smoky Mountains of East Tennessee and western North Carolina, with the concentration of structures being about the same in each state. A few cantilever barns were also reported to exist in a section of mountainous

CANTILEVER BARN AREAS OF
EAST TENNESSEE

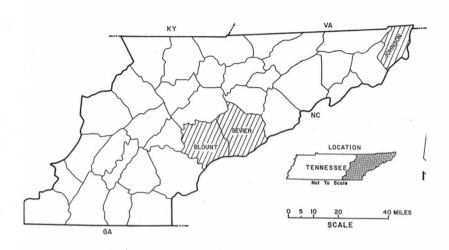

Map 12.1. Cantilever barn areas of East Tennessee. Barns are scattered through the region but are concentrated in Blount, Sevier, and Johnson Counties.

southeastern Kentucky and in a narrow ribbon straddling the border of eastern West Virginia and western Virginia.[5] However, a recent attempt to map the distribution of the barn found the structure to be virtually non-existent in North Carolina.[6]

The cantilever barn served to support the general or mixed farming system associated with southern Appalachia. Prior to this century the economy of East Tennessee and Southwest Virginia was dominated by small yeomen farms and self-sufficient agriculture, with corn, hay, wheat, and oats being the principal crops produced and swine, cattle, and sheep the most important livestock raised. The horse served as the region's principal work animal, but oxen and mules occasionally were used.[7]

The typical cantilever barn in Blount and Sevier Counties in Tennessee is a double-pen or double-crib structure, with a pen simply being a four-wall unit of horizontal log construction.[8] The barn consists of ground-level log cribs and an overhanging frame upper floor supported by log beams or cantilevers.[9] The log cribs usually are separated by a central passage or runway. A majority of the barns have overhangs on all four sides, with most of the remaining structures having overhangs on front and rear only (fig. 12.1, 12.2). Lower cribs were used as animal stalls and the upper floor was a hay-

Fig. 12.1. The most common double-crib cantilever barn type in mid-East Tennessee. The frame upper-level loft overhangs the lower-level log cribs in front and rear and on both sides. Note that the areas beneath the side overhangs have been enclosed.

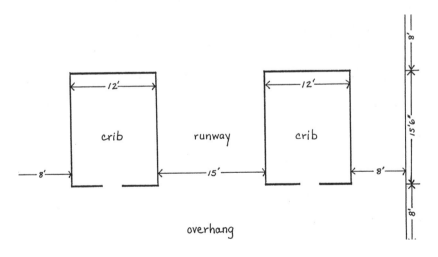

Fig. 12.2. Plan of most common double-crib cantilever barn type. Reproduced courtesy of the author.

loft. Perhaps the most important function of the overhang was to provide a dry area in which to feed barnyard animals, especially cattle.[10] One scholar recently stated, however, that the "survival" of an overhang or forebay on American barns "was most likely the result of tradition."[11]

This barn type was identified by Glassie, who believed the structure diffused to the southern Appalachian region from the Midland Culture hearth in Pennsylvania, "where similar barns may be very rarely found."[12] Architectural historians Marian Moffett and Lawrence Wodehouse, however, argue that cultural diffusion does not explain the presence of cantilever barns in mid-East Tennessee, and they claim that the large number of barns in Sevier and Blount Counties near Knoxville suggest that the structure was invented in that section of the state.[13] According to Moffett and Wodehouse, "Someone, perhaps from within Sevier County, must have originated the [barn] form, and it met with sufficient local enthusiasm that the cantilever principle was applied to single-crib, two-crib, and four-crib types. Family connections, geographical proximity to an existing cantilever barn, and possibly the social prominence of several early barn builders seem to us to account for both the distribution and small-scale variation in these barns."[14]

They further reject the Pennsylvania barn as the forerunner of the cantilever barn and state that the structure was modeled after cantilevered blockhouses built in East Tennessee to protect early settlers from Indian attacks.[15]

The barn has been widely promoted as Tennessee's only unique contribution to America's indigenous architecture, and it has received so much publicity in local and regional newspapers that it has become a part of the regional identity and popular culture of mid-East Tennessee.[16]

Upper East Tennessee Barns

In the late 1980s, I discovered a few cantilever barns in Johnson County, in the upper East Tennessee corner (map 12.1). Later, while completing a building survey for the Tennessee Historical Commission, I identified more than fifty cantilever barns in Johnson County and concluded that the cantilever barn was the dominant agricultural structure in the county during the nineteenth century.[17] The discovery of so many barns in Johnson County also significantly alters Moffett and Wodehouse's recent map, purported to show the distribution of cantilever barns throughout East Tennessee. Their map identifies only six cantilever barns in Johnson County.[18]

A comparison of form and construction characteristics reveals that most of the cantilever barns in Johnson County are similar to those in

Fig. 12.3. Typical Johnson County double-crib log barn, with cantilevered overhang on front and rear of structure. Reproduced courtesy of the author.

Blount and Sevier Counties, Tennessee. That is, they are double-crib units with upper-level frame overhanging lofts. The most common barn in Johnson County has the overhang projecting on the front and rear only and not on the ends, as is typically the case in Blount and Sevier Counties (fig. 12.3). There are, however, a few barns in Johnson County that exhibit the overhang on all four sides. The county also has more single-crib cantilever barns than are found in Blount and Sevier Counties, and a higher percentage of Johnson County's barns have posts to support the cantilevered overhangs.

Southwest Virginia Barns

Buchanan County
In 1989 I serendipitously encountered a few cantilever barns on the Cumberland Plateau along the Kentucky–Virginia border near the Breaks Interstate Park, and the barns have forms similar to those in Blount and Sevier Counties in Tennessee. Most of the barns in the Breaks area are found in Buchanan County, Virginia (map 12.2), and two of the structures are triple-pen units with the middle pen or crib

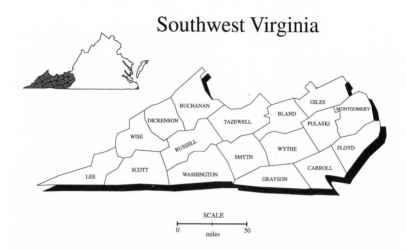

Map 12.2. The counties of Southwest Virginia.

used as a threshing floor (figs. 12.4, 12.5).[19] The great majority of the double-crib barns in the Knoxville area are separated by an open runway or central passage, but some do have central threshing floors similar to those in the Breaks area. A few of the Breaks area barns also have end cantilevers, a feature that Moffett and Wodehouse claim give East Tennessee barns uniqueness (fig. 12.6).

Subsequent field research in Buchanan County, Virginia, indicates that the cantilever log barn was the dominant barn type in the county from the 1830s or 1840s until the 1930s. This finding requires that maps of the cantilever barn be modified once again because no one has previously mentioned the existence of the barn in far Southwest Virginia. Field reconnaissance revealed the presence of at least sixty cantilever barns in the county, and thirty barns outside the Breaks area have been inventoried. Of those, twenty-two are double-crib log barns with a frame upper floor. All but one of the double-crib barns have a central runway, with the cribs of the other barn separated only by a log wall. Five of the barns also had overhangs on all four sides, making them nearly identical in form to the "unique" barns of East Tennessee. Eight single-crib structures with frame second floors were also identified. The upper level overhangs projected outward on all four sides on three of the structures; extended over two sides on five of the barns; and projected over three sides on one of the buildings (figs. 12.7, 12.8).

The log cribs on Buchanan County barns tend to be square or nearly square, with the most common crib dimension being 12 feet by 12 feet.

Fig. 12.4. Triple-crib cantilever barn, Buchanan County, Virginia. Note the areas under rear and end overhang have been enclosed. Reproduced courtesy of the author.

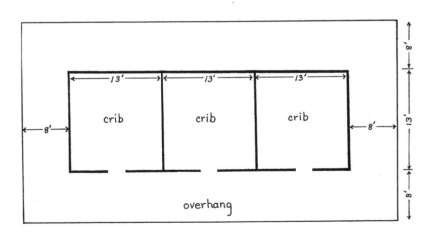

Fig. 12.5. Plan of Triple-crib cantilever barn shown in fig. 12.4. Reproduced courtesy of the author.

Fig. 12.6. Cantilevered end or side overhang of Buchanan County barn shown in fig. 12.4. Reproduced courtesy of the author.

Fig. 12.7. Single-crib log barn with overhang on all sides, Buchanan County, Virginia. Reproduced courtesy of the author.

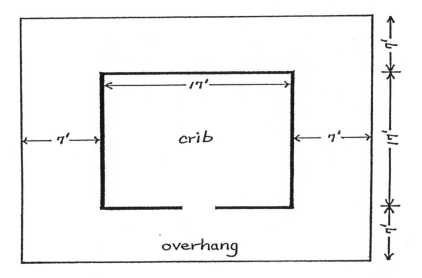

Fig. 12.8. Plan of single-crib barn shown in fig. 12.7. Reproduced courtesy of the author.

That dimension is also a common one for cribs in mid-East Tennessee barns, but most log cribs in Tennessee are more rectangular than Buchanan County cribs. In Blount County, most common crib dimensions are 12 feet by 16 feet, 12 by 14 feet, and 12 by 18 feet.[20] However, rectangular cribs can also be found in Buchanan County, where units of 12 feet (front) by 14 feet (side), 12 by 16, and 12 by 20 have been identified.

In the overwhelming majority of the cantilevered double-crib barns in both Buchanan County and East Tennessee, doors are placed in the front of the crib as opposed to being placed in the runway side of the crib. That pattern of door placement indicates that barn cribs in both areas function as stables for livestock. In other log barn areas, where crib entrance is typically from the runway, cribs tend to serve primarily as grain or hay-storage facilities.[21]

Cantilever projections range from 6 to 10 feet in length on Buchanan barns, with the most common dimension being 8 feet. Those dimensions are similar to those on barns in Blount County, Tennessee, where overhangs range from 3 to 12 feet but are dominated by lengths of 8 to 10 feet. The width of the runways or central passages for Buchanan County barns is also similar to the widths of Blount County barns. They range from 4 feet to 15 feet in Buchanan County, and from 6 to 20 feet in Blount

County, Tennessee. The most frequently observed runway width in Buchanan County is roughly 10 feet, and in Blount County the most common widths are 10 feet and 12 feet.[22] Those widths would allow for a horse-drawn wagon to enter the runway, and there hay could be transferred from the wagon to the upper hayloft.

The presence of the cantilever barn in several parts of Appalachia allows one to question the assertion of Moffett and Wodehouse that the barn was invented in mid-East Tennessee. It is unlikely that independent invention of the same barn occurred in three areas located relatively close together. It is also unlikely that Johnson County, Tennessee, or Buchanan County, Virginia, were the recipients of the diffusion of the barn from mid-East Tennessee because such a movement would have been counter to the primary migration pattern of early settlers to East Tennessee—that is, a southwesterly flow down the Great Valley from Virginia and Pennsylvania.

The Valley of Southwest Virginia

My recent field research on the cantilever barn also has focused on Washington, Smyth, and Wythe Counties, located in the Valley of Southwest Virginia (map 12.2). This area may be critical to an understanding of the cantilever barn because the area to the southwest contains cantilever barns and the area to the northeast (at least beyond Roanoke) is dominated by the Pennsylvania forebay bank barn. The Pennsylvania barn was "transported" to western Virginia largely by Germanic settlers, who migrated southward from Pennsylvania into the Shenandoah Valley of Virginia during the eighteenth century. If the cantilever barn evolved from the Pennsylvania barn, perhaps there is evidence of a transition in barn form in the Valley of Southwest Virginia.

Twenty-eight cantilevered log barns were identified in Washington, Smyth, and Wythe Counties. Although there are several versions of the barn, none has the exact form as those in East Tennessee. In each of the three counties, most of the barns are double-crib structures that have log upper floors, and most use the cantilevers simply to support the barn roof. Several, however, have the cantilevers placed low enough to allow for the creation of additional second-floor space. Some also have end cantilevers. Most of the barns have central, earthen runways between the cribs, but several of the structures, especially in Wythe County, have wooden threshing floors.

An excellent example of a two-level, double-crib barn with cantilevered overhangs on four sides is the Copenhaver barn, erected in Smyth County near the town of Marion during the 1830s (fig. 12.9). The log

Fig. 12.9. Cantilevers support porch roof on all sides of double-crib barn in Smyth County, Virginia. Reproduced courtesy of the author.

cribs, each 23 feet, 9 inches square, extend to the eave level of the structure and are separated by a wooden threshing floor (20 feet, 7 inches wide), which is slightly elevated above ground level. The doors to the ground-level animal stalls are on the front of the cribs. Openings for pitching hay to and from the second-floor mows are found on the runway walls of each crib. A "porch" roof extends outward 8 feet on all sides of the structure, and the roof is attached to large, unsupported cantilevered beams. The front overhang shelters a feeding area for barnyard animals, as evidenced by the presence of a hollowed-out log feed trough and a hay rack attached to the exterior front of one of the cribs. However, the function of the overhangs on the rear and ends of the structure is not so clearly understood.

Recent field research by Warren E. Roberts in southern Indiana indicates that some German American double-crib log barns in DuBois County are similar to a few of the cantilever barns in the Valley of Southwest Virginia.[23] The barns in both areas (Virginia and Indiana) not only have cantilevered beams supporting front and rear porch roofs but also typically have two cantilevers on each crib, with the cantilevers projecting from the side walls of each crib. The presence of similar barns in southern Indiana and southwestern Virginia would suggest that the barn was carried westward and southwestward by settlers migrating from Pennsylvania.

The Pennsylvania Barn

Several of the cantilevered barns erected in Wythe County were log versions of the Pennsylvania forebay bank barn, and at least one of those barns remains on the landscape today. The Pennsylvania barn is a two-level structure with a bank or ramp entrance to the second floor and a second-floor overhang or forebay extending several feet over the first floor on the side opposite the bank. The lower level functioned as a stabling area for animals and in the multifunctional upper level were located the hayloft, granary, threshing floor, and storage areas for farm equipment. The developed form of this structure in Pennsylvania usually had a stone lower floor and a timber-frame upper floor, but examples of brick and stone barns are also numerous.[24]

The origin and development of the forebay bank barn has been the subject of considerable debate. Some scholars, such as Henry Glassie, have argued that the Pennsylvania barn is an American development. He stated in 1970 that "the bank barn resulted from meshing the multi-level banked notion brought from Central Europe and Northwestern England with the double-crib barn idea from Central Europe."[25]

Glassie's idea about the origin and development of the forebay-bank barn has been vigorously attacked during recent years by geographers Terry G. Jordan and Robert F. Ensminger, who conducted detailed field investigations (independently of each other) in Central and Alpine Europe during the late 1970s and early 1980s. They both found examples of log forebay bank barns and "evolved" non-log models in central and eastern Switzerland. Both Jordan and Ensminger convincingly proposed that several permutations of the Pennsylvania barn were transferred directly from Europe and that the barn did not go through an evolutionary process in America.[26]

The Kettering barn is a log forebay bank barn in Wythe County. The building merits detailed examination because it is a tri-level structure and not the prototypical two-level Pennsylvania barn (fig. 12.10).[27] The barn was erected along Mill Creek near the town of Rural Retreat in 1816 by Lawrence Kettering, a Revolutionary War soldier of German descent.[28]

The Kettering barn is a large, double-crib structure with side-

Fig. 12.10. Log double-crib Pennsylvania barn, Wythe County, Virginia, with frame forebay supported by cantilevers. View of barn's central threshing floor is obscured by front corncrib addition. Reproduced courtesy of the author.

facing gables, and roof ridge running parallel to the front and rear of the building. The log cribs have rectangular forms with the east crib having a front dimension of 19 feet, 10 inches and the side extending 29 feet, 4 inches. The west crib is also 19 feet, 10 inches in front, but has a side dimension of 28 feet. The central runway is 18 feet wide and is entered from ground level on the hillside. The barn is supported by a stone (masonry) foundation, which is nearly 4 feet high in the front of the building but becomes gradually lower on the sides because the structure is built into a low angle hillslope.

A frame forebay or overhang, supported by 14 cantilevered beams, 7 in each crib, extends the second floor outward 8 feet in the front of the structure. A rear section, which extends the structure by 8 feet on the hillslope, may have been an addition to the structure, because there are no large beams connecting the rear shed to the log cribs. The upper-level log cribs were used as hay mows, and the forebay section east of the runway served as a granary for wheat and oats. A wooden structure, 4 feet wide by 18 feet long and about 4 feet high, was built into the forebay and subdivided into 4 separate grain bins of equal size. The runway or central passage functioned as a threshing floor for wheat and oats, and when not in use for threshing, served as a storage facility for the wagon and perhaps other equipment.

Of significance is the fact that the central runway or threshing floor of the Kettering barn does not lead to a true second floor, but rather occupies a position intermediate between the ground floor and the floor of the upper-level hay mows. The runway height is certainly different from that of the non-log Pennsylvania barns in the Shenandoah Valley of Virginia and the Delaware Valley of southeastern Pennsylvania, and it appears to be different from the runway height of log barns in those areas as well. Is the low placement of the runway a sign of its future deletion—for the purpose of creating a ground-level open passage between the log cribs? Further research is needed to answer that question and to determine the extent to which the tri-level Kettering barn is different from other log Pennsylvania barns.

The identification and examination of log Pennsylvania barns in other parts of western Virginia may provide hints about the development of the cantilever barns in southwestern Virginia. For example, I recently identified a log Pennsylvania bank barn in Augusta County (near Staunton) with the overhang on both the front and rear of the structure (fig. 12.11). If one removed the bank and viewed the barn from the side, it would look quite similar in form to some of the barns in East Tennessee. Several other Pennsylvania barns with multiple overhangs were present in the Shenandoah Valley and at least one such barn was also located in Botetourt County, Virginia.[29] I also discovered a similar barn with front and rear forebay at Ferrum College's Blue Ridge Farm Museum. This barn was built about 1800 in Callaway, Virginia (in Franklin County near Ferrum). Does the presence of a front and rear overhang on the bank barn and on the cantilever barn suggest the possibility of an antecedent barn type in Pennsylvania or Europe that had the overhangs but not the bank? Recent research by Ensminger identified bank barns in Pennsylvania with overhangs on two, three, and four sides, and Hubert G. H. Wilhelm located several barns with front and rear overhangs in southeastern Ohio.[30] However, cases of nonbank barns with multiple overhangs have yet to be reported in areas where the Pennsylvania barn is dominant.

Conclusion

My field research requires that the maps of the cantilever barn be ex-

Fig. 12.11. End view of Pennsylvania bank barn with overhang on front and rear of structure; Augusta County, Virginia. Reproduced courtesy of the author.

panded to include parts of Southwest Virginia. Broad parts of the region, however, have yet to be examined, and future field surveys will almost certainly expand further the geographic range of the cantilever barn. The discovery of numerous cantilever barns in Johnson County, Tennessee, and Buchanan County, Virginia, make it highly unlikely that the barn was invented in mid-East Tennessee, as claimed by Moffett and Wodehouse.

This research, coupled with previous work, indicates that there are several varieties of the cantilever barn. It appears that different types tend to cluster into barn "micro-regions." Because the Pennsylvania bank barn has antecedents in sections of mountainous Central Europe, especially Switzerland, may we assume that cantilever barn clusters in the United States are synonymous with areas of Germanic settlement? That explanation would seem plausible for the valley counties of southwestern Virginia, especially Wythe County, where double-crib log barns are referred to simply as "German barns," and it might be plausible for Johnson County, Tennessee, because numerous German settlers migrated to the area from the Shenandoah Valley, where the Pennsylvania barn is the most pervasive landscape feature.[31] However, it might be more difficult to attribute the presence of the cantilever barn in the Knoxville area or Buchanan County to the strong influence of Germanic settlement.

At this point, we are perhaps left with more questions than answers in our search for the origin of the cantilever barn. For example, to what extent was the cantilever barn an adjustment to an agricultural system in southwestern Virginia that might have been different from that found in the Shenandoah Valley, where the standard Pennsylvania barn was pervasive? John Fraser Hart has suggested that the Pennsylvania barn is absent in much of Southwest Virginia because farmland in the region was inferior to land in the Shenandoah Valley, farms were smaller in Southwest Virginia, and corn replaced wheat as the dominant crop in the region.[32] Less emphasis on wheat would reduce the need for a threshing floor, and lack of affluence might rule in favor of construction of barns much smaller and simpler than the Pennsylvania barns of the Shenandoah Valley.

With respect to the varieties of the cantilever barn in Southwest Virginia and East Tennessee, did an evolutionary process occur in the region, or were all the permutations of the barn present at one time in southeastern Pennsylvania or even Europe and simply transferred to new locations? The answer may be somewhere in the middle, with cultural transfer dominating but some adaptation of barn form taking place in local communities.

Additional field research is needed to establish and account for the distribution of the cantilever barn, to record its form and construction characteristics, and to determine when and by whom individual barns were constructed. Definitive statements on the origin, diffusion, and development of the cantilever barn can be made only after such field investigations have been completed in the United States and in Europe. Such studies should be conducted immediately because the number of cantilever barns in some areas, especially southwestern Virginia, is decreasing rapidly. Failure to study them will result in the loss of a valuable link to the past cultural heritage of the region.

Notes

1. See, for example, Henry Glassie, "The Pennsylvania Barn in the South," *Pennsylvania Folklife* 15 (2) (1965–66): 8–17; Henry Glassie, "The Pennsylvania Barn in the South," pt. 2, *Pennsylvania Folklife* 15 (4) (1966): 12–25; Henry Glassie, *Pattern in the Material Folk Culture of the Eastern United States* (Philadelphia: Univ. of Pennsylvania Press, 1968); John Fraser Hart, "Types of Barns in the Eastern United States," *Focus* 43 (1) (1993): 8–17; Fred Kniffen, "Folk Housing: Key to Diffusion," *Annals of the Association of American Geographers*

55 (1965): 549–77; and Allen G. Noble, *Wood, Brick, and Stone*, vol. 2 (Amherst: Univ. of Massachusetts Press, 1984).

2. Glassie, *Material Folk Culture of the Eastern United States*, 74–101; Glassie, "Pennsylvania Barn in the South," 8–19; Robert D. Mitchell, "The Formation of Early American Cultural Regions: An Interpretation," in *European Settlement and Development in North America: Essays on Geographical Change in Honour and Memory of Andrew Hill Clark*, ed. James R. Gibson (Toronto: Univ. of Toronto Press, 1978), 85; Wilbur Zelinsky, *The Cultural Geography of the United States* (Englewood Cliffs, N.J.: Prentice-Hall, 1973), 100.

3. Glassie, "Pennsylvania Barn in the South"; Marian Moffett and Lawrence Wodehouse, *The Cantilever Barn in East Tennessee* (Knoxville: School of Architecture, Univ. of Tennessee, 1984); John Morgan and Ashby Lynch Jr., "Log Barns of Blount County, Tennessee," *Tennessee Anthropologist* 9 (2) (1984): 85–103.

4. Marian Moffett and Lawrence Wodehouse, *East Tennessee Cantilever Barns* (Knoxville: Univ. of Tennessee Press, 1993), xii.

5. Glassie, "Pennsylvania Barn in the South," 18.

6. Moffett and Wodehouse, *East Tennessee Cantilever Barns*, 1.

7. The 1850 Census of Agriculture reveals that in Wythe County, Virginia, in 1850 there were 3,696 horses but only 88 asses and mules and 152 working oxen; James L. Douthat, *Early Wythe Settlers, Wythe County, 1810–1850* (Signal Mountain, Tenn.: Mountain Press, 1984).

8. For background on horizontal log construction in the eastern United States, see, for example, Terry G. Jordan, *Texas Log Buildings* (Austin: Univ. of Texas Press, 1978); Jordan, *American Log Buildings* (Chapel Hill: Univ. of North Carolina Press, 1986); Kniffen, "Folk Housing," Fred Kniffen and Henry Glassie, "Building in Wood in the Eastern United States: A Time-Place Perspective," *Geographical Review* 56 (1966): 40–66; and John Morgan, *The Log House in East Tennessee* (Knoxville: Univ. of Tennessee Press, 1990).

9. As Allen G. Noble pointed out, "The term crib can be confusing because it is applied in two ways. In its simplest application, it refers to a pen composed of logs . . . [and] used for crop or equipment storage or animal shelter. A crib may also be a more specialized structure, often of frame construction, used essentially for the storage of corn left on the cobs" (Noble, *Wood, Brick, and Stone*, 171).

10. For a discussion of the various functions of the overhang or forebay on Pennsylvania barns, see Joseph W. Glass, *The Pennsylvania Culture Region: A View from the Barn* (Ann Arbor, Mich.: UMI Research Press, 1986), 12–16; and Terry G. Jordan, "Some Neglected Swiss Literature on the Forebay Bank Barn," *Pennsylvania Folklife* 37 (2) (1987–88): 75–80.

11. Hubert G. H. Wilhelm, "Midwestern Barns and Their Germanic Connections," in *Barns of the Midwest*, ed. Allen G. Noble and Hubert G. H. Wilhelm (Athens: Ohio Univ. Press, 1995), 70.

12. Henry Glassie, "The Old Barns of Appalachia," *Mountain Life and Work* 40 (2) (1965): 28.

13. Moffett and Wodehouse, *East Tennessee Cantilever Barns*, 17, 26–27.

14. Ibid., 27.

15. Ibid., 17.

16. See, for example, Geneva Allen, "Cantilevered Barns," *Knoxville News-Sentinel*, Mar. 4, 1987; Vic Weals, "That Old Log Barn Might be Unique to this Region,"

Knoxville Journal, Sept. 13, 1984; Don Williams, "Good Bye Old Barns," *Knoxville News-Sentinel,* Jan. 8, 1989.

17. Building surveys for East Tennessee counties, including Blount, Johnson, and Sevier, are on file at the Tennessee Historical Commission, Nashville.

18. Moffett and Wodehouse, *East Tennessee Cantilever Barns,* 123.

19. One of the barns was described in Peter M. Letcher, "The Breaks, Virginia," *Pioneer America* 4 (2) (1972): 1–7.

20. John Morgan and Ashby Lynch Jr., "The Log Barns of Blount County, Tennessee," *Tennessee Anthropologist* 9 (2) (1984): 90.

21. Henry Glassie, "The Double Crib Barn in South Central Pennsylvania," pt. 4, *Pioneer America* 2 (2) (1970): 23–34; and "The Pennsylvania Barn in the South," 13.

22. Morgan and Lynch, "Log Barns of Blount County," 90.

23. Warren E. Roberts, "Early Log Crib Survivals," in Noble and Wilhelm, eds., *Barns of the Midwest,* 33–34.

24. Eric Arthur and Dudley Witney, *The Barn: A Vanishing Landmark in North America* (Toronto, Canada: A and W Visual Library, 1972); Noble, *Wood, Brick, and Stone;* and Alfred L. Shoemaker, ed., *The Pennsylvania Barn* (Kutztown, Pa.: Pennsylvania Folklife Society, 1955).

25. Henry Glassie, "The Double-Crib Barn in South Central Pennsylvania," pt. 4, 25.

26. Robert F. Ensminger, "A Search for the Origin of the Pennsylvania Barn," *Pennsylvania Folklife* 30 (2) (1980–81): 50–71; Jordan, *American Log Buildings,* 99–115.

27. The Kettering barn was previously described in John Morgan, "A Pennsylvania Log Barn in Western Wythe County, Virginia," paper presented at New River Symposium, Beckley, W.Va., Apr. 1992.

28. Personal interview with Hilda George, Alpharetta, Ga., Feb. 12, 1992.

29. Robert F. Ensminger, *The Pennsylvania Barn* (Baltimore: Johns Hopkins Univ. Press, 1993), 75–79; Glassie, "Pennsylvania Barn in the South," part 2, 16, 21.

30. Hubert G. H. Wilhelm, "Double Overhang Barns in Southeastern Ohio," *Pioneer America Society Transactions* 12 (1989): 29–36.

31. *History of Johnson County, 1986* (Mountain City, Tenn.: Johnson County Historical Society, 1985).

32. John Fraser Hart, "Types of Barns in the Eastern United States," 13–15.

Works Cited

Allen, Geneva. "Cantilevered Barns." *Knoxville News-Sentinel,* Mar. 4, 1987.

Arthur, Eric, and Dudley Witney. *The Barn: A Vanishing Landmark in North America.* Toronto: A and W Visual Library, 1972.

Dornbush, Charles E. *Pennsylvania German Barns: Twenty-First Yearbook of the Pennsylvania German Folklore Society.* Allentown, Pa.: Pennsylvania German Folklore Society, 1955.

Douthat, James L. *Early Wythe Settlers, Wythe County, 1810–1850.* Signal Mountain, Tenn.: Mountain Press, 1984.

Ensminger, Robert F. "A Search for the Origin of the Pennsylvania Barn." *Pennsylvania Folklife* 30 (1980–81): 50–69.

———. "The Pennsylvania Barn: A Study in the Continuity of Form." *Pennsylvania Geographer* 21 (1983): 14–20.

———. *The Pennsylvania Barn.* Baltimore: Johns Hopkins Univ. Press, 1992.

Gibson, James R., ed. *European Settlement and Development in North America: Essays on Geographical Change in Honour and Memory of Andrew Hill Clark.* Toronto: Univ. of Toronto Press, 1978.

Glass, Joseph W. *The Pennsylvania Culture Region: A View from the Barn.* Ann Arbor, Mich.: UMI Research Press, 1986.

Glassie, Henry. "The Old Barns of Appalachia." *Mountain Life and Work* 40 (2) (1965): 21–30.

———. "The Pennsylvania Barn in the South." *Pennsylvania Folklife* 15 (2) (Winter 1965–66): 8–19.

———. "The Pennsylvania Barn in the South." Pt. 2. *Pennsylvania Folklife* 15 (4) (Summer 1966): 12–25.

———. *Pattern in the Material Folk Culture of the Eastern United States.* Philadelphia: Univ. of Pennsylvania Press, 1968.

———. "The Double-Crib Barn in South Central Pennsylvania." *Pioneer America* 1 (1) (1969): 9–16.

———. "The Double-Crib Barn in South Central Pennsylvania." Pt. 2. *Pioneer America* 1 (2) (1969): 40–45.

———. "The Double-Crib Barn in South Central Pennsylvania." Pt. 3. *Pioneer America* 2 (1) (1970): 47–52.

———. "The Double-Crib Barn in South Central Pennsylvania." Pt. 4. *Pioneer America* 2 (2) (1970): 23–34.

Hart, John Fraser. "Types of Barns in the Eastern United States." *Focus* 43 (1) (1993): 8–17.

History of Johnson County, 1986. Mountain City, Tenn.: Johnson County Historical Society, 1985.

Jordan, Terry G. *Texas Log Buildings.* Austin: Univ. of Texas Press, 1978.

———. "Alpine, Alemannic, and American Architecture." *Annals of the Association of American Geographers* 70 (1980): 154–80.

———. "A Reappraisal of Fenno-Scandian Antecedents for Midland American Log Construction." *Geographical Review* 73 (1983): 58–94.

———. *American Log Buildings.* Chapel Hill: Univ. of North Carolina Press, 1985.

———. "Some Neglected Swiss Literature on the Forebay Bank Barn." *Pennsylvania Folklife* 37 (2) (1987–88): 75–80.

Jordan, Terry G., and Matti Kaups. "Folk Architecture in Cultural and Ecological Context." *Geographical Review* 77 (1987): 52–75.

———. *The American Backwoods Frontier: An Ethnic and Ecological Interpretation.* Baltimore: Johns Hopkins Univ. Press, 1989.

Kauffman, Henry J. "The Log Barn." In *The Pennsylvania Barn.* Edited by Alfred L. Shoemaker. Kutztown, Pa.: Pennsylvania Folklife Society, 1955.

Kniffen, Fred. "Folk Housing: Key to Diffusion." *Annals of the Association of American Geographers* 55 (1965): 549–77.

Kniffen, Fred, and Henry Glassie. "Building in Wood in the Eastern United States: A Time-Place Perspective." *Geographical Review* 56 (1966): 40–66.

Letcher, Peter M. "The Breaks, Virginia." *Pioneer America* 4 (2) (1972): 1–7.

Mitchell, Robert D. "The Formation of Early American Cultural Regions: An Interpretation." In *European Settlement and Development in North America: Essays on Geographical Change in Honour and Memory of Andrew Hill Clark,* edited by James R. Gibson, 66–90. Toronto: Univ. of Toronto Press, 1978.

Moffett, Marian, and Lawrence Wodehouse. *The Cantilever Barn in East Tennessee.* Knoxville: School of Architecture, Univ. of Tennessee, 1984.

———. "The Cantilever Barn in East Tennessee." *Pioneer American Society Transactions* 9 (1986): 17–22.

———. *East Tennessee Cantilever Barns.* Knoxville: Univ. of Tennessee Press, 1993.

Morgan, John. *The Log House in East Tennessee.* Knoxville: Univ. of Tennessee Press, 1990.

———. "A Pennsylvania Log Barn in Western Wythe County, Virginia." Paper presented at New River Symposium, Beckley, W.Va., Apr. 1992.

Morgan, John, and Ashby Lynch Jr. "The Log Barns of Blount County, Tennessee." *Tennessee Anthropologist* 9 (2) (1984): 85–103.

Noble, Allen G. *Wood, Brick, and Stone: The North American Settlement Landscape.* 2 vols. Amherst: Univ. of Massachusetts Press, 1984.

Noble, Allen G., and Hubert G. H. Wilhelm, editors. *Barns of the Midwest.* Athens: Ohio Univ. Press, 1995.

Roberts, Warren E. "Early Log-Crib Barn Survivals." In *Barns of the Midwest,* edited by Allen G. Noble and Hubert G. H. Wilhelm, 24–39. Athens: Ohio Univ. Press, 1995.

Shoemaker, Alfred I., ed. *The Pennsylvania Barn.* Lancaster, Pa.: Pennsylvania Dutch Folklore Center, 1955.

Weals, Vic. "That Old Log Barn Might Be Unique to this Region." *Knoxville Journal,* Sept. 13, 1984.

Wilhelm, Hubert G. H. "Double Overhang Barns in Southeastern Ohio." *Pioneer America Society Transactions* 12 (1989): 29–36.

———. "Midwestern Barns and Their Germanic Connections." In *Barns of the Midwest,* edited by Allen G. Noble and Hubert G. H. Wilhelm, 62–79. Athens: Ohio Univ. Press, 1995.

Williams, Don. "Good Bye Old Barns." *Knoxville News-Sentinel,* Jan. 8, 1989.

Zelinsky, Wilbur. *The Cultural Geography of the United States.* Englewood Cliffs, N. J.: Prentice-Hall, 1973.

Selected Bibliography

Alvord, Clarence, and Lee Bidgood. *The First Explorations of the Trans-Allegheny Region by the Virginians, 1650–1674.* Cleveland: Arthur H. Clark Co., 1912.

Bailyn, Bernard, and Philip D. Morgan, editors. *Strangers Within the Realm: Cultural Margins of the First British Empire.* Chapel Hill: Univ. of North Carolina Press, 1991.

Beeman, Richard R. *The Evolution of the Southern Backcountry: A Case Study of Lunenburg County, Virginia, 1746–1832.* Philadelphia: Univ. of Pennsylvania Press, 1984.

Billings, Warren M., John E. Selby, and Thad W. Tate. *Colonial Virginia: A History.* White Plains, N.Y.: KTO Press, 1986.

Briceland, Alan V. *Westward from Virginia: The Exploration of the Virginia–Carolina Frontier, 1650–1710.* Charlottesville: Univ. Press of Virginia, 1987.

Bridenbaugh, Carl. *Myths and Realities: Societies of the Colonial South.* Baton Rouge: Louisiana State Univ. Press, 1952.

Caruso, John A. *The Appalachian Frontier: America's First Surge Westward.* New York: Bobbs-Merrill Co., 1959.

Chalkley, Lyman. *Chronicles of the Scotch-Irish Settlement of Virginia.* 3 vols. 1912. Reprint, Baltimore: Genealogical Publishing Co., Inc., 1980.

Draper, Lyman C. Collection. Microfilm. State Historical Society of Wisconsin, Madison.

Farmer, Charles J. *In the Absence of Towns: Settlement and Country Trade in Southside Virginia.* Lanham, Md.: Rowman and Littlefield, 1993.

Fischer, David Hackett. *Albion's Seed: Four British Folkways in America.* New York: Oxford Univ. Press, 1989.

Glassie, Henry. *Pattern in the Material Folk Culture of the Eastern United States.* Philadelphia: Univ. of Pennsylvania Press, 1968.

Hart, Freeman H. *The Valley of Virginia in the American Revolution, 1763–1789.* Chapel Hill: Univ. of North Carolina Press, 1942.

Hart, John Fraser. "The Spread of the Frontier and the Growth of Population." *Geoscience and Man* 5 (1974): 73–81.

Hatley, Tom. *The Dividing Paths: Cherokees and South Carolinians through the Era of Revolution.* New York: Oxford Univ. Press, 1993.

Hoffman, Ronald, Thad W. Tate, and Peter J. Albert, editors. *An Uncivil War: The Southern Backcountry during the American Revolution.* Charlottesville: Univ. Press of Virginia, 1985.

Hofstra, Warren R. "Land, Ethnicity, and Community at the Opequon Settlement, Virginia, 1730–1800." *Virginia Magazine of History and Biography* 98 (1990): 423–48.

———. "The Virginia Backcountry in the Eighteenth Century: Origins and Outcomes." *Virginia Magazine of History and Biography* 101 (1993): 485–508.

Jordan, Terry G., and Matti Kaups. *The American Backwoods Frontier: An Ethnic and Ecological Interpretation.* Baltimore: Johns Hopkins Univ. Press, 1989.

Kegley, F. B. *Kegley's Virginia Frontier.* Roanoke, Va.: Southwest Virginia Historical Society, 1938.

Kercheval, Samuel. *A History of the Valley of Virginia.* 4th edition. Strasburg, Va.: Shenandoah Publishing House, 1925.

[Lederer, John]. *The Discoveries of John Lederer.* Edited by William P. Cumming. Charlottesville: Univ. Press of Virginia, 1958.

Lemon, James T. *The Best Poor Man's Country: A Geographical Study of Early Southeastern Pennsylvania.* Baltimore: Johns Hopkins Univ. Press, 1972.

McCleskey, Nathaniel Turk. "Across the First Divide: Frontiers of Settlement and Culture in Augusta County, Virginia, 1738–1770." Ph.D. diss., College of William and Mary, 1990.

———. "Rich Land, Poor Prospects: Real Estate and the Formation of a Social Elite in Augusta County, Virginia, 1738–1770." *Virginia Magazine of History and Biography* 98 (1990): 449–86.

McWhiney, Grady. *Cracker Culture: Celtic Ways in the Old South.* Tuscaloosa: Univ. of Alabama Press, 1988.

Merrell, James H. *The Indians' New World: Catawbas and Their Neighbors from European Contact through the Era of Removal.* Chapel Hill: Univ. of North Carolina Press, 1989.

Mitchell, Robert D. *Commercialism and Frontier: Perspectives on the Early Shenandoah Valley.* Charlottesville: Univ. Press of Virginia, 1977.

———, editor. *Appalachian Frontiers: Settlement, Society and Development in the Preindustrial Era.* Lexington: Univ. Press of Kentucky, 1991.

Nobles, Gregory H. "Breaking into the Backcountry: New Approaches to the Early American Frontier, 1750–1800." *William and Mary Quarterly* 3d ser., 46 (1989): 641–70.

Roeber, A. G. *Palatines, Liberty, and Property: German Lutherans in Colonial British America.* Baltimore: Johns Hopkins Univ. Press, 1993.

Thorp, Daniel B. *The Moravian Community in Colonial North Carolina: Pluralism on the Southern Frontier.* Knoxville: Univ. of Tennessee Press, 1989.

Tillson, Albert H., Jr. *Gentry and Common Folk: Political Culture on the Virginia Frontier, 1740–1789.* Lexington: Univ. Press of Kentucky, 1991.

———. "The Southern Backcountry: A Survey of Current Research." *Virginia Magazine of History and Biography* 98 (1990): 387–422.

Wayland, John W. *The German Element of the Shenandoah Valley of Virginia.* Charlottesville, Va.: The Michie Co., 1907.

Wolf, Stephanie Grauman. *Urban Village: Population, Community and Family Structure in Germantown, Pennsylvania, 1683–1800.* Princeton: Princeton Univ. Press, 1976.

Wust, Klaus. *The Virginia Germans.* Charlottesville: Univ. Press of Virginia, 1969.

Contributors

MICHAEL B. BARBER received a B.A. in anthropology from the College of William and Mary, an M.A. in sociology and anthropology from Kent State University, and has completed coursework for a Ph.D. in anthropology from the University of Virginia. Mr. Barber is currently employed by the United States Department of Agriculture—Forest Service, George Washington and Jefferson National Forests in Virginia as heritage resource program manager. Mr. Barber has published and presented numerous papers on archaeology with a focus on paleoethnozoology, the Contact Period of the interior, and the Virginia iron industry.

EUGENE B. BARFIELD received a B.A. from Radford University in liberal arts and has completed master's degree classwork in archaeology and anthropology at Indiana University, Bloomington. Mr. Barfield is currently an archaeologist with the United States Department of Agriculture—Forest Service in the George Washington and Jefferson National Forests of Virginia. His research interests include the Paleoindian diet in western Virginia, various quarry sources utilized by Native Americans in western Virginia, and late Pleistocene environments affecting Virginia's earliest inhabitants.

MARILYN DAVIS-DEEULIS holds a Ph.D. in American literature from the University of North Carolina at Chapel Hill, where she is presently on leave as a research assistant professor. She directs a National Endowment for the Humanities Focus Grant for UNC entitled "Regional Print Culture in the Classroom and Library." Her book on Caroline Hentz's diary and southern readers, *The Bold Atmosphere of Mrs. Hentz,* is forthcoming; she is completing a second study concerning women's reading culture on the old Virginia frontier.

ELLEN ESLINGER, who received the bachelor of science degree from Northern Illinois University and her doctorate from the University of Chicago, is currently a member of the history faculty at DePaul University. Her research interest in Virginia history has focused primarily on the great leap across the mountains to Kentucky. Her dissertation explored the social context of early camp meeting revivalism, and the importance of slavery on the frontier became apparent to her during the course of that research.

WARREN R. HOFSTRA is professor of history at Shenandoah University. He holds a M.A. degree from Boston University and a Ph.D. from the University of Virginia. In addition to teaching in the fields of American social and cultural history, he directs the Community History Project of Shenandoah University. His research and writing focuses on regional studies with an emphasis on the Shenandoah Valley. He has published in the fields of social and economic history, material culture, geography, and archaeology.

KENNETH W. KELLER is professor of history at Mary Baldwin College. He received his Ph.D. from Yale University. Dr. Keller is the author of *Rural Politics and the Collapse of Pennsylvania Federalism* (1982). He has contributed articles to numerous journals, including *Pennsylvania History, The Pennsylvania Magazine of History and Biography, The Virginia Magazine of History and Biography, Labor History, American Presbyterians: The Journal of Presbyterian History, The Missouri Historical Review, The Encyclopedia of Southern History,* the *Reader's Encyclopedia of the American West,* the forthcoming *Dictionary of Virginia Biography,* and the third edition of the American Historical Association's *Guide to Historical Literature.*

RICHARD K. MACMASTER did his undergraduate work at Fordham University and earned a doctorate at Georgetown University. He has taught at Western Carolina University, James Madison University, and Bluffton College. He is the author of several books on Virginia history, including *The Five George Masons* (1975). He organized the Shenandoah Valley Historical Institute in 1981. Since 1994, he has been a Fellow of the Young Center for the Study of Anabaptist and Pietist Groups at Elizabethtown College.

ANN E. MCCLEARY'S interest in Shenandoah Valley vernacular architectures comes from her experience conducting architectural survey for the Virginia Division of Historic Landmarks and from her work in researching and maintaining the historic farms as curator of research and programs at the Museum of American Frontier Culture. She holds a master's and doctorate degree in American civilization from Brown University, and has taught history and American studies at James Madison University.

TURK MCCLESKEY is an assistant professor of history at the Virginia Military Institute. He received a B.A. degree in history from the University of Texas at Austin and a Ph.D. in history from the College of William and Mary. His research and publications focus on colonial Virginia west of the Blue Ridge.

ROBERT D. MITCHELL, professor of geography at the University of Maryland, College Park, was educated at the University of Glasgow, Scotland, the University of California at Los Angeles, and the University of Wisconsin, Madison, from which he received his doctorate degree. His principal research interests focus on European colonization of North America, particularly landscape transformation, frontier settlement, and colonial urbanism. He is the author of *Commercialism and Frontier: Perspectives on the Early Shenandoah Valley; North America: The Historical Geography of a Changing Continent;* and editor of *Appalachian Frontiers: Settlement, Society, and Development in the Preindustrial Era.*

JOHN MORGAN is an associate professor of geography at Emory and Henry College. He studied at East Carolina University and the University of Tennessee, where he earned his Ph.D. His research focuses primarily on present and past landscapes of the U.S. South, especially Appalachia, and he is the author of *The Log House in East Tennessee* (1990).

MICHAEL J. PUGLISI holds a bachelor of arts degree in history from James Madison University and the doctoral degree from the College of William and Mary. He is currently associate dean of academic affairs and assistant professor of history at Marian College. He previously taught at Emory and Henry College. He is the author of *Puritans Besieged: The Legacies of King Philip's War in the Massachusetts Bay Colony* (1991).

J. SUSANNE SCHRAMM SIMMONS received her B.A. in history and political science from Bridgewater College and an M.A. in history from James Madison University. She has worked as a museum educator and as an independent researcher. She is currently employed as a social studies teacher by the Augusta County School Board.

GAIL S. TERRY holds a bachelor of arts degree in history from the University of Tennessee and a doctorate from the College of William and Mary. She has won several national fellowships, including the J. Franklin Jameson Fellowship sponsored by the American Historical Association and the Library of Congress and a Paul W. McQuillen Fellowship at the John Carter Brown Library in Providence, Rhode Island. She is currently teaching history at Middlebury College and working on a study of migration and the making of an elite that focuses on the Preston and Christian families.

Index

African Americans, 15, 108, 129–33, 159; free blacks, opportunity, 130–31, 160–63, 168; frontier society, 130, 161–66, 168, 184–85, 203–4; in historiography, 7, 129–30; indentured servants, 162; Indians, relations with, 174, 181–83, 184, 185; literacy, 132, 162, 194–204; population, 131, 132, 160, 163–64, 168, 173, 179–81, 184–86; race relations, 130, 161–63; traditional views on, 7, 15, 129; treatment by courts, 161–63, 165–67; *see also* Slavery

Agriculture: and barn construction, 276, 290; commercial, 12, 37, 38, 40, 55, 61, 100–101, 104, 116, 197–98; German, 12, 56, 62, 100–101, 104, 116; hemp production, 61, 164; land quality, 32, 33, 34; mixed farming, 37, 38, 66, 168, 276; Native American, 136, 138; Scotch-Irish, 62; and slavery, 164, 168, 176, 180–81, 197–98; tobacco, 37, 164

Alderson, Rev. John, 85, 88, 93, 94
Alexandria, Va., 40, 116
American Revolution: changes in political practice, 212, 227–28, 229, 233–34, 239–41
Amerindians. *See* Indians
Anabaptism, Anabaptists, 103
Anderson, John, 165–66
Anglican Church, Anglicans, 83, 87, 93
Archaeological Society of Virginia, 138–39
Archaic Indian period, 135–36
Architecture: barn construction, 251, 275–90; Continental Plan, 259, 261, 263; county surveys, 250, 256–57, 270–71, 278; cultural and ethnic influences, 117, 221–22, 249–51, 258–71, 275, 278, 284, 286, 289–90; German house plans, 117, 221–22, 250, 253, 257–65, 268; Historic American Buildings Survey, 254–55; in historiography, 252–71, 278; I-house design, 61,